Child Parent Relationship Therapy (CPRT)

CHILD PARENT RELATIONSHIP THERAPY (CPRT)

A 10-Session Filial Therapy Model

Garry L. Landreth
Sue C. Bratton

Published in 2006 by
Routledge
Taylor & Francis Group
270 Madison Avenue
New York, NY 10016

Published in Great Britain by
Routledge
Taylor & Francis Group
2 Park Square
Milton Park, Abingdon
Oxon OX14 4RN

Routledge is an imprint of Taylor & Francis Group

Printed in the United States of America on acid-free paper
10 9 8 7 6 5 4 3 2 1

International Standard Book Number-10: 0-415-95110-0 (Hardcover)
International Standard Book Number-13: 978-0-415-95110-4 (Hardcover)
Library of Congress Card Number 2005014279

Library of Congress Cataloging-in-Publication Data

Landreth, Garry L.
Child-parent-relationship (C-P-R) therapy : a 10-session filial therapy model / Garry L. Landreth, Sue C. Bratton.
p. cm.
Includes bibliographical references and index.
ISBN 0-415-95110-0 (hardbound)
1. Parent-child interaction therapy. 2. Play therapy. 3. Parent and child. I. Bratton, Sue. II. Title.

RJ505.P37L36 2005
618.92'891653--dc22 2005014279

Taylor & Francis Group
is the Academic Division of Informa plc.

Visit the Taylor & Francis Web site at
http://www.taylorandfrancis.com

and the Routledge Web site at
http://www.routledge-ny.com

TABLE OF CONTENTS

PREFACE

This book is about changing the mental health structure of families, communities, and ultimately society, by changing the nature of relationships in families through a process of helping parents become therapeutic agents in their children's lives. We now know that in a matter of a few weeks, parents are quite capable of learning and incorporating into their relationships with their children and spouses therapeutic skills once thought to require years of graduate education and training.

What we have written in this book about Child Parent Relationship Therapy (CPRT): A 10-Session Filial Therapy Model is an extension of our experiences with children in play therapy as they expressed themselves through the process of play in the safety of a caring relationship that released their inner dynamic potential that had been previously unknown to significant adults in their lives. We have long held a deep and abiding belief in the ability of parents to establish the same kind of therapeutic relationship with their own children by learning and incorporating the basic attitudes and skills of child-centered play therapy in special play relationships, referred to as filial therapy.

We believe the future mental health of adult populations lies squarely on the shoulders of mental health procedures that empower parents to become therapeutic agents with their own children. We must not wait until children become adults to attempt to impact their mental health, for by then a lifetime of less than the best has been lived out. That is not a very progressive or satisfying way for a society to go about the experience of living life. Mental health professionals must actively engage in the process of giving their skills away to families—that is the future.

We are indebted to the many parents who have shared their lives with us in our CPRT groups. From those parents, we have learned how to be more facilitative in our roles as filial therapists and how to use ourselves more fully in developing relationships with parents in our CPRT training groups. From parents, we have learned what works and what does not work very well in the training process. In general, parents have helped to perfect the 10-session filial therapy model into a dynamic, therapeutic, and educational process that changes lives.

The intent of this book is to provide the essential structure, skills, materials, and resources needed to learn how to effectively conduct CPRT training. To that end, some of the unique features of this book are

- Specific instructions for implementing the group process and teaching components of the 10-session CPRT model.
- Detailed instructions for structuring the 10 sessions of CPRT training.
- Insights of filial therapists in training about difficult dimensions to pay attention to in facilitating a CPRT group.
- Transcripts of the interactions in 10 CPRT sessions for one group of parents afford an opportunity to experience the filial therapy training process.
- One mother's personal struggles are highlighted in each of the filial therapy training transcripts, revealing her development of insight and the dynamic changes in her attitude and behavior.
- Transcripts of parent-child play sessions provide insight into how parents apply the skills learned.
- Answers to questions parents ask about CPRT training.
- Suggested solutions to problems that arise in CPRT training.

- Application of the 10-session CPRT model in various settings is explained.
- Four-year and 13-year follow-up interviews provide an unusual opportunity to evaluate the continuing and long-range effects of the 10-session CPRT model.
- A review of research on the 10-session CPRT model, which is helpful in justifying CPRT to insurance panels and managed care.

READERS' NOTE:

Therapists may want to consult this book's companion, *Child Parent Relationship Therapy (CPRT) Treatment Manual: A 10-Session Filial Therapy Model for Training Parents (2006)* published by Routledge. The treatment manual contains treatment outlines, a therapist study guide, parent handouts, CPRT resources, and supplemental training materials needed for conducting the 10-session training model. The CPRT Treatment Manual also contains a CD-Rom allowing the therapist to print the therapist notebook, parent notebook, and all additional material needed.

For further information visit the Taylor & Francis Website at www.taylorandfrancis.com or call 800-634-7064.

ACKNOWLEDGMENTS

The rewarding shared opportunity with our spouses, Monica and David, to be parents is the most significant experience in which we have invested our lives. Our children, Kimberly, Karla and Craig (G.L.L.) and Lauren (S.C.B.), have made the journey through parenting a wonderful experience as we have struggled to live out the principles of Child Parent Relationship Therapy on a daily basis with them. They have reaffirmed our faith in the process. This book is dedicated to Monica and David and our children. Without their inspiration, love and encouragement this book would not have been possible.

We would also like to acknowledge the contributions of our graduate students whose enthusiasm about CPRT and its positive impact on families has been a significant factor in writing this book. We are especially grateful to our many doctoral students who have contributed to the research on the effectiveness of this model. A special thanks to Mary Morrison, Angela Sheely, Jenny Findling, Yumi Ogawa, April Shottlekorb, Charlie Myers, Rinda Thomas and Eric Dafoe, for their feedback and assistance in preparing and editing the manuscript.

CHAPTER 1

HISTORY, DEVELOPMENT, AND OBJECTIVES OF CHILD PARENT RELATIONSHIP THERAPY (CPRT): A 10-SESSION FILIAL THERAPY MODEL

In *Play Therapy: The Art of the Relationship*, Landreth (2002) stated that if the mental health of future adult populations is to be significantly impacted in positive ways, greater effort must be made to substantially improve the mental health of all children. His position was that the skills of those in the mental health professions must be given away through training to parents, who are in the best position to profoundly impact the lives of future adults. Therapists helping parents to become therapeutic agents in their children's lives is the most efficient way to significantly improve the mental health of adult populations of the future.

Antecedents of Filial Therapy

Precedents for training parents to be therapeutic agents in their children's lives can be traced to the early part of the 20th century. In 1900, Sigmund Freud (1959) successfully used the father of a 5-year-old boy in the treatment of the child by instructing the father in how to respond during play sessions with the boy. The treatment was carried out by the father at home, and Freud contended the changes made in the child's behavior would have been impossible without the father's interaction. As early as 1949, Dorothy Baruch advocated planned play sessions at home modeled after Axline's (1947) play therapy sessions for the purpose of allowing children to work out their personal issues and enhancing parent–child relationships.

A dramatic example of the effect of play therapy–type home play sessions was reported by Natalie Fuchs (1957). With the advice and encouragement of her father, Carl Rogers, the founder of client-centered or person-centered therapy, she employed regularly scheduled special playtimes based on procedures suggested in Axline's (1947) writings and achieved significant results in helping her daughter overcome emotional reactions related to toilet training. Moustakas (1959) provided one of the earliest detailed descriptions of these special play therapy–type home play sessions between parent and child:

> Play therapy in the home is essentially a relationship between a child and his mother or father through which the child discovers himself as an important person, sees that he is valued and loved, and recognizes his irreplaceable membership in the family. It is a way through which the child opens himself to emotional expression and in this process releases tensions and repressed feelings....He learns to count on regular meetings with the parent once or twice a week for one-hour periods in which he is the center of the experience. A variety of play materials are made available to him at this time....The parent does not tell him what to do, but sits nearby watching him closely and showing interest and regard....In the play therapy relationship created in the home, the child finds that his

> parent really cares, wants to understand, and accepts him as he is. (pp. 275–277)

These earlier experiences of parents conducting special play sessions at home differed from filial therapy in that the parents did not receive regularly scheduled systematic training, close supervision, or the opportunity to explore their feelings and reactions with peers in a group process/therapy type format. Baruch (1949) and Moustakas's (1959) recommendations were for children who did not have identified clinical problems.

Child-Centered Play Therapy

Filial therapy applies the constructs and skills of child-centered play therapy (CCPT) to parent and child relationships in a manner similar to the relationship between a play therapist and a child. As in CCPT, the parent is taught to facilitate a permissive and growth-producing atmosphere in which the child can reach her full potential. Child-centered play therapy is based upon the theoretical constructs of nondirective therapy developed by Carl Rogers (1942) and further developed and expanded by Rogers (1951) as client-centered therapy. CCPT is grounded in a belief in the innate human capacity of the child to strive toward growth and maturity and an attitude of deep and abiding belief in the child's ability to be constructively self-directing. Rogers (1986) summarized the essence of the approach:

> The person-centered approach, then, is primarily a way of being that finds its expression in attitudes and behaviors that create a growth-producing climate. It is a basic philosophy rather than simply a technique or a method. When this philosophy is lived, it helps the person expand the development of his or her own capacities. When it is lived, it also stimulates constructive change in others. It empowers the individual, and when this personal power is sensed, experience shows that it tends to be used for personal and social transformation. (p. 199)

It is this *formative tendency* that all persons—indeed, all of nature—possess that forms the foundation for the child-centered approach to working with children (Rogers, 1951).

These constructs were applied to working with children through play therapy by Virginia Axline (1947), a student and colleague of Rogers. She successfully applied nondirective (client-centered) therapy principles (i.e., belief in the individual's capacity for self-direction) to children in nondirective play therapy. Her approach was later referred to as client-centered play therapy and then as child-centered play therapy. Axline (1950) summarized her concept of play therapy:

> A play experience is therapeutic because it provides a secure relationship between the child and the adult, so that the child has the freedom and room to state himself in his own terms, exactly as he is at that moment in his own way and in his own time. (p. 68)

The child-centered approach to play therapy, like client-centered therapy with adults, is based upon a process of **being with children** as opposed to a procedure of application. It is not so much a process of reparation as it is a process of becoming. Thus, the focus is on the child, not the problem. The child-centered play therapist makes no effort to control or change the child, based on the theory that the child's behavior is at all times internally motivated toward self-realization, positive growth, improvement, independence, maturity, and enhancement of self. The child's behavior in this process is goal directed in an effort to satisfy personal needs as experienced in the unique phenomenal field that for that child constitutes reality. A fundamental rule of thumb in child-centered play therapy is that the child's perception of reality is what must be understood if the child and behaviors exhibited by the child are to be understood (Landreth, 2002). (*This concept that the child's phenomenal field constitutes reality for the child is central to Child Parent Relationship Therapy and is the basis for the structure of much of the training.* ***Rule of Thumb: Look through the child's eyes.*** *The parent is to avoid judging or evaluating even the simplest of the child's behaviors—a painting or stacked blocks, and works hard to try to understand the internal frame of reference of the child.*)

In child-centered play therapy, it is the relationship that is the agent of change. Child-centered play therapy is an experience for children in which the therapeutic process emerges from a shared living relationship developed on the basis of the therapist's consistently conveyed acceptance of children and confidence in their ability to be of help to themselves, thus freeing children to risk using their own strengths. Virginia Axline (1947) concisely clarified the fundamental principles that provide guidelines for establishing and maintaining a therapeutic relationship and making contact with the inner person of the child in the play therapy experience. Landreth (1991, pp. 77–78) revised and extended Axline's eight basic principles as follows:

- The therapist is genuinely interested in the child and develops a warm, caring relationship.
- The therapist experiences unqualified acceptance of the child and does not wish that the child were different in some way.
- The therapist creates a feeling of safety and permissiveness in the relationship so the child feels free to explore and express self completely.
- The therapist is always sensitive to the child's feelings and gently reflects those feelings in such a manner that the child develops self-understanding.
- The therapist believes deeply in the child's capacity to act responsibly, unwaveringly respects the child's ability to solve personal problems and allows the child to do so.
- The therapist trusts the child's inner direction, allows the child to lead in all areas of the relationship, and resists any urge to direct the child's play or conversation.
- The therapist appreciates the gradual nature of the therapeutic process and does not attempt to hurry things along.
- The therapist establishes only those therapeutic limits that help the child accept personal and appropriate relationship responsibility.

These principles all point to the development and maintenance of a strong therapeutic relationship. Moustakas (1959) further emphasized the therapeutic value of children experiencing this kind of relationship: "Through the process of self-expression and exploration within a significant relationship, through realization of the value within, the child comes to be a positive, self-determining, and self-actualizing individual" (p. 5).

Filial Therapy: A Radical Approach

The development of filial therapy was an evolutionary process for Bernard Guerney (1964), a child-centered play therapist who ascribed to the theoretical principles of client-centered therapy as conceptualized by Carl Rogers and the play therapy principles of Virginia Axline. Early in his professional career, in the 1950s and early 1960s, Bernard Guerney (personal communication, October 22, 1992) viewed parents as potential effectual allies in the treatment of their children and began to contemplate the need to involve parents more directly in the therapeutic process. Guerney's first step in the process of involving parents in the therapeutic process of helping their children was to include parents in the playroom as observers, followed by discussions with parents to explain what they had witnessed in the play sessions. His next step in the evolutionary process was to give parents more of a role in the therapeutic process.

These successful experiences led him to conceptualize a training program in which parents would be trained in basic child-centered play therapy skills to become the therapeutic agent in their children's lives, based on the view that play is the primary way children express themselves and work through issues. Guerney's premise for his innovative approach was that children's problems are often the product of parental lack of parenting knowledge and skill. Furthermore, he proposed that children's problematic behaviors that were influenced by parental attitudes could be more effectively ameliorated under similar conditions. This was a revolutionary idea, because a prevailing attitude in the mental health field in the 1950s and early 1960s was that children's problems are usually a product of the pathology of the parents. This shift from viewing the parents as pathological to being the primary therapeutic agent of change in their child's life was a radical departure for the time.

In 1964, Bernard Guerney published the first article, "Filial Therapy: Description and Rationale," explaining the principles and results of filial therapy. In that article, he described the importance of parents as key to the filial therapy approach:

> The parent–child relationship is nearly always the most significant one in a child's life. Therefore, if a child were provided the experiences of expression, insight, and adult acceptance in the presence of such powerful

> people as parent, every bit of success the parent achieves in carrying out the therapeutic role should be many more times more powerful than that of a therapist doing the same thing...a relatively small amount of affection, attention, interest, and so on, from the parent can be expected to be more therapeutic than a larger amount from a therapist. (p. 309)

Because the parent potentially has more emotional significance to the child than does the therapist, the objective of this approach is to help the parent become the primary change agent in the child's life by using the naturally existing bond between parent and child; thus, the term *filial therapy* was coined by the Guerneys. (Louise Guerney participated with her husband in the early research and development of filial therapy at Rutgers University and has continued as one of the leading proponents of this innovative approach to helping children and families.) Stover and Guerney (1967) proposed further advantages of using filial therapy over play therapy. Utilizing parents as the agent of change would empower parents, reducing feelings of guilt and helplessness parents may experience when dependent upon a professional to help their child. Additionally, as parents learn more effective ways of interacting with their child, there is greater potential for long-lasting change as parents continue to utilize these acquired skills and attitudes throughout their child's life.

The next step in development of this revolutionary approach was the establishment of a sound research program to verify the effectiveness of this program of parent training. The Guerneys' early research results on filial therapy were highly encouraging and provided a strong foundation for the research that followed (Chapter 21 provides an overview of their early, groundbreaking research).

In the initial stages of development, the Guerneys (personal communication, March 8, 1995) conceptualized filial therapy as a structured treatment program for children with emotional problems and accepted only couples for filial therapy training. Using a small group format, parents were trained in basic child-centered play therapy principles and skills. Husbands and wives were not placed in the same groups, though, because there were concerns about marital issues dominating the training sessions. Experience and success with their model quickly resulted in a shift in attitude, and they found that when couples were allowed in the same group, they could deal with some marital issues appropriately.

Another important learning was that filial therapy groups composed of parents whose children all had similar personality dynamics, such as acting-out behaviors, were not very effective because the parents had similar dynamics of their own, and they reinforced each other's negative behaviors because they had difficulty viewing each other's children from a different perspective as parents who have children with other kinds of problems might do. This same concern does not apply to groups composed of parents whose children have a similar issue that has nothing to do with dynamics: children with learning disabilities, children with chronic diabetes, etc. These children share a common problem, but they are different in terms of their personality and dynamics. Heterogeneous groups are preferred.

Originally, the Guerneys met with filial groups for 2 hours once a week for about a year. Their experience and success led them to streamline training procedures so that groups now meet 2 hours once a week for about 5 to 6 months. Research on these shorter groups has produced comparable results to those of the longer groups. Ginsberg (1997) and VanFleet (1994), both protégés of the Guerneys, have successfully adapted the Guerneys' model for use with individual parents.

Development of the Landreth 10-Session Filial Therapy Model/Child Parent Relationship Therapy (CPRT)

I have, throughout my professional career as a high school counselor, university professor, and consultant, been involved in working with parents through counseling and training experiences. For many of my early years as an assistant professor teaching play therapy and carrying play therapy cases, I was involved in teaching parents "Lessons from Play Therapy for Parents" but without any emphasis on having playtimes. I had an intensifying belief that if what I did in the playroom was helpful to children, then parents could develop those same kinds of attitudes and learn to utilize those same kinds of skills with their children. Play therapists should be giving their skills away to parents and teachers. We should not hide our skills behind the door of the playroom. When I read the Guerneys' work in filial therapy, I immediately resonated to this dynamic structure of training and supervising parents that incorporated the facets of teaching, supervision, play therapy, and group process, dimensions that are exciting to me and have occupied my professional focus. Here was a model that allowed me to meld my fascination with group process, my passion for play therapy, and my love of teaching. Filial therapy was a natural fit.

Long-term therapy has always been a problematic concern for me as I believe we do not fully comprehend the potential of the human organism for growth and change. My doctoral dissertation focused on the effects of collapsing the time between group counseling sessions in time-limited settings. Therefore, I was naturally attracted to the possibility of reducing the number of filial therapy training sessions from what was at that time typically a year of training. I had already learned from my counseling experiences with parents in the Albuquerque, New Mexico public schools, and parents who brought their children for counseling and play therapy sessions at the University of New Mexico counseling clinic where I was a graduate assistant and intern, that it was very difficult for parents to stay committed for long periods of time. I had similar experiences with parents in the Pupil Appraisal Center (later named the Child and Family Resource Clinic), which employed a multidiscipline approach to children with learning problems and that I helped found in 1967 at the University of North Texas. In public schools, the typical semester of 15 to 17 weeks is a natural break, and many parents have difficulty carrying through with a commitment beyond that time frame. Therefore, my first filial therapy groups were structured around a 15-week model.

Although these experiences were rewarding, maintaining consistent attendance at training sessions in the last four or five sessions was very difficult; I began to experiment with 12 sessions, but still had problems with dropouts. A 3-month commitment seemed to parents to be much too long, so I decided to try 10 sessions and had immediate attendance success. During these early experiences with filial therapy, I was encouraged to find Arthur Kraft's (1973) book, which provided a case description of his use of 10 sessions of filial therapy training.

The immediate problem confronting me in developing my 10-session model was how to efficiently cover all the material and training experiences I thought necessary in only 10 two-hour sessions. The training content, method, and style of presentation, as well as the sequence of training in the 10-session model, was greatly influenced by my years of experience teaching master's and doctoral level courses in child-centered play therapy and by my experiences in play therapy in the Pupil Appraisal Center at the University of North Texas, where I joined the faculty as an assistant professor in 1966.

The process element, that is, the involvement of parents in the learning process, facilitation of interaction within the group, utilization of a therapeutic modality, and general emphasis on group process, in the 10-session model was an outgrowth of my experiences in teaching master's and doctoral level courses in group counseling. In the early years of developing the 10-session model, I trained a multitude of filial therapy groups primarily in off-campus settings in my role as a consulting supervisor in private counseling agencies in the late 1970s. Refinement of the 10-session model was a function of my experiences in these settings. Because the term *filial therapy* was not familiar to parents, in the late 1980s I began to market my approach to parents as, Child–Parent–Relationship (C-P-R) Training. Later, after successful experiences with filial therapy in these private counseling agencies, I began to teach graduate courses in filial therapy in my department on the University of North Texas campus. Further refinement of the 10-session structure led to formally naming the model Child Parent Relationship Therapy (CPRT) to distinguish it from other filial therapy models. The resulting structure of the 10-session CPRT training model is described in detail in later chapters.

The second task was to verify the effectiveness of the 10-session model through rigorous research. The 10-session filial therapy model has been researched in 33 studies involving over 800 participants representing a wide range of child and parent populations. Of these studies, 27 measured the effectiveness of this model, using a pretest and posttest comparison or control group design, and obtained statistically significant findings on the vast majority of measures. Many of the studies used the rigorous dimension of rater analysis of videotapes of parent and child play sessions to evaluate parents' demonstrated ability to apply the empathic skills of child-centered play therapy. Chapter 21 provides the reader with a summary of the findings for all 33 studies conducted on this model.

Definition of Filial Therapy

Since the use of filial therapy is rapidly becoming an accepted practice in the mental health field, it seems important to provide a definition that identifies and standardizes the practice of filial therapy. In the CPRT model, *filial therapy is defined as*

> *a unique approach used by professionals trained in play therapy to train parents to be therapeutic agents with their own children through a format of didactic instruction, demonstration play sessions, required at-home laboratory play sessions, and supervision in a supportive atmosphere. Parents are taught basic child-centered play therapy principles and skills including reflective listening, recognizing and responding to children's feelings, therapeutic limit setting, building children's self-esteem, and structuring required weekly play sessions with their children using a special kit of selected toys. Parents learn how to create a nonjudgmental, understanding, and accepting environment that enhances the parent–child relationship, thus facilitating personal growth and change for child and parent.*

Objectives of CPRT

The focus of CPRT is on the importance of the relationship between the parent and child and on the inner person of the child, what the child is capable of becoming. This relationship is viewed as the vehicle for the process of change. Therefore, the objective is to help the parent relate to the child in ways that will release the child's inner directional, constructive, forward-moving, creative, self-healing power. As in child-centered play therapy, CPRT is not focused on solving specific problems or a "quick fix," but rather is structured to enhance the relationship—in this case between the parent and child, with the parent serving as the therapeutic agent of change.

The overall aim of CPRT is to enhance and strengthen the parent–child relationship through improved family interactions and problem-solving strategies and through increased feelings of familial affection, warmth, and trust. CPRT offers significant benefits for both children and parents. Therapeutic goals for children are similar to those for children in play therapy, including a reduction of symptoms, development of coping strategies, and an increase in positive feelings of self-worth and confidence. Broad therapeutic goals for parents include a greater understanding and acceptance of the child's emotional world, the development of more realistic and tolerant perceptions and attitudes toward both self and child, the development of more effective parenting skills based on developmentally appropriate strategies, and last, but not least, to help parents recapture the joy in parenting.

Specific play session objectives include helping parents: (a) understand and accept their child, (b) develop sensitivity to their child's feelings, (c) learn how to encourage their child's self-direction, self-responsibility, and self-reliance, (d) gain insight into self in relation to the child, (e) change their perception of their child, and (f) learn child-centered play therapy principles and skills. Through didactic instruction, demonstration play sessions with children, viewing of videotapes, role-playing, and supervision of parents' play sessions, parents' sensitivity to their children is enhanced, and parents learn how to create a nonjudgmental, understanding, and accepting environment in which children feel safe enough to explore other parts of themselves as persons and other ways of relating to their parents.

References

Axline, V. (1947). *Play therapy: The inner dynamics of childhood.* Cambridge, MA: Houghton Mifflin.

Axline, V. (1950). Entering the child's world via play experiences. *Progressive Education, 27,* 68–75.

Baruch, D. (1949). *New ways in discipline.* New York: McGraw-Hill.

Freud, S. (Ed.). (1959). Analysis of a phobia in a five-year-old boy. In *Collected papers* (pp. 149–289). New York: Basic Books.

Fuchs, N. (1957). Play therapy at home. *Merrill-Palmer Quarterly, 3,* 89–95.

Ginsberg, B. G. (1997). *Relationship enhancement family therapy.* NY: Wiley & Sons.

Guerney, B. (1964). Filial therapy: Description and rationale. *Journal of Consulting Psychology, 28*(4), 303–310.

Kraft, A. (1973). *Are you listening to your child? How to bridge the communication gap through creative play sessions.* New York: Walker.

Landreth, G. (1991/2002). *Play therapy: The art of the relationship.* New York: Routledge.

Moustakas, C. (1959). *Psychotherapy with children: The living relationship.* New York: Harper & Row.

Rogers, C. (1942). *Counseling and psychotherapy.* Boston: Houghton Mifflin.

Rogers, C. (1951). *Client-centered therapy.* Boston: Houghton Mifflin.

Rogers, C. (1986). Client-centered therapy. In I. Kutash & A. Wolf (Eds.), *Psychotherapist's casebook* (pp. 197–208). San Francisco: Jossey-Bass.

Stover, L., & Guerney, B., Jr. (1967). The efficacy of training procedures for mothers in filial therapy. *Psychotherapy: Theory, Research, and Practice, 4,* 110–115.

VanFleet, R. (1994). *Filial therapy: Strengthening parent–child relationships through play.* Sarasota, FL: Professional Resource Press.

CHAPTER 2

UNIQUE FEATURES OF CPRT

There are many significant and dynamic features of CPRT that set this model apart from other parent training programs. The following parent–child dimensions and training dimensions make CPRT a unique form of parent training.

Parent–Child Interaction Dimensions

Parent–Child Relationship

The primary focus of CPRT is on enhancing and strengthening the parent–child relationship by equipping parents with basic child-centered play therapy skills that have been proven to be necessary and effective dimensions in facilitating the development of positive relationships. Most other parent training programs focus primarily on teaching specific techniques or problem-solving skills to be utilized in the correction or extinguishing of specific child-related behaviors. CPRT is based on the rationale that the relationship between parent and child is the essential and curative therapeutic dimension for improving and correcting children's problems and preventing the development of future problems.

Communication Is Play Based

Unlike other parent training models that rely on verbal skills stressing family discussions or parent–child discussions to resolve problems, CPRT and other forms of filial therapy rely on the child's natural means of communication—play—as the primary medium for communicating the child's feelings, needs, wants, wishes, fantasies, experiences, and thoughts. In filial therapy, play is the communication medium for understanding the child and building the parent–child relationship. Children are comfortable with the medium of play and can, therefore, more easily lead the play experience/relationship to focus on dimensions important to them. The child's communication through play is, thus, less restricted.

Symbolic Expression

Since play is the child's natural medium of expression and CPRT/filial therapy is play based, it is the only parent training model that allows children to express their emotions fully, and through the safety of symbolic expression. Parents are taught that children's play behavior has meaning and demonstrations with toys are used to convey examples of how a child's play with the selected toys may relate to events, fears, etc., in the child's life. Parents are taught to be sensitive to possible meanings in their child's play. However, they are not expected to figure out or understand symbolic meaning in a child's play, only to be sensitive to the importance of the play and the therapeutic value of play. The important factor is that the child has an opportunity to play out potentially significant messages. The playing out is more important than whether or not the parent understands the symbolic meaning.

Child Takes the Lead

In the special playtimes, the child is allowed to lead. The parent does not initiate topics of conversation, content of play, how the time will be spent, or offer suggestions for solutions to problems. The child leads throughout the 30-minute special playtime, and the parent follows. The focus of the time together is determined by the child, regardless of previous child behaviors that may concern the parent. In most other parent training programs, content and direction of parent–child interactions are determined by the parent. Allowing the child to lead provides the child with opportunities to experience what responsibility feels like.

Acceptance Rather Than Correction

In CPRT, there is no emphasis on correcting a child's behavior. The focus of the training is on developing skills to be utilized during a special 30-minute playtime. For 30 minutes, the parent is to be accepting of the child and the child's decisions within appropriate boundaries or limits. The child is allowed to make decisions related to the playtime, what the child will play with, how the child will play, etc., and the parent accepts those decisions. The parent does not correct the child, except in situations where previously identified limits are needed, does not wish the child were different, and allows the child to make mistakes without interfering or offering suggestions. For 30 minutes, the child is in charge and is accepted as she is.

Training Dimensions

Group Process/Group Therapy

The process or group therapy component of CPRT is unique and vital to the success of CPRT because parents often have strong reactions to their children and feelings about themselves and their family members that they need to process in order to be fully present and emotionally available to learn what is being taught in the CPRT training sessions. This process is described in the following self-critique of a graduate student in a supervised filial therapy practicum experience.

> I recognized that Ashley and her husband had an argument on the way to the filial session, and it was obvious that she was going to have a hard time listening until she was able to process how she was feeling right then; so I put my training agenda aside to help her process her feelings. I learned that this kind of flexibility is crucial to filial training. Taking the time to allow Ashley to express

> her feelings and be heard before I asked her to listen to my training points facilitated the development of rapport and trust in our relationship in addition to clearing her system so she could listen. Allowing her to explore her feelings facilitated not only the expression of her feelings but also a greater awareness of her own needs. I believe this will help her to have more effective play sessions with her son because she will better understand the power and process of reflection which I modeled. On a personal note, once again I learned the power of reflection. I did not try to help her come to a resolution in her argument with her husband, but I simply reflected and followed her lead. My reflections facilitated some interesting insights. At the end of the session, she reported feeling much better.

Parents' strong reactions to their children and feelings about themselves and their family members also need to be processed in CPRT training so parents can be fully present and emotionally available to their children as is called for in the special play sessions. One mother described the necessity of processing as "I grew up in a highly dysfunctional family, and I'm experiencing some really strong gut reaction feelings about my parents that are probably preventing me from hearing the emotional messages communicated by my child in our playtimes." The didactic/therapeutic dimensions of filial therapy training sessions and the processing of the parents' special play sessions with their children often reminds parents of emotional wounds and issues with their own parents that have been pushed aside over the years. These issues are explored in the context of their interference with the parents' role of relating to their children as therapeutic agents of change, not in the context of "There is something wrong with you that you need to change," or as personality issues that need to be corrected. Therefore, this component of filial therapy is referred to as group process or as a group therapy type component.

Parents are not in CPRT to receive group therapy. They need training and development of relationship skills. But they also need to develop insight into personal issues that interfere with their relating to their children as change agents, and the processing of personal issues facilitates the inner growth required to enable parents to incorporate the new skills and apply the new behaviors required.

During a CPRT training session focused on developing the skill of reflecting children's feelings, Angela seemed particularly resistant and adamantly questioned the importance of reflecting her child's feelings. In a later training session, she shared:

> I've been thinking about reflecting a child's feelings, and I now understand why it is important. As a child, I would tell my mom I didn't want to stay home with my father when she went out shopping. My mom ignored my pleadings, and my father sexually abused me. I grew up not trusting my feelings and not trusting myself because my mother didn't listen to my feelings. I now realize that when you validate children's feelings, you teach them to trust themselves.

Processing her childhood experience and current feelings in the filial group freed Angela to identify, emotionally relate to, and validate her child's feelings. Angela's sharing her insight also reinforced the leader's emphasis on the importance of reflecting children's feelings and provided added impetus for the other parents to invest energy in validating their children's feelings.

Hearing other parents' experiences breaks down barriers of defensiveness and isolation. Therefore, the leader is active in facilitating interaction among parents and helping them to feel included in the group. The power of the group was summed up by Emily in the last training session as she described what had impacted her in the CPRT training:

> Dr. Landreth could sit there and tell us all day that there are other parents like us who are struggling, to try to make us feel better, but knowing that there are other people we can see, hear, and touch makes a big difference. It helped me so much to hear you-all describe your problems and struggles with your children.

The critical importance of the group process/group therapy component of filial therapy was supported in Eardley's (1978) research. A model of filial therapy structured exclusively around didactic training components coupled with the utilization of demonstrations and required parent–child play sessions with supervision feedback was found to be less effective than a model of filial therapy incorporating a combination of didactic training components and group process components. The effectiveness of filial therapy training is dependent on parents actively processing personal issues related to themselves, their children, the play sessions, and their family.

Future Focused

CPRT training is future focused. Most other parent training models are grounded in past relationships and happenings with an emphasis on correcting the way the child has been. CPRT is focused on what the child is capable of being or becoming, not what the child has done. Therefore, minimal time is spent on parents recounting their children's behaviors. Responding to children on the basis of past behaviors restricts children to continue to be the way they have been.

If significant adults in children's lives perceive them as being incapable of change, then children are bound to their past. It is not possible for a child to become what the child is capable of becoming until a significant adult in the child's life believes the child is capable and responds to the child as though the child were capable. CPRT is based on a belief in the child's capacity for positive self-directed change and, therefore, focuses on the child's potential rather than the child's problem.

Experientially Based

CPRT is primarily experientially based, relying on the principle of learning by doing. Most other parent training models use a lecture–discussion format to teach principles and procedures considered to be important. The experiential approach engages parents more quickly, maintains a high level of parent interest and involvement, and provides opportunities for the trainer to supervise the development of skills. The experiential approach also engages or draws out parents who are hesitant, quiet, or somewhat reserved about talking in a group. This process can be seen in the following description in a filial therapist's report.

> Maria has really surprised me. At first, she was quiet and did not participate in the group discussion. She seemed to become more comfortable in the third session, and then really seemed to explode with excitement once she began the play sessions with Adam. Wow, the excitement and enjoyment she had was exciting to me! She was faithful in bringing her videotapes each week. On the videotapes, it was evident that she understood the skills we taught and was applying them. In fact, I was surprised at the pace at which she really learned the skills. By the fifth training session, Maria began to share her feelings about the playtimes and began asking how she should respond in specific situations outside the play session.
>
> She also began sharing what she was learning with her husband and even videotaped him in a play session with Adam, then brought the video, with her husband's permission, for us to view. As we viewed the video of his play session, Maria pointed out how he should have responded and in general took on the supervisor role. She reported that the play sessions were fun for her and for Adam, that Adam was treating his sister better and was much more obedient and cooperative at home. Adam's teacher reported that his behavior in the classroom was much more positive, he was more socially interactive and more cooperative at school.

Practicing new skills in a role-playing format in the training sessions prior to implementation of the special play sessions increases the confidence level of parents and helps ensure the new skills will be used correctly in parent–child interactions in the required at-home special play sessions. One filial therapist observed:

> It is not enough for a parent to tell you she understands limit setting. I am sure Margaret did understand. However, it is different when the parent is put in the position of actually setting a limit without having had enough rote memorization of how to state the limit. Margaret did set a limit in her play session, but it was set in the way that

> she would have done it in the past because she couldn't remember how to actually state the limit in the new way. I can really see the value of role-playing and how beneficial it is to practice in a group where a parent can observe others doing it, too.

The most dynamic part of experiential learning occurs in the required parent–child special playtimes as parents implement their new role of therapeutic agent with their child. These special play sessions are usually times of exciting discovery for parents about themselves and their children and are often reinforcing times for parents as they successfully implement new skills.

The experiential approach of role-playing during training sessions and then having special play sessions that are viewed by other parents in the group allows parents to engage in the process of giving supportive feedback and encouragement. Peer group support is more powerful in influencing parental behavior than comments made by the CPRT trainer. These dimensions are vital in building parents' confidence in trying new ways of responding to their children.

Building a Relationship Rather Than Correcting a Problem

The focus of CPRT training is on equipping parents with the skills necessary to develop a therapeutic relationship with their children. There is no emphasis on correcting a specific problem a child may have. The rationale for this approach to parent training is that improving the parent's relationship with a child will positively impact the underlying causes of the problematic behavior, which will in turn result in positive changes in the behavior of concern. The person of the child and the parent's relationship with the child is always more important than the problem the child may have. Therefore, CPRT training sessions focus on developing therapeutic relationship skills rather than on techniques or methodology for correcting problems.

Changing the Child's Perception

A central objective of CPRT training is to change the child's perception of the parent and the parent–child relationship rather than to change the child's behavior. Behavior is viewed as a function of perception. Therefore, a change in perception will result in a change in behavior. In CPRT, parents learn how to establish an understanding, accepting, and empathic play session environment in which the parent comes to be viewed by the child as an ally, because for 30 minutes the parent gives up any attempt to correct or change the child. Parents learn how to look through their child's eyes, to assume their child's perceptual frame of reference.

Focus on Parental Efficacy vs. Changing the Child

Parents who come for filial therapy often feel out of control, believing what they need to learn is a method to control their child. While most parent training models prescribe strategies for changing the child, that is not the objective in CPRT training. Rather, this approach focuses on changing the parent through increased parental efficacy. Parents who feel more confident in their ability to respond appropriately to their children feel more in control.

How parents feel about themselves, their sense of adequacy as a person and a parent, significantly affects their interaction with their children and thus their children's development. Parenting is at best a difficult, stressful, and often frustrating process for even the most skillful and dedicated parent. When difficulty occurs in the parent–child relationship and things just are not going well, parents are susceptible to self-blame, and doubt their adequacy as a parent. Research has shown that parental efficacy can have a profound impact on any number of the dimensions of children's development. Rohner (1986) reported that the children of parents who were warm, accepting, and nurturing exhibited more positive social skills. Children who were experiencing difficulties with social skills had parents who were rigid, authoritarian, and cold. Other studies concluded that parents scoring high in internal locus of control appear to influence their children's development in positive ways (Schaefer, 1981; Swick & Graves, 1986). Swick, Gladstone, and Hayes (1988) noted that parent interventions designed specifically to increase parents' sense of control resulted in improvements in children's behavior.

The dynamics of the relationship between parent and child most assuredly affect children's development, and a major factor in this relationship is the parent's attitude and perception of self, as related to parental locus of control. Parent's perception of self affects their locus of control, which in turn influences the direction and extent of parental guidance and involvement in their children's lives. Generally, when a child experiences some developmental difficulty or parents experience prolonged difficulty in their interpersonal relationships with their children, parents feel out of control, they believe they can do nothing, and they feel inadequate. Therefore, a major objective in CPRT is supporting and encouraging parents. The sensitive therapist will convey faith in the parent's ability to grow in understanding and acceptance of the child and to have a positive impact on the child's development. Parents need assistance in learning skills that encourage the development of positive parent–child relationships. To assume that most parents already know what these skills are and how to utilize them is incorrect because relatively little effort has been put forth in our society to teach parents how to interact with their children in effective ways.

As parents learn the basic child-centered play therapy skills of reflective responding and therapeutic limit setting, they gradually begin to perceive themselves as being capable because they have new tools to utilize in their interactions with their children. As a result, parents feel empowered and their self-perception is improved. Changes in self-perception result in changes in parental behavior. As parents feel more confident and in control in their role as a parent, they are able to shift their focus from controlling their child to accepting their child as being capable of positive self-directed change. This change in perception on the part of the parent is a powerful therapeutic dimension that frees the child from defending a rigid perception of self, thus enabling the child to change. Thus, a major focus in CPRT is helping parents develop a more realistic and tolerant view of their children.

Understanding the Relationship vs. Purpose of Behavior

In CPRT training, the emphasis is not on understanding the purpose of behavior, but rather on understanding the child, the child's emotional needs, and the importance of the relationship with the child. It is not necessary to understand the why of behavior. It is always important to understand the child. Parents are often more concerned about understanding why their children behave as they do rather than understanding their child as a person. This need to have an answer seems to be motivated by a belief that if the parent can just find an answer to why her child behaves the way he does, that will solve the problem. This solution-focused approach reinforces a need for control and overlooks the importance of the person of the child.

Internal Locus of Control vs. External Locus of Control

CPRT and other forms of filial therapy are unique in emphasizing the importance of responding to children in ways that develop an internal locus of control. The accomplishment of this objective is facilitated in developing a relationship with the child in which the parent's responses communicate a belief in the child's ability to respond responsibly by returning responsibility for decisions in the special playtime to the child. This belief in the child is grounded in developmentally appropriate boundaries that are established in such a way as to allow the child to develop inner control. This is not a completely permissive relationship. There are limits on behavior. However, the behavior being expressed by the child is viewed in the context of the relationship, and understanding the child is more important than stopping the behavior.

Understanding the child means responding to the intrinsic variables related to the child's motivation, perception of self, independence, and need for acceptance. In the CPRT relationship, the objective is not to stop a child's behavior. Statements such as "Stop that, don't do that" and "You can't do that" promote the development of an external locus of control. The focus in the CPRT approach is on understanding the unique perspective of the child, the child's feelings, what the child wants, and what the child is trying to communicate. Therefore, rather than trying to stop the behavior, the objective is to communicate understanding of the child—"You would like to pull that doll's head off," "You're angry at me"—and to respond to the child in such a way as to allow the child to stop himself: "The doll's head is not for pulling off," "I'm not for hitting," "The Play-Doh is for playing with on the cookie sheet." These responses allow the child to say "No" to self and they facilitate the development of an internal locus of control in the child. Significant change comes from within the child, and this belief is modeled by the parent responding in ways that empower the child.

Required Laboratory Sessions

CPRT training is very systematic and follows a structure that involves parents in an ongoing learning experience that does not leave the acquisition or practice of skills to chance. CPRT/filial therapy is the only parent training model of its kind that requires a structured laboratory experience. Unlike other parent training models that wait for an opportune time, usually initiated by a child's behavior, to utilize a new technique or skill, parents in filial therapy are required to have a scheduled 30-minute special playtime with their child of focus (the child identified by the parent as needing help) once a week in their home or other designated location. During this special playtime, parents are to practice child-centered play therapy skills learned in the training sessions.

Specific Set of Play Materials

Parent–child special play sessions utilize a specific set of play materials that have been found to facilitate a wide range of children's play behaviors and emotional expressions. In the special play times, play materials are used by children in the act of play to communicate their personal world. Since the toys and materials selected for the play sessions are a significant therapeutic variable, parents are not allowed to introduce other toys into the playtimes unless they have been approved. All play materials do not automatically encourage the expression of children's needs, feelings, and experiences.

Skills Are Required To Be Practiced Only During Special Play Times

The general expectation in parent training programs is that skills learned will be practiced by parents 24 hours a day, 7 days a week. Such expectations build in failure experiences because even the best- intentioned parent is not able to always put into practice new techniques or acquired skills 24 hours a day. Parents get caught up in emotional experiences, they become overly stressed, or their lives become so hectic that they simply forget to try to apply new procedures, and then they feel guilty because they failed. CPRT is structured to promote success by requiring parents to utilize skills learned only during the designated 30-minute special playtimes. This time-limited requirement helps elicit cooperation from even the most resistive parents. As one parent put it, "I can do almost anything for just 30 minutes once a week, but all day every day is an impossibility for me."

Skills Are Generalized

Since the skills learned are not problem/correction focused, they can be generalized to situations outside the special playtimes. Even though parents are required to use the skills only during the special playtimes, parents quite readily begin to spontaneously respond to their children at other times in a manner similar to the way they have been responding during the special playtimes. This transfer of new parent behaviors outside the special playtimes occurs naturally and is an indication that the new behaviors have been incorporated into the parents' natural way of responding. Parents in CPRT training often report they even find themselves responding empathically or giving choices in their work experience encounters.

Supervision

A critical component of CPRT training is the structure and provision of supervision experiences. CPRT training is a very structured approach to learning. Nothing is left to chance. There is no guesswork about whether or not parents have learned the skills or are able to appropriately utilize the skills. Parents are required to videotape their special playtimes and present the video to be viewed during training sessions, or parents bring their child to the training setting and the training group observes special playtimes through a two-way mirror. When these options are not available, parents have a special playtime in the training setting and the training group sits in the room and observes.

It is essential that the filial therapist know whether or not parents have learned the skills. Parents' descriptions of how they have utilized the skills during special playtimes are often incomplete and perceptually biased, especially during the early stages of training. Parents simply are not aware of many of their negative communication behaviors. There is no substitute for direct observational supervision or seeing one's self on video. It should be pointed out that the primary focus of supervisory feedback, even in cases similar to the session described in the next paragraph, is always on positive behaviors parents have exhibited during the special playtimes.

The importance of supervision in the learning process and the necessity of insisting that this part of the training model not go overlooked for any parent can be seen in the following report of a filial therapist in our training program.

> Jeanie didn't bring a videotape of her play sessions with her child until our final training session. Until then, her reports sounded like she was utilizing the skills she was learning. After viewing her video, however, it was obvious she just didn't understand the principles and didn't know how to apply the skills. There were no reflection of feelings, virtually no tracking responses, almost all verbal interchanges were in the form of questions, and she maintained control during the entire play session. I wish I had seen this video in one of the earlier training sessions so I could have worked with her on developing her skills. She would have benefited from some intensive one-on-one role-playing. If she continues having the play sessions the way she is now responding, I'm not sure there would be any point. It was really disheartening to see this kind of play session at the end of the training, especially since she really seems to want to do the best she can for her children and thinks she is doing things the correct way. I really hope she will take another filial therapy class!

The inclusion of a structured approach to supervision in the CPRT/filial therapy training model is unique among parent training programs.

Applicable to a Wide Range of Parents

CPRT has been demonstrated through rigorous scientific studies to be effective with a wide range of parents and problematic behaviors of children (see Chapter 21 for an in-depth review). Parents from all rungs of the socioeconomic scale have been able to learn and effectively utilize the skills taught in CPRT. CPRT has been shown to be effective with a wide range of parental populations such as incarcerated parents, immigrant parents, parents of emotionally disturbed children, Native American parents living on a reservation, parents residing in a domestic violence shelter, nonoffending parents of sexually abused children, parents of chronically ill children, parents of children with speech problems, single parents, parents of children with learning difficulties, and other populations. Research results have been so robustly positive with a wide range of parents and in severe training circumstances that there can be no doubt as to the efficacy of CPRT with most parent populations.

Trainer Qualifications

Filial therapists generally have a master's degree in a mental health field such as counseling, psychology, or social work; specific training and supervision in play therapy; and advanced clinical experience in play therapy, as well as group therapy. Filial therapists are expected to be able to train parents to use the child-centered play therapy skills while at the same time attending to and facilitating group dynamics. Other parent training models may only require a few hours of training for a nonprofessional person to be considered qualified to train parents.

References

Eardley, D. (1978). *An initial investigation of a didactic version of filial therapy dealing with self-concept increase and problematic behavior decrease.* Unpublished doctoral dissertation, The Pennsylvania State University, University Park.

Rohner, R. (1986). *The warmth dimension: Foundations of parental acceptance/rejection theory.* Newbury Park, CA: Sage.

Schaefer, E. (1981). Development of adaptive behavior: Conceptual models and family correlates. In M. Begab, H. Haywood, & H. Garber (Eds.), *Psychological influences on retarded development: Vol. 1. Issues and theories in development.* Baltimore, MD: University Park Press.

Swick, K., Gladstone, D., & Hayes, J. (1988). *In search of themselves: Special needs children in a preschool setting.* Unpublished report on the Special Needs Learner Project, University of South Carolina's Children's Center, College of Education, University of South Carolina, Columbia.

Swick, K., & Graves, S. (1986). Locus of control and interpersonal support as related to parenting. *Childhood Education*, *62*, 26–31.

CHAPTER 3

TRAINING AND SUPERVISION OF CPRT FILIAL THERAPISTS

The field of play therapy is still a developing area in the mental health profession, and filial therapy is an even more recent, innovative and unique modality within the field of play therapy. Only a handful of university counseling, psychology, or social work programs offer graduate training in filial therapy. This chapter presents some guidelines for training in the CPRT filial therapy model, essential personal characteristics of filial therapists, and important variables in facilitating a CPRT/filial therapy group.

Training Experiences

Training and supervised experience in play therapy are prerequisites for becoming a filial therapist. This is a logical sequence because filial therapists must be able to teach play therapy skills to parents and supervise parent–child play sessions. In our counseling program at the University of North Texas, graduate students in filial therapy training are required to complete a 3-hour graduate credit course in Introduction to Play Therapy that has a supervised mini-practicum component and a 3-hour graduate credit course in

Group Play Therapy that has a practicum component prior to enrolling in a 3-hour graduate credit course in Filial Therapy with a 10-session filial therapy supervised practicum component. As a part of the supervision experience for the filial therapy course, graduate students watch videotapes of their filial therapy sessions and write a weekly self-critique paper focusing on topics such as what went well, areas for improvement, and what I learned about myself. A goal of this experience is that the process of self-observation and self-evaluation will continue after the graduate student is no longer in a formal educational experience. All practicing therapists should be engaged in a process of continually learning about self in the therapeutic relationship. This exploration is not likely to occur if the process has not been initiated and experienced in a training setting.

Some graduate students colead filial therapy groups in our training program and others lead filial groups by themselves. The criteria for placement in a coleading experience is based on the graduate student's knowledge, clinical experience, self-confidence, attitude, insight into self, and general professional maturity. There are distinct **advantages to coleading a filial therapy group**, as is evident in the following graduate student's self-critique:

> I enjoyed the experience of working with a coleader. It made leading the group easier by **taking some of the pressure off each of us**. If I forgot a point, my coleader was able to cover it. I felt more confident because I wasn't always "on the spot" or the focus of attention. I could pull some of my thoughts together while my coleader was running the show. An unexpected learning was **how important communication between the two of us was** between sessions, not only for processing the experience, formulating assessments of individual parent needs, and planning for the next training session, but also to keep our relationship open and honest about our reactions to each other, and what we noticed in each other during the sessions. I benefited greatly from our different styles of leadership, and I learned a great deal from the way she responded to parents and the way she picked up on cues that I had missed. **An important learning for both of us was how to read each other** so we would know when to take the lead without interrupting or monopolizing.

A caution about coleading a filial therapy group is that **one of the leaders may assume a role that is not active enough**, as is evident in a graduate student's self-critique:

> I learned that I have difficulty asserting myself. I have to continually work on this. My coleader did the majority of the speaking/leading in this first session, and I did not assert myself. As a result, I feel like the group members did not fully understand what my role was; whether I was a coleader or simply there to "aid" the group leader. This was frustrating to me because I wanted our roles to appear equal. My coleader and I have designed a more structured outline for the second session in order to prevent this from becoming the rule rather than the exception.

Regular supervisory sessions are needed to work on these and other issues inherent in coleading a filial therapy group. Differences in style of leadership can also present a problem:

> I am learning that it can be difficult to colead a group because of difference in styles. I like to let the group process "happen" and Stacey enjoys the "teaching" aspect of working with a group. We are open with each other about this issue and taking steps to reconcile these differences in the form of a compromise so we both get our needs met.

Supervised Experience

In addition to completing the introduction to play therapy, group play therapy, and filial therapy courses, graduate students are required to complete a supervised Practicum in Play Therapy in the Center for Play Therapy and an internship where they can continue clinical experiences in play therapy and filial therapy. Although training in play therapy and filial therapy are generally viewed as essential prerequisites to becoming a filial therapist, little attention has been focused in the professional literature on the crucial role supervision plays in facilitating the development of effective play therapists and filial therapists.

Even though most supervisors would agree that the general purpose of supervision is to facilitate the filial therapist's personal and professional development, the personal dimension is often only minimally focused on in supervisory relationships. Too often, supervision is a cognitive process focused on instructing and educating the therapist, questioning his decisions, identifying mistakes, providing information, interpreting parents' motivation, and offering suggested ways to respond to parents. Since the filial therapist's own inner struggles and conflicts can inhibit the progress of a filial therapy group, the filial therapist should engage in a process of learning about self. Learning what skills to teach in CPRT/filial therapy is not nearly as important as developing an awareness of the dynamics of the process of teaching those skills and how to utilize one's self in facilitating the learning process of parents. We propose that it is more important to focus the supervision experience on the attitudes of the filial therapist rather than techniques, on feelings rather than content, on the relationship rather than specific responses, and on accepting rather than evaluating. Supervision is a critical element in training filial therapists, especially in the areas of therapist reactions, feelings, and attitudes; insight into self; pacing in presenting material; facilitation of the group process; and gaining insight into parents' emotional needs. Beginning filial therapists need assistance in understanding themselves and the underlying inner motivations and dynamics of parents.

It is the person of the therapist that is the most significant factor in determining the effectiveness of the CPRT therapy experience. The therapist's understanding of self is more important than what the therapist knows, some intellectual knowledge, for it is the person of the therapist and how the therapist uses herself in the context of the CPRT therapy group that parents react to most. A goal of supervision is that the therapist will develop self-understanding and self-acceptance so the therapist will be able to spontaneously incorporate the person she is into the training experience with parents. To do this, the therapist must engage in a process of learning about self.

The therapist's emotional reactions to resistive parents, the process of teaching, and the pressure of the amount of material to be taught can inhibit the therapist's natural use of self and, therefore, should be processed in the supervisory relationship. It is the dynamics of the inner person of the therapist that largely determine whether or not the experience with parents is therapeutic. Therefore, the supervisory relationship must be therapeutically oriented in order to deal with the dynamics of the emotional issues of the filial therapist in training.

The self-critique of a filial therapist in training illustrates the importance of supervision in dealing with some of these personal dimensions.

> I experienced a range of emotions about parents missing training sessions, including anger, disappointment, and sadness. However, I suppose I have had enough actual experience as a counselor to avoid self-blame and feeling as though the problem related to me as a counselor. I also ran a gamut of feelings about some parents' fear of doing something different with their children, and these feelings progressed to impatience with the parents' obvious reluctance to hold special playtimes or be observed on video. A particularly growth-promoting experience for me in this filial therapy class was the continuous exploration of my feelings and thoughts in supervision during the process of the filial therapy sessions. I was able to achieve an understanding of my feelings as I processed them. I came to realize that these parents were no different from anyone else who was trying to break an ingrained habit, and parenting behaviors may well be some of the most difficult to alter. I came to realize that, just as we try to help parents view the world from their children's eyes, I, too, must step outside my perspective and view the parents' world from their perspective in order to be of help to them.
>
> Eventually, as I worked through my intense feelings toward the parents, I reached the core of my feelings: my anger at parents for their shortcomings went directly back to my own guilt for not having done with my own child all the things I know today. If I am candid with myself, I must admit that this is part of my reaction. This awareness will hopefully prevent my own baggage from interfering with the process of training. Now that I am aware of the potential, I will hopefully recognize my feelings earlier in filial therapy groups and be able to work through them before they negatively affect my ability to relate to parents.

Development of this kind of insight into self is essential for the filial therapist to be able to put personal reactions aside, understand the needs of parents, and facilitate an understanding and accepting atmosphere in the CPRT therapy group. A resistive or overtly rejecting and hostile parent can cause an inexperienced filial therapist to experience feelings of frustration and anger, as indicated in the following self-critique by a graduate student:

> I feel frustrated and irritated at parents in the group who don't contribute or volunteer information to the group. I know that it is my job to include these particular parents and seek feedback from them, yet I find myself feeling agitated when they are not actively contributing to the group.

Another graduate student wrote:

> Towards the end of this session, I was feeling very frustrated with a particular parent. It appeared that he was challenging me and trying to "prove me wrong." I was feeling very upset and irritated at him. Looking back on the experience, I think I was wanting him to agree with me on the specific topic. I need to be more comfortable with parents not agreeing with what I am teaching them.

CPRT training groups may stimulate a wide range of emotional reactions in inexperienced filial therapists, and they will, therefore, need an opportunity to process those reactions in a supervisory relationship.

Essential Personal Characteristics of Filial Therapists

The characteristics essential for an effective filial therapist are basically the same characteristics considered to be necessary for effective play therapists. The development of these characteristics is a function of the training and supervision the filial therapist receives that facilitates insight into self and an understanding of and sensitivity to the inner dynamics of children and parents. **Filial therapists need self-understanding and insight** into their own motivations, needs, blind spots, biases, personal conflicts, and areas of emotional difficulty, as well as personal strengths. Therapists should not assume they can keep their own values and needs compartmentalized and separate from their relationships with parents. Personal needs and values are a part of the person of the therapist and thus become a part of the relationship with parents. Therefore, training and supervision of filial therapists must incorporate a process of self-exploration that will promote self-understanding, thus minimizing the potential impact of the therapist's motivations and needs.

A focus of the supervision relationship should be on developing **therapist qualities that facilitate the learning environment** in the filial therapy relationship. **Warmth and caring** must be integral parts of the filial therapist's personality and readily experienced by parents as warmth, kindness, and friendliness. Warmth and caring increase parents' confidence and encourage open expressions of emotions and thoughts. The ability to warmly accept parents is predicated on the therapist's ability to understand and accept himself.

The **attitude of the therapist is the key to the learning environment** in CPRT because it is the therapist's attitude that sets the tone in the CPRT group and quickly permeates the entire training experience. Parents are impacted much more by the person of the therapist than by the knowledge of the therapist. Effective filial therapists appreciate their own uniqueness and are therefore able to accept the uniqueness of parents. The filial therapist is **intentional about creating an atmosphere** with parents that optimizes learning opportunities.

The effective filial therapist is relatively **free of threat and anxiety** and is thus **open to receiving parents as they are**, as they present themselves in the filial therapy group. The therapist is able to turn loose of his world of reality and to experience the parent's world of reality. This open-minded dimension allows the therapist to receive fully and with accuracy the meanings communicated by parents verbally and nonverbally in their interactions in the group. Many parents are fearful of rejection of the person they are or rejection of the kind of parent they are when they enter CPRT training. Experiencing **acceptance** helps them to lower their defenses and consider the possibility of incorporating new parenting skills into their relationships with their children. Acceptance means prizing the unique person of the parent and does not imply approval of all of the parent's behaviors.

Because parents are always in a process of becoming, the therapist should project a **future-mindedness** in relating to parents by not restricting them to the past through attitude or verbal responses. This means not restricting parents to ways they have previously described themselves as being, but being open to perceiving ways in which parents have changed. Therefore, the therapist is always engaged in a process of trying to catch up to where the parent is this week. This future-mindedness does not project or lead the parent into the future, but is an attitude of receptivity to the parent being in a continuous process of becoming.

The effective filial therapist acts and responds out of **personal courage** by admitting mistakes, by being vulnerable at times, and by admitting inaccuracies in personal perceptions. Personal courage is needed to take risks and to act on intuitive feelings in response to parents' sharing. Personal courage based on inner confidence may be required when a parent is angry, resistive, or defensive. Therapists who have low tolerance for these behaviors and lack self-understanding may respond inappropriately by being defensive or by rejecting the parent. Such situations call for a high degree of **patience**. The therapist is able to be patient with parents because of her willingness to accept her own imperfections and to forgive herself for not being perfect; that is, to accept her own humanness. Therefore, no need exists to have the parent be perfect. The effective filial therapist is **personally secure** and thus recognizes and accepts personal limitations without any sense of threat to her feelings of adequacy. A supportive supervising relationship is essential to help beginning filial therapists feel personally secure.

Being real means being vulnerable enough to admit "I don't have solutions to all the problems parents describe with their children." Being real is dependent on a high degree of self-understanding and self-acceptance, which implies having insight into self: being aware of and accepting one's own feelings and reactions with insight into the accompanying motivations. A therapist who lacks self-understanding of her own motivations may inappropriately project rejection to the parents whose experiences and value systems are different. This struggle can be seen in the self-critique of a filial therapist in training:

> This was my fifth filial therapy session, and **I am still struggling with being judgmental of parents**, expecting more from them than I should. I have difficulty

> accepting that people are doing the best they can versus making improvements to do it "better." I have a tendency to think that people should always be working on themselves, their issues, and their relationships. This expectation of people often impedes my ability to really hear them, to be supportive and to provide helpful interventions.

Filial therapists should work through such issues in supervisory relationships.

Realness is an attitude of willingness to allow parents to experience the many parts of the person of the therapist, not just the professional self. Beginning filial therapists often experience difficulty allowing the uniqueness of their person to be seen:

> Observing myself on video reminded me of how task-oriented I can be, and how I often have a difficult time **focusing on the current moment**. I can be so worried about the future that I am not present in the present. I learned how my driven behavior affects every area of my life. I was reminded of how I desire to be seen as intelligent and professional. I have a tendency to become too distant and disconnected as the informative group leader. I will attempt to **balance the professionalism with sincerity and vulnerability**.

CPRT training can really be fun and exciting, and the therapist should be comfortable enough with herself to relax and enjoy the process. The humorous part of the therapist should be readily interjected into the training experiences with parents. A **sense of humor** helps parents to relax, puts them at ease, and helps them to share personal dimensions of their lives. Well-placed **humor can make learning fun** for parents and can be used to help get points across to parents that might be difficult for them to accept, as in the following filial therapy interaction.

Pat: (a single mom) Things are really hectic at my house in the mornings. I'm trying to get to my university classes on time, and Josh is in the front room in his pajamas watching TV. I take his breakfast in to him and feed him while he's watching TV.

Dr. L.: (interrupts) Excuse me, Pat. How old is Josh? (This fact was already know by Dr. L.)

Pat: He's 5, and that's not all. After I feed him, I dress him, and I'm still late getting to my classes.

Dr. L.: (looking at his notes) Pat, I don't remember you telling us Josh has both arms broken.

Pat: They're not.

Dr. L.: Are his legs broken?

Pat: No.

Dr. L.: Is he in a full body cast? (group laughs)

Pat: Not yet! (group laughs) (silence as Pat thinks) OK, I get the message. He's old enough to feed himself and dress himself. I've known I should do that, but just haven't done it. I just need to give him the responsibility for doing so. OK! Tomorrow I will do it!

Dr. L.: So you haven't done what you knew was the best thing to do, but I hear your commitment now. Next week, I'll check on you to find out how it went.

As in play therapy, the effectiveness of the filial therapist is largely dependent on the relationship the therapist creates with parents in the training setting and the extent to which the therapist is able to facilitate the creation of a therapeutic relationship between parents and their children in specially structured play sessions. It is the parent–child relationship that is created in the play sessions that makes the experience unique, not the toys or the setting, for most parents already play with their children.

Learning How to Lead a CPRT Group

A part of graduate students' supervision experience in our program is the requirement that they engage in a process of self-critique and self-analysis related to their experiences in leading CPRT training groups. The following excerpts, selected from lengthy self-critiques because they represent diverse reactions, provide insight into beginning filial therapists' experiences, some points of learning about themselves, and their discovery of important variables in facilitating a CPRT group that merit attention by most filial therapists. A striking dimension in these critiques is the depth of insight into self these inexperienced filial therapists developed.

Mike: If I can touch parents where their needs are, I have done well. Filial therapy is about enriching the relationship between parent and child to enhance the healthy growth of the child. I have found that while doing that, the parent's self-esteem goes up, their effectiveness goes up, and, therefore, their level of health and well-being also increases. I really enjoy filial therapy.

I have also learned that **when I move too quickly through the material, the parents do not learn** what I think they learn. I must take the time to get feedback from the parents and not move so rapidly next time. If what I am teaching them sparks new thinking, they will be involved in their own thought process. If I do not wait for them to do all of their processing, they will draw inaccurate conclusions from the other snatches that they catch on the way. They will get lost while I jump too quickly to another subject.

Valerie: I need to **improve my ability to respond to parents' nonverbal communications, reflect their feelings more often, and model the skills I am teaching them to use**. I often felt clueless when the opportunities to respond arose. **My need to be liked and looked on as an authority interferes** with my willingness to observe and respond to nonverbal cues. I feel silly admitting that I know the material, believe in it, and use it myself, but can't even see how to model these behaviors for parents! This fear of not being liked by the parents, coupled with my fear of not having answers to parents' questions, places undue stress on me to perform rather than lead and guide. Sometimes on the videotapes of my filial group, I sounded "preachy." I believe this is the result of my need to be an expert in every way when I lead this filial group.

Margaret: I need to **improve my skill in redirecting parents and keeping them on track** when they are relating information. Occasionally, we ran out of time because we had spent too much time allowing parents to share too many details about problems at home. On numerous occasions, I recognized after the fact that I should have gently interrupted a parent, summarized the topic, and generalized the point to other parents. Secondly, I need to **utilize more insightful questions when processing information from parents**. Instead of merely accepting a report about a play session or a homework assignment, I need to challenge parents more by asking what they learned from these experiences, what they recognized about their child that they hadn't known before, what they learned about themselves, etc.

Mary: There is a fine line between being a therapist and a teacher. The therapist in me wanted to be understanding and empathetic when a parent missed a training session or did not have a playtime one week. However, the teacher in me was disappointed when either situation occurred. I had one parent who did not have her playtime two weeks in a row. She used reflective listening with her son and saw immediate results in his response. However, she had difficulty being disciplined in scheduling and conducting special playtimes. I should have been **firmer with her when she reported that she did not have a play session** those weeks. I did not want the parent to get mad and not come back to class, so I was hesitant in how to handle this situation. (Supervisor comment: Ask the parent, "Can I get a commitment from you that you will have a session this week?")

Kay: I recognized that I was not as comfortable in the teaching role as I am in a counselor role. Partially, this is due to my lack of experience in this role and with this material, but I felt that I was not as genuine while teaching as I normally am. **It was obvious on my videos when I felt uncomfortable** by watching my body language and listening to my tone of voice. I spoke faster, looked down at my notes a lot, used excessive hand gestures, and my tone of voice was higher pitched than usual while teaching the filial group. I will need to continue to be aware of this and, hopefully, with more experience I will become more comfortable. I also learned that **when I lack confidence in myself, my level of genuineness tends to decrease and is evident through my nonverbal cues**.

Karen: I feel positive about the improvement that I have made in my ability to **keep the parents on track**. During the early training sessions, I had to focus on keeping the parents on task during role-playing sessions, and on **returning responsibility to answer questions back to the parents** instead of providing them with the answers. As the training sessions progressed, I improved in using nonverbal cues, such as handing out papers, as a means of indicating that we were ready to begin the next topic. I also improved in being able to use what the parents said to focus the conversation back on the topic at hand and then continue with the next topic for discussion. In addition, I am improving at being more direct, at being **able to redirect off-task conversations in an inconspicuous manner, and at providing more structure in guiding the length of conversations**. I am now more able to insist that parents stay on task during the role-playing experiences and ask questions at a later time.

Matt: My most significant learning from leading a filial therapy group is: **Never underestimate the power of filial therapy**, even three or four sessions. I met with Greta and watched a video of her play session with her daughter. She did an exceptional job setting limits in the play session. She reported that she has been giving choices outside the playtimes, and they are working. Her daughter is now going to sleep an hour earlier and sleeping much better through the night. Greta is also using the limit setting and choices successfully at work. She reported feeling more in control of herself with her daughter and stated that her daughter feels more secure. During the supervision time, Greta brought up some personal issues, and I asked if she would consider individual counseling to help her with these issues. She said that she would and planned to call the counseling center. I am incredibly surprised by how much these parents and their children have changed in just a few sessions of filial therapy.

Randy: In this first filial therapy session, one area for improvement that I noted is my overuse of verbalization. Filial therapy has a teaching aspect, and in that vein, I can really "get into it." I have a hard time not talking. **I need to learn to be quiet sometimes**. I think this happens because I do enjoy teaching and being in charge. I also can be prone to having some lack of faith in myself, which means I might tend to overdo the talking in an effort to ensure I am making my point.

Janet: Looking back on the first session, I recognize several areas for improvement. If I could go back and redo the session, I would definitely **talk more slowly**. Mallorie and I raced through the material, as if we were trying to "cram in" as much information as possible. Sometimes I talked so fast that I could not understand myself! The parents just nodded and did not complain about the quick pace. However, the quizzical looks on their faces should have been my clue to slow down. Every once in a while, I paused momentarily and asked "Any questions?" Of course, none of the parents replied. They were probably shell-shocked! Instead of asking for questions, I should have said, "Tell me what you understand." This statement focuses on what they know, rather than pointing out what they do not understand. I need to **pay more attention to group dynamics**. I felt as if I was teaching a class rather than facilitating a group. I know I missed several opportunities to get in touch with the parents. I especially want to **look for reactions of group members while one of the parents is speaking**. Often, a parent in the group may have experienced the same problem and could identify with the parent that is sharing. Focusing on these dynamics would strengthen the cohesiveness of the group.

In the third filial therapy training session, one couple was having marital problems. The tension between them was obvious, yet I ignored it altogether. **I was so**

uncomfortable with the tension between the couple. I was afraid to refer to their angry feelings because I was unsure of what reaction they would have. I was reluctant because I feared an avalanche of blaming and accusations between them. This is my issue, because I have always tried to avoid conflict. This avoidance hinders my ability to be honest with these parents. I must work on this.

The group dynamics in the sixth session were fabulous. The parents seemed relaxed and comfortable with each other. They supported and encouraged each other. The couple who experienced marital difficulties were getting along beautifully! The father gave especially vibrant feedback to several other parents. I really enjoyed this group.

Shelly: One area, which needed improvement in this third session, was more involvement from the parents. I think Janet and I felt so rushed that **we did not stop and involve the parents enough**. We needed to do more role-playing. During the next session, we are going to focus on role-playing and helping the parents to get involved. We also need to do a better job of **relating to Tasha, who appears not to believe a lot of what we say. We need to help her to become more directly involved and interactive with the other parents**. I think I am scared that she will ask me a question, and I will not know the answer! This is compounded by my reaction that a question means the parent has doubts. **I need to let the parents develop their own answers at times.** I also learned in this session how much life a session has. I was so tired before the filial group, but once it started I became alive and full of energy.

Gail: I was uptight about presenting information to my filial therapy group due to my perfectionism. I always feel that I have to do it right even though I know intellectually that there is no specific right way. **I did tend to get into a lecture mode in this first session, instead of keeping the interaction more casual.** I do have a need to be in control, to make sure something is being accomplished.

I became more relaxed in the second session after I began to focus more on the material and information and less on me, and this resulted in a better flow. I am beginning to realize how much of my life was programmed toward accomplishment, and I am working to keep this need under control. In the fourth session, I became **aware of just how important role-playing is helping these new ways of responding to become second nature** to these parents.

Justin: I have learned that **parents change when they are ready** and often in ways which I least expect, but they do change. I was continually surprised by the changes I saw in my filial group members, and these changes often occurred when I was experiencing the greatest doubt. In almost every case, I learned the lesson of **trusting the process**. I also learned that by sharing my experiences with other counselors in supervision, we can maintain enthusiasm and hope, even when we are experiencing difficulties.

I have learned in leading my filial group that I have a great opportunity to be creative and to **put my own unique spin on the process**. It reminds me of my brother, a jazz musician. He took tons of theory classes, but when it came to improvisation, he said he had to put all the theories and techniques and exercises on the shelf, and **play from his heart**. The same holds true for me as I attempt to integrate what I have learned.

CHAPTER 4

CRITICAL COMPONENTS IN FACILITATING THE PROCESS OF CPRT

The CPRT process is characterized by **two key components: a didactic component and a group process component in the context of a safe, reassuring, supportive, nonthreatening environment** that encourages parents to explore feelings, attitudes, and perceptions about themselves, their children, and parenting. This safe, accepting environment also facilitates risk taking that leads to behavioral change. In her ethnographic study of the process of the Landreth 10-session CPRT filial therapy model, Lahti (1992) concluded that the careful, skilled balancing of the didactic element of filial therapy with a group process/therapy element is a unique aspect of filial therapy's nature and may be the primary key to the manner in which filial therapy effectively facilitates change.

Group Process Component

The supportive format in a CPRT group often resembles group therapy as the leader responds empathically to parents' issues and emotional reactions related to their family or their role as parents. Likening the emotional exploring and supportive component of CPRT to group therapy does not imply that the objective is to provide group therapy, only that some aspects of the group interaction and process take on the nature of group therapy for short periods of time as parents explore their feelings about themselves, their children, and their families. When Mary complains that she can never do enough for her daughter, the leader responds, "You're feeling frustrated and helpless, sometimes." The transition from this empathic group therapy type element of exploring an emotional issue to the didactic element can be accomplished by limiting the group therapy exploration to a few minutes of interaction, making an empathic reflection that summarizes the parent's feeling, and then making a teaching point that is related to the content of the parent's sharing:

> Mary, that was a very frustrating experience for you. Group, just as you need someone to understand your frustration, when your child is frustrated, your child needs to know you understand, and understanding is communicated by reflecting your child's feeling. For example, "That is really frustrating to you when the pieces won't stick together." Let's work on reflecting feelings now.

The struggle to maintain an effective balance between the didactic and process dimensions of CPRT was expressed by a filial therapist in training:

> The area I need to make the most improvement in is related to balancing teaching with counseling. I am more comfortable teaching the information related to filial therapy and less comfortable addressing the emotional needs of parents as they arise in the group. Although I recognize these needs, I struggle with how I should address them, how often and how in-depth I should go. I know I do not want the session to focus fully on counseling. However, I believe I am currently missing many opportunities to quickly address emotional needs of parents which would allow them to better focus, and I am missing many opportunities to role-model how reflecting feelings and communicating understanding can be impactful, the very skills I am training them to use with their children.

The implementation of this kind of insight will make CPRT groups more dynamic and effective.

In CPRT training, it is common that the discussion of relationship skills elicits in parents current and/or long-standing intense feelings and reactions about their children. Parents need time to process these feelings in order to clear their cognitive and emotional systems before they can incorporate and integrate the new concepts, principles, and skills being taught. Processing parents' reactions and feelings about their children promotes the beginning of change in parents' perceptions about their children. The filial therapist must maintain a delicate balance between the didactic and process dimensions without being rigid in covering the scheduled training material or allowing the group to become bogged down in the group therapy dimensions of the process. A filial therapist in our training program described the process as:

> The crunch of trying to get in all of the training agenda in each training session nagged at me in every session, and I sometimes felt myself become annoyed when parents would go into a drawn-out story about their children. About halfway through the 10 training sessions, I learned how to loosen my grip on the agenda of the sessions in order to meet more of the personal, emotional needs of the parents. As the weeks went on, I became more relaxed about this, realizing that parents occasionally need to vent their feelings in order to clear their systems so they can concentrate and really learn the content of the training. I also became much better at redirecting a parent when it was time to move on. I have been taught my whole life not to interrupt people, so this task took some effort. However, when I realized just how little time we had per session, it did not take me long to accomplish this goal and actually become pretty good at it.

It is imperative that the leader intersperse the teaching component of CPRT with building **group cohesiveness**, especially in the first two or three training sessions. This is accomplished when the therapist generalizes parent disclosures to help parents identify with each other by asking questions such as "Does this sound familiar to anyone else?" or "Anyone else ever yell at your child?" and "What was that like for you?" when a parent responds affirmatively. When parents nod their heads understandingly as a parent describes a problem, the leader can comment, "So the rest of you know what that is like." This **linking of parents** helps break down barriers of isolation and the feeling "I'm the only one who feels this way" or "I'm the only one who ever yells at her child."

If a parent describes a point of difficulty in a play session, the leader can ask, "Group, what rule of thumb applies here?" The leader can also encourage group interaction by inviting parents to respond to each other's questions: "Linda, how would you suggest Erika respond when her son wants to paint her glasses?" This question not only facilitates interaction but also decreases parents' dependence on the leader for solutions by inviting parents to contribute their ideas. If a parent seems to be thoughtful about something, the leader can invite sharing: "Angela, what are you thinking?" The guiding principle for the leader is careful adherence to the **Rule of Thumb: The leader is a facilitator of interaction, not just a trainer**. An objective is that as the training progresses, the interaction among the parents will increase, and they will be more actively supportive and offer suggestions to each other.

The development of group interaction and group cohesiveness is described in the following filial therapist's report:

> The family that has struggled with the father's severe medical problems has seen a sharp increase in angry outbursts from their 3-year-old daughter, Melissa. As the group discussed ways to facilitate healthy expression of feelings, Melissa's mother had a sudden flash of insight and burst out, "We're not validating her anger!" Melissa's parents stopped trying to distract her and started reflecting her feelings and had extremely positive results. Another very positive experience in the filial therapy group has been the parents' dedication to the group and support of each other. The father with health problems became wheelchair-bound for about 2 weeks during the training, and yet he continued to come to the group and even did his play sessions from his wheelchair. This same couple brought a book to help a child adjust to the birth of a new baby and gave it to the parents who are expecting. Another group member was obviously

struggling with the filial skills, and when he showed his videotape, the other group members worked very hard to find and reflect his strengths. It was really wonderful to see these parents trust us as leaders and trust each other enough to allow themselves to be very vulnerable in the process of learning new ways to relate to their children. These parents felt safe enough to struggle openly with self-doubt and feelings of inadequacy in the parent role and were genuinely supportive of each other in these struggles.

The group process components that are facilitative to the process of CPRT are highlighted in the following transcriptions of dialogues between Dr. Garry Landreth and parents who participated in one of his 10-session CPRT training groups. The group process components illustrated by selected transcriptions are

- Normalizing and generalizing individual parental concerns and fears to the group
- Encouraging a parent to explore thoughts and feelings more fully
- Building group cohesion to encourage or teach members

Normalizing and Generalizing Individual Parental Concerns and Fears to the Group

Scenario 1: One parent may disclose information to the group about her child or herself that may feel shameful or embarrassing. Hearing similar happenings or reactions from other parents normalizes the disclosure and creates a safe environment for all parents, encouraging them to reveal their own similar experiences so the disclosing parent realizes she is not alone in her feelings or experience.

Debbie: I think my daughter is of average intelligence, and strong willed. I am rejecting her as a person because I am having so many problems with her.

Dr. L.: So she is demanding and bossy. How do you react to her when she is bossy?

Debbie: Honestly? Extremely violently.

Dr. L.: I gather from the way you say that that you get really angry sometimes. Any of the rest of you get angry with your children?

Kim: Yes, absolutely.

Scenario 2: Sometimes generalizing to the group opens up an opportunity for another parent to discuss more fully her own concerns associated with those revealed by the first parent.

Sonya: His dad has always been the one who disciplines him. There have been problems at school, but since his dad moved out of the house, he has gotten better at school. I am just losing patience.

Dr. L.: Anyone else lose your patience when reacting to you children?

Nita: Yes, I do.

Dr. L.: What is that like for you?

Nita: I get angry and say things that I wish I had not said.

Encouraging a Parent to Explore Thoughts and Feelings More Fully

Scenario 1: When a parent has made an emotionally laden comment, the parent is encouraged to talk more, so that the parent may put words to the thoughts and feelings that often huddle beneath the surface of a first response.

Dr. L.: Let's see what the video of your play session looks like, Laura.

Laura: The play sessions are more about just allowing me to appreciate my son more than anything else.

Dr. L.: Laura, add to that.

Laura: We were having a really hard time, and I didn't like a lot of his behavior. Being a single parent, I feel so much that I'm always the one who has to discipline him, and that I forget to just enjoy and play with my children. So the play sessions have allowed me to do that, with joy.

Scenario 2: Encouraging a parent to elaborate allows the parent to describe specific events or situations that are troublesome, which in turn allows the therapist to teach the group about filial therapy skills that will benefit the entire group.

Dr. L.: Well, how were your playtimes this week?

Kathy: Ours started a little bit late Thursday night because we went out to eat, but we had the session right after we ate.

Dr. L.: You did have it.

Kathy: Yes, we had a pretty good one.

Dr. L.: Tell us some specifics. What happened in the playtime?

Kathy: He wanted to play with some different games this time. He really didn't ask me to do anything with him. So I just sat there and watched him. And sometimes when I told him that I saw what he was doing, he'd say, "Mom, I know that already. I know what I'm doing already."

Dr. L.: Let's work on that. Say to him, "Well, I'm just really interested in what you're doing, and I want to let you know that I see what you're doing. I don't know any other way to say it."

Emily: Very good, because I had the same problem with my child. She would tell me she didn't want me to tell her what she was doing. She got really agitated with me for doing it.

Dr. L.: It may also be that your children feel that you're tracking them a little too closely.

Building Group Cohesion to Encourage or Teach Members

Scenario 1: Asking parents to explain skills or teaching points to parents who were absent not only builds group cohesion, but also secures parents' commitment to the process and abets accountability. Knowing that they may be called on to describe a skill or explain a rationale to the group increases parents' attention and understanding.

Dr. L.: Well, we need to do some review of last week's session. Last week we worked on limit setting. What I'd like to do, Sonya and Kim, is let you all do a little bit of review about limit setting for the others who weren't here.

Sonya: Oh yes, I remember.

Dr. L.: If you would tell everyone what you remember about limit setting, that would help them learn it.

Sonya: How about telling them about ACT?

Dr. L.: OK.

Sonya: Dr. Landreth gave us an acronym, ACT. "A" means acknowledge the feeling or the want of the child, such as, "I know you want to stay up later," or "I know you want to hit me or your sister," or "I know you feel angry." Then "C" is for communicate the limit, such as "It's time to go to bed," or "It's bedtime," or "It's not OK to hit me," whatever you need to say to communicate the limit. "T" is for targeting the choices. All together, you would say something like, "I know you feel angry, but it's not OK to hit me. You may hit your stuffed animals." Then Dr. Landreth gave us an assignment to write down two times when we used ACT setting limits.

Scenario 2: Rather than teach and provide all the answers in the group, the leader allows parents to apply their newly learned skills and abilities and become a part of the solution in which all group members learn.

Dr. L.: Your son is too subtle. If he picked up a hammer, you'd know he was going to hit the mirror, but he does a lot of things that are on the borderline, doesn't he?

Nita: Yes, a lot, and it's hard to know whether or not to set a limit.

Dr. L.: So what would you all like to suggest? Laura, what would you suggest?

Scenario 3: Use group management skills to involve all parents, and encourage parents to direct comments to each other to obtain the most power from parents' observations.

Dr. L.: My, such patience, Laura. Not once in your playtime did I hear you say, "Now hurry up. You've been washing your hands there a long time now. Now hurry up." Group, I want you all to give Laura some feedback. What did you see and what did you hear?

Debbie: (Looking at Dr. L.) She stayed right with him.

Dr. L.: You all tell Laura. Don't tell me, tell Laura.

Nita: I agree. You didn't overtrack.

Sonya: You didn't overtrack. You stayed right there. You look relaxed, real comfortable, real calm. You look like you've done this for years.

Kathy: I liked your facial expressions.

Kim: You varied your responses. He knew you were interested.

Teaching Components

Presenting the information to be learned in **simple one-item teaching points** is the key to parents learning and assimilating new information. Giving parents too much information in one training session or presenting complex information is overwhelming to parents. If parents do not feel they can quickly implement a new skill, they are not very likely to attempt to use the new skill. One parent noted, "There was a lot of information, but it wasn't overwhelming because it was presented one step at a time."

Simple homework assignments and concise informational handouts are provided to reinforce teaching points made in the training sessions. A parent commented:

> I'm amazed at how simple the homework is. It makes me aware of how I respond to my child. The homework makes a real difference in the effectiveness of this class. Sometimes it takes a direct assignment to make me stop the busy work and learn to relate to my child.

The simplicity of the homework and presenting this new approach to parenting in small incremental steps reduces parents' anxiety about trying something new and motivates them to attempt the assignments.

An overriding objective in CPRT is to **empower parents**. This is accomplished by creating a safe, supportive, nonthreatening atmosphere in the group and by being understanding of parents' difficulties, accepting of their weaknesses and mistakes, encouraging of their efforts, supportive of their struggles to try new behaviors, and actively communicating a belief in their capability. This last dimension is perhaps the most crucial. **Rule of Thumb: It is difficult to believe in yourself if no one believes in you.** This attitude of belief in the parent frees the parent to risk being imperfect and reduces parents' dependence on the leader. Focusing on parents' positive behaviors, successes, effectiveness, and accentuating parents' progress inspires confidence, reduces defensiveness, and engenders the courage to change. **Active affirmation** of parents' efforts is considered to be a critical key to the effectiveness of CPRT.

Employing a variety of teaching tools such as **stories, analogies, and metaphors to emphasize teaching points** helps to maintain a high level of parent interest and facilitates the learning process. Parents may have difficulty recalling a teaching point in isolation, but when the point is attached to a short, interest-catching story, **parents will remember the story and then the teaching point**. Such stories are most effective when they are inserted during parents' disclosures to clarify or support parents' efforts or to teach a new principle. This seems to make the stories personally meaningful.

Catchy "Rules of Thumb" also help make teaching points easier for parents to remember. When teaching major principles, the rule of the day is **repetition, repetition, repetition**. For example, the four therapeutic messages "I am here," "I hear you," "I understand," and "I care" are reviewed at a pertinent point in each training session.

Modeling by the therapist is a key component of the teaching process. The **therapist's responses to parents should consistently model basic child-centered play therapy principles and skills**, thus enabling parents to personally experience the impact of skills they are being asked to use with their children. Modeling allows parents to learn these principles and skills by experiencing. This learning can be emphasized by the therapist first reflecting a parent's feelings and then asking the group, "What did I just do?" The therapist may have to identify for the group what he did and then elicit help from the parent whose feelings he reflected to explain the impact of the reflection. One parent's reaction at the end of the first CPRT training session was, "I've taken lots of parenting classes, but I already see a difference in filial training. I will experience it!"

The therapist can use **self-disclosure** about his efforts and mistakes as a parent to illustrate teaching points and to model permission to make mistakes. Hopefully, the therapist will also be secure enough to point out the mistakes he makes in videos or live demonstration play sessions. Such disclosures create a more relaxed atmosphere in the group and seem to remove parents' self-imposed pressure to be perfect.

Modeling is also utilized by **showing videotapes of the therapist's play sessions** or by the therapist conducting a live play session to demonstrate the kind of responses hoped for by parents in their play sessions. When viewing a video, the video should be stopped frequently to point out skills and specific responses that have been emphasized in the training sessions. A parent commented on the benefits of viewing videos of the therapist's play sessions:

> Watching Dr. Landreth's videos was an added dimension that we've never gotten in other parenting classes. Seeing how he responded made learning the skills come alive. You can't get that from a book or from someone just telling you how to do it.

When **viewing the video of a parent's play session**, the video should be stopped frequently to validate and affirm the parent's efforts. **The focus is on what the parents are doing correctly** rather than focusing on mistakes. The therapist's focus on providing positive feedback models for parents how they are to give feedback to each other. The therapist can help parents to begin thinking about the meaning of their children's play by making comments such as "He did a lot of nurturing and taking care of you during the medical kit play." It is also helpful to call attention to patterns or themes in the play sessions and to infer children's needs and motives based on their play behavior. This provides insight and encourages parents to move to a higher skill level. After watching herself in a play session with her child, a mother said, "That was a real growth experience for me. I wasn't aware of my behaviors until I saw myself in the video."

The teaching components that are facilitative to the process of CPRT are highlighted in the following transcriptions of dialogues between Dr. Garry Landreth and parents who participated in one of his 10-session CPRT training groups. The teaching components illustrated by selected transcriptions are

- Modeling acceptance, reflective listening, and focused attention
- Fallibility of therapist (as expert)
- Encouraging parental strengths
- Utilizing specific instruction
- Providing concrete examples
- Imparting expert knowledge
- Using analogies to increase parent awareness
- Encouraging role-play and practice of skills
- Making suggestions for improvement
- Identifying what is learned from events in special playtimes
- Identifying shifts or changes in behavior (in child or in parent)
- Facilitating insight
- Clarifying

Modeling Acceptance, Reflective Listening, and Focused Attention

Acceptance

Scenario 1: A critical aspect of CPRT is the parent's acceptance of the child, practiced through many different skills in special playtimes. The therapist models acceptance in sessions with parents, so that parents may experience what that type of acceptance feels like; parents can, in turn, practice acceptance of their children in the playtimes.

Laura: My special playtime is supposed to be on Tuesday afternoon, but Tuesday was a really hectic day, and I forgot the playtime. Then Thursday I finally remembered and had the playtime just before his bedtime. I can remember to go to my university class, but I forget my son.

Dr. L.: Your life gets really hectic sometimes, and you feel guilty about forgetting your special playtime, but the important thing is that you did have it. The rule of thumb that applies here is the most important thing may not be what you do, but what you do after what you have done. You love your son and made a special time for him. That's an important message.

Scenario 2: The therapist should take every opportunity to acknowledge and label parents' acceptance of their children's feelings during training sessions with parents.

Emily: I reflected what he was doing. I didn't say, "You're stabbing them in their private areas." I just simply stated, "Oh, you're stabbing the baby, and now you're stabbing the mom."

Dr. L.: That was enough.

Emily: And then he started slashing furniture with the rubber knife. He was just a little animal. At that point, I said, "You look really angry." That's when he threw the knife down and crawled up in my arms, and that was it.

Dr. L.: The important thing is that your child got to express his feelings, and he felt understood. His feelings were accepted, not necessarily the act, but the feelings were accepted.

Reflective Listening

Scenario 1: The therapist models reflective listening skills, in addition to teaching parents these skills, so that parents experience being heard and practice the same reflective listening with their children.

Sonya: I have two children, both are girls. I am a single parent, divorce pending, and it is harder than I thought it would be. Right now, I think my older daughter is trying to tell me something.

Dr. L.: And you are not quite sure what it is.

Sonya: Sometimes she shows me with her anger that she is scared. Since my husband and I separated, there is no consistency with visitation. She loves her daddy, and he is just not there; he never was. I try to open up the arena to talk about stuff, but I sense that she feels it is not okay to talk. She has started doing some things that I am confused about.

Dr. L.: I hear two things: that you are trying to be all things to her and that is not quite possible. The other thing is you want so much to understand what your daughter is saying to you, but she can't sit down and say it. That's one of the things that I am going to work on: to help you become a keen observer of your child's play and to learn as much as you possibly can from your child's play.

Scenario 2: Parents' descriptions of their interactions with their children provide occasions for the therapist to model reflecting feelings.

Kathy: This playtime was NOT an enjoyable experience for me at all. He was violent the whole time. He was attacking me.

Dr. L.: He was trying to hurt you, and the whole experience wasn't very satisfying for you.

Kathy: Yeah. He hit me with the plastic reflex hammer while he was playing doctor, and I said, "You may play with the hammer, but you can't hurt me."

Dr. L.: So you were able to set a limit.

Kathy: Yeah, but I was exhausted. By the time the playtime was over, I was really glad to stop.

Dr. L.: So you were able to set a limit, but it sounds like the playtime was an emotionally draining experience for you.

Kathy: Yes. We come from an abusive situation, and when I see him act like that, I can see his father. I just get kinda petrified.

Dr. L.: You were really frightened and wanted out of there.

Focused Attention

Scenario 1: CPRT training emphasizes teaching parents to focus attention on their children. The therapist points out occasions when parents give their undivided attention to their children and makes sure parents recognize the positive impact of this kind of attention.

Dr. L.: This segment of your video is an example of when your facial expression says a lot more than any words can ever say. You reflect his feelings with your face. Watch your face. No words. Everything about your face says, "I'm here with you, I hear you. I understand. I care." I hear your message in your face. You're excited about that. It's fun for you. You say no words, and yet you conveyed everything you needed to convey to him.

Laura: I don't think he ever looked at me.

Sonya: I think so. Yes, he's checking.

Dr. L.: Watch this. (plays video) He did see you—right there. (stops video) Children don't miss a thing. This is a delightful scene right here, clearly enjoyed by both of you.

Scenario 2: During a training session, the therapist models focused attention, often recognizing a parent's nonverbal behavior and asking the parent to comment so that other parents have the opportunity to experience the benefits of focused attention.

Debbie: That's the thing that I'm still having trouble with—being in the middle of the crisis, and being able to step back out of the crisis.

Dr. L.: And be objective.

Debbie: And be objective from it, and know that it's OK, too. That I don't have to react, that I can step back and get in control of my own emotions, and then decide what to do.

Dr. L.: Laura, you were reacting to that, when Debbie said she can step back.

Laura: When my son does these things, the first thing I do now is just tell myself that he is not really doing this just to get me. I used to feel, "You are doing this on purpose to get me." But when I take myself out of it, then I handle the whole situation a lot better, and I'm a lot happier, and he's a lot happier.

Fallibility of Therapist (As Expert)

Scenario 1: If parents believe their filial therapist is an infallible expert in child behavior, they may feel intimidated and inadequate, leading to possible reluctance to participate or unwillingness to demonstrate newly learned skills and techniques. The therapist can weave personal commentary on his own mistakes in parenting into his groups, as well as oversights he has made while in playtimes with children. These disclosures help parents realize there is no standard of perfection, and no one is capable of doing everything right at all times with children.

Dr. L.: Let's check some more of this video of my session with this little girl. (Video is played.) Do you realize what I just missed?

Sonya: That she was happy.

Dr. L.: Yes. You would think that after doing this for 25 years that I would have caught that. But I'm just like you all are. I'm not perfect either. I slip up lots of times, Sonya. I still don't know why I didn't respond to her feeling. It's so obvious she's delighted with that. I think I got too caught up in what she was doing with her hands, just tracked that, and I missed her feeling. So if I miss her feeling after all these years of experience, surely it must be OK if you miss your child's feelings now and then.

Debbie: Is it OK if we follow up after missing a feeling?

Dr. L.: Yes, I get a chance to come back to it. (Video is played.) Just a little slow, but I finally got around to saying, "That surprised you."

Scenario 2: By relating his parenting mistakes with his own children or in play sessions, the therapist reduces parents' fears that he will judge them as a parenting expert incapable of erring.

Dr. L.: When my oldest daughter was three years of age, we were visiting in my parents' home in another state. It was 9:30 at night. Out of the kitchen came my 3-year-old daughter. By the way, I just told you something really important about me. It's 9:30 at night, and my 3-year-old daughter…

Debbie: Is still awake.

Dr. L.: Yes, she is still awake. So what does that tell you, Debbie? I'm just like the rest of you. I didn't always put her to bed at the time she should have been in bed. I'm like the rest of you. I don't always do what I should all the time as a parent.

Encouraging Parental Strengths

Scenario 1: Teaching parents new and different skills is a basic part of CPRT. The therapist can employ modeling as one method of demonstrating to parents the impact of allowing their children the freedom to decide in play sessions.

Dr. L.: These toys on the list can only be played with for 30 minutes once a week.

Emily: What if my son already has a bottle that he uses once or twice a week; I'll open the playroom door and it's in his mouth, and he's saying, "goo-goo-ga-ga," because he was never nurtured as an infant, and so he still wants to play that way. Do I now take that bottle he's had for the last year in our home away, and tell him this is only for this special playtime? How do I handle that?

Dr. L.: You can decide that. It can be OK either way.

Scenario 2: Parents can learn that the therapist will not provide all the answers for them. Parents learn to trust their children's abilities.

Dr. L.: Nita, how was your session?

Nita: It was great.

Dr. L.: What made it great?

Nita: He played with the toys he never even picked up before. He had never even opened the Tinkertoys box. He opened the box.

Dr. L.: He finally opened the Tinkertoys.

Nita: I was going to ask you something. If he names things wrong during the special playtime, I can't tell him he's wrong, right? You know, parents are supposed to label things correctly.

Dr. L.: What do you think my answer is?

Nita: Your answer would be "No." But in the play session, I thought, "I can't let him get away with thinking that's what that is." But I didn't say anything. It's like he was waiting for me to tell him that he was wrong. And I just sat there.

Dr. L.: So you passed the test.

Scenario 3: The therapist recognizes parents' successes in giving their children the lead.

Kim: He wanted me to tell him if it was the right color when he did the color drawing. He had two different colors of sun. He knew the right answer. He was waiting for me to tell him, to see if I'm listening, I guess. I didn't tell him.

Dr. L.: So you let him be in charge.

Utilizing Specific Instruction

Scenario 1: Highly didactic methods can be used to teach parents specific information, such as how to build their childrens's' self-esteem.

Dr. L.: I want to show you two minutes of a videotape of a 4 ½-year-old child with me in the playroom. I want you to focus on how many times you hear me make a self-esteem–building response. This will just be a review of what we've talked about many times before. A self-esteem–building response is when you give your child credit for knowing or doing something, such as "You stacked those just as high as you wanted." Count how many times you hear a self-esteem–building response. (Video is played.)

Dr. L.: How many did you hear?

Kim: I got eight.

Sonya: I got 12.

Scenario 2: Homework assignments tasking parents with practicing very specific exercises are given to hone parents' skills.

Dr. L.: I'd like you to specifically work on building up your child's self-esteem in the 30-minute session this week. That will be one of your assignments: to give your child credit. "You figured out how to make that work," or "You can count all the way to three!" Give your child credit for all the little things they do in the 30-minute play session.

Providing Concrete Examples

Scenario 1: The therapist utilizes his own experience in play sessions to teach parents.

Dr. L.: At this point in the video, the child and I just walked into the room. I'm going over to be closer to the child, so he'll know I'm interested. Now, let's talk about what you saw me do.

Sonya: You gave him space when he came into the room, which gave him his freedom, or space.

Dr. L.: I let the child move away and settle in, and then I went over to the sandbox. What else did you see me do?

Sonya: You let him pick what he wanted to do.

Dr. L.: Yes, I let him choose. He's in the lead. This is his time to play with any of the toys that he chooses to play with.

Scenario 2: Setting therapeutic limits is a crucial aspect of CPRT, and one in which most parents have no training and limited skills. Therefore, the therapist uses didactic methods and provides specific examples to help parents master the new language.

Dr. L.: I'm going to ask you to pick a special place that these playtimes will occur. If the kitchen is not a private place, and there are other people in the house, and you can't have a private time, then you may need to choose a place like your bedroom. If there is a carpet, then you'll have a big beach-type towel, or a big piece of cardboard, and when the child pulls the Play-Doh out, you say, "The Play-Doh is for playing on the towel," a new way to set a limit.

Scenario 3: Parents often need help in making an appropriate response that is specific.

Dr. L.: (Group has been watching a video of a parent's playtime.) He's asking you to do something that you really don't want to do.

Kathy: That's right.

Dr. L.: He's asking you to use a word that you don't want to use. So, what would you like to say to him?

Kathy: "I don't want to say that."

Dr. L.: Sounds great to me.

Kathy: OK, but I thought I was supposed to do what he wants me to do through this whole playtime.

Dr. L.: There are limits.

Emily: Well, if he wants to mark on the wall, you're not going to let him mark on the wall.

Kathy: No, that's true, I'm not.

Dr. L.: There are limits. This is not a completely free or completely permissive relationship.

Imparting Expert Knowledge

Scenario 1: The therapist, while acknowledging lack of perfection, is nonetheless a mental health professional trained in knowledge of children's behavior. There are opportunities during group sessions for the therapist to impart knowledge to parents.

Dr. L.: When you say, "You're just so angry at me because you don't want to go to bed," your goal at that moment is that tomorrow night or the next week your child will say "I'm angry" instead of saying "I hate you." When your child says, "I hate you," my suggestion is that you not take it personally, because you're not a "hateable" person. I suggest that you wonder, "What is my child trying to say to me?" and then respond.

Scenario 2: The therapist can reframe parents' pejorative descriptions of their children's behaviors into an interpretation of the behavior that is either more positive or more developmentally aligned with the children's ages. Often, parents are assisted in recognizing the part they play in the difficulty.

Dr. L.: In this video of your play session, your son surely is doing lots of exploring. I don't know how you all view that, but when your child is curious and does lots of exploring, that is a very positive thing. It is helpful to be able to look at such behavior and say, "Oh, I'm so thankful my child is interested in things," rather than, "Oh goodness, he gets into things all the time." You wouldn't want the opposite of that: a child who never gets into anything, is never interested in anything, is always quiet and calm, who never pulls anything out, and only does exactly what he's told to do. That would not be a very creative, spontaneous, outgoing sort of child. So it's a very positive thing when your child does lots of exploring.

Laura: But we try to conform them to the other way.

Dr. L.: Oh, yes. It's called lack of tolerance on our part. But for 30 minutes in these play sessions, your child gets your full tolerance and patience, Laura.

Using Analogies to Increase Parent Awareness

Scenario 1: Some teaching points may elude even the most earnest parent. Analogies can be used as another tool to explain points to parents.

Dr. L.: I hear you saying that maybe she was feeling both ways.

Debbie: Well, she was probably, yes. I would say she was angry.

Dr. L.: Then respond to that more.

Debbie: But I feel like, in that particular thing, she's manipulative.

Dr. L.: Oh, so you know what she is doing.

Debbie: Right, but validating her feelings at bedtime doesn't change the fact that it's bedtime.

Dr. L.: And it's not expected to.

Debbie: OK, well that's maybe in my mind.

Dr. L.: These responses work even when they seem not to be working. Let me explain. Have you ever cut your finger? You put medicine on it, and you put a bandage on it, and 30 minutes later you take the bandage off; the cut is still almost exactly like it was, so you wipe the medicine off and throw the bandage away. Have you ever done that?

Debbie: No.

Dr. L.: You leave the medicine on. Why?

Kim: So it will slowly heal it.

Dr. L.: You assume it will eventually begin to be helpful.

Scenario 2: Parents are often more capable of understanding teaching points when the essence is portrayed in an everyday situation.

Dr. L.: Have you ever gone to the doctor when you have had a really sore throat, and he said, "Take this twice a day for 7 days?" You take it for one day, wake up the next morning and your throat's still sore, so you throw the pills away? No, you don't do that. Why?

Debbie: You know you have to give it time.

Dr. L.: You assume that it's going to work, and it is working. You just don't see an immediate result. And with these responses, you won't always see immediate results. Over time, your child comes to realize that you understand, and so she doesn't have to push so hard to get her message over to you.

Encouraging Role-Play and Practice of Skills

Scenario 1: Role-playing and practice are essential to learning the new skills taught in CPRT.

Dr. L.: Let's do some quick role-playing. You two can be partners, you two are partners, and you two are partners. The person closest to me in each pair is the child first. Let's work on two things. Limit setting: those of you who are the children, do some things like threaten, "I'm going to paint on the wall," or "I'm going to cut this," or "I'm going to break this," and let your "parent" set a limit. And also, just play. Those of you who are the parents, practice what you saw in the videotape we just watched; make tracking and self-esteem, building responses and set limits. (Group role-plays.)

Dr. L.: Children, give some feedback to your parents. Tell them how they did, be specific. No generic praise. (Group gives feedback in pairs.)

Dr. L.: Now let's change roles. Children, you're now the parent, so switch roles. (Group role-plays.)

Dr. L.: OK, children, you can stop and give your parents some feedback. Tell them how they did. (Group gives feedback in pairs.)

Scenario 2: The therapist encourages parents to think through situations and come up with responses in advance of being faced with the dilemma, to give the parents a greater sense of agency over the new skill or technique.

Dr. L.: Let's just see how it will work, if you practice that response ahead of time so that you already have it. If he should start to shoot you with the dart gun, you say, "I'm not for shooting." Then you go to the next step, "I'm not for shooting. You can pretend the Bobo is me and shoot the Bobo," and you point to the Bobo.

Sonya: Can you set the limit that "I'm not for shooting," and if the child persists, say, "If you insist on shooting me, then

I will have to remove the gun from the playroom." Can you set that kind of limit?

Dr. L.: That will work. You figured it out.

Making Suggestions for Improvement

Scenario 1: Parents are sensitive to criticism of their parenting skills, so care must be given to the means and methods of making suggestions for improvement. The therapist gives parents the opportunity to search for alternatives and assists them in crafting responses that will enhance the parents' relationships with their children.

Debbie: My daughter insists on having other toys. She's just disinterested in the play session. She just wants to go play with her friends.

Dr. L.: So what might you say to her, if you were reflecting her feelings?

Debbie: I did the 5-minute thing. I said let's play for 5 more minutes. And then in exactly 5 more minutes, she asked again.

Dr. L.: Be sure to reflect her feelings. "Oh, if you can't have other toys, then you just don't want to play at all. It doesn't seem as much fun to you if you can't have the toys you want." That might be the beginning of her expressing her anger. And you open the door by being understanding. That may open the door for her to stick it out. Let us know next week how it works out.

Scenario 2: Instead of telling parents they said or did something incorrectly, the therapist often frames his alternatives as suggestions or variations.

Dr. L.: There could be a variation on that response. Instead of saying, "That can be whatever you want it to be." When he said "What's this?" and then almost immediately banged it on top of his head, you said "I think that's what that's for." I think that is a very appropriate response. One of the things I hope you all begin to do is vary some of the things that we've worked on here so that your response becomes more "you." It doesn't have to always be said just the way we might work on it here.

Scenario 3: A specific suggestion may need to be made to counter a parent's natural instincts to teach and show.

Kathy: I told him I hoped we got the handcuffs off. He wanted to take them off and I didn't know he could. So I took them off.

Dr. L.: I heard you say also, "I don't think you can."

Kathy: Maybe I shouldn't have done that.

Dr. L.: Did you know he couldn't?

Kathy: No, I didn't know for sure that he couldn't, but...

Dr. L.: Therefore, you let the child try. And then it's his decision about whether or not he figures out that he can't take them off. You give him credit. In that way, he gets to feel powerful in a more positive way, because it seems to me he wants to feel powerful, to push you around, make you say things. Maybe that's not so good. He can feel powerful by doing something constructive. He figures out how to take the handcuffs off, and then he hears a self-esteem–building response from you, and he feels powerful in a more positive way.

Identifying What Is Learned from Events in Special Playtimes

Scenario 1: While interpretation is not emphasized in CPRT, parents are assisted in recognizing their children's feelings and often unspoken notions.

Dr. L.: If you put yourself in your son's spot, and your mom likes being in this session with you, looks forward to it, has fun while you're together, how would your son feel? How would that make him feel?

Kim: Pretty special.

Dr. L.: Yes, special.

Kim: Loved.

Dr. L.: Loved. Yes. And that he's important. "I'm important because she wants to be with me." That's a special gift you're giving.

Scenario 2: The therapist encourages parents by letting them know how effective even the smallest change in a parent's behavior has been on a child's outlook.

Sonya: A lot of times, my daughter just wants me to acknowledge her feelings on something. Like the time when she said: "I don't like you. You're not my friend anymore." I haven't been feeding into that. I just kind of check in that she is angry or frustrated. Usually, she's angry. I just say, "Sounds like you're very angry because I won't do what you want me to do," and it works great.

Dr. L.: At that moment then, your child knows that her message has been received by you. "Mom understands." They hear the labeling coming back that touches their feelings. And at that moment, too, you get a chance to teach your child an appropriate label: this is anger; it's not that I hate you.

Identifying Shifts or Changes in Behavior (in Child or in Parent)

Scenario 1: The therapist helps parents recognize shifts in their own behavior and/or their children's behavior after the playtimes.

Emily: The last time he did this it ended up a full-scale temper tantrum where his caseworker had to sit physically in front of her door to keep him in the room. It's different now because he'll just talk very calmly. There's no temper tantrum, there's no arguing.

Dr. L.: At home he's really different and has been consistently different with you in the way he reacts.

Emily: Yes, he is.

Dr. L.: So something has really changed.

Emily: Yes.

Scenario 2: Parents can discover new aspects of their relationship with their children and new aspects of themselves about which they may have been unaware.

Dr. L.: It's almost as though, Nita, you're saying, "I've rediscovered how to be a loving mother."

Nita: Yes, I used to think that everything has to be in control, and perfect, and that makes for a perfect love. Now, I've found that I can leave everything scattered around me, and I can take care of myself, too.

Dr. L.: So, your life is different.

Nita: He knows he can do other things. He knows he can hit the pillow. He laughed because Mom did it—I did it. He watched me hit the pillow, as something he could do.

Dr. L.: As I listen to you, Nita, one of the things that occurs to me is that it's almost as though you're saying, "I'm more free now."

Nita: Yes, I was in the "the mommy" trip.

Dr. L.: And this is a different place.

Nita: Yes.

Facilitating Insight

Scenario 1: Parents are often surprised that just a few playtimes will result in a change in their children's behavior.

Kim: I was shocked to see him clean each brush and put it back. I was concerned that he was going to mix them, but he put them back in the right places. And he washed each one of them, cleaned them up, and cleaned the whole sink after all that.

Dr. L.: Why is it that your children will take this kind of responsibility in this 30-minute playtime?

Kim: This is his choice. It wasn't because Momma was standing there telling him to do it. And he wasn't standing there saying, "I'm not going to do it just because you're telling me to."

Dr. L.: No struggle.

Debbie: No battles.

Dr. L.: And when your children are free to make some of these kinds of decisions, they naturally move toward taking care of themselves and the situation without a lot of hassle. What an important discovery! How could we discover that unless there is a free time for your child to play when you're not the teacher, you're not the boss, and you're not correcting. Your child's self-direction just comes forward. The only way you could have discovered that is in this kind of free time. This works!

Scenario 2: Parents are given tools to help their children begin to learn the skills the children will need as they grow up and become responsible members of society.

Nita: I might say, "I can see you're very angry with me, but I'm not for kicking and hitting and calling names. You may tell me you're angry with me, or you can hit the Bobo or the floor."

Dr. L.: Sounds great. You got all the steps in there, and now he has a choice. He can say it or he can act it out. Could it be that your children, lots of times, just didn't think of any other way of doing it?

Sonya: You know, what's real interesting is that we adults go through life trying to find out what our choices are, in buying a car, in doing all these things. The more choices we get, the more freedom we feel like we have to choose what is best for us.

Dr. L.: It's important for children to find out what their choices are, and learn how to make decisions. When you make a decision, what happens? Where's the responsibility? On the person who makes the decision. So you're helping your child learn what it feels like to be responsible.

Clarifying

Scenario 1: Parents are taught how to help their children stop their own behavior. Choice giving is integral to this process.

Dr. L.: In limit setting, it's really important that you point to what the acceptable item is when you give a choice. You always point to the acceptable choice. In this approach, we don't grab hold of the child, literally or figuratively, and stop them. The objective is to help them to learn inside themselves to say "No" to self. They start to do something and we say, "The wall is not for marking on, the paper is for marking on." Now, if the child chooses not to mark on the wall, and go mark on the paper, the child has stopped himself. He has said "No" to self. Where we're headed with this is when your child is 13 or 15, and they're out somewhere else, not under your thumb, they need to stop themselves because someone else may not stop them. They'll need to say "No" to themselves, and they need to know what that feels like.

Scenario 2: Parents learn that it is not their responsibility, but their children's, to stop the children's behavior. Children *are* able to learn how to do this.

Emily: Having the play sessions has brought a different dimension to my son and me, and things are much better. We had started some of the limit setting before the play sessions, but we didn't always follow through. Now, we're not about to do that. A lot of times, I would just stop the behavior, and now I've watched him so many times: he'll clinch his fist, and he'll hold it like this, but he doesn't act with it.

Dr. L.: So, he's stopping himself.

Conclusion

A variety of group process elements and teaching points have been presented as critical components of the 10-session CPRT model.

Clearly, this listing of excerpts from actual group dialogues does not represent a complete array of skills and methodologies that help create the environment for change in the CPRT approach. Nonetheless, these excerpts serve to illuminate the breadth of topics and skills that this model incorporates.

References

Lahti, S. (1992). *An ethnographic study of the filial therapy process*. Unpublished doctoral dissertation, University of North Texas, Denton.

CHAPTER 5

CPRT SKILLS, CONCEPTS, AND ATTITUDES TO BE TAUGHT

The child-centered play therapy skills, concepts, and attitudes taught in Child Parent Relationship Therapy are presented in this chapter in greater detail to provide the filial therapist with a theoretical framework and a deeper understanding of these principles and procedures. Experienced play therapists who are well grounded in the child-centered theoretical approach are likely already familiar with these basic skills and concepts. For these play therapists, this information can serve as a review of the necessary skills and concepts to be taught in the 10-session CPRT model.

The material in this chapter is taken extensively from Landreth's book *Play Therapy: The Art of the Relationship* (2002) and some limited use is made of the material in Giordano, Landreth, and Jones' book *A Practical Handbook for Building the Play Therapy Relationship* (2005).

Objectives of the Parent–Child Playtime

The focus is on the child and all that the child is capable of becoming. The relationship is viewed as the vehicle for the process of change. Therefore, the overall aim is for the parent to relate to the child in ways that will release the child's inner-directed capacity for constructive forward-moving growth. With this in mind, the filial therapist helps parents focus on the following objectives for the special playtime:

1. **Establishing an atmosphere of consistency and predictability for the child.** The child cannot feel safe or secure in a relationship that contains no limits. A feeling of security and predictability is promoted by the consistency of the parents' responses and behavior in the playroom.
2. **Understanding and accepting the child's world.** Acceptance of the child's world is conveyed by being eagerly and genuinely interested in whatever the child chooses to do in the playtime. Acceptance also means being patient with the pace of the child's play. Understanding is accomplished by relinquishing adult reality and seeing things from the child's perspective.
3. **Encouraging the expression of the child's emotional world.** Although the play materials are important, they are secondary to the expression of feelings by the child, which they facilitate. In the playtime, there is an absence of evaluation of feelings. Whatever the child feels is accepted without judgment.
4. **Establishing a feeling of freedom.** An important aspect of the special playtime is that the child feels or senses the greater freedom available in this setting to express his thoughts, feelings, and needs in ways that may not be permissible at other times. However, this is not a totally permissive relationship; parents learn to allow their child more freedom within secure limits. Allowing the child to make choices also creates a feeling of permissiveness.
5. **Facilitating decision making by the child.** This is accomplished largely by refraining from being an answer source for the child. The opportunity to choose which toy to play with, how to play with it, what color to use, or how something will turn out creates decision-making opportunities that, in turn, promote self-responsibility.
6. **Providing the child with an opportunity to assume responsibility and to develop a feeling of control.** Actually being in control of one's environment may not always be

possible. The significant variable, though, is that children feel in control. Children are responsible for what they do for themselves in the 30-minute playtime. When parents do for children what they can do for themselves, children are deprived of the opportunity to experience what self-responsibility feels like. *Feeling in control* is a powerful variable and helps children develop positive self-esteem.

Structuring the Special Playtime

Structuring is a very important skill and means more than simply planning ahead and setting up the toys. The word *structuring* is used in this instance to mean helping the child understand the nature of the play session. It involves verbally letting the child know such things as "During our special playtime, you can play with the toys in lots of the ways you want to" or "You get to decide…that's up to you." These statements are freeing in that they convey to the child responsibility for direction. Words should be chosen carefully to communicate to the child freedom, self-direction, and the parameters of the relationship. Boundaries on freedom are conveyed by the words *"in a lot of the ways,"* which in effect communicates limits on behavior. This is a key phrase. The words *"any way you want"* are avoided because this is not a time of complete freedom. Parents sometimes introduce a child to the playtime with "This is our playtime, and this is a place where you can play with the toys *any way* you wish," only to have to withdraw their absolute approval as they are about to be shot with the dart gun or as the child throws the airplane at the lamp.

More important than words are the ways the parent nonverbally communicates the specialness of the playtime in the first play session. The parent is encouraged to enter the play session with eager anticipation. Since this is the child's time, the parent should sit down, preferably on the floor or at the child's level, further communicating to the child interest and willingness to allow the child to lead. Remaining standing may result in the parent towering over the child and conveys that the parent is in charge or is about to do something else, so the child waits expectantly. The parent should move closer to her child when the child is intent and focused on her play, and join in when invited. It is important for the parent to be comfortable, not detached, during her play sessions with her child.

The parent can also be involved in and be a part of the child's activity without physically following the child around the room. The parent can be quite active by shifting body posture or by leaning forward to be closer to the child's activity to convey interest and involvement.

In supervising parents, we have often observed parents turning their head 90 degrees to track children with their eyes while the rest of their body remained motionless and projected away from the child, communicating only minimal involvement with the child. When the parent's whole body turns toward the child, and the parent conveys genuine interest and full attention, the child feels the parent's presence.

RULE OF THUMB:

The parent's toes should follow his/her nose.

Some parents have a need for the child to have fun in the playtime. Seven-year-old Clarice stands in the middle of the toys whining, "You don't have any good stuff. I don't wanna stay here." The parent says, "Honey, look at all the fun things to play with in our kit. See the dolls over there. You could play with them." An accepting parent does not coerce the child to play or talk. Pushing the child to play or talk ignores the child's feelings and deprives the child of opportunities for decision making and self-initiative.

Helping Parents Enter the Child's World

Although parents occupy time and space with their children, many do not *know* or *understand* their children. Children need time for emotional sharing with their parents. A major goal for the parent–child play session is to help parents learn how to facilitate this kind of relationship with their children. The process begins by helping the parent become more sensitive to and understanding of their child's emotional world by entering into the child's world of play. Hopefully, the uppermost thought in the parent's mind at such times is "I want to know my child better." The parent is taught to wonder, "Does the love, the warmth I feel for my child show in my face? Does my tone of voice reveal kindness? Does my child know that I think he is important, the most important person in the world at this moment? Do my eyes show that? Is my caring about how my child feels inside being communicated? Do my words convey that caring?"

Children, too, are wondering such things as: "What are we going to do? Why is this time different? Why are you talking differently? Will you like what I do? What can I do to make sure you approve of me? What do I do if you don't tell me what you want? What if I make the wrong choice?"

RULE OF THUMB:

Be sensitive to the child's world.

Through the process of accepting the child's attitudes, feelings, and thoughts, the parent enters the child's world. In this way, the child feels understood and accepted by the parent, and a deeper parent–child bond begins to develop.

A New Kind of Language: Communicating "Being With"

The typical approach in parent–child interactions is characterized by an attitude of evaluation of the child based on what is known about the child and previous circumstances. Seldom does a parent strive to understand the immediate internal frame of reference of the child, the child's subjective world, to genuinely "be with" the child. Sensitive understanding of the child occurs to the extent the parent is able to put aside personal experiences and expectations and appreciate the personhood of the child, as well as the child's activities, experiences, feelings, and thoughts. Children are not free to explore, to test boundaries, to share frightening parts of their lives, or to change until they experience a relationship in which their subjective experiential world is understood and accepted. The attitude of the parents is essential in "being with" their child in such a way that the child feels understood and accepted. This depth and dimension of understanding means remaining free of a stylized role and participating deeply and meaningfully in the work of understanding the child. This means putting aside the tendency to evaluate and judge, and to see from the viewpoint of the child.

Responding to children in a way that communicates sensitivity, understanding, and acceptance and conveys freedom and responsibility is for many parents like learning a foreign language and requires a drastic shift in attitude and a restructuring of words used in responses. From this new perspective, children are viewed as being capable, creative, resilient, and responsible. The objective of CPRT is to help parents develop an attitude of genuinely believing *their children are capable* of figuring things out for themselves, within the boundaries of their developmental capabilities, and communicating this attitude through responses to their children in the play session.

The parent communicates "being with" by being a verbally responsive participant in his child's play. The child may often be engrossed in play and not talkative about what is being played out, and no feelings are evident or sensed by the parent. At such times, the parent can respond to the child's nonverbal play by what is being observed. "You're using lots of colors to make that." "Now, you're putting her in the bed." "That one just crashed right into the other one." These responses, which are referred to as "tracking responses," communicate the parent's involvement, interest, and understanding. Parents are taught to avoid lengthy responses that disrupt the child's focus, resulting in the child being caught up in using energy to try to understand what the parent is saying, which tends to change the direction of the child's expression. **Responses should be short and interactive**, much like a conversation.

The parents also communicates his understanding of his child through accurate reflection of the child's level of affect. The parent should avoid getting overly excited beyond the child's level of affect about little happenings such as, "Oh, my! Isn't that wonderful! You found a colored rock in the box!" This kind of excitement may cause the child to feel something is wrong or to distrust her own reaction because she does not feel equally excited. Expressing affect beyond the level expressed by the child is structuring and will lead the child into expressing affect and behaviors beyond what the child is genuinely feeling. For example, this can be seen when David hits the bop bag with minimum effort and the parent responds with, "Wow! You really socked him that time!" Then, David proceeds to hit the bop bag with more force and looks at the parent for approval.

Another typical parent response that prevents the parent from fully "being with" the child is questioning. Questions place the parent in a leading, controlling position. Generally, **if the parent has enough information on which to base a question, enough information is available on which to make a statement**. Generally, questions imply a lack of understanding. "Did that make you angry?" communicates the parent's lack of understanding, yet the parent does sense the child feels angry or he would not ask the question. The parent should trust what has emerged in his own intuitive system and make a statement, "You feel angry about that." Empathic statements go into the child's heart and soul. Questions go to the mind to be processed and evaluated.

- **Conveying an Understanding of the Child's World: the "Be-With" Attitudes**

Only when the child begins to become accustomed to the special playtime and the new verbal language of the parent will the child begin to express and explore the emotionally meaningful experiences that have been experienced. The parent must wait for this development. It cannot be rushed or made to happen. This is the child's time, and the child's readiness or lack of readiness to play, talk, or explore must be respected.

When the child experiences the freedom and permissiveness of directing his own play in the context of an empathic and caring relationship with his parent, the child develops self-discipline and perseverance that comes from the sustained effort required to carry out or complete a self-selected activity or project. The process of independently choosing an activity, directing the action, and relying on self for the outcome enhances self and develops self-reliance.

The parent's responsibility in the relationship can be summed up in the following four healing messages, referred to in CPRT training as the **"Be-With" Attitudes**. The parent works hard to communicate to the child at all times, not just in words, but with his total person.

1. **I am here.** Nothing will distract me. I will be fully present physically, mentally, and emotionally. I want to be so fully present that there will be no distance between myself and my child. I want to enter fully into my child's world, to move about freely in my child's world, to sense what my child senses, feel what my child feels. Once I have achieved this kind of knowing contact, it is easy to know when I am not in touch with my child. Can I enter so fully into my child's world that I have no need to evaluate or judge my child?
2. **I hear you.** I will listen fully with my ears and eyes to everything about my child, what is expressed and what is not expressed. I want to hear my child completely. Can I experience, hear, my child as she is? To accomplish this kind of hearing, I must be secure enough within myself to allow my child to be separate from me.
3. **I understand.** I want my child to know I understand what she is communicating, feeling, experiencing, and playing, and so will work hard to communicate that understanding to my child. I want to understand the inner depth and meaning of my child's experience and feelings. The crucial dimension in special playtimes is the communication of this kind of understanding and acceptance to the child.
4. **I care.** I really do care about my child and want my child to know that. If the parent is successful in communicating fully the first three messages, the parent will not be perceived as a threat, and the child will allow the parent into his world. Then, the child will know the parent cares. This kind of caring releases the dynamic potential that already exists in children.

- **Conveying Acceptance: a Necessary Dimension of "Being With"**

Acceptance grows out of a genuine and sincere interest in one's child, a belief that he can assume responsibility for himself. Children who experience such an atmosphere of acceptance in their special play session with their parents learn that they can depend on others for support while developing their own sense of adequacy and independence. Acceptance is communicated through the parent's patience and willingness to trust the process. Patience allows the parent to see things from the child's perspective. The parent's acceptance is reflected in refraining from offering advice, suggestions, or explanations, and in not questioning or interrupting the child. The parent's empathic responses communicate understanding and acceptance to the child, thus freeing the child to be more creative and expressive.

By empathically reflecting happenings and feelings, the parent expresses respect for the child and affirms the child's right to have feelings and to express herself through actions. Even when the parent must set limits on the child's behavior, the parent conveys acceptance of *the child*. Acceptance, then, occurs in conjunction with permissiveness, but does not necessarily imply approval of what the child is doing.

The parent's attitude and expression of acceptance encourages a child to explore thoughts and feelings further. When a child's feelings are expressed and accepted by the parent, they are experienced with less intensity by the child. The child then is more fully able to integrate and deal with feelings by expressing positive and negative emotions in a more focused and specific way. Focusing on the child's feelings validates the person of the child rather than the importance of the problem.

Allowing the Child to Lead to Facilitate Self-Direction and Responsibility

Parents are usually in the position of being "the expert." Children look to parents for direction, permission, and answers. During the play session, the parent is not the teacher or a person who corrects children's responses. During play sessions, a child is able to call a "giraffe" a "horse" without being corrected.

The child can add five plus one and get an answer of seven. In addition, the child can choose to spell any way the child decides. This is an accepting and permissive environment. The child can learn spelling and addition outside the play session.

- **Returning Responsibility to a Child and Facilitating Decision Making**

The child leads and the parent follows. The child decides what toys to play with and how to play with the toys, within appropriate boundaries. The child is allowed to solve problems. The parent has no solutions. During the 30-minute playtime, the parent has no information the child needs. The child directs the drama.

- **What Is Meant by Returning Responsibility and Facilitating Decision Making?**

When children ask questions or seek assistance, the parent will make a response that returns the responsibility to the child. These responses encourage children to make their own decisions and to take responsibility for a current concern. For example:

Child: What should I play with first?

Parent: In here, you can decide what you want to play with first.

- **Why Facilitate Responsibility and Decision Making in the Child?**

Children can learn how to make decisions and take responsibility for themselves at a young age. These skills are developed throughout childhood and will prepare children to make decisions during the teen years and into adulthood. Children who are provided opportunities to learn decision making and self-responsibility become self-directed, self-motivated, and feel a sense of control in their lives.

Responsibility is learned through experience. When parents make decisions for children that children are capable of making themselves, children are deprived of a learning opportunity. Instead of developing self-responsibility, children learn to become dependent upon the parent.

Allowing a child the freedom to engage in the process of decision making provides opportunities for the child to project his own personal meaning onto the item or material. This inner experience of making decisions strengthens the child's self-concept and provides the child with experiences that can become incorporated into a changed perceptual view of self. This is a growth process that will enable the child to respond emotionally to future problems and situations in a more effective way. Therefore, the parent refuses to accept responsibility for making decisions for the child during the playtime, no matter how insignificant the decision may seem to be. To the child's question, "What color is the moon?," the parent replies, "The moon can be any color you want the moon to be." Thus, the child is encouraged to accept responsibility for self and, in the process, discovers personal strengths.

Therapeutically facilitative responses return responsibility to the child, thus helping her to feel in control and to become intrinsically motivated. The parent conveys a belief in the child, by allowing the child to make decisions, and is committed to providing opportunities for self-direction by avoiding interfering with the process.

At the beginning of the first playtime, a child often wants the parent to identify what to do, what things are used for, and how to "undo" difficult things. The child may hold up a toy that the child obviously knows the name for and ask, "What's this?" This is a moment when the parent does not know for sure the motivation behind the question. To name the item may inhibit the child's creativity, structure the child's expression, or keep responsibility in the hands of the parent. Responsibility could be returned to the child by responding, *"That can be whatever you want it to be."* Similar responses, depending on the child's request, might be *"You can decide"* or *"That's something you can do."* If the child needs help to complete a task she is not capable of completing without assistance, the parent can respond, *"Show me what you want done."* These responses allow a child to assume responsibility and to make a decision and, typically, by the end of the session the child is stating what things are without asking for the parent's decision.

Children will often answer many of their questions if the parent simply will not be so quick to reply. A thoughtful "Hmmmm" by the parent may be all that is needed.

- **Example Parent Responses That Return Responsibility**

1. Child: (picks up handcuffs and asks) What are these for?

   Parent: In here, you can decide what those are for.

2. Child: (picks up baby bottle and asks) What is this?

   Parent: That can be whatever you want it to be.

3. Child: What color are elephants?

   Parent: You can paint elephants any color you want them to be.

4. Child: (struggling to get glue bottle open)

   Parent: Hmm, you are really working hard to get that open.

   Child: Here, open this for me. Please.

Parent: Show me what you want done.

5. Child: How do you spell happy?

Parent: You can spell happy any way you want.

- **Example Parent Responses That Facilitate Decision Making**

Child: (Enters the play and looks around the room. Parent–child play session was in a clinic.) What should I do?

Parent: In here, you can decide what you want to play.

Child: (Walks toward the arts and crafts table and pulls out a piece of paper.) I know what I can do.

Parent: You figured out what you want to do.

Child: I am gonna make a picture for my teacher.

Parent: You've got a plan and know just what you want to do.

Child: (Begins to pick out colors from the markers/crayons and starts drawing.) I'm gonna make a rainbow.

Parent: You know just what you want to do and how to make it.

Child: Yeah…what colors should I put in my rainbow?

Parent: You can decide what colors to use.

Child: I think I'll use blue and red because they are my favorite colors.

Parent: You figured out a way to decide what colors to use.

Reflecting a Child's Nonverbal Play Behavior (Tracking)

- **What Is Acknowledging Nonverbal Behavior?**

The parent responds to the child's actions and nonverbal play. The parent describes what the parent sees, hears, and observes the child doing. For example:

> You are pushing *that* (car) right through *there* (tunnel).
> You are putting lots of sand in that (bucket).

Note: The parent does not identify the item until the child does.

- **Why Acknowledge Nonverbal Behavior?**

When children provide little to no verbal content to respond to and are not expressing any particular emotion, acknowledging children's behavior helps children feel the parent is interested in their world, cares about their world, and that the parent is striving to understand their world.

- **Rationale for Not Labeling Toys**

Toys used during the playtime should not be identified or labeled until the child has verbalized an identifying label for the item. Labeling a toy anchors the child to reality and interferes with the child's creativity and fantasy. Once the parent has identified the item as a truck, it can no longer be a school bus or an ambulance. Referring to a toy as "it," "that," "her," or "him" allows the child to decide what she wants the toy to be. When the child picks up the car and puts it into the box, the parent responds, "You just put that right in there." The child is now free to continue with her original intent that the car is a giant bug. This response also communicates to the child that the parent is *with her*. When the parent labels toys and behaviors according to an adult perspective, inaccurate assumptions and responses may be made. If a child is pushing a block into the sand and the parent responds by stating, "You are pushing that block deep into the sand." The child could be pretending that the block is a bulldozer, a spaceship, or an animal. A response that avoids labeling would be **"You're pushing that into the sand."** When a parent inaccurately labels a toy, some children will correct the parent and some will not. Children may feel restricted and less understood by a parent if the toy is inaccurately labeled. Not labeling toys creates a freer environment that encourages the child to be creative and to use toys in other ways than in a conventional manner.

- **Guidelines for Responding to Nonverbal Play Behavior**

1. **Responding infrequently:** If the parent is silent during the child's play, the child will begin to feel watched or that the parent is uninterested in the child. Instead, the parent wants

the child to feel as though the parent is a part of the play. This is similar to being in a conversation with an adult. Adults know that a person cares and hears them when the person listens and verbally responds. In a like manner, the parent listens with ears and eyes and verbalizes what she hears and sees.

2. **Responding too frequently:** If the parent acknowledges nonverbal behavior too frequently, the parent may sound like a sports commentator providing play-by-play action. This type of commentary does not sound genuine and conversational. The child may experience the comments as intrusive. The goal is for responses to be genuine and conversational, interactive—a genuine attempt to convey the "Be-With" Attitudes: I'm here, I hear you, I understand, I care.
3. **Acknowledging nonverbal behavior: Personalizing the response:** Begin the response with "You're" or "You are." This personalizes the message and places the focus on the child instead of the toy. It also promotes a feeling of the child being in control. For example: The child is playing with a car, which he has previously identified as a car, and is driving it around in large circles. ***"You're driving that car around and around"*** (focus is on the child; helps the child feel empowered). **"That car is going around and around"** (focus is on the toy; depersonalized message, does not help the child feel important or empowered). During the first play therapy session, the parent may be more talkative and acknowledge nonverbal behavior more frequently to help alleviate the child's uneasiness. If the child is absorbed in play, fewer responses may be needed.

- **Example Parent Responses That Acknowledge Nonverbal Behavior**

Child: (Pushes a truck across the carpet.) Vrrmm.

Parent: You're pushing that right across there.

Child: (Gets up and begins looking around the room.)

Parent: Looking around for something else.

Child: (Puts the plastic soldiers on the carpet and begins to set up a scene using all the toys he has brought over.)

Parent: You've got all you want for now and you are getting them the way you want them.

Child: (Puts the plastic soldiers in a straight line, then begins to build a wall around them.)

Parent: You're lining them up and making a wall around them.

Child: (Begins to enact a battle with the plastic soldiers.) Pow, bang, boom.

Parent: Sounds like they are really fighting.

Reflecting a Child's Verbalization (Content)

- **What Is Reflecting Content?**

The parent repeats in slightly different words something that the child has said. For example: The child is working in the corner and states, "There is going to be a big earthquake soon. No one can keep it from happening; not even Superman." Parent responds, **"No one can help stop the earthquake."** The child places the dishes on the floor and states, "It's time for dinner, everyone come to dinner this very minute." Parent responds, **"You're letting everyone know that dinner is ready to *eat*."**

- **Why Reflect Content?**

Reflecting content helps the child know that you hear and understand the content of her message. It also provides the child with the opportunity to hear the message so that she can hear what she has said. This helps validate her perspective and clarify her understanding of self. When presented with a choice to reflect feeling or content, respond to the child's feeling or combine a feeling and content response. If a child's feelings are not obvious, listen to the tone of voice the child uses to help discern the feeling within the message.

- **Example Parent Responses That Reflect Content**

Child: An earthquake is happening.

Parent: Here comes an earthquake.

Child: Batman and Robin are here! (Child drops figures on the earthquake.)

Parent: Batman and Robin dropped some things on the earthquake.

Child: But they can't stop it.

Parent: No matter what they do, it's not enough to stop that earthquake.

Reflecting a Child's Feelings/Wants/Wishes

Because most parents' life experiences have not taught them to value and express emotions, the most difficult filial skill to teach is helping parents identify and reflect their children's feelings, wants, and wishes. Parents need to be aware of feelings that they avoid or are uncomfortable dealing with in their lives. Sometimes these same feelings are difficult to acknowledge in the child. Examples of responses that recognize the child's feelings, wants, and wishes are "You seem frustrated that...," "You look happy...," "You're angry that...," "You're confused...," "You look excited...," "You are sad...," "You really like...," "You don't like...," "You really want...," "You wish...."

- **Why Reflect Feelings/Wants/Wishes?**

Reflecting feelings communicates understanding and acceptance of children's feelings and needs. It also shows children that you are interested and that you want to understand them. This process helps children understand, accept, label, and communicate. If a feeling, desire, or need is expressed and goes unrecognized, children may think that the feeling or expression is not acceptable.

- **Guidelines for Reflecting Feelings/Wants/Wishes**

1. Look into the child's eyes for clue to feeling.
2. After you've decided what child is feeling, put the feeling word into a short response, personalize the message by beginning the reflection with "you." For example: "You seem sad," "You're really mad at me right now."
3. At the beginning of reflections, avoid repetitive use of phrases such as "sounds like."

- **Example Parent Responses That Reflect Feelings**

Child: I like to go to school because I get to play with my friend.

Parent: You like school and have fun with your friend.

Child: (Goes to the paper and begins to draw.) Yeah, but sometimes we have to read.

Parent: Sounds like you don't like to have to read at school.

Child: (Begins to play with the dartgun.) I like this.

Parent: You found something else you like.

Child: Yeah! I can use this to shoot things!

Parent: You are really excited about what you can do with that.

Child: Yeah—look how far I can shoot it!

Parent: You are really proud of yourself.

Self-Esteem Building and Encouragement

One goal of filial therapy is for the child to build esteem by internalizing her own positive statements about herself. Praise is defined as nondescriptive evaluative statements containing words such as wonderful, good, great, and beautiful. These words evaluate the child or the child's product (a painting, block tower, etc.). The evaluator holds the power and the child learns to need additional praise in order to feel good about herself. This type of praise does not make a positive long-term impact on the child because it lacks description. If the child relies on external praise and evaluations, her peers, family members, and other adults' comments define what she thinks and how she feels about herself.

On the other hand, comments that acknowledge time, effort, and hard work describe the process of creating a picture or block tower. This type of message can be internalized. "I worked hard to make this tower." Thus, the parent's recognition of efforts and hard work can be integrated into the child's self-concept and beliefs about herself. The child learns to acknowledge her own personal qualities, commitment, and effort.

Responses should always be personalized and address the presence of the child. Responding to David, who is busy banging on the Bobo, by saying "David really likes hitting that Bobo" causes the child to feel talked about as a non-person. *"You really like hitting that Bobo"* addresses the child personally. *"You"* gives the child credit and recognizes ownership.

Some parents are prone to inappropriately include themselves in the interaction. Beth talks about playing soccer and how much she wanted to win but her team lost. The parent responds with, "Sometimes it feels bad when we lose and want to win." The parent was not a part of the happening, and the use of "we" shifts the focus away from the child.

- **Encouragement vs. Praise**

Praise judges a child's abilities and self-worth. It tells the child what *you* think about his or her abilities. Praise teaches the child to value "self" based upon other's positive and negative comments and, as such, facilitates an external locus of control. The child learns to allow others' ideas and beliefs to direct his or her life. Examples of praise include such statements as: "Great job!," "What a beautiful picture," "You're such a good boy," "That looks awesome," "You're good at that," and "What a fantastic tower."

Conversely, encouragement acknowledges the child's *effort*. It helps a child develop an internal locus of control and to become self-directed and self-responsible. Children who are intrinsically motivated do not need others' praise and comments to determine self-worth. They are able to applaud their own efforts and accomplishments. Encouraging responses include such statements as: "You are making it just the way you want," "You did it," "You got it," "You are trying hard," "You worked hard," "You really like your [picture]," "You know just how you want it to go," "You are proud of [your tower]," "Sounds like you know a lot about [dinosaurs]," and "You know how to: count [feed the baby, build the blocks, write your name, etc.]," The statement "you know how to" reflects ability instead of making a judgment as to the child's ability ("You're good at counting").

Scenario 1: Child draws a picture, then asks, "Look mommy, do you like my picture?"

Example of Praise: **"That's a beautiful picture!"** This type of response reinforces the child's need for a positive external locus of evaluation. If a child can make a beautiful picture, she can also make a picture that displeases the parent.

Example of Encouragement: **"You worked hard on that picture."** This type of response helps a child learn to give credit to him or herself and to appreciate his or her own abilities. The child will learn to be proud of self and will not formulate ideas about self-concept solely based upon other's evaluation.

Scenario 2: Child cooks dinner and hands the parent a plate with a pretend chicken leg on it, then asks, "How do you like it?"

Example of Praise: **"This dinner is delicious!"** This response evaluates and judges the cook's performance. This encourages the child to be motivated by your comments and praise.

Example of Encouragement: **"You worked hard making this dinner just for me."** (Show admiration in tone of voice.) This response focuses on the child's work and effort. It encourages the child to develop internal motivation. The child will become self-motivated instead of relying on praise from others.

- **Example Parent Responses That Facilitate Encouragement and Esteem Building**

Child: (Child builds a very tall tower out of blocks.) Look at this. Isn't it awesome?

Parent: You really like the way it turned out.

Child: Yeah. But what do you think of the tower?

Parent: You put a lot of time into making it and you look proud of your work.

Child: I am proud of my tower. (Walks over to the construction paper and begins to write multiplication problems on the paper.) I know how to do multiplication.

Parent: You know how to multiply numbers.

Child: (Child multiplies the numbers 20 times 20. Writes the answer 400 under the problem.) Look at this! (Pride in voice.)

Parent: You're excited and proud of your ability to do multiplication.

Child: (Writes another multiplication problem and the answer.) I had to do so many worksheets for homework before I could do this.

Parent: You put a lot of work and effort into learning how to do multiplication.

- **Encouraging a Child Who Needs Help Completing a Task**

1. When you see a child struggling to complete a task, don't jump in to help. Wait until the child asks for help. Encourage the child while he or she is working on the task: **"You are really working hard to get that done." "You are figuring out a way to get that open."** Every time you do something for a child without allowing her to struggle with figuring it out for herself, you rob her of the opportunity to feel competent and capable.
2. Encourage the child to complete age-appropriate tasks on his own. For example, a 3-year-old child may have difficulty taking off a lid that has been tightly put on a plastic jar. It is appropriate to work together as a team to open the jar lid. While working on the task together, encourage the child: **"You are working hard."**
3. Don't complete a task for a child who has not made an attempt at the task and asks for help.
4. If a child a) tries to accomplish the task, b) asks you for help, and c) the task seems challenging for someone his or her age, respond: **"Show me what you want done."** This response encourages the child to make decisions about how he would like you to help. This approach also helps the child focus on what specifically needs to be done to accomplish the task.

Therapeutic Limit Setting

Limit setting is one of the most important aspects of parent–child play sessions and is also the most problematic for most parents. Consistent limits provide structure and security for children and are critical to a healthy parent–child relationship. Parents often feel insecure about trying to limit their children's behavior in a new way and they may be slow to apply limits. Sometimes the parent is reluctant or inconsistent in setting limits because of a desire to be liked by the child.

- **Basic Guidelines in Limit Setting**

Permissiveness in the special playtime does not mean the acceptance of all behaviors. Limits provide children with an opportunity to learn self-control, that they have choices, what making choices feels like, and how responsibility feels. Therefore, when limits should be set and are not, children are deprived of an opportunity to learn something important about themselves. In therapeutic limit setting, children are given the opportunity to choose. They therefore become responsible for themselves and their own well-being in the special playtime.

The parent's belief that children will choose positive cooperative behavior is a significant and impactful variable in the play process. Children are more likely to comply with limits when they experience respect for themselves and acceptance for their feelings and behaviors—both positive and negative. Therefore, the parent will be most helpful by focusing on the child's unexpressed need for defiance, for example, while continuing to express fundamental understanding, support, valuing of the child, and a genuine belief in the child.

In therapeutic limit setting, *the focus and emphasis is always on the child in order to clearly convey where the responsibility lies.* A response such as "We don't draw pictures on the wall" is inappropriate because the parent has not the least inclination to draw pictures on the wall. Yet the use of "we" and "our" implies the parent is a part of the process.

- **When and How to Present Limits**

A common question among parents is when to set limits. Should limits be set as a part of the general introduction at the beginning of the first playtime, or should the parent wait until the occasion calls for the setting of limits? Providing a long list of limits at the beginning of the first playtime is not necessary. This tends to set a negative tone and interferes with the objective of establishing a climate of freedom of expression. Since the special playtime is a learning experience for children, the best time to learn is when the limit issue arises. Self-control cannot be learned until an opportunity to exercise self-control occurs.

RULE OF THUMB:

Limits are not needed until they are needed.

The establishment of total limits rather than conditional limits seems to work best. Total limits are less confusing to children and help the parent to feel more secure. "You may put a little paint on the table" leaves the issue wide open as to how much paint. A total limit would be *"The table is not for painting on."* The child now knows exactly what is not permissible. Conditional limits, such as "You can't kick the door hard," can become the basis for arguments. What the parent thinks is hard may not be perceived by the child as hard, and so the child may attempt to convince the parent. The parent should never engage in an argument with a child. The best procedure is to just restate the original limit or issue and then reflect the child's feelings or desire. "You would like to convince me that you didn't shoot the lamp, but the lamp is not for shooting."

Parents are reminded that, although the establishment of limits is an essential component of the special playtime, limits should be minimal and enforceable. It is important for the filial therapist to help parents determine the few limits that need to be established to promote safety and security in the parent–child relationship. The need for consistency and follow-through in applying limits cannot be overstated. Parents who do not follow through harm their relationship with their child by sending the message "You cannot count on me to do what I say."

- **Rationale for Therapeutic Limits**

Although it may seem strange to say so, and even more difficult to appreciate in the midst of confrontation by an aggressive, angry child, the child's desire to break the limit has greater significance than the exhibited behavior. Although the behavior being expressed is really secondary, the child's behavior too often captivates the parent's attention and energy in an attempt to stop it. **All feelings, desires, and wishes of the child are accepted, but not all behaviors.** Destructive behaviors cannot be accepted, but the child can be granted permission to express herself symbolically without fear of reprimand or rejection. The therapeutic rationale for limit setting during the 30-minute play session is contained in the following six statements and accompanying discussions.

1. **Limits provide physical and emotional security and safety for children.** Although the atmosphere in the playtime is conducive to a greater feeling of permissiveness than exists in a child's relationships outside the playtime, basic commonsense health and safety limits prevail in the playtime. A child may not stick a pencil up his nose or cut himself with the scissors. Likewise, the child may need to be protected from potential guilt, as in the case when a child wants to draw with markers on the parent's face, pour glue on the parent's clothes, or shoot the parent with the dart gun. Although a child may express a desire to hit the parent, break a toy, or damage furniture, such behaviors are limited in order to prevent accompanying feelings of guilt and anxiety. In responding to situations described here, the parent always maintains an accepting attitude of the child's feelings and desires.

   The growth potential in children cannot be maximized in settings where children feel insecure. When no boundaries and no limitations on behavior exist, children feel insecure and usually experience anxiety in such situations. Limits provide structure to the environment and the relationship so children can feel secure. Some children have difficulty controlling their own impulsiveness and need the security of experiencing limits being set in a way that provides them with an opportunity to gain control of their own behavior. Limits, therefore, help to assure the emotional security of children. When children discover where the boundaries are in the playtime relationship and experience those boundaries being adhered to consistently, they feel secure because there is predictability in the relationship and setting.
2. **Limits protect the physical well-being of the parent and facilitate acceptance of the child.** The inherent growth potential in children is facilitated by the parent's acceptance and warm caring, and it is limit setting that allows the parent to remain empathic and accepting of the child throughout the

playtime. For the parent to maintain a warm, caring, accepting attitude toward a child who is hitting the parent in the face with a toy sword is virtually impossible. In this situation, the parent will very likely experience feelings of resentment and rejection, which will in turn be communicated to the child at some level. **Any form of direct aggressive physical acting out or attack on the parent should be prohibited.** Such behaviors are not to be tolerated under any circumstances because they will interfere with the parent's empathic acceptance of the child.

3. **Limits facilitate the development of decision making, self-control, and self-responsibility of children.** In the midst of experiencing the welling up of intense emotion, children are often unaware of their behavior and so are equally devoid of feelings of responsibility. Limit setting addresses the immediate reality of the situation and indirectly calls attention to the child's behavior through statements such as *"The wall is not for painting on."* How can children develop a feeling of responsibility if they are unaware of what they are doing? And how can they experience a feeling of self-control if they are too defensive to change their behavior? Therapeutic limit setting does not stir up feelings of defensiveness that often accompany parents' attempts to stop a behavior. Rather than focusing on what the child is doing that is unacceptable, the parent focuses on the child's feelings or desires and matter-of-factly states the rule. This can be seen clearly in the statement *"You would like to play with the Play-Doh on the carpet, but the carpet is not for putting Play-Doh on,"* as opposed to "Billy, don't put that on the carpet."

   The child's need—to get Play-Doh on the carpet, to be messy, to break the limit—is accepted and communicated to the child in very specific and concrete ways by providing acceptable alternatives, such as *"You can play with the Play-Doh on the tray"* (pointing to the tray). No attempt is made to stop the expression of the feeling or the need. Such a statement clearly indicates to the child a permissible way to express herself. Now the child is confronted with a choice: to act on the original impulse or to express herself through the alternative behavior. The choice is the child's and the parent allows the child to choose. **The decision is the child's and responsibility accompanies decision**

making. If the child chooses to play with Play-Doh on the tray, it will be because the child decided to and exercised self-control, not because the parent made the child.

4. **Limits anchor the playtime to reality.** When the parent verbalizes a limit, the experience is quickly changed from fantasy to the reality of a relationship with an adult where certain behaviors are unacceptable, as is true in the world outside the playtime, except that in the playtime substantially fewer limitations are established on behavior. When the parent interjects *"You would really like to dump that Play-Doh on the carpet, but the Play-Doh is not for dumping on the carpet. You can dump the Play-Doh on the tray,"* the child is confronted with the reality of having crossed an unacceptable boundary, has been presented the opportunity to choose what will be done next, and experiences the accompanying responsibility.

5. **Limits promote consistency.** Some homes are characterized by inconsistency in behavior on the part of adults who have difficulty maintaining rules. In these homes, what was prohibited today may or may not be prohibited tomorrow. What was allowed today may or may not be allowed tomorrow. An accepting attitude on the part of the adult this morning may or may not be evident this afternoon.

   One of the ways the parent establishes a consistent environment in the playtime is through the introduction and use of consistent limits. Limits are presented in a consistently nonthreatening manner, and the parent is consistent in seeing that the limits are adhered to—not in a rigid manner, but in a consistent manner. The parent can be patiently understanding and accepting of the child's wish or desire and still not accept the behavior. **Limits, therefore, help to provide the structure for a consistent environment.** What was prohibited last time is prohibited in this playtime, and what was allowed in the last playtime is allowed in this playtime. Thus, the playtimes have predictability. Without consistency, there can be no predictability, and without predictability, there can be no security.

6. **Limits protect the playtime materials and room.** Allowing random destruction of toys could become an expensive process and at the same time would not be helpful to the emotional growth of the child. Therefore, *"Bobo is for hitting, not*

stabbing with the scissors." Although it might be great fun for the child to jump on the dollhouse and smash it to pieces, it would probably not be repairable and should be protected with *"The dollhouse is not for jumping on."* Less expensive items also are not for breaking or smashing. These are opportunities for limit setting, and thus opportunities for the child to learn something valuable: how to bring self under control. The playtime is not a place of limitless freedom where the child can do anything.

An important consideration, however, is that children have an opportunity to appropriately express their feelings through acceptable items. Just limiting the behavior is not sufficient. Therefore, every playtime box should have some inexpensive items that are for smashing, breaking, or throwing. Egg cartons seem to fit this purpose quite well. They can be stacked and kicked over, jumped on and smashed, broken apart, thrown, and painted. Play-Doh can be suggested as an acceptable substitute for smashing.

Actually, the number of limits set during a playtime is minimal and involves setting limits on behaviors in the following areas: (a) harmful or dangerous behavior to the child and parent, (b) behavior that disrupts the routine or process (continually leaving the room, wanting to play after time is up), (c) destruction of room or materials, (d) taking toys from playtime, and (e) socially unacceptable behavior.

- **Procedures in Therapeutic Limit Setting**

The process of setting limits is a carefully thought out procedure designed to convey understanding, acceptance, and responsibility to the child. The objective of the parent is not to stop the behavior but rather to facilitate the expression of the motivating feeling, want, or need in a more acceptable manner. **The parent is a facilitator of expression rather than a prohibitor of action.**

Rather than attempting to stop behaviors, the parent's objective is to respond to the child in such a way that the child is left with the responsibility for changing her behavior. If the parent tells the child what to do, then the parent is responsible. When the parent trusts the child's capacity to respond responsibly and communicates, *"The lamp is not for throwing at. The bop bag is for throwing at,"* the child is then free to decide what to do next and is thus responsible.

The parent is encouraged to carefully examine his attitude and intent when faced with the need to set limits and to give thoughtful consideration to how best to communicate the actual limit. A different message is obviously communicated in each of the following statements to a child who is about to draw on the wall.

It's probably not a good idea to draw on the wall.
You can't draw on the wall.
Maybe you could draw on something else other than the wall.
The rule is you can't draw on the wall.
The wall is not for drawing on.

- **Steps in the Therapeutic Limit Setting Process**

Parents are taught the 3-step A-C-T method of limit setting to facilitate the process of communicating understanding and acceptance of the child's motives, to make the limit clear, and to provide acceptable alternative actions and behaviors. When limit setting is needed, the parent can remember to **ACT** in instituting the steps in the process sequence.

A—Acknowledge the child's feelings, wishes, and wants.
C—Communicate the limit.
T—Target acceptable alternatives.

STEP 1. Acknowledge the child's feelings, wishes, and wants. Verbalizing understanding of the child's feeling or want conveys acceptance of the child's motivation. Simply setting the limit without acknowledging the feeling might indicate to the child that his feelings are not important. Verbalizing an empathic understanding of the feeling often helps to defuse the intensity of the feeling. This is especially true in the case of anger and is often all that is needed for the child to begin modifying his behavior. Acceptance of the feeling or desire often satisfies the child, and a need for the act no longer exists. **Feelings should be reflected just as soon as they are recognized:** *"You're angry at me."* Once the block of wood is in flight across the room, acceptance of the feeling can no longer be a deterrent.

STEP 2. Communicate the limit. Limits should be specific and should clearly delineate exactly what is being limited. No doubt should exist in the child's mind as to what is appropriate and what is inappropriate, or what is acceptable and what is unacceptable. Limits that are "fuzzy" or unclear interfere with the child's ability to accept responsibility and to act responsibly.

The parent may not always be able to follow these steps in sequence. The urgency of the situation—the child is about to throw the truck at the window—may necessitate stating the limit first, *"The window is not for throwing things at,"* and then reflecting, *"You want to throw the truck at the window, but the window is not for throwing at."* In this example, no feelings are evident, so the child's desire is reflected.

STEP 3. Target acceptable alternatives. The child may not be aware of any other way to express what is being felt. At that moment, the child can only think of one way to express himself. At this step in the process of limit setting, the parent provides alternatives to the child for the expression of the action. This can involve pointing out a variety of different alternatives to the child. A more durable or appropriate object may need to be selected for the expression. *"The dollhouse is not for standing on. You may choose to stand on the chair."* A different surface may be needed to draw on: *"The wall is not for drawing on. You may choose to draw on the paper or the egg carton."* A substitute may need to be selected to replace the parent as the recipient of aggressive behavior: *"Ellen, I'm not for hitting. The Bobo is for hitting."* A nonverbal cue pointing toward the alternative(s), in conjunction with the verbalized alternatives, is especially helpful in diverting the child's attention from the original source of focus and facilitating the process of choice making. Using the child's name helps to get the child's attention.

The following interaction shows how the A-C-T model is applied when 6-year-old Robert is just as angry as he can be at his parent, picks up the dart gun, and glares at his parent as he begins to load the dart gun.

Parent: Robert, I can see you are really angry at me.

Robert: Yes! And I'm going to shoot you good!

Parent: You are just so angry at me you would like to shoot me. (Robert now has the gun loaded and begins to take aim at the parent.) But I'm not for shooting. (Robert interrupts before the parent can go on with the limit.)

Robert: You can't stop me. Nobody can! (points the gun at the parent)

Parent: You're so powerful no one can stop you. But I'm not for shooting. You can pretend the Bobo is me (parent points toward the Bobo) and shoot the Bobo.

Robert: (Swings the gun around, takes aim at the Bobo, and yells) Take that! (as he shoots Bobo)

The important consideration here is that the feeling is expressed and the child has assumed responsibility for both feelings and controlling behavior. This is a significant step in the therapeutic process of learning self-control and self-direction, and that feelings are acceptable.

- **When Limits Are Broken**

When a child is reluctant to abide by the limit and pushes the boundary, the parent does not threaten the child or extend a consequence to the next playtime. Choices and consequences should apply only to the current play session. Each play session should be an opportunity for a new beginning for a child.

When a child persists in expressing or pursuing the original behavior and continues to break an established limit, verbalizing an additional step to the limit setting sequence may be necessary. Before explaining this step, a caution is in order. Too often parents become overly involved in trying to force the acceptance of the limit and move much too quickly to implement this final step. **Patience is the rule of the day.** In most instances, the first three steps should be gone through in sequence at least two or three times before verbalizing the final step. This final step should rarely be used.

STEP 4. State final choice. At this point, an ultimate or final choice is presented to the child. The parent either indicates the child can choose by his behavior to have the item placed off limits for the rest of the playtime or presents leaving the playtime as the ultimate choice. This step must be carefully stated so the child clearly understands he has a choice and that whatever happens will be the result of his choice. *"If you choose to shoot me again, you choose [not to play with the gun anymore today] [to end our playtime]."* Limits presented in this manner are neither punishment nor rejection of the child. If the child shoots the parent one more time, the child has clearly indicated by action the choice to leave the playtime or to stop playing with the gun, depending on which choice was presented. In this process, leaving the playtime or having the gun removed is not the parent's choice. Therefore, the child is not rejected.

Children need to realize they have a choice and that consequences are related to their behavior. Therefore, once this final choice has been presented, and the child has indicated the choice by his behavior (either stops shooting or shoots one more time), the parent must follow through and see that the child's choice is carried out. Therefore, if the child chooses to break the limit again, the parent stands up and says, *"I see you have chosen to end our special playtime for today."*

- **Situational Limits**

Taking Toys or Materials from the Playtime

This experience can really tug at the parent's emotions when a child begs ever so pitifully, "Can I please just take this little car to play with? I really want it to play with my truck and police car." The parent's first reaction may be "Sure, why not? There are lots of other toys here and even another one just like that one." There are two basic reasons for not allowing toys to be taken out of the special playtime box. Limiting the use of the toys to the special playtime enhances the specialness of the playtime and facilitates the development of learning how to delay the need for gratification.

To a child's request to take a toy out of the playtime box, the parent could respond: *"Having that car to play with would be fun, but the toys are for staying in the playtime box so they will be here next time for our special playtime."* This response generalizes to all the toys, thus preventing the necessity for restating the limit on the next 10 items the child wants to take out of the playtime box and shows great respect for the child with "so they will be here next time for our special playtime."

Leaving the Playtime

Allowing a child to go in and out of the playtime at random during the session is not permitted. The 30-minute play session is a consistent structure the parent provides for the child each week. Children need to learn that they cannot run away from the responsibility of seeing things through and that commitment to a relationship means staying and working things out, especially when a limit has been set or the child has just expressed some angry or frightening feelings. Allowing children to leave the room and return at will can turn the experience into little more than a game. The parent may want to inform a child that if the child chooses to leave, he chooses for the special playtime to be over for that day.

In most cases, the preferable procedure is not to allow a child to leave the playtime until the scheduled time is up, except to get a drink or to go to the bathroom. Usually a rule of one trip out for a drink and one trip out to the bathroom is sufficient. However, this cannot be adhered to rigidly because some children may genuinely need to go to the bathroom more than once. To help avoid this problem, parents should take the child to the bathroom prior to each playtime and a small pitcher of water and a small cup or two can be brought into the playtime.

Time Limits

A 30-minute playtime is sufficient and whatever time span has been communicated to the child should be adhered to. The parent should remind the child when 5 minutes are left in the session. Young children who do not have a clear conception of time and children who are completely immersed in their play may need an additional one-minute time "warning." These reminders help children to get ready to end the experience and give them an opportunity to complete the task at hand or to move quickly to something else they had planned to do. This latter behavior is typical of many children and speaks of their planning ahead in their play.

References

Giordano, M., Landreth, G., & Jones, L. (2005). *A practical handbook for building the play therapy relationship*. Lanham, MD: Aronson.

Landreth, G. (2002). *Play therapy: The art of the relationship*. New York: Routledge.

CHAPTER 6

THE 10-SESSION CPRT TRAINING PROCESS

Utilizing a small group format, parents are trained in basic child-centered play therapy (CCPT) principles and skills. As in CCPT, Child Parent Relationship Therapy is not focused on solving specific problems or a "quick fix," but rather is structured to enhance the relationship, in this case between the parent and child, with the parent serving as the therapeutic agent of change. Play is the primary way children express themselves and work through issues. Therefore, CPRT/filial therapy utilizes play as the means to facilitate interaction and enhance the relationship between parent and child. Parents practice these new skills with their child in weekly 30-minute special play sessions and report their experiences to the group.

The combination of didactic instruction coupled with required parent–child play sessions and supervision in a supportive atmosphere provides a dynamic process that sets filial therapy training apart from most parent training programs, the majority of which are exclusively educational in nature. These key training components are critical to the successful CPRT training process and cannot be overstated. The filial therapist's greatest challenge throughout the

10-session training—and it is a challenge even for the most experienced therapist—is balancing the parents' need for support and encouragement with the need to cover the training curriculum in order that parents learn the attitudes and skills necessary to conduct successful home play sessions with their children.

Weekly Parent–Child Play Session

The importance of the weekly 30-minute parent–child play session cannot be overstated; it is the essential element in the success of Child Parent Relationship Therapy (CPRT). The parent's weekly application of play sessions provides the structure for all learning and change. Parents are trained in the use of child-centered play therapy procedures in order to create an accepting and nonjudgmental play session environment in which their children can freely express their thoughts, feelings, and behaviors, within certain limits. The basic principles for the filial play sessions include:

1. The child should be completely free to determine how he will use the time. The child leads and the parent follows without making suggestions or asking questions.
2. The parent's major task is to empathize with the child, to understand the intent of his actions, and his thoughts and feelings.
3. The parent's next task is to communicate this understanding to the child by appropriate comments, particularly, whenever possible, by verbalizing the feelings that the child is actively experiencing.
4. The parent is to be clear and firm about the few "limits" that are placed on the child. Limits to be set are time limits, not breaking specified toys, and not physically hurting the parent.

Because the parent's major task is to empathize with the child, the parent develops a new perceptual awareness of the child and her potentialities. Moreover, because the parent is taught to follow the child's lead, the child is free to express fully her own developing creativity, resourcefulness, and, in turn, experience the accompanying responsibility. For 30 minutes, the child is free, within appropriate boundaries set by the parent, to direct one's self, to be creative, to be bossy, to be silly, to be somber, to be serious, and to just enjoy the fullness of being alive at that moment without any fear of parental rejection. Within this potent context, change occurs within both parent and child, and the parent–child relationship is enhanced.

Although there are situations when parent–child play sessions may be conducted at the therapist's office/playroom, the emphasis is on helping parents learn to conduct these special play sessions at home with their child. Therefore, time is spent during training helping parents select the necessary toys and choose a location for play sessions. The location should be one that allows for movement and a degree of messiness without the need for excessive limits. The therapist must emphasize the importance of establishing a consistent time and place to conduct playtimes. Our experience is that most parents have a great deal of difficulty with providing consistency in their children's lives, and finding a time to hold play sessions is no exception. Parents are asked to treat the filial play session "appointment" time the same as an important meeting with their employer—one that they would not dare miss! Since parents are expected to demonstrate the skills they have been taught **only** during the limited time of the scheduled once-a-week 30-minute play sessions, they are not threatened by the magnitude of having to completely change their approach to parenting. Chapters 8 and 9 of this text provide more suggestions regarding helping parents plan for and successfully conduct the weekly play session.

Child of Focus

Parents are asked to select one child between the ages of 2 and 10 years that they will focus on during the 10-session training period. Because the focus is on the parent–child relationship, special playtimes are always conducted with *one* child and *one* parent. The therapist helps the parent decide which child would likely benefit the most from the weekly play sessions. In some cases, the child who needs the parent the most may not be the child exhibiting the most behavioral difficulties. Parents with more than one child often have difficulty choosing. The therapist addresses parents' concerns that invariably arise about other children in the family not having a special playtime and suggests "special" activities for the other children to be involved in while the parent conducts a play session with the "child of focus" (e.g., a relative taking other children to the park or for an ice cream cone). If both parents or caregivers attend the training, each one selects a different child of focus (assuming there is more than one child in the family) to conduct weekly play sessions with for the duration of CPRT training. In the case of an only child and both parents participating, the child receives a play session with each parent each week.

Although CPRT is typically utilized with children ages 2 to 10, the basic child-centered principles and skills can be adapted for infants and preadolescents. For older children, instead of a "play" time, more developmentally appropriate activities, such as baking cookies together, building a birdhouse, crafts, model airplane project, etc., are substituted, with the focus remaining on allowing the child to lead or choose the activity.

Training Structure: Balancing Didactic and Group Dynamic Components

CPRT is a blending of didactic elements with timely exploration of feelings and emotional reactions in the group as parents interactively share feelings about themselves and their children. The expression of these feelings and exploration of their underlying dynamics in the group setting helps parents to develop insight and prevents emotions from building up and being acted out at home. Therefore, skill and experience in facilitating group therapy, as well as expertise in play therapy, is essential for the professional contemplating employing CPRT. Filial therapists must have sufficient training and supervised experience in play therapy to develop the self-confidence necessary to effectively model and demonstrate specific play therapy skills for parents. Inexperienced filial therapists often have a tendency to get caught up in exploring parents' feelings to the exclusion of providing the necessary training. Maintaining a sensitive balance between teaching specific skills and exploring emotional experiences is essential. Exclusive group therapy is not the order of the day. Parents also need to learn new skills of parenting.

Filial therapists who lack training and experience in group facilitation often make the mistake of allowing a parent to dominate group discussions, resulting in the other group members feeling left out and unimportant. All parents need the opportunity to share. The group format and the time-limited structure of the 10-week model requires a skilled therapist to balance the didactic and dynamic components of the CPRT training. There are specific skills that must be taught, modeled, and practiced in each session to ensure that parents will experience success in their special play sessions at home. For the novice filial therapist, there are significant benefits to employing a coleader to help share the responsibility of covering the required weekly curriculum, while attending to group dynamics and individual parent needs.

Another important attribute for the successful CPRT facilitator is spontaneity and creativity. Parents are more motivated to learn these new skills when the information and skills are presented in the context of their own lives. When the facilitator can seize the opportunity to teach or reinforce a skill as an issue spontaneously presented by a parent, the potential for learning is enhanced. The potential for learning can be further heightened if the facilitator uses the opportunity to explore feelings and emotional reactions in the group. Encouragement of even the smallest success must be offered throughout the process. Generalizing a specific comment made by a parent to include the other parents' experiences is another important strategy the facilitator should utilize to maximize learning. Chapter 4 provides the reader with an in-depth description of the group process component and provides case examples to illustrate the process.

Group Format

The basic format is six to eight parents and the therapist sitting in a circle (avoid tables, which create a barrier) engaged in a discussion, with lively interaction among parents. Ten parents in a group is too large for the necessary supervision of each parent's weekly play sessions and places too many restrictions on group interaction, a prerequisite to effective group process. The group feeling that develops and group cohesiveness are important dimensions of the CPRT process. Therefore, groups are closed, with no new participants added after the second session. It is just not possible for parents to catch up on the material missed in the first few sessions. CPRT training is also possible with an individual parent or a couple, and many times may be the training mode of necessity for professionals in private practice when getting a group together for training is not possible. One caution is that when couples are included in a training group, relationship problems may emerge in the sharing that goes on and the leader may need to work extra hard to keep the discussion focused on the training objectives.

Our preference is the group setting because of the group dynamics feature and the vicarious learning that is always available to parents; however, variations of the 10-session weekly group format are provided in Chapter 20, including the application of the principles and procedures of CPRT with individuals and couples. Other variations of the model consist of collapsing the 10 sessions into 5 weeks, with twice-per-week group training sessions, and an intensive application of the model in which sessions are held daily (specifically for use in shelters and other "in-patient" settings where parents and children are living for short periods of time). Also described is an intense 1-weekend model, as well as a researched modification of the 10-session model in which the curriculum is taught during 4-hour blocks over 4 weekends.

Training Format

Lengthy lectures are avoided and, as often as possible, the focus is kept on the parents. In addition to the set training curriculum, teaching points and training information are carefully introduced in connection with spontaneously expressed parent concerns about their children. This interspersing of information in the context of parents' current struggles results in the information being received and incorporated by parents in a more meaningful manner. Solutions to concerns and new ways to respond to children often originate within the group. Homework assignments are given at each session to help maintain involvement between sessions. Therapists are cautioned against overwhelming parents with homework or the amount of content presented during a session. Homework assignments are faithfully reviewed at the beginning of the following session to communicate to parents the importance of these assignments. Experiential activities, including demonstrations, role-play, and supervision of videotaped home play sessions are crucial to parents' success in learning the skills and are utilized liberally throughout each training session.

Supervision Format

An essential component of this model is the structure and provision of supervision, particularly the requirement for parents to videotape their play sessions for supervision purposes. One to two parents are scheduled each week to bring their videotape for viewing in the group. Preferably, the therapist arranges for the assigned parents to come to the clinic or office playroom for videotaping; however, most parents have video cameras and can record their play sessions at home (although the chance of equipment problems or parents "forgetting" to videotape are greater with home sessions). There is no substitute for parents being able to view themselves and each other; the opportunity for vicarious learning is unparalleled. The ability to view parents' skills firsthand is invaluable to the therapist, and most importantly, provides the opportunity for accurate and supportive feedback.

Essential Training Elements

Our approach emphasizes the vital importance of parents experiencing success in order to gain confidence in their new role. We carefully structure training experiences to ensure that parents feel successful. Although Chapter 2 describes these training features in detail, we consider these five elements so important to the overall success of training that they are briefly summarized here.

1. CPRT is a strength-based parent training model, rather than a problem-focused approach. Parents are encouraged to focus on their children's strengths, as well as their own, and to build on those strengths. The focus is on the future and developing potential rather than trying to correct the past.
2. Parents are asked to practice the skills they are learning only during a weekly 30-minute special play time. They are not asked or expected to completely change the way in which

they interact with their children; in fact, they are initially told specifically not to practice these skills outside of the playtime. This avoids the sense of failure that would inevitably ensue if parents were expected to utilize these new skills in all their interactions with their children. Typically, as parents gain confidence in their skills, they will gradually begin to spontaneously and successfully utilize their new skills outside of the play sessions.

3. Considerable focus is placed on helping parents select the time and place they will conduct the play sessions each week, focusing on helping them commit to a set time when they are not likely to be stressed or hurried and can be emotionally available to the child.
4. The combination of didactic instruction within a supportive group atmosphere provides parents an experience of safety, support, and encouragement. This type of environment is critical in order for parents to express their vulnerabilities, share their failures as parents, and begin to take risks that promote growth and change.
5. Supervision of parents' videotaped and/or live play sessions holds parents accountable for learning and allows them to receive accurate and supportive feedback from the filial therapist and the other group members within a meaningful context.

Selection of Parents

The research on this model (see Chapter 21) supports its use with diverse populations and a broad range of presenting issues, including incarcerated mothers, incarcerated fathers, mothers residing in a domestic violence shelter, immigrant Chinese parents, Native American parents, nonoffending parents of sexually abused children, parents of chronically ill children, and parents of children with learning difficulties, to name a few. The child-centered relationship established in the special play sessions makes filial therapy an ideal therapeutic medium for parents from different cultures.

The reasons parents are referred for CPRT training have been varied and have included many of the more typical child adjustment problems and parent–child relationship difficulties, as well as children who were experiencing behavioral and emotional difficulties.

Even in well-adjusted, stable families, experiences occur that may result in temporary disruptions in parent–child interactions or emotional reactions on the part of the child that make it essential that the parents be especially sensitive to the child's emotional reactions and needs (i.e., birth of an infant; stressful academic difficulty; difficult to manage child; night fears; moving from one home to another; death of a parent, sibling, or close friend; a parent who is too involved in work and absent from home; loss of a job or major change in parent income; involvement in an auto accident). These experiences can result in children being fearful, anxious, clingy, or they may withdraw or act out. Many parents do not know how to respond adequately in appropriate emotionally nurturing ways to such reactions or behaviors. Their natural tendency is to try to stop the behavior rather than to try to understand the child.

Many parents attend CPRT training groups simply because they want to be better parents. A recent trend in filial attendees is grandparents (and other relatives) who have recently received custody of their grandchildren. Several affluent families have sent their live-in nannies to learn how to conduct the special play sessions. Recently, a young nanny in her early 20s was enrolled by the parents of a 14-month-old who were concerned that the nanny be sensitive to the emotional development and needs of their child. She did a superb job of responding empathically to the 14-month-old in their scheduled play sessions, which were videotaped for critique in the weekly parent group sessions. One 6-month-pregnant mother-to-be signed up for the training because she wanted "to get an early start on practicing the special play techniques." She borrowed a friend's child to practice on during the training period and was one of the most excited parents in the group. A couple expecting for the first time enrolled in another group, and both parents-to-be had weekly play sessions in their own home with the children of a relative. The parents of a 5-year-old girl sought out the training because they felt it was important for the father to build a relationship bond with his child before he began serving a prison sentence. CPRT can be a preventative approach that can be helpful for all families, not just those experiencing severe problems.

The overwhelmingly positive findings on the research for this model suggest that CPRT is a more effective intervention than traditional play therapy, and in a shorter amount of time. However, clinical rationale would prohibit the use of CPRT with all parents and children. Parents who are experiencing a significant amount of emotional stress often have difficulty focusing on the needs of their children. In this case, many parents need to undertake their own therapy before they are capable of learning and facilitating the skills of therapeutic play with their children. Also, as most child therapists have experienced, many parents are unwilling or unmotivated to participate in their child's therapy. Issues of guilt, resentment, time, money, and effort are just a few of the reasons for nonparticipation by parents.

In addition to parental issues that prohibit participation in filial play therapy training, a child may not be best suited for this approach. On occasion, a child's emotional issues might extend beyond the capability of the parent. In a case where a child is significantly emotionally disturbed, a parent may not be able to provide a child with an effective therapeutic experience. Yet, research supports that if a child and a parent are both firm candidates, filial therapy would be the treatment of choice (Bratton et al., 2005).

Practical/Logistical Issues

Marketing CPRT

Over the years, we have used several terms interchangeably to market the 10-session model to parents, because the term filial therapy was not familiar. Marketing this program as Child–Parent–Relationship (C-P-R) Training met with the most success, hence that title stuck. We also liked the play on the term "CPR," as parents readily identified that term as a method of saving a life. Similarly, we believe that the application of filial therapy training can save the child–parent relationship. Examples of marketing strategies, inluding a flyer, article, and brochure, are included in Bratton, Landreth, Kellam, and Blackard (2006) *Child Parent Relationship Therapy (CPRT) Treatment Manual: A 10-Session Filial Therapy Model for Training Parents* published by Routledge.

Initial Parent Intake

We recommend meeting with individual parents prior to the first group session for several reasons—most notably, screening for group membership. Other goals of the parent intake are (a) developing rapport, (b) addressing parent questions about CPRT training and how it can benefit both parent and child, (c) establishing fees, (d) administering assessments, (e) gathering background information, and (f) obtaining informed consent. A major objective is to help the parent select the "child of focus." We believe that conducting parent intakes prior to training contributes significantly to the success of the first session. The filial therapist is freed from the majority of administrative responsibilities and can focus full attention on group process and training elements.

Training Setting

The optimal setting for conducting the training is a play therapy room in a clinic with a two-way mirror and a space for providing childcare for the children of the parents in the group. This type of setting allows for live demonstrations, observations, and role-play. Also necessary for training is a television and VCR, one with the appropriate inputs for various patch cords to accommodate a variety of video recording formats.

Child Care

Providing child care is important, particularly for single parents who often lack financial resources and/or the necessary support systems to assist in caring for their child while they attend training. Children seem to enjoy coming to the clinic and seeing where their parents are coming to learn "special ways of playing with them." Providing child care on-site also allows the therapist to conduct live demonstrations for parents to observe play session skills firsthand. Because of the length of the training groups, snacks should be provided for the children. In some cases, with disadvantaged families, we have provided a light meal for children and parents.

Goals and Objectives

The overall goal of Child Parent Relationship Therapy is to enhance and strengthen the parent–child relationship. Consistent with the principles of child-centered play therapy, the relationship is viewed as the vehicle for the process of change. Therefore, the objective is to help the parent relate to the child in ways that will release the child's inner directional, constructive, forward-moving, creative, self-healing power. Overall, therapeutic goals for children include a reduction of symptoms, development of coping strategies, an increase in positive feelings of self-worth and confidence, and a more positive perception of parents. Broad therapeutic goals for parents include a greater sensitivity to their children's emotional worlds, more positive perceptions of their children, and the development of more effective parenting skills. Specific goals for parents and children, as well as the family, are as follows.

Goals for Parents

- Increase their understanding, acceptance, and sensitivity to their children, particularly their emotional worlds.
- Learn child-centered play therapy principles and skills.
- Learn how to encourage their children's self-direction, self-responsibility, and self-reliance.
- Develop more realistic and tolerant perceptions and attitudes toward self and child.
- Gain insight into self in relation to the child.
- Increase parental self-acceptance and confidence in their ability to parent.
- Develop more effective parenting skills based on developmentally appropriate strategies.
- Rediscover the "joy" of parenting their children.

Goals for Children

- Communicate thoughts, needs, and feelings to his parent through a medium of play.
- Experience more positive feelings of self-respect, self-worth, confidence, and competence through feeling accepted, understood, and valued.
- Change any negative perceptions of the parent's feelings, attitudes, and behavior through increased trust and sense of security.
- Reduce or eliminate problematic (self-defeating) behavior.
- Develop an internal locus of control (self-control), become more self-directing, take responsibility for actions, and ultimately choose more appropriate ways to express needs and get needs met.
- Develop effective problem-solving skills.

Goals for Parent–Child Relationship

- Strengthen the parent–child relationship and foster a sense of trust, security, and closeness for both parent and child.
- Improve family interactions and expression of affection.
- Increase level of playfulness and enjoyment between parent and child.
- Improve coping and problem-solving.

10-Session Training Content

A brief summary of the content and focus for each CPRT training session is provided below as an overview of the 10-session model. Chapters 7 through 16 provide an in-depth description of the content and procedures followed in each training session. The 10-session training curriculum, including training outlines for the filial therapist and a complete set of parent handouts are included in the Bratton, Landreth, Kellam, and Blackard (2006) *Child Parent Relationship Therapy (CPRT) Treatment Manual: A 10-Session Filial Therapy Model for Training Parents* published by Routledge.

Training Session I: Training Objectives and Reflective Responding

The primary objective in this initial session is to create a safe environment for parents, one that encourages parents to share their parenting struggles openly with each other. Toward this goal, ample time is spent with parents introducing themselves and describing their families, with particular emphasis on the child they have chosen to conduct filial play sessions with. The therapist gives an overview of the training objectives, emphasizing the goal of parents developing sensitivity to their children's emotional worlds. The concept of reflective responding is introduced and demonstrated, with a focus on identifying and reflecting feelings.

Training Session 2: Basic Principles of Play Sessions

Parents are introduced to the basic principles, guidelines, and goals for the play sessions. A list of toys to be used during the special playtimes is provided, with the therapist demonstrating and sharing the rationale for each. The therapist demonstrates or shows a videotape of a typical play session, followed by parent role-play of skills observed. Parents are asked to put their toy kit together and decide on a specific time and location for the home play sessions and report back next session.

Training Session 3: Parent–Child Play Session Skills and Procedures

The major focus for this session is preparing parents for their first home play session. Parents are given a handout that outlines basic filial play session "Dos and Don'ts" for conducting play sessions. The essential play session skills of structuring, allowing the child to lead, and "being with" are demonstrated by the therapist, followed by parent role-play of those skills. The therapist provides parents with a play session procedures checklist to help them prepare for their sessions. Parents are instructed to conduct their first play session at home during this week, and 1–2 parents are selected to videotape their play sessions to bring for focused supervision during the next session.

Training Session 4: Supervision Format and Limit Setting

The major focus in this session is for parents to report on their first home play session with their children, with the majority of this time spent reviewing the videos of the parents whose play sessions were videotaped. The viewing of videotaped parent–child play sessions provides a rich opportunity for vicarious learning and group empathy. The therapist uses examples from the video and from parents' comments to reinforce play session skills and to encourage and support parents. The primary objective is to find something positive in each parent's sharing. The therapist reviews and demonstrates all play session skills. The skill of limit setting is introduced, demonstrated, and role-played by parents. Two parents are scheduled to be videotaped for the next week's session.

Training Sessions 5: Play Session Skills Review

This session follows a similar format to Session 4, with an emphasis on supporting and encouraging parents as they learn and practice their new play session skills. To avoid overwhelming parents, no new skills are introduced, although limit setting is a continued focus. The majority of the session is again spent with the therapist supervising parents' home play sessions (including parent self-report and videotape critique of 1–2 parents), with an increased focus on parents' self-awareness, particularly in relation to their children. Play session skills are reviewed and demonstrated, as needed.

Training Sessions 6 Through 9

These sessions all follow the same general format. Each session begins with parents reporting on their home play session, followed by focused supervision on the 1–2 parents assigned to videotape their play sessions. Although no new play session skills are introduced after Session 5, related topics are presented each week to enhance parents' learning and generalization of skills to outside the play session. Session 6 introduces choice giving as a method of empowering children and as the fourth step in limit setting. Self-esteem–building responses are taught in Session 7, and the related topic of encouragement versus praise is presented in Session 8. Helping parents begin to generalize the skills they have learned and apply them to everyday happenings is the focus of Session 9. Each week, 2 more parents are scheduled for videotaping. (Our goal is that over the course of *training*, each parent will have two opportunities to be videotaped and receive focused feedback.)

Training Session 10: Evaluation and Summing Up

The final session is used primarily as a review and to bring closure to the group, with an emphasis on parents recognizing the progress they and their children have made. The therapist encourages and reinforces their comments through the examples of progress they have shared in previous sessions. The importance of continuing home play sessions is emphasized and parents are asked to sign a contract, making a commitment to continue the play sessions for *x* number of weeks. A follow-up group session is scheduled (usually in 4–6 weeks). Parents address a postcard to be mailed later as a reminder.

Follow-up Training Session

Parents briefly share their experiences in their play sessions since the last meeting, focusing on changes they have observed in themselves and in their children. The therapist utilizes this sharing time to briefly review the basic filial principles, but the primary aim is to encourage and support each parent's growth since the beginning of training. Generalizing play session skills to typical parenting struggles is also emphasized. Parents are asked for examples of when they have used their new skills successfully. If there is enough interest, another follow-up training session can be scheduled to be held in 2–3 months. Parents who are interested again address a postcard to be mailed as a reminder.

Case Study

Chapters 7 through 16 provide detailed descriptions of content and material for each of the 10 training sessions. To provide the reader with an opportunity to examine the 10-session therapy process as it was lived out by an experienced filial therapist and a group of parents, a partial transcript is provided at the end of each chapter. This is a rare opportunity in filial therapy literature to "get inside" the personal perceptual world of individual parents and follow them in their experiential journey through CPRT training. The therapist was Dr. Garry Landreth and the training sessions were held in a play therapy room in the Center for Play Therapy at the University of North Texas for videotaping purposes and to provide ready access to toys for role-playing practice and demonstration experiences. The CPRT training group featured in the transcripts was composed of 7 mothers, all of whom completed the 10 weeks of weekly, 2-hour training sessions following CPRT methodology. The dynamics of providing CPRT training, dealing with unexpected happenings, responding to parents' emotional expressions, answering questions, the importance of being flexible in responding to parental needs, and the role of the therapist in providing therapeutic dimensions as well as training dimensions cannot be communicated in a description of the content to be covered in each training session. These dimensions can only be known by going inside a functioning CPRT group.

Excerpts selected from each training session focus primarily on only a few of the parents in the group to provide insight into the dynamics of the experience for individual parents and the CPRT process across the 10 sessions of training. For clarity, the following are the names and presenting issues for the "child of focus" for each of the 7 parents (all names are pseudonyms): Debbie and 4-year-old Rachel, described as demanding and bossy (also mentions her infant, Josh, throughout the training); Sonya and 2 ½-year-old Jenny, described as fearful; Emily and 4 ½-year-old foster son Chris, described as abused, neglected, and angry; Nita and 3-year-old Jeff, described as acting out and having a low sensory threshold; Kathy and 4-year-old Cody, described as angry and acting out; Kim and 4-year-old Toby, described as developmentally delayed and diagnosed with Attention Deficit Disorder; and Laura and 6-year-old Dawson, described as angry, demanding, and jealous of 2-year-old sister. In each session, attention is focused especially on one mother, Debbie, to highlight her personal struggles, the learning process as she experienced it, her development of insight, and the dynamic changes in her attitude and behavior.

Case of Debbie and Her Daughter

Debbie was a married, stay-at-home mother with two children, 4-year-old Rachel and 3-month-old Josh. Her initial intake at the clinic revealed that she felt isolated, depressed, angry, and overwhelmed by parenting. The marriage relationship is characterized by lack of communication and inability to connect with each other on most matters of importance. Debbie felt as though she was parenting by herself with no support from her husband in efforts to parent. "I do all the parenting by myself. He undermines me. I put Rachel to bed at night, later she wakes up, he decides she is hungry and feeds her. Then she's wide awake and tearing around the house, and I'm supposed to take care of her." (Several years later, Debbie described this time as "the darkest period of my marriage.") She felt out of control and felt everything in the home was out of control. Many little factors seem to create an explosive situation. Debbie felt powerless to create the kind of home and be the kind of parent she would like to be because "I don't know what a home and family is supposed to look like. I don't know what is normal for a family. I have no role model."

She wanted a sense of peace and calm in her home but didn't know how to make that happen. "I have no building blocks to create a home. I have no routine in my life." Debbie didn't have a sense of home, didn't know how to stay home and create order and routine. "When Rachel was a tiny baby, I would put her in a car seat and be gone all day long. I would come home just before my husband came home from work. The house was always a disaster area."

Debbie didn't know how to build routine into her life, her home, and her children. Yet, she wanted this desperately. "I want to figure things out, to make my home better, to be a better parent. I need skills so I won't feel so overwhelmed and angry toward my children. I need to know what I am supposed to do. I'm hungry for information."

Chapter 17 provides a more in-depth assessment of the parent–child relationship struggles and the impact of CPRT on Debbie and her child. Included in the chapter are (a) an interview shortly after the conclusion of the 10 training sessions to assess the immediate impact of the CPRT training on Debbie and her daughter and; (b) a 4-year and a 13-year follow-up interview with Debbie to provide the reader with an unusual opportunity to evaluate the continuing and long-range effects of 10 sessions of CPRT training as experienced by Debbie.

References

Bratton, S., Landreth, G., Kellam, T., & Blackard, S. (2006). Child Parent Relationship Therapy (CPRT) Treatment Manual: A 10-Session Filial Therapy Model for Training Parents. NY: Routledge.

Bratton, Ray, Rhine, & Jones (2005). The efficacy of play therapy with children: A meta-analytic review of treatment outcomes, *Professional Psychology: Research and Practice*, 36(4).

Glover, G. (2001). Cultural considerations in play therapy. In G. Landreth (Ed.), *Innovations in play therapy: Issues, process, and special populations* (pp. 31–41). Philadelphia: Routledge.

Guerney, B., Jr. (1964). Filial therapy: Description and rationale. *Journal of Consulting Psychology, 28*, 304–360.

Guerney, B., Jr. & Stover, L. (1971). *Final report on filial therapy for grant MH18264-01*. Pennsylvania State University.

CHAPTER 7

CPRT TRAINING SESSION 1: TRAINING OBJECTIVES AND REFLECTIVE RESPONDING

Overview

Parents are introduced to the basic premises and objectives of Child Parent Relationship Therapy (CPRT), emphasizing children's use of play to communicate their experiences, thoughts, and feelings. Training focuses on helping parents develop sensitivity to their children's emotional world through the skill of reflective responding. Parents are taught the essential "Be-With" Attitudes—I'm here, I hear you, I understand, and I care—as the way to nonverbally convey empathy to their children. Parents introduce themselves and their family and briefly discuss parenting concerns. The primary objective in Session 1 is to structure the group training format to create a safe and comfortable environment for parents to share, with particular emphasis on linking parents' experiences to help them see that they are not alone in their parenting struggles. This chapter concludes with the partial transcript of CPRT Session 1 for the group of parents introduced in Chapter 6 and illustrates the focus on group dynamics, with key concepts and teaching points skillfully woven throughout.

Materials

Suggested materials include: *CPRT Session 1–Treatment Outline;* name badges for parents; *C-P-R Training: Parent Notebook* (we suggest printing the complete parent notebook with 10-session training materials and homework in a 3-ring binder for parents); parent information form with list of parents/child of focus/age, etc. (with room for additional notes); and Session 1 handouts and homework, including: *Session 1 Parents Notes & Homework, Feelings Response: In-Class Practice Worksheet, Feelings Response: Homework Worksheet,* and *Child–Parent–Relationship (C-P-R) Training: What Is It and How Can It Help.* Additional materials include: *Life's First Feelings* video *(video source and locations of segments on the video are found in the CPRT Treatment Manual)* and video clip demonstration of play session skills of reflection of feeling and allowing the child to lead (optional).

> *Note: The* CPRT Treatment Manual *that is available through the publisher, Routledge, provides the complete curriculum for Child Parent Relationship Therapy (CPRT), including detailed training session outlines for each of the 10 sessions, reproducible parent handouts, and additional supplemental handouts and materials for each training session. Included with the Treatment Manual is a CD-ROM containing all parent handouts and leader's outlines for ease of reproduction of materials. References for supplemental resources to enhance training are also included in the* CPRT Treatment Manual.

Content and Procedure

Since many of the training points and skills listed in the procedure sections for each CPRT training session are described in detail in Chapter 5, "CPRT Skills, Concepts, and Attitudes to Be Taught," or in the transcripts at the end of chapters 7 to 16 that describe the

10 training sessions, a complete description of a training point may not appear in the procedure section for each of the CPRT training sessions. The reader is reminded that the transcripts of filial therapy sessions contain only portions of the interactions in the 2-hour CPRT training sessions. Therefore, some of the material described in the training format may not show up in the partial transcript. Including a complete transcript for each session would have been too cumbersome.

Informal Greeting and Group Sharing

Session 1 begins informally with the therapist greeting parents as they arrive, distributing name tags and parent notebooks, and facilitating casual conversation between parents in order to begin to build rapport and connections. Remind parents that it is critical that they bring their notebooks with them weekly. As an option, refreshments can be served as parents arrive and fill out any necessary paperwork that is missing from their files (consent forms, background information, child behavior checklists, etc.). Prior to this first group meeting, the therapist should have talked with each parent, either by phone or in person. The goal of the initial parent interview is to screen parents for appropriateness for CPRT training, to begin to develop rapport with parents, and to briefly explain what CPRT (filial therapy) training is and how this approach can help alleviate child and/or family difficulties *(refer to Chapter 6 for more information on screening parents and the initial interview).* At this time, parents can be provided with the handout, *Child–Parent–Relationship (C-P-R) Training: What Is It and How Can It Help.* Ideally, all necessary paperwork will be obtained from parents prior to the first training session, either at the initial interview or, for those parents contacted by phone, by mailing packets to complete and return prior to the CPRT start date. If all else fails, schedule parents who have not completed required forms to come early to the first training. The objective is to take care of the majority, if not all, of the administrative activities prior to the beginning of class. Allow approximately 15 minutes for this informal sharing time before introducing training content. This informal sharing is a weekly ritual aimed at helping parents feel supported and connected. The transcript included at the end of this chapter illustrates how an experienced CPRT therapist who is also an experienced group leader facilitated group dynamics during this initial sharing. This kind of interaction would not be possible if the therapist had not met with parents individually and obtained necessary paperwork prior to the first group session.

CPRT Training Objectives and Essential Concepts

Begin by giving a brief overview of the basic premises that CPRT is based on. Refer to Session 1 handouts when appropriate, reminding parents to take notes about assignments and main points. The main points (discussed below) can be elaborated on or explained in simpler terms, depending on the needs of the particular group of parents. Refer to the handout, *Child–Parent–Relationship (C-P-R) Training: What Is It and How Can It Help*, but do not overwhelm parents with lengthy explanations. It is not necessary to try to anticipate all the questions parents might have or explain the entire CPRT process. Encourage parents to ask questions and use their questions as a springboard to emphasizing key points. Training points do not necessarily need to be introduced sequentially or all at once, and are never delivered lecture style. That would be boring to parents. Provide a bit of information here and there so parents don't get overwhelmed. Encouraging parents to ask questions helps maintain interest and enthusiasm. Ideally, parents' questions and comments are utilized to link parents' experiences and facilitate group dynamics, with teaching points interspersed as illustrated in the transcript at the end of this chapter. Major points are always more powerfully delivered when introduced at a relevant point in the discussion. *However, depending on previous group therapy and psychoeducational experiences, the beginning CPRT therapist may initially feel more comfortable adhering to a more structured outline; the CPRT curriculum allows for both structure and flexibility in presentation.*

The importance of facilitating a group process where parents feel supported, while presenting key concepts, cannot be overstated. **The rule of thumb for the day is warm acceptance and lots of encouragement.** Recognize that a major strength for these parents is simply that they are there—their presence and willingness to take time out of their busy schedules communicates their love and care for their children. The following key concepts should be introduced during Session 1. Again, these points do not have to be delivered in order or all at once. The ideal is to intersperse teaching points within group process.

- **Play is the child's language.**
  Children use play to communicate their experiences, thoughts, feelings, and wishes. Although children use both words and actions to communicate, young children communicate more meaningfully through the concrete world of play and activity. Play is more than just fun for children, they can also use play to make sense of a confusing or disturbing event and work through their problems. CPRT focuses on helping parents to be "keen observers" of their children's play. Learning to understand their **children's play provides parents with a window to their children's inner worlds**.
- **The goal is to prevent problems by teaching parents to understand what their children need.**
  CPRT training gives parents the tools they need to better understand their children—to better understand what their children are saying through the toys. When children feel understood, they feel better. There is a direct connection between how children feel and how they behave. **Children who feel better behave better!**
- **CPRT training strengthens parent–child relationships.**
  Parents are the most important and influential people in children's lives. A secure, loving relationship with a parent is the greatest predictor of a child's future happiness and success in life. A strong relationship is especially important in times of stress! Filial play sessions ***provide closer, happier times for parents and children—and build warm, special memories!*** Ask parents what they want their children to remember most about them 20 or 30 years from now.
- **Focus on the donut, not the hole!**
  The focus in CPRT is on the relationship (the donut—the good stuff), not the problem (the hole—what's missing, what needs to be fixed). The greatest strength a parent brings to parenting is her relationship with and love for her child; no matter how difficult the situation, the desire for a close parent–child relationship is a strength to be built on. The importance of encouraging parents by focusing on

what they are doing right is critical to the success of CPRT training. Only then will parents be able to do the same for their child. The most significant growth in parents over the 10 sessions of training generally occurs in this area.

Note: Donuts can be served as a refreshment, allowing the therapist to demonstrate this concept by holding the donut up and asking parents, "What is the first thing you notice about the donut?" The majority of parents respond "the hole." The therapist uses parents' responses to emphasize that is what we do as parents—focus on the hole, what is missing—rather than the donut—all the good stuff.

Emphasize to parents that during these 10 sessions they will be focusing on their strengths and their children's strengths.

- **Goal is for parents to change what they do for only 30 minutes each week.**
  This element of CPRT training is what sets it apart from other parenting training models, with the idea that setting aside a carefully chosen 30 minutes a week to practice these skills will promote consistency, and ultimately contribute to parent success. Emphasize to parents that they are not expected to change everything they do with their children. No one could do that! Therapists, who are also parents, can use personal stories to emphasize this point. Emphasize that it will be **the most important 30 minutes per week that parents will ever spend**. Parents committing to spend only 30 minutes per week of focused attention playing with their children really does make a difference! Research shows that these once-per-week special playtimes significantly improve children's behavior, significantly impact the parent–child relationship, and significantly reduce parenting stress (see Chapter 21). CPRT therapy is based on the premise that as the parent–child relationship is strengthened, children develop more confidence and self-control, and, as a result, behavior problems improve.
- **Parents can learn play therapy skills and become therapeutic agents for their children.**

Explain to parents that in 10 sessions they will learn the same basic play therapy skills that graduate students learn in a 15-week semester course. In this method, the parent is viewed as the therapeutic agent for the child, rather than the professional. Emphasize that parents will not be play therapists when finished with training, but that they will have learned some of the skills play therapists use to help children experiencing problems. Research shows parents can be just as effective in learning basic play therapy skills (Elling, 2003), and just as effective (in some cases more effective) as professionals in helping children with their problems (Bratton, Ray, Rhine, & Jones, 2005). Explain that role-play and video demonstrations of play sessions will be used to teach skills. Reassure parents that they will have many opportunities to observe and practice before they start their play sessions. The filial therapist's encouragement and modeling of the courage to be imperfect is critical in this initial stage of training. If the filial therapist is a parent, using personal stories to report the therapist's own failures as a parent helps parents feel less threatened and more willing to take risks.

- **CPRT skills help parents regain control as a parent.**
  The idea of "control" is very appealing to parents. Our experience is that the majority of parents come to CPRT training feeling out of control as parents and feeling that their children have far too much control. They think what they want is to be in control of their children! The therapist's job is to help parents understand that regaining control as a parent means developing control over themselves and how they respond to their child. Let them know that the skills they will be learning will give them the tools they need to respond purposefully and effectively to their children in difficult situations. They will know what to do and what to say—that is what is meant by control. This concept is easily introduced during the group sharing time, as there will always be a parent who reports events that allow the therapist to respond, "Sounds like there are times that you don't feel in control," as a segue into discussing how CPRT training will help.

Emphasize that not only do these new skills help parents feel more in control, they also help parents teach their children self-control. To illustrate this point, introduce the **Rule of Thumb: Be a thermostat, not a thermometer in your child's life**. *Respond (reflect) rather than react. Your child's feelings are not your feelings. When your child's feelings and behavior escalate, you can respond in a helpful way, rather than simply reacting and allowing your feelings and behavior to escalate, too.* In-control parents are like thermostats in their child's life. Out-of-control parents are like thermometers. They only react to what is there.

> *Note: You can introduce this concept by asking parents, "What is the difference between a thermometer and a thermostat?" Thermometers simply react to the temperature: the temperature goes up, the thermometer goes up—it doesn't do anything to regulate or help the situation (room temperature). On the other hand, thermostats respond to the slightest change in temperature, taking immediate action to respond in a way to help the situation (room temperature). Thermostats create an environment that is more comfortable and pleasant.*

Emphasize to parents: **In 10 weeks you will be different and your relationship with your child will be different!** (Modify the statement, if needed, to reflect the actual length of training.) Using metaphors, rules of thumb, visuals, stories, or demonstrations to illustrate points often helps parents understand more readily and, most certainly, helps them retain the learning.

Getting Acquainted: Parent Introductions and Selecting Child of Focus

Parents introduce themselves and describe their family. Avoid going around the circle asking each person in turn to share. In describing their families, parents are asked to select one child they will focus on during the 10 sessions of training. This is the child that the parent will have special play sessions with, 1 per week for 10 weeks. Usually the child of focus is the child most in need of help or the child to whom the parent is having the most difficulty relating. Some parents who have more than 1 child in the desired age range for filial play sessions, 2 to 10 years of age, may need help in deciding which child needs them most right now. To facilitate consistency for the child, **parents are instructed to work with only one child during training**. This strategy is also designed to insure parent success in applying CPRT skills, by focusing all their efforts on one child in their play session each week.

Initially, most parents are eager to have play sessions with all of their children, but the therapist must hold firm. Allowing parents to commit to conducting play sessions with more than one child per week is setting them up for failure. Most parents have difficulty in consistently conducting a 30-minute play session each week with 1 child, much less 2 or more. However, some parents can be very resistant to the notion that their other children will be left out. Suggesting that parents plan special activities of another nature (e.g., baking cookies) for children not receiving special play sessions minimizes resistance. Parents are instructed that they may start play sessions with other children at the end of the 10 weeks. Parents often need help in understanding that it is okay for one child to need them more right now and that the other children are learning a valuable lesson in delayed gratification. They, too, will get to have special play times with "daddy," but they will have to wait 7 more weeks (for younger children, marking on a calendar is helpful).

When both parents attend a CPRT training group and have only one age-appropriate child, each parent has a weekly special playtime with the child. When both parents attend and there are two age-appropriate children, each parent chooses a child of focus. All play sessions are conducted by the same parent. Alternating sessions between parents interferes with the building of trust and the development of themes across sessions. Helping parents select their child of focus during the initial parent interview avoids lengthy discussions that detract from time allotted for parents to share what has brought them to CPRT training.

In their descriptions of their children, parents generally focus on the problems they are having. These descriptions usually result in strong emotions being shared. "I am so angry at my son! I can't stand him!" Such feelings should be quickly generalized in the group by the therapist. "Anyone else ever get really angry at your child?" This protects the parent and helps to prevent overwhelming guilt by **normalizing the parent's experience**. In this way, parents quickly begin to perceive that **they are not alone in their struggles**. As parents share, the therapist clarifies and reflects content and feelings related to parent disclosure, listening carefully for underlying messages that reveal what the child really needs, rather than the problem presented. The therapist must skillfully limit the amount of time each parent shares by acknowledging the parent's concern or feelings and refocusing back to the group. For example, "Debbie, sounds like you really have your hands full, and we're going to be helping you work on that in your special play sessions with Rachel."

Use what parents disclose as an opportunity to explain more about the training and special play sessions and work in a few teaching points. At an appropriate point, introduce the **Rule of Thumb: The most important thing may not be what you do, but what you do after what you have done.** We are certain to make mistakes, but we can recover. It is how we handle our mistakes that makes the difference. (This rule of thumb and the accompanying story are described in the transcript of CPRT training Session 1 at the end of this chapter.) The therapist can use personal stories to effectively illustrate "Rules of Thumb" and other teaching points and hold parents' attention.

Beware of falling into the trap of trying to solve parents' problems. If parents could hear a quick solution and go home and apply it successfully, they wouldn't need to attend CPRT training. They can find lots of advice on TV, in magazines, and in books—advice that focuses on the problem. The problem isn't the problem! It's the relationship and the parents' view of their child that needs work, and that takes time—**there is no quick fix!** An effective strategy for addressing parents concerns is to briefly let them know you heard their concerns and that you're going to make a note of that to come back to in a few weeks. *(Always write parent concerns down and do come back to them in Sessions 9 and 10, when the focus is on helping parents generalize their play session skills to specific parenting issues.)*

The therapist records details of parents' descriptions of their child of focus for reference during training sessions. These notes are also read to the CPRT group in Session 10 to provide a benchmark for parents to evaluate their children's progress and to provide a base for discussing each parent's contribution to her child's growth and behavior change.

Reflective Responding

Reflective responding is the primary skill taught in CPRT training, a skill that teaches parents to **listen with their eyes as well as their**

ears and to respond empathically to their children, **without asking questions**. Parents use reflective responding in play sessions to communicate to their child what they see their child doing, what they hear their child saying, and what they experience their child feeling. Reflective responses provide a mirror for the child to see herself more clearly. Most importantly, this way of responding **helps children feel understood, valued, accepted, empowered, and capable**.

Parents are taught the essential **"Be-With" Attitudes—I'm here, I hear you, I understand, and I care**—as the way to nonverbally convey empathy and understanding to their children. These attitudes are the foundation that reflective responding is built on. The most skillful parent response will not be effective in communicating empathy unless the child perceives these underlying attitudes. The concept of parents "being with" their child, fully and without distraction, during play sessions cannot be overstated.

Reflecting Feelings

The most difficult aspect of reflective responding is helping parents identify and reflect their children's feelings, wants, and wishes. The majority of skill development in Session 1 is spent on the skill of identifying and reflecting feelings. Chapter 6 contains more information and examples for teaching the skill of reflection of feelings.

Most parents' life experiences have not taught them to value and express emotions. When parents first begin to identify their children's feeling, instead of reflecting the feeling, "You look sad," their tendency is to ask a question, "Are you sad?" Help parents understand that questions imply "I don't understand," while reflections are much more powerful and convey "I'm listening and I understand." Reflecting a child's feelings communicates acceptance of feelings and needs, which in turn helps the child feel understood and helps the child better understand and label his own feelings. We have found that using the analogy of a mirror helps parents understand how this works. The parent is like a mirror for her child; the parent accurately "reflects" back to the child what she heard and saw in the child's face (labels the feeling); then the child can "see" or understand her feelings more accurately from the "reflection." The more often and accurate the reflections, the more understood the child feels. The mirror can be a powerful analogy to help parents understand that a child's view of self is essentially what is mirrored back by the significant adults in his life. Children whose mirror reflects acceptance, encouragement, and affirmations will feel accepted, valued, and worthwhile.

Children whose parents accurately reflect their feelings also learn by example to verbally communicate their feelings. Conversely, children whose feelings are unrecognized by parents can learn that the expression of feelings is not acceptable. Some parents will likely express concern that if they accept their children's feelings, they will be condoning unacceptable behavior. Even if this issue is not raised, it will likely be a concern for some parents; therefore, some discussion of the difference is warranted.

Life's First Feelings Video

This video is a dramatic illustration of the importance of reflective responding and helps parents understand and identify feelings. Have the video cued to the segment in the early part of the video showing the infant's emotional reaction when the mother shows no facial affect in response to child. (Video source and locations of segments on the video are found in the CPRT Treatment Manual.) Ask for parent reactions to the video segment and use their reactions to emphasize teaching points. Parents generally comment on the dramatic impact of the mother's nonresponsiveness to her baby. These kinds of comments provide an opportunity to discuss the importance of parents' nonverbal responses, as well as the critical importance of children being responded to in a way that matches how they are feeling. Children perceive as much or more from what they see in their parents face as they do from what their parents say.

It is helpful to ask parents if they can think back to when their child was an infant (like the one in the video) and ask, "How many of you think it was easier to understand what your child needed at that age?" "How many of you enjoyed your child more?" Parents generally respond that it was much easier to understand their children's needs as infants and that they enjoyed their children more. Explore with them what has changed (they began walking, getting into things, saying "no," etc.). Point out that with an infant you spend more time looking into their face for a clue to what they need, because they cannot tell you.

Hand out *Feelings Response: In-Class Worksheet* (depicts emotions of anger, happiness, sadness, and fear). Next, show the second segment of the *Life's First Feelings* video to illustrate a variety of emotions *(the location of this segment on the video is described in the CPRT Treatment Manual).* The segment shows black-and-white drawings of different facial expressions and identifies the emotion that accompanies the facial expression. Ask parents to specifically notice the four feelings on the worksheet and how the expression of those feelings develops in the child's facial expression. Parents have the most difficulty distinguishing between sad and angry; therefore, more time focused on these two emotions is warranted. Stop the video periodically and make observations and teaching points.

Feelings Response: In-Class Practice Worksheet

The facilitator should read scenarios provided on worksheet with obvious emotion expressed in voice and nonverbals, and then ask parents, as a group, to identify how the child is feeling. After parents have agreed on the feeling—for example, "excited"—have them write it in the blank. Next, ask the group to use the feeling word and begin with "you" or "you're" and make a short reflection of feeling response, "You're excited," or "You're excited that Grandma and Grandpa are coming." Follow the same procedure to complete the other three examples. Parents are then given the handout, *Feelings Response: Homework Worksheet* (see Figure 7.1), and instructed to use the format on the practice sheet to identify those same four emotions in their child of focus this week and make a reflective response for each emotion (being a mirror for the child's emotions). Remind each parent to: (a) look into her child's face for a clue to what the child is feeling; (b) identify a feeling word; and (c) matching the child's intensity of feeling, make a short reflection of feeling beginning with "you" or "you're" and using the feeling word they identified. Parents are then to use the homework sheet to write down what the child did or said, what the child felt, and the parent's response. The importance of going through this step by step cannot be overemphasized—parents have great difficulty with this seemingly easy assignment. Remind parents of the importance of bringing the completed sheet to the next training session. If time permits, more practice on identifying and reflecting feelings is beneficial—parents have the most difficulty with this skill. A very effective training strategy is to find three or four video clips, each depicting a situation where a child is obviously showing a feeling. Stop the video after the "happening" and ask parents how the child was feeling and then help them turn the feeling word into a "you" statement.

C-P-R TRAINING FOR PARENTS

Feelings Response: Homework Worksheet - Session 1

Directions: 1) Look into child's eyes for clue to feeling. 2) After you've decided what child is feeling, put the feeling word into a short response, generally beginning with "you", "you seem sad", "you're really mad at me right now". 3) Remember the importance of your facial expression & tone of your voice matching child's (empathy is conveyed more through non-verbals than verbals).

HAPPY

Child: *(what happened/ what child did or said)* ______________________

____

____

Child Felt: ______________________

Parent Response: ______________________

____

____

Corrected Response: ______________________

____

____

SAD

Child: *(what happened/ what child did or said)* ______________________

____

____

Child Felt: ______________________

Parent Response: ______________________

____

____

Corrected Response: ______________________

____

____

MAD

Child: *(what happened/ what child did or said)* ______________________

____

____

Child Felt: ______________________

Parent Response: ______________________

____

____

Corrected Response: ______________________

____

____

SCARED

Child: *(what happened/ what child did or said)* ______________________

____

____

Child Felt: ______________________

Parent Response: ______________________

____

____

Corrected Response: ______________________

____

____

Figure 7.1 C-P-R Training for Parents—Feelings Response: Homework Worksheet #1.

Role-Playing Experiences

Role-play and demonstrations are critical experiences for parents. When working with individual parents or couples, parents can practice with their children, but the group format does not generally allow for the space or time to accommodate this activity. Instead, parents need many opportunities to role-play with each other, after first seeing the therapist demonstrate what they are expected to do. Coleaders are invaluable for this activity.

In Session 1, parents are asked to practice reflective listening and responding by first role-playing an adult listening to an adult. That assignment is generally less threatening than starting out asking parents to role-play their children. Allow time for parents to role-play reflective responding, and introduce the activity by saying, "Let's practice reflective listening and responding." Group parents in pairs. The therapist first role-plays with a parent volunteer to demonstrate reflective responding (or with a coleader, if available). Ask the parent to talk about something that happened at home this week with a child. Ask parents to watch and listen closely to what you do, as this is your way of teaching them what you want them to do in practicing reflective listening with their parent partner. Role-play and then ask parents to identify what they saw and heard you do. Parents then role-play. Ask parents to talk about something that happened with their child that week, and the parent partner is to reflect content and feelings. Listeners are instructed that they may not offer any solutions, suggestions, or stories of their own. After 3 minutes, parents switch roles. Then the group reacts to the role-playing. If time permits, a video clip demonstration of reflecting feelings and/or allowing the child to lead can be shown.

Homework Assignments

1. *30-second burst of attention.* Tell parents that you have a special homework assignment for them to do with their children—and that it will only take 30 seconds! Ask parents how many have had difficulty with their child wanting their attention at the least opportune moment; for example, when the phone rings. Generally, all hands go up! Explain to parents: "The next time your child wants your attention while you're on the phone, ask the person on the phone, 'Can you hold for thirty seconds? I'll be right back.' Then bend down to your child and for 30 seconds focus your undivided attention

on your child, prizing what your child is saying or showing you, as if that is most important in all the world to you at that moment. When the 30 seconds are up, let the child know that you need to finish talking on the phone and go back to your conversation." (See transcript of CPRT session at end of this chapter for a transcribed example of how to present this to parents.) Let parents know that this may not work all the time, but it does work for many parents. This assignment is offered in the first session because it is easy for parents to grasp and it really does work most of the time. This assignment also gives parents a brief experience of the power in providing for their children's need for focused attention. Giving parents a useful skill to try after 1 week of training that has a high probability of success also encourages and motivates them to want to learn more. Ask parents to report back next week.

2. Notice a new physical characteristic about your child of focus—could be freckle, shape of ears, etc. Explain that the reason for this assignment is to have parents practice becoming keen observers of their children during the special play sessions. The value in parents' simply noticing their children is not to be underestimated. Most parents will initially protest that there couldn't be anything physical about their children that they hadn't seen before. We have never had a parent who came back without finding something!
3. Bring a favorite picture of your child of focus. Instruct parents to bring in a picture that makes them want to smile, the one that most tugs at their heart when they look at it. Explain that they will share their pictures of their children the following week.

   Note: Most parents bring pictures of their children as infants or toddlers, which provides for additional teaching points for the following week!

4. *Feelings Response: Homework Worksheet.* Remind parents to complete and bring the following week. End by reminding parents to bring their C-P-R Training: Parent Notebook the following week and ask them for any paperwork (given at initial parent intake) that they did not return prior to class. Suggest that if they haven't already told their children about

why they are coming to CPRT Training they should tell their children, "I'm taking a class to learn how to play with you." Optional: Close session with a motivational story or poem, such as "If I Had My Child to Raise over Again" (found in *Chicken Soup for the Soul*; see CPRT Treatment Manual for reference). This poem can be used to motivate parents to do something different *now* to make a difference in their relationship with their children, instead of looking back and wishing they would have done things differently. Parents need to leave Session 1 motivated to commit to the 10 weeks. You are asking them to make a huge commitment.

5. Remind parents of the Rule of Thumb for this week.

Introduction to the CPRT Transcripts

The partial transcripts at the end of the chapters that describe the process and content of the CPRT training sessions are from a single filial therapy training group with 7 parents, no spouses. The therapist was Dr. Garry Landreth and the training sessions were held in a play therapy room in the Center for Play Therapy at the University of North Texas for videotaping purposes and to provide a comfortable and safe atmosphere for the parents. A secondary benefit of this setting was that role-playing practice and demonstration experiences could be easily entered into.

Excerpts selected from each training session focus primarily on only a few of the parents in the group to provide insight into the dynamics of the experience for individual parents and the CPRT process across the 10 sessions of training. In each session, attention is focused especially on one mother, Debbie, to highlight her personal struggles, the learning process as she experienced it, her development of insight, and the dynamic changes in her attitude and behavior. Chapter 13 provides a transcript of Debbie's play session with her daughter, a revealing look into the dynamics of some of her child's behaviors. An interview shortly after the conclusion of the 10 training sessions affords an opportunity to assess the impact of the CPRT training on Debbie and her daughter. A 4-year and 13-year follow-up interview with Debbie in Chapter 17 provides an unusual opportunity to evaluate the continuing and long-range effects of 10 sessions of CPRT training as experienced by Debbie. This is a rare opportunity to "get inside" the personal perceptual world of individual parents and follow them in their experiential journey through filial therapy training.

The dynamics of providing CPRT training, dealing with unexpected happenings, responding to parents' emotional expressions, answering questions, the importance of being flexible in responding to parental needs, and the role of the therapist in providing therapeutic dimensions as well as training dimensions cannot be communicated in a description of the content to be covered in each training session. These dimensions can only be known by going inside a functioning CPRT group. These transcripts provide an opportunity to examine the CPRT process as it was lived out by the therapist and parents.

Partial Transcript of CPRT Session 1

(Group met in a play therapy room.)

Dr. L.: Let me tell you a little about this training and then I would like to answer any questions you have. My objective is not to change your life or change everything you do with your child, but to teach you in 10 weeks as much as I possibly can about how to structure a special playtime with your child. Play is important because toys are like words for your child and play is their language. I'll teach you skills that I teach my beginning play therapists on this campus because I believe that what we do as a professional in this room, and what I do in this room with children like yours and other children, is helpful. So I am going to teach you what I know about play therapy. Not that you will be play therapists, but you'll have some of those skills so that when you have these special playtimes you will know how to reflect your child's feelings and communicate what you see your child doing.

The purpose behind that is so that your child will feel that you understand, that you are interested in what they do, that you are interested in them, and that you care. So, we'll be working on your relationship with your child. We have found that these special playtimes help improve children's behaviors. And then as we go along, we will work on some of the things that you are concerned about. Your special playtimes will begin in another couple of weeks.

I'll teach you what to do in the special playtimes before I ask you to have the special playtimes with your child. I'll do some role-playing here with you to practice new skills, we'll watch a videotape or two of my playtimes, and I'll let you see me demonstrate the skills with children like yours. Then you will begin your special playtimes at home.

I guess most of all I want you to know right off I'm not trying to change your life or that the things we do here you must go home and do every hour. I couldn't do that, I don't do these things all the time with my children either. But I will expect you to do them for 30 minutes once a week. Does that sound like something you could try, for 30 minutes?

I talked with each one of you a little on the phone, but you may still be thinking, "Well, I still don't know exactly what he meant or what I'm suppose to do." And I'd like to answer any of those questions if you have any.

Kathy: Will this help us learn how to set limits and improve our children's behavior when they're out with us?

Dr. L.: I gather by the way you are asking that question that's something that happens quite a bit for you.

Kathy: Yes, it does. Like last night, we went to get ice cream, and he ran behind the counter to choose his toppings. I had to run back there to get him. And sometimes some of the things he does like that I feel kind of silly. You know, having to go behind the counter and get him.

Dr. L.: Any of the rest of you ever have your child do something out in public that was awkward for you or that you felt a little embarrassed about?

Group: Yes.

Dr. L.: It happens to all of us, doesn't it? Children don't always do things just the way we would like for them to. I've noticed that and I'm sure you've experienced that, too. Kathy, the answer to your question is yes. One of the things we will work really hard on is called therapeutic limit setting. We won't get to that today. But we will in a few weeks, and I will teach you how to help your child learn self-control. I think that's what you're after.

Kathy: That's right. Like when I say it's time to come in off the bicycle, he doesn't think I mean it. His reward for being good is going to do something special, and then if his behavior hasn't been what it's supposed to be, then we don't go. How do we live with each other after that? He knows that will push my buttons. He just pushes my buttons until we fall apart.

Dr. L.: Until you feel like exploding.

Kathy: Right, and he does, too. He just gets angry and angrier the longer and longer we don't get to do it. But he knows he's not going to because his behavior hasn't been appropriate.

Dr. L.: Sounds like there are some times when you don't feel in control.

Kathy: There's a lot of times, a lot of times, yes.

Dr. L.: One of the things we will work on is returning control to you. Not necessarily always controlling your child. Because control means…

Sonya: (nods her head and smiles)

Dr. L.: Sonya, go ahead and finish that.

Sonya: Controlling yourself, or your reactions and feelings with a child.

Dr. L.: Because you will know what to do. When you know what to do and how to apply a new skill, then that gives you control. One of the things we will work on, Kathy, is how to help your child follow through without bribing.

Nita: (nods her head)

Dr. L.: You struggle with that some, Nita?

Nita: We go on spells. We have to use a lot of bribery.

Sonya: I have a question. So we will never actually have the children in here?

Dr. L.: Yes, once or twice during this training, I will ask you to bring your child to this room and be videotaped in a playtime. The purpose will be for us to see each other. I'm going to let you watch me, and then after you have practiced your skills here and you're more comfortable, you will bring your child in here, and we'll make a videotape and then bring the videotape to one of our sessions for feedback. After the first three training sessions, we'll watch a parent play session every time we meet.

Debbie: What is the purpose of the play therapy? What's the objective?

Dr. L.: I don't expect you all to be play therapists, but I will teach you some of the skills I know so you will be a therapeutic agent to your child, you'll be helpful to them. The purpose of the special playtimes is to build a better relationship with your child and to work on things like teaching your child self-discipline. Your child might start throwing sand on the floor and sand is not for throwing on the floor; so I'll teach you how to set limits so your child will stop themselves rather than you having to jump up and stop them. It'll help you teach your child self-control. Are there some other questions?

Nita: I don't like to say I'm bossy, or controlling, but I am an overfunctioning type of personality, and I see that a lot in my relationship with my son Roger. I'm really intent on becoming more self-aware and changing more things with me than I am with him.

Dr. L.: That's what we'll be working on. When I talk about returning control to you that means first you must become aware of what you do before you can be in control.

Nita: So we will address our behaviors and reactions, too? All mothers know children can just do things that can send you way off into outer space. If you weren't so busy and pressured, and could take some time to think about it, you might be able to think it through and understand the behavior. But in day-to-day life, it's not so easy. And really, I think my son's biggest problem sometimes is me. He's a lot like me, too.

Dr. L.: I hear what you're saying there about pressure, and one of the things I want you all to know is I believe parents are doing the best they can under the circumstances. Sometimes the circumstances are not very good, you have a lot to do. I heard you say, Emily, you have five foster children?

Emily: I have three foster, two biological.

Dr. L.: You have your hands full. My experience is that children don't always wait until we're at our best to ask for something they need. How many of you have children that are 4 years old or younger? When do 4 and 3 and 2-year-olds seem to want your attention the most? When you're doing what?

All: Cooking, on the phone, in the bathroom.

Dr. L.: It seems automatic, doesn't it? When the phone rings, that's when they discover something they must show you at that moment and no later. There is a little technique that you can use when your child must have your attention, like when you're on the phone. It's called a 30-second burst of attention. It works this way: You're on the phone, here comes your child and must show you their startling discovery right now, and so you say to your friend on the phone, "Excuse me, I'll be back to you in 30 seconds." You put the phone down, and you give your child 30 seconds of undivided attention. You prize what your child is saying or showing you, and then you say, "Thank you so much for showing me that, thank you for telling me that, now I'm going to talk on the phone," and you pick the phone up.

This will not work all of the time with all children, but it will work most of the time with most children. If you don't put the phone down and give your child a

30-second burst of attention, what will you do? (Parent demonstrates hand pushing away.) We keep pushing our child away for 10 minutes while we try to carry on a conversation and in the process we are rejecting our child, which is not what you really want to do. You don't want your child to feel rejected by you. So, better that your friend waits for 30 seconds than for your child to feel rejected. One of your assignments this week is to give your child a 30-second burst of attention and tell us next week how it worked out. You will need to bring a notebook each week to write down your assignments and points to practice in your special playtimes. Some of you don't have a notebook with you, so here's some paper to write on today.

Dr. L.: To get better acquainted, let's go around the circle and you tell us about your family, how many children you have, and what their names are. While you do that, begin to think about the child, age 2 to 10, that you would like to have these special playtimes with. I know you don't have time in your busy week to have special playtimes with five children. I ask that you choose one child to start with. Later we'll talk about adding a second child to have a special playtime with. Think of the child who needs you most or the child you seem to be having the most difficulty with, and that's the child we will call the child of focus that you will have your special playtime with every week, without fail. Once you start having your special playtimes, I'll ask you not to let anything interfere.

Debbie: I'm Debbie and I have a 3 ½-month-old son and my daughter Rachel, who is 4. She is going to be the child that I do my special playtime with.

Dr. L.: Tell us about your daughter.

Debbie: I think she is a sensitive child, but she is extremely strong willed, and I've gotten to the point where I am rejecting her as a person because I am having so many problems with not knowing how to deal with her. I have always thought if you just spank a child, they'll do what they are supposed to do and everything will be fine, but it just does not work. I have to learn what she needs. She would throw sand and go past her 30 seconds and onto the next minute, and she would tell me to clean it up.

Dr. L.: So she's demanding and bossy.

Debbie: Very.

Dr. L.: How do you react when she is bossy?

Debbie: Extremely violently. I become a 3-year-old, too. We're like these two kids that are having a fight, and it doesn't matter what I say, she doesn't do it.

Dr. L.: Sounds like you get angry sometimes. Do any of the rest of you get angry at your children?

All: Yes.

Dr. L.: Sonya, what is it like when you get angry at your child?

Sonya: Sometimes I yell at her, and I know I shouldn't.

Debbie: I don't know what to do. When we're picking up pizza at the store and she wants a toy, when I tell her "No" she just sprawls herself out on the floor and just lays there in a screaming fit, and I have a choice. I can publicly beat her, or I can ignore her. I'm feeling very frustrated and very angry. She's making a demonstration and there's something that has to be done. But I'm wishy-washy, and sometimes I'll ignore her or sometimes I'll have to leave. And I don't think that's right.

Dr. L.: So you're left feeling angry, frustrated, and defeated.

Debbie: Isn't she winning?

Dr. L.: Not the way we will work it out.

Emily: Have you tried to validate her feelings by saying, "I understand that you want this toy"? Then explain why she can't have it and then set up an odd job she can do to earn the money. Maybe that will increase her self-respect.

Debbie: I haven't got into the earning money because she just turned 4.

Dr. L.: So money may not be that important to her.

Debbie: Yeah, for the last 2 years, she has slept in our bed, and it is my husband's problem. I'm working with my own inabilities and also against my husband who thinks our daughter is a friend.

Dr. L.: So he has trouble following through with discipline sometimes.

Debbie: It just doesn't exist.

Dr. L.: Debbie, I hear several people reacting and the reaction is, "You have your hands full."

Debbie: That's why I'm here.

Dr. L.: And we're going to work on that. Let's go on. Nita, tell us about your family.

Nita: My name is Nita, my husband and I have a son who turned 3 a few weeks ago. My son was one of those babies who didn't get over colic until he was 4 ½ months old. He would cry an average of 8 to 9 hours a day, every day. He did not sleep more than 4 hours a day until he was 26 months old. So it is just his temperament. He is very active; he walked very early, and crawled by 5 months. He's very intense; everything is life or death with him. Always has been, always will be, I guess. He has a very low sensory threshold. I was so sure it was me and the experts say no, he is a more difficult child.

Sonya: When you say "low sensory threshold," do you mean he takes in everything easily, like sense of touch and sense of sight?

Nita: In order to get him to sleep, his room has to be pitch black, and he has to have a sound machine on. He will be half asleep, the sun will go behind a cloud, and he will sit up and say, "Where'd the light go, Mom?" He is real light sensitive, also about clothing and bright colors. He gets worked up so easily that he can't enjoy a lot of things. I have to protect him in a way, and he is kept on a very rigid schedule. If he gets off his schedule, he just disintegrates, and he gets a sensory overload.

Dr. L.: He feels out of control.

Nita: I'm a little concerned about his self-esteem. He used to be good about working on things and trying. But since we've been remodeling the house, and I've been in the hospital with this pregnancy, I've been getting more tired and cranky. He just seems to be giving up faster and saying, "I just can't do it, Mommy. I just can't do it!" I used to think that would not be a problem for him, self-esteem, but I'm beginning to think that's not as strong as I thought it was.

Dr. L.: So you're exhausted, the house is in turmoil, and he seems to be reacting to all of that. Kathy, tell us about your family.

Kathy: My son is 6, and right now I feel that sometimes he's more in control of me than I am of him. We're going through him saying "No" and "Shut up." There are a lot of things I don't like that he's telling me, like "I don't have to." I feel like he is stronger physically than I am. He's built a lot like his dad. We're in the process of a separation right now. And that's hard on him. I've got him for 2 weeks at a time all to myself. If I have my back turned for a minute, he knows what he can sneak into that will fire me up, and he will do it. He wears me out physically. He gets angry, kicks me, pinches, and scratches when he can't get what he wants. I am having a hard time setting limits.

Dr. L.: Sounds like you feel he is out of control.

Kathy: At school he has been mean and hateful, so they put him in time out.

Dr. L.: So whatever he's reacting to, he's reacting to it everywhere.

Kathy: Sometimes I lose my patience and I just yell at him.

Dr. L.: Let's work on that. Along the way I am going to share with you some rules of thumb, and there is one that really fits right here: The most important thing may not be what you do, but what you do after what you have done. I, like you, am an emotional person. You are not to go away thinking, "Oh, Garry Landreth does all of those wonderful things with his children all the time." I don't.

I do some of these good things some of the time when I can remember to. But there are times that I yell at my kids just like you yell at your children, and I don't mind you knowing that.

Let me show you how this rule of thumb works. I came home one afternoon and my wife had had it up to here with our 5-year-old daughter, and in about 30 minutes, I had had it up to here with our 5-year-old daughter. The next thing I know, I'm yelling at her. I have never taught parents, "Go home and yell at your children. It's good for them." I don't believe that. But, here I was doing something I don't believe in. And the next thing I knew, I was threatening her: "If you don't stop that I will…" Does that sound familiar? Here I was doing two things that I don't believe in and I don't teach.

I blew the relationship right there; we had this big break in our relationship that afternoon. But I don't believe that was the most important thing that I did that day with my daughter. Two hours later, I was sitting on the side of her bed, and I said, "Karla, this afternoon when I yelled at you, I shouldn't have done that. I know better. But Karla, this afternoon, I was so angry at you, I couldn't think of anything else to do." She was lying there taking all this in. When I finished, she said, "Daddy, you could have said, 'I'm mad at you,'" which is exactly what I teach. And I had to be reminded of that by a 5-year-old. What did my 5-year-old daughter learn that day?

Emily: That even Dad makes mistakes.

Dr. L.: That Dad makes mistakes, and…?

Debbie: That you can say, "I'm mad at you."

Dr. L.: That you can say, "I'm mad at you," and…?

Sonya: To apologize?

Dr. L.: That it's okay to admit you made a mistake. Don't you wish all children and adults could do that? That's hard to do. And there's only one way our children will learn to do that. Someone must teach them by doing it. I believe that you are your child's best teacher. I want you to free yourself to use yourself more effectively. My daughter also learned that you can recover a relationship. The most important part of that day was the recovery of our relationship when I sat on the bed. I just described something important there. If you have something important to say to your child, sit down. If you stand in the room, the message to the child is, "She's not going to be here very long." If you sit down on the bed, the message to your child is, "She's going to be here for a while. I may have to compromise." If you stand up, they think, "She will leave quickly." If you sit down, they think, "This is going to take a while."

(Parents continue to discuss the Rule of Thumb and the implications for themselves.)

Kim: I'm Kim and I have three children, 4 years, 3 years, and 2 months. The reason I am here is my oldest son was born premature. He is in the early childhood intervention program. He has been diagnosed with Attention Deficit Disorder, and he had real bad ear infections for 2 years. His speech has been diagnosed at 24 months. He's in physical therapy and speech therapy, and I'm going to help him at home, so he's going to be the child I'll be working with. My 3-year-old is extremely precocious and very smart. And she adds to the problem because she's way ahead, and he's behind.

Dr. L.: Tell us some more about what your son is like as a person.

Kim: When he had his ear infections, we thought he could hear us, but he couldn't. So he's completely in his own little world. Some of his symptoms are like autistic symptoms.

Dr. L.: Just thinking about him as a person, what is he like?

Kim: He doesn't have very good self-esteem. He's behind; so you have to look at him like he is at a 2-year-old level. But he's large for his age, and he's adorable. You have to keep telling yourself, "He's 2, not 4."

Dr. L.: What else is he like?

Kim: He's real affectionate, real well meaning, and real sweet. We have a new baby, and he's aggressive with her. But it's not to be mean; the doctors say his sensory skills are low, and he has to touch and feel his world.

Dr. L.: So he likes contact, and he likes to feel. What bothers you most about him?

Kim: His low self-esteem. I'm real worried about him, and my husband is real worried about him, too.

Dr. L.: How do you know he has low self-esteem?

Kim: He's very frustrated; he wants to do what his sister is doing. His motor skills are at about 24 months. I think he knows he is behind.

Dr. L.: So he's impatient with himself?

Kim: Very. You would think he was autistic, if you didn't know everything.

Dr. L.: The special playtimes will be a wonderful opportunity for him to learn to be patient with himself as you are patient with him. And as you are patient with your child, he will become more patient with himself. You will get a chance to work on that in the playtimes.

Kim: We were never taught to be parents.

Dr. L.: Sometimes that is frustrating, because nothing we have had has taught us to be parents. It's just expected we will know it. In here, we are going to work on some things that are helpful for parents to do. Emily?

Emily: I have two biological children. They are 4 and 10. I don't have any problems with them. They are pretty good, well-rounded kids. I have three foster children, ages 4 ½, 6 ½, and 7 ½. I think the 4 ½-year-old is the one I'm going to concentrate on. He came into foster care after being abandoned by his mother eight times. Because of that, he has very poor respect for anything of authority, starting with the mother figure, which is me. He has been diagnosed with Posttraumatic Stress and Pervasive

Developmental Disorder. He is about a year behind chronologically where he should be functioning. He is an extremely intelligent child. He has been with us for 1 year and we will be adopting him in 1 month.

Dr. L.: You love him a lot.

Emily: I do. He is a special kid, and he can be a brat and a half. I think what I want to focus on is his anger toward his mother because of the physical abuse and the abandonment that has happened to him.

Dr. L.: What is he like on a daily basis?

Emily: He is a charmer, but….he's as big as our 6-year-old girl. He's a gorgeous kid, and he knows it.

Dr. L.: You said he's a charmer, but…

Emily: He goes through severe bursts of anger. I feel it's not the issue of he can't have a cookie after supper that night. It's more of an issue of at some point in his life, his mother didn't let him have a cookie, and therefore he pitched a fit and got beat up for it. And he tests me on a day-to-day basis. "How bad do I have to be?" About 6 months ago, he was peeling the wallpaper, peeling the carpet up. This kid has a lot of problems. I set the limits, I had followed the limits, and I had not lost my cool with him. When it was all over that evening and I said, "No matter how angry I get, no matter how mad you get, and no matter how destructive you are, I will always love you." And he said, "No, you won't."

Dr. L.: So it's almost as if at times he's trying to find out if you really love him. What I'm hearing most, Emily, is that you are understanding of this little boy. Even when he's angry and difficult to deal with, you understand that it's not necessarily you that he's angry at. Okay, Laura.

Laura: I'm a single parent and I still like to say I have five children and one's in heaven. I have a daughter that's 15 and a son that was 9 that died January 1st, and a son that is 6, another son that is 4, and a daughter that is 22 months. Dawson, the 4-year-old, will be my focus child. The problems that he and I have are that I hung onto him like he was my last child and the 22-month-old came. She was my bonus. Dawson has a lot of anger and is very resentful of the time I spend with the 22-month-old. He is very demanding of my time. He is difficult to control. Sometimes he will just disappear out of the house at all hours and go hide under other trailer homes in our area. I put deadbolt locks on the doors of our house, but he can still get out the windows. One time he was gone for 2 ½ hours before we found him.

Dr. L.: That must have been a really frightening situation.

Laura: Yeah. When I found him, I just held him and cried. He has been a real challenging and trying child.

Dr. L.: What makes him challenging, Laura?

Laura: He tests me a lot, and I feel physically and emotionally drained after I have had to deal with him.

Dr. L.: Sounds like several of you have children who test you and push the limits a lot.

Laura: I know that if I stay with the limits and keep insisting that he abide by the limits, they will work. But it's really hard to do. I think that if a child knows you will give out or give up in 3 hours, the child will test you for 3 hours until you fall apart.

Dr. L.: That sounds like a frustrating and exhausting situation with Dawson. Is there anything he does that particularly bugs you?

Laura: He is very demanding of my time.

Dr. L.: I'm not sure you're saying this, but it sounds to me like you are saying, "I can never escape from him."

Laura: Sometimes he will even get into my bed or grab my hair to keep my attention focused on him.

Dr. L.: He wants all of you, and that's really draining on you. That's something we will work on. Sonya, tell us about your family and your child of focus.

Sonya: My name is Sonya, I have two girls; they're cute and sweet. One is 2 ½ and the other is one. I've been a single parent for almost a year now. The divorce is pending, but there will be no reconciliation. It's harder than I thought it would be. Being a single parent wasn't planned. Right now I'm concerned with the 2-year-old because I think she's trying to tell me something.

Dr. L.: And you're not quite sure what it is.

Sonya: Right. Sometimes she'll talk about being scared. Every once in a while she will get very clingy, and she's usually not like that. She is very articulate, and she does a lot of things that 4-year-olds do. We use time out a lot. We don't use physical disciple. Ever since we've been separated, there's no consistency in visitation. She loves her daddy, he's just not there, and he never really was very available physically or emotionally. It's hard for me to separate emotionally what's her pain and what's mine. I try to open up the arena for her to talk, but I think she senses that some topics aren't okay, like if she's missing her daddy or if she's scared or angry. She has started doing some things I am a little confused about.

Dr. L.: Seems as though you are trying to be all things to her, and that's not quite possible.

Sonya: Yeah, it makes me tired.

Dr. L.: It also seems to me that you are saying that you would like so much to understand what your daughter is trying to say to you, but she can't just sit down and say it. And that's one of the things I'm going to work on, to help you all understand your child's play behavior. For the 30 minutes of your special playtime, you will be a keen observer of your child's play. You will learn as much about your child as you possibly can through their play because play is the way that children talk.

They will act out the message with these toys. I will ask you to make notes about your special playtimes, and you will bring your notes here and say, "This is what my child did with these toys," and I will try to help you understand what your child is trying to say to you so that you become a reader of your child's play behavior. Let me shift gears with you. (Emily leaves the session.) It is so important that we notice our children. (Debbie leaves her chair beside Dr. L. and moves across the room into Emily's chair.)

Debbie: No offense. (group laughs)

Dr. L.: No offense taken. You can see better over there.

Debbie: You do look like Mr. Rogers.

Dr. L.: Well I take that as a compliment. I admire Mr. Rogers. Your assignment is to notice something physical this week about your child that you have not noticed before. You may notice a dimple or a freckle you hadn't noticed before. Study your child and try to find something physical you hadn't noticed before. My reason for this assignment is to have you practice becoming a keen observer of your children. When you start your special playtimes, I will say, "Now I want you to become keen observers of your child's play. I want you to listen to your child with your eyes." What your child sees in your face is also important. Let me show you how important this is. (Turns on VCR and shows segment of *Life's First Feelings* video showing an infant's emotional reaction when no emotion is shown in the mother's face.)

Nita: That almost makes me sad, because part of the reason I'm here is because when my son was younger than 2, I was tuned into him and able to pick up on his cues even though he screamed night and day, and now I can't do that. I thought somehow that when he got over all these difficulties that I would be more tuned in, but I don't feel as connected. Maybe you just don't connect when they're not nursing anymore.

Dr. L.: One of the things you will learn here is how to be more in tune with your child, and that begins by watching what shows on your face, because our children react to what they see or don't see on our faces.

Debbie: My daughter will say "Mommy!" and move my face to look at her.

Dr. L.: And that's the message I wanted you to get, that children react to what they see on our faces. The second assignment is to identify these four emotions in your children this week. (Dr. L. hands out the *Feelings Response Worksheet.*) Before we work on this sheet, let's watch more of the video to identify your children's emotions. (Shows more of the video depicting facial expressions that accompany emotions and stops.) If you saw that emotion in your child, you would let your child know what you saw in her face by saying, "You're interested in that." As you see each one of these emotions, begin to practice responding in your mind: "You're angry, you're interested, you're sad." Whatever the emotion is, start with "You" and then say it in your mind.

Let's watch some more of the video and you can practice responding in your mind to what you see. (Plays more of the video and stops.) Many parents mistake anger for unhappiness. The child in the video has been left, Mom walks away, and the child reacts with anger. The mom comes back and tries to make the child happy, but it doesn't work because the child is angry, not unhappy.

Debbie: I don't know how to differentiate between unhappy and angry.

Dr. L.: And I don't expect you to, yet. I'm just trying to introduce you to the whole range of emotions. (Plays more of the video and stops.) What I would like for you all to do this week is identify in your child the four emotions on this sheet. Let's make sure we are all on the same track. The first emotion on the sheet is…

Group: Happy.

Dr. L.: If you see your child being happy, how could you respond?

Kim: You look happy.

Dr. L.: You look happy. You're happy. You're happy about that. Have you noticed the word I start with almost every time?

Group: You.

Dr. L.: "You" points to the child and says, "I understand you're happy. You really like that." And the second feeling on the sheet?

Group: Sad.

Dr. L.: If your child is sad about something, you will say…

Sonya: You look sad.

Dr. L.: You look sad. You're sad about that, or you're really sad. I noticed, Sonya, as you said, "You look sad," your eyebrows squinted and feeling showed in your face. Remember, as was shown on the video, your child responds to what shows in your face. And, Sonya, you looked like you understood the sadness. *(The remaining feelings depicted on the worksheet are identified and discussed.)*

Nita: I just realized I do that, except, I make it a question and say, "Are you sad?"

Dr. L.: And that says you don't understand.

Nita: Why do I do that? Why do I have to put everything into a question?

Dr. L.: It's typical. It says, "I don't understand," and yet, you already know the answer. When you ask, "Are you sad about that?," you already see sadness. It is a lot more powerful to say "You're sad" than to say "Are you sad?" because the question says "I don't understand." There are four healing messages I will remind you of each time we meet, because we are going to work really hard on conveying them to your child. The first message is "**I'm here.** I am fully here. I won't be distracted." The second message is "**I hear you.** I hear your emotions. I hear your play"—and you hear that with your eyes—"I'm here. I hear you." The third message is **"I understand."** When you say, "You look sad about that," or "You're angry," you are saying, "I understand," rather than asking, "Does that make you angry?" Have you ever had an adult do that to you? You were so angry and they said, "Are you mad?" as though they had no idea you were mad. We want to communicate I'm here, I hear you, I understand. And the fourth message is **"I care."** If you communicate the first three messages, then the fourth one falls into place.

This week when you see one of these emotions, respond and reflect back to your child their emotion, sort of like looking in that mirror and reflecting back to your child their emotion. You're going to hold their emotion up to them and show it back to them by putting a label on it. After you have done that, write down what your child did and what you said. It might be "My kindergartener was really happy about the paper she brought home and I said, 'You're really happy about the happy face on your paper.'"

Bring the faces sheet with you next time, and we will go over this assignment. Let's practice reflective listening. (Puts parents into groups of two.) The person closest to me in each pair, you talk about something that happened with your child this week. The other person is the listener, and you reflect what you hear. Here's the way it will work. Kim, tell me something that has happened in your home this week. You all watch me, and you will see what I want you to do.

Kim: My son took out a dozen eggs and decorated the kitchen floor with them. It was yuk.

Dr. L.: Sounds like a frustrating thing to have eggs all over the floor.

Kim: I overreacted. It was just a dollar's worth of eggs.

Dr. L.: You wish you hadn't reacted so strongly because it was only some eggs. What did you all hear me doing? I'm mirroring back what Kim is saying. Mirror back the words. Now you try it in your groups. Listeners, for 3 minutes you may not tell anything that happened to you or offer a suggestion to fix a problem.

(Parents practice in pairs.)

Dr. L.: Sometimes your child will play without saying anything. They're just playing in the sandbox. (Dr. L. scoops up sand in the sandbox and pours it into pile.) You would say,

"You're just scooping that sand and pouring it right there and making a big hill of sand." You just state what you see. That's called tracking. Our reflecting back is like what they see in our face. Let's change roles and reflect back.

(Parents practice in pairs.)

(Group discussion about role-playing.)

Dr. L.: I sense that you all want to learn everything there is to learn today, and I don't expect that. I just want you to try this on, see how it feels, come back next week, and we will talk about it. Next week, I will give you a list of toys to put together for your special playtime.

(Dr. L. ends the session by going over homework assignments.)

References

Bratton, S., Landreth, G., Kellam, T., and Blackard, S. (2006). Child Parent Relationship Therapy (CPRT) Treatment Manual: A 10-Session Filial Therapy Model for Training Parents. NY: Routledge.

Bratton, S., Ray, D., Rhine, T., and Jones, L. (2005). The efficacy of play therapy with children: A meta-analytic review of treatment outcomes, *Professional Psychology: Research and Practice, 36(4).*

Elling, E. R. P. (2003). A comparison of skill level of parents trained in the Landreth Filial Therapy Model and graduate students trained in play therapy. (Doctoral dissertation, University of North Texas, 2003). *Dissertation Abstracts International, 64* (06), 1983.

CHAPTER 8

CPRT TRAINING SESSION 2: BASIC PRINCIPLES FOR PLAY SESSIONS

Overview

The primary focus for Session 2 is to begin preparing parents to conduct their 30-minute home play sessions by reviewing reflective responding and familiarizing parents with the basic principles for play sessions. Next, the therapist emphasizes the importance of structuring and setting the stage for conducting a successful home play session, which includes parents gathering the special toys needed for their filial play kit and deciding on a consistent time and place to hold their weekly play sessions that will ensure privacy and freedom from distractions from other family members.

The partial transcript of CPRT training Session 2 found at the end of the chapter illustrates essential therapist skills needed to facilitate a supportive atmosphere while presenting key concepts and points to be covered. Important therapist skills and attributes demonstrated include encouragement and support of parents' initial attempts at reflective responding; the ability to balance parent support with teaching new concepts, spontaneity, and immediacy in presenting concepts in teachable moments; and a sense of humor.

The importance of setting the stage for the first play session is emphasized, and the basic structuring skills of facilitating the child's freedom to decide and allowing the child to lead are demonstrated and role-played. Parents are reminded of the importance of conveying the four messages taught in Session 1: I'm here, I hear you, I understand, and I care.

Materials

Suggested materials include: *CPRT Session 2–Treatment Outline;* parent information form with pertinent notes on each parent (with room to add additional notes); homework assigned in Session 1, including extra copies of any homework worksheet; and Session 2 handouts and homework, including: *Session 2 Parent Notes & Homework, Basic Principles of Play Sessions, Toy Checklist for Play Sessions,* and an optional practice worksheet on reflective responding skills. Additional materials include: an optional display poster of the "Be-With" Attitudes, a sample filial play kit, photograph of toys set up for a play session, and an optional video clip that demonstrates structuring and setting the stage in a play session (creating an environment of permissiveness and allowing the child to lead). If a video clip is not available, arrange ahead of time to demonstrate with a child of a parent in the CPRT group.

> *Note: All handouts listed above, as well as a training session outline for the therapist, additional supplemental parent handouts, and resources for this training session are found in the* CPRT Treatment Manual *and accompanying CD-ROM, available from the publisher, Routledge.*

Content and Procedure

This session begins, as all sessions, with the therapist facilitating approximately 10 minutes of general discussion of how each parent's week has been, with a goal in mind of building rapport with parents, providing support, and facilitating connections between parents. This informal group discussion time also allows a few minutes for latecomers to arrive before reviewing weekly homework assignments and, in this session, provides the therapist an opportunity to model reflective listening and responding to feelings as a lead-in to reviewing parents' homework assignment to notice and respond to their children's feelings. This informal sharing time in the group provides an opportunity to check in with parents to see if anyone had a chance to use the 30-second Burst of Attention strategy. Since this skill is not directly related to what parents will be asked to do during their home play sessions, there is no need for the therapist to spend a lot of time on this activity. Remember, the goal in introducing this in the first session was to give parents an easy-to-use skill that they could immediately put to use outside of play sessions, generally with a measure of success.

As stated in Session 1, it is the therapist's responsibility to **find something to support and encourage in each parent's response** as they share about their week—when possible. Some parents' responses would challenge even the most experienced CPRT therapist, so those responses are best ignored! Continue to utilize the strategy of saying, "That's something we'll work on later. I'm going to make a note, so I won't forget," when parents get off topic and want the therapist to give them a quick solution to a problem.

> Reminder: it is very important to write down parents' concerns and come back to them in Session 9 or 10 when you are helping parents generalize their skills to responding to issues that arise outside of their play sessions. Your goal is to let parents know you heard them, their problems are important, you care, and you will address their concerns later.

Review Homework

Begin session by asking parents to turn to the *Feelings Response: Homework Worksheet.* We have found that most parents have difficulty with this assignment; therefore, it is important to spend time reviewing the skill. The therapist must be encouraging and supportive as parents make their first attempts at sharing their reflective responses in front of group members by focusing on the part of a parent's response that was appropriate and ignoring the part that wasn't. For example, in the Session 2 transcript that follows, Kim shares her response to her child's happiness, "You look happy there. Are you excited about that?" The therapist offers encouragement and helps the parent feel successful by focusing only on the first part of her response, "I heard you begin with 'You.' 'You look happy...'" and proceeds to turn that part of her response into a teaching point. **Remember: Encouragement is the order of the day!**

A parent may share a concern that when she reflected her child's feeling, the child didn't respond. It's important to emphasize to parents that when they are using these new skills, **they should not expect something back from their children**. Explain to parents: "Your child probably won't say, 'Yeah, you're right.' But your child hears you and takes it in. Sometimes you may get a smile or a nod that lets you know your child heard you, but sometimes your child may just take it in and continue what she was doing."

A typical problem that arises as parents begin to use the skill of reflective responding is that some parents report that reflecting their child's feelings didn't seem to help. Of course, all parents would like to see quick and dramatic results for their efforts; but for some parents this is more of a need than for others. The therapist must caution parents to be patient; that **these new ways of responding therapeutically to their children are working, even when they seem not to be working**.

In essence, the therapist is asking parents to **trust the process**, when most parents have had no similar experience on which to base their trust. The therapist may find it helpful to use an analogy that parents can relate to, such as asking parents what they do when they cut their finger badly. Parents know from experience that although you respond immediately by putting some medicine and a bandage on the wound, it doesn't work (heal) immediately. But they would not remove the bandage and wash off the medicine after a few hours, just because the wound had not healed yet; they would trust that over time, by continuing to apply the medicine, the wound would heal. Their experience has taught them that they have to be patient and trust the process of healing; and the deeper the wound, the longer the process of healing. This analogy is used in the partial transcript of Session 2 at the end of this chapter.

For parents who are having difficulty identifying and responding to feelings, remind them, again, to first stop and think of the feeling word that best describes what they see in their children's faces and/or hear in their children's voices, and then take that word and make a short statement, beginning with "you." (Parents often get confused and depersonalize their attempt at reflection by saying: "David is really angry" or "My, *we* really are angry today!") Remind them that beginning with "you" personalizes the response: "You are really angry." The therapist can also demonstrate reflective responding with a parent volunteer role-playing as her own child or use a demonstration video clip to reinforce this skill (refer to Chapter 5 for more examples and strategies for teaching reflective responding). Typically, a few parents will not have completed this assignment or will have forgotten to bring their worksheet, but encourage them to participate by giving an example of a time during the week when they remember their child feeling ____ and help them formulate a response. **The message is that homework and practice are important—and you will hold them accountable!**

Share Favorite Picture and Physical Characteristic of Child

Next, ask parents to report on their second homework assignment, to notice something new about their child, a physical characteristic that they hadn't noticed before. Introduce the purpose of this activity by discussing the power of simply noticing and really *seeing* their child. Just by using their eyes, they can begin to know and understand their child better. This discussion can be coupled with having parents show their favorite picture of their child as they report on something new they noticed in their child. Our experience is that parents typically bring pictures of their children as babies or toddlers, which can lead to a brief but lively discussion of why that stage in their children's development holds more special memories than their children's current developmental phase. (Hint: less discipline problems and power struggles!) Sharing pictures is another way of enhancing parent connectedness in the group and developing rapport among group members. In addition, this activity focuses parents on children's strengths—what they love most or enjoy most about their children.

Filial Play Sessions—Basic Principles and Structuring of Play Sessions

The major portion of Session 2 is spent on helping parents begin to prepare for their home play sessions. The therapist begins this process by introducing the *Basic Principles of Filial Play Sessions* handout. This handout introduces four basic principles that are critical to parents' successes in conducting play sessions with their children. Focus primarily on the four principles *(parents can read over play session goals later at home, if group time is limited).*

1. The parent sets the stage by structuring an atmosphere in which the **child feels free** to determine how he will use the time during the 30-minute play session. The **child leads** in the play and the **parent follows**. The parent follows the child's lead by showing keen interest and carefully observing the child's play, **without making suggestions or asking questions**, and by actively joining in the play when invited by the child. *For 30 minutes, the parent is "dumb" and doesn't have the answers; it is up to the child to make his own decisions and find his own solutions.*
2. The parent's major task is to empathize with the child; to understand the child's thoughts, feelings, and intent expressed in play by working hard to **see and experience the child's play through the child's eyes**. *This task is operationalized by conveying the "Be-With" Attitudes, below.*
3. The parent is then to **communicate this understanding to the child** by (a) verbally describing what the child is doing/playing, (b) verbally reflecting what the child is saying, and (c) most importantly, by verbally reflecting the feelings that the child is actively experiencing through his play.
4. The parent is to be clear and firm about the few "limits" that are placed on the child's behavior. Limits are stated in a way that gives the child responsibility for his actions and behaviors—helping to foster self-control. Limits to be set are time limits, not breaking toys or damaging items in the play area, and not physically hurting self or parent. **Limits are to be stated only when needed**, but applied consistently across sessions. *(Your therapist will help you in deciding when to set limits and provide you with lots of opportunities to practice this important skill over the next several weeks.)*

Goals of Filial Play Sessions

1. To allow the child—through the medium of play—to communicate thoughts, needs, and feelings to his parent; and then, for the parent to communicate that understanding back to the child.

2. For the child to experience more positive feelings of self-respect, self-worth, confidence, and competence through feeling accepted, understood, and valued, and ultimately develop self-control, responsibility for actions, and learn to get needs met in appropriate ways.
3. To strengthen the parent–child relationship and foster a sense of trust, security, and closeness for both parent and child.
4. To increase the level of playfulness and enjoyment between parent and child.

Selection of Toys for Filial Play Kit

Next, the therapist introduces the importance of setting the stage for a successful play session by careful planning and preparation, which begins by collecting the required toys. The therapist provides parents with the *Toy Checklist for Filial Play Sessions* and gives a brief discussion of the overall rationale and importance for inclusion of specific toys and materials within three broad categories: (a) real-life/nurturing toys include: small baby doll, nursing bottle, doctor kit (with stethoscope and three Band-Aids), two toy phones, doll family, domestic animal family, wild animals, play money, car/truck, and plastic kitchen dishes; optional toys in this category include: puppets, doll furniture, and small dress-up items; (b) acting-out/aggressive release toys include: a dart gun, rubber knife, piece of rope, aggressive animal or two, small toy soldiers (12–15 of two different colors—to specify two teams, good guys and bad guys, etc.), inflatable bop bag, and a mask (Lone Ranger type); optional toys in this category include: toy handcuffs with a key; (c) creative/expressive toys include: Play-Doh, crayons, plain paper, child's scissors, transparent tape, egg carton, ring toss game, deck of playing cards, soft foam ball, and two balloons; optional toys in this category include: a selection of arts and crafts materials in a ziplock bag, Tinkertoys or small assortment of building blocks, binoculars, tambourine (drum or other small musical instrument), and a magic wand. *The Toy Checklist for Filial Play Sessions* in the CPRT Treatment Manual provides more detailed description of toys.

Explain briefly that the toys included in the filial play kit were carefully selected because they provide opportunities for a wide range of expression, mastery, imagination, fantasy play, creativity, and activity. Caution against including mechanical toys that limit children's creativity. Remind parents that the toys collected for the filial play kit should be selected with safety in mind to keep limit setting to a minimum. Emphasize that toys need not be new; in fact, old is better! Lastly, inform parents that the filial play kit toys are to be used only during play sessions to convey the specialness of this time. Landreth (2002) provides additional information on rationale for toy selection criteria, but avoids lengthy explanations. Additional rationales can be provided as toys are demonstrated.

Parents need to see the actual toys they are being asked to collect. Be sure the demonstration kit reflects the instructions given to parents by including old toys, broken crayons, and inexpensive toys found in dollar stores. If the training sessions are being held in a play therapy room in a clinic, the therapist can point out the difference in quality of toys for the playroom (which are purchased for durability) and the quality of toys for the filial play kit. Under no circumstances should you use the playroom toys to show parents what toys they need to collect—parents tend to be literal and will think they must find the same quality toys. Playroom toys are generally far too expensive and many would be hard to find. Parents find it helpful for the therapist to briefly show each toy and explain the rationale for including specific toys, particularly the nursing bottle and the dart gun. These are the toys parents generally express the most concerns about including in the play sessions. As each toy is shown, this is a good time to briefly demonstrate how to respond to a child's verbalization or play activity involving the toy.

We find it helpful to be very specific in all matters related to toys by demonstrating such things as how to store the toys, how to arrange the toys, etc. A small, sturdy cardboard box with a lid, such as the type that reams of copy paper are delivered in, is free and can double as a dollhouse and container for toys. The deep box lid can be used as the dollhouse by drawing lines on the inside to designate rooms and drawing or cutting out windows and doors on the sides *(again, it is helpful to show parents exactly what you are describing)*. Toys need to be kept in a container that can be easily stored out of sight to avoid the child's wanting to play with the toys at other times during the week. The therapist can suggest a location such as the parent's closet or the trunk of a car to avoid conflicts over use of toys outside of play sessions. Either in this session or the next it is helpful for parents to see the filial play kit arranged for a play session. A photo example of a filial play kit arrangement is included on the CD-ROM that accompanies the *CPRT Treatment Manual* for ease of copying for parents. Parents are instructed to find an old quilt or blanket to arrange the toys on, to serve as a boundary for the play area, and to protect the carpet. The therapist can also suggest that parents provide a cookie sheet or similar flat, easy-to-clean surface for children to use for Play-Doh (to contain the mess) and to be used as a hard surface for drawing on.

The therapist will need to provide suggestions on places to obtain toys, emphasizing that they do not need to be new. Focus on sources where toys can be obtained at little or no cost to the parent, such as from attic storage, neighbors, relatives, garage sales, dollar stores, and toy aisles at grocery stores and drugstores. The filial toy checklist also includes inexpensive ideas for making toys or using common household items to substitute. Some toys on the list can be obtained from toys the child already has; however, parents are to make sure the child understands that **toys and materials put in the special playtime box can only be played with during the special playtime**. For an older child, parents can add more craft items. Adaptations for younger children are primarily related to safety and messiness due to lack of experience or coordination with art materials.

Unless emphasized, most parents will not understand the rationale for the toys being used only during play sessions and may be tempted to haphazardly pull some toys from the child's room for weekly play sessions. Remind parents that the requirement for a special kit of toys is very important to maintaining the specialness of the parent–child play sessions and for providing children with a variety of toys specially selected to facilitate their children's expression. Because **children use play to express their thoughts, feelings, and needs to parents**, the selection of toys is important. **Toys are the child's words!** This is also a good time to discuss children's need for opportunities to learn to delay gratification. The therapist can use this opportunity to briefly role-play what limit setting would look like in the case of the child wanting to play with toys outside of a play session: "I know that you really want to play with the special toys now, but these toys are for our special playtime; you will get to play with them tomorrow right after school." The therapists ends the discussion of toy selection by asking parents to commit to gathering the majority of all of the toys listed by the next week's class.

Choosing a Place and Time for Filial Play Sessions

The therapist then introduces the second critical element in setting the stage for a successful play session: planning ahead for where and when parents will have their play sessions. Suggestions are made for suitable locations to hold play sessions—locations that insure privacy, freedom from distractions, and minimal worry about mess and breakage of treasured or expensive items. The location chosen is also dependent on whether other family members are home at the time the play session will be held. Ideally, play sessions can be held when no one else is at home, particularly siblings. In this case, the kitchen area is ideal, because it meets the criteria stated above and has the added bonus of having easy access to water for cleanup. If play sessions must be held when other children are in the home, the location must be in a room with a door that can be closed during the sessions. Locations to avoid are the child's room, because of the distractions of other toys, and the living room, where there are too many concerns about mess and breakage of family possessions.

The therapist emphasizes **the importance of consistency in holding play sessions on the same day and at the same time each week**, a time that the child looks forward to and can count on. This time should be a time the parent can commit to without fail and ideally will be a time free of interruptions from other family members. Consistency builds a sense of predictability and routine for the child; these are necessary conditions for children to feel secure. Play sessions should not be scheduled during the first 30 minutes after the child arrives home from school. Children, like adults, need time to unwind. Most importantly, the therapist asks parents to choose a time when they are generally feeling the most rested and patient and the least stressed and rushed, a time when they can be most emotionally available and free to focus fully on their children, without distractions. Introduce the **Rule of Thumb: You can't give away that which you don't possess**. *As your child's most significant caregiver, you are asked to give so much of yourself, often when you simply* *don't have the resources within you to meet the demands of parenting. As parents, you may be deeply aware of your own failures, yet you can't extend patience and acceptance to your child while being impatient and unaccepting of yourself.*

Introduce this analogy by asking parents what the flight attendant says when demonstrating the use of oxygen masks in the case of emergency (having one as a prop adds interest). Most parents answer that the flight attendant informs passengers to first put the mask on themselves and then put the mask on the child. Use this analogy to reinforce the concept that parents cannot help their children unless they first take care of themselves. With this in mind, the therapist asks each parent to give *careful* thought to deciding on a time and place to hold his play session and to report back the following week on what he has decided.

Role-Play and Demonstration of Basic Filial Play Session Skills

The therapist needs to make sure to allow time in the training session for demonstration and role-play of the skills covered in *Basic Principles of Filial Play Sessions*, most importantly, the structuring skill of "allowing the child to lead" without giving suggestions or asking questions. This is a difficult role for parents to assume, because their experience as a parent is that it is their job to be in charge, have all the answers, make the decisions, and tell the child what to do. Asking the parent to follow the child's lead requires a huge role shift for parents; therefore, much practice and patience is needed. Remember that parents must first stifle their natural urge to direct and initiate before they can begin to apply these new skills successfully. Remind parents that the attitude of fully being with their children goes along with the attitude of allowing children the freedom to lead the play. Both are necessary elements for setting the stage for successful filial play sessions. Review the "Be-With" Attitudes: I'm here, I hear you, I understand, and I care.

The therapists helps parents generate possible responses to anticipated scenarios involving their children asking them for help, or wanting parents to solve a problem for them, or even the inevitable "Why is...?" These kinds of situations are pitfalls for parents to slip back into the comfortable role of problem-solver (refer to chapter 4 for strategies and examples of how to teach parents to follow their children's leads and various responses to challenging situations). The therapist can either conduct a live demonstration with one of the parents' children (if on-site child care is provided) or show a demonstration video clip focusing on these skills. If time permits, it is helpful for the therapist to briefly role-play with a parent, with the parent assuming the role of the child. Parents are then paired up for role-play, taking turns being the parent and the child, practicing play session skills learned thus far. **(Role-playing should occur in each training session.)**

Homework Assignments

1. Ask parents to collect toys and materials on filial play kit checklist—brainstorm ideas and sources and suggest parents share resources.
2. Ask parents to select a consistent time and an uninterrupted place in the home suitable for the play sessions and to report back the following week.
3. Remind parents to complete a worksheet on reflective responding (parents are given several scenarios of what children have said or done in play sessions; they are to write their responses, practicing their reflection skills).

   Note: the *CPRT Treatment Manual* contains sample worksheets.

4. Remind parents of the Rule of Thumb for this week.

5. Close with motivational book, story or poem, such as *I'll Always Love You* by Robert Munsch. This children's book provides a lighthearted, yet touching, example about the importance of the parent–child relationship. Parents need to leave this session motivated to begin preparing for their home play sessions. **In order for parents to be successful in holding their first home play session after training Session 3, it is critical that parents leave Session 2 prepared and motivated to gather the required toys and begin to plan for when and where they will hold their play sessions, including making plans for other family members that will insure privacy and a minimum of distraction.**

Partial Transcript of CPRT Session 2

Dr. L.: Well, how has the week been?

Debbie: Pretty good.

Dr. L.: What made it a pretty good week?

Debbie: When I got home Monday, Rachel came in from day care, and I just did 30-second bursts of attention when she'd want my attention. I didn't go follow her around when she wanted my attention. In the past, she has acted like a little witch in public, and this time she acted like a little lady. We went to the awards banquet, and she sat and ate her cookies. She sat in her chair through the awards ceremony, and she was just an angel. It was unbelievable.

Dr. L.: Really different.

Debbie: It was really different.

Dr. L.: It sounds like she was controlling herself. She sat in the chair.

Debbie: Uh-huh, she did, and she had her little dress on, and usually that's just another explosion point.

Dr. L.: Disaster time.

Debbie: Yeah, yeah—embarrassing. And when she said "Mommy, this," "Mommy, that," I just gave her the 30 seconds of attention, and she would go on. That was the interesting thing; she didn't want anything more than just that little speck of attention. She just wanted to say something, and we enjoyed the awards banquet.

Dr. L.: Sounds like a really delightful time for you, and, I gather, for a change.

Debbie: Yes, for a big change.

(Nita enters late. She is 8 months pregnant and is carrying two pillows.)

Dr. L.: Come in, come in.

Nita: I'm gonna have to just get comfortable because I've been hemorrhaging again.

Dr. L.: Oh, bless your heart.

Nita: So, I just brought my pillows, and I'll just kind of recline. (She sits on the floor and leans back against a table.)

Dr. L.: That's fine. You just make yourself comfortable. I'm glad you're here.

Nita: Well, I wasn't gonna come, but I thought, oh, I hate not to come because we've had a really rough week, and I thought you all wouldn't mind because I'm sure you've been in similar circumstances.

Emily: With the exception of Dr. Landreth, maybe.

Dr. L.: No, I can't say I've been there. (Group laughs.) Are you okay?

Nita: I'm okay, yes. It's gonna be rough getting to 36 or 40 weeks, so I almost feel like I need this more than ever. Because Jeff's starting to—

Dr. L.: He's starting to react?

Nita: To feel the tension. Never knowing if I'm gonna have to go to the hospital and not knowing whether or not there will be a nursery or a bathroom; we have our whole house torn up right now, because we assume that I will go the 40 weeks.

Dr. L.: So everything's disrupted right now.

Debbie: How many weeks are you?

Nita: I'm 32, so I have a good chance of the baby surviving, like 90% chance, if he were to come now.

Kim: I had one at 32 weeks, and he's fine.

Nita: How long did he stay in the hospital?

Kim: Twelve to thirteen days, and he went back after three months, but he's fine. He's huge.

Nita: Good, that makes me feel better. When they said he'd be about 5 pounds, I thought, "Oh!"

Emily: Still, 5 pounds is a good size for a preemie. It really is. A lot of full-term babies barely weigh 5 pounds.

Nita: It seems tiny.

Dr. L.: I hear what you're saying, though, it's a scary time.

Nita: Yes, not knowing is, I think, almost worse for us than if we knew exactly what we were having to deal with; it's just not knowing.

Dr. L.: Um-hmm, I guess that's true in a lot of our experiences, isn't it? If we could just know what's around the corner.

Nita: Right.

Dr. L.: In this case, what's around the corner in the pregnancy, but also what's around the corner with what's your child going to do next, or, will it get any better after this? Well, let's check on what it was like for you to identify emotions this week. Did everybody bring their sheet with you? Okay, what I'd like to do is go around and each one of you share with us what happened, and what you said in reflecting the feeling to your child in the first episode, the happy situation. Sonya, you want to start? We'll just go around.

Sonya: My daughter is Jenny. She's 2 ½, and for Valentine's Day I got her this big huge balloon. It's almost as big as she is, and it was a surprise when she got home from preschool. She looked real surprised and then, when she said, "Is that for me?" I said, "Oh, I see a happy face," and she said, "I am! I am!" and she was hopping up and down.

Dr. L.: So, she knew that you understood she was happy.

Sonya: Um-hmm.

Dr. L.: And I gather, from what you said there, that seemed to increase her happiness.

Sonya: Yeah.

Dr. L.: Generally, when you're happy and someone understands that you're happy and verbally reflects your happiness to you and shares it with you, what happens to your happiness?

Sonya: It feels better.

Dr. L.: Yes, it increases. What happens when you share your sadness with someone, or if you've been hurt and you share your hurt with someone, and they understand?

Laura: For me, I am able to get rid of more of it.

Dr. L.: It decreases—that's very interesting the way we're made. You share your hurt and it decreases. It's less hurtful because somebody understands. You share your happiness and it increases your happiness because somebody understands. Debbie, did you get a chance to reflect happiness?

Debbie: I didn't write it down, but I told Rachel we would take her to McDonald's when we picked her up from school, and she was real happy, so I said, "I see you're happy," and she said, "Oh, yes, I'm happy."

Dr. L.: So she knew you understood.

Emily: I picked Chris up one day right before lunch, and we spent the afternoon going out to eat, shopping, and got him new shoes. At various times, he was just real happy, and he looked at me one time and said, "I like it when it's just us, Mom." And, I said, "Well, it seems to make you very happy, Chris, whenever you get so much attention from me." And he just smiled. He didn't say thank you, he just smiled.

Dr. L.: That's another good point you've mentioned there, that I haven't mentioned to you all. We should not always expect something back. It may be enough that your child smiles, or that they seem to take it in. They won't always give you a response back, but I heard you say, "I knew he had heard me, and he knew that I understood," even though he didn't say, "Yeah, you're right."

Kim: My experience is the same. I usually don't stop and just talk to him. I could tell he was thinking, "Why are you talking to me?" I noticed he was happy, he smiled bigger. He was happier.

Dr. L.: What did you say to him when he was happy?

Kim: Well, we were taking cupcakes to school. We made cupcakes for Valentine's, and he was just bouncing. I told him, "You look happy there. Are you excited about that?" And he just got more happy.

Dr. L.: I heard each one of you begin with "You." "You look happy," which helps your child identify "this is for me."

Sonya: Jenny has just recently potty-trained herself, and I would tell her, "I am so proud of you," and so now, when I go to the potty, she tells me, she says, "I am so proud of you, Mommy. Thank you."

Dr. L.: What we want to do is give our children credit. They need to feel good about what they've done because of the effort they've put into it, not because of whether or not it makes us proud.

Kathy: We went skating, and Cody learned how to do an airplane with one foot. I was real proud of him for learning a new trick, and I told him, "I'm really proud of you."

Dr. L.: I'm not a skater, but having tried it once or twice, I can tell you that took great effort. He had to work hard to do that.

Kathy: Oh, he did.

Dr. L.: So, instead of saying, "I'm proud of you," you could say, "You really worked hard to do that just right."

Debbie: So that's like what you told us last week about telling our children what we see them doing. "Oh, I see you're coloring that picture," and "I see you're doing this," sort of adds to what they're doing. Is that like giving them credit?

Dr. L.: Yes, you noticed your child. Since we've touched on that, let's go back to that first assignment. Your first assignment was to notice something new about your child. This all fits together. Your words say, "This is what I notice with my eyes, what I see," or "This is what I hear with my ears." You notice things about your child with your eyes. What did you notice about your child? Kim, did you notice anything new or different about your child?

Kim: Yes, I noticed that Toby pulls his ears forward when he's playing, if he's thinking about his cars or whatever. So, I took him to get his ears checked Friday morning, and the doctor said they're clear; so, it's just a character trait. He pulls his ears forward and she said, well, a lot of little boys do that, pull their ears forward. I never noticed that before.

Dr. L.: I hear a very sensitive mom in what you described. You noticed something you needed to check out. Sonya, what did you notice?

Sonya: While I was trimming Jenny's toenails, I noticed how really pretty her feet are. Her younger sister has Fred Flintstone feet. They're square, but Jenny's are really pretty. I had never really noticed her feet.

Dr. L.: But, this time, you did. You took them in. You appreciated her feet.

Sonya: Yeah, they were pretty.

Dr. L.: And, the important thing is that we see what we're looking at. Lots of times we look, but we don't see. We just know our children are there. I hear you saying, "I really saw her feet."

(All parent reports of what they noticed about their child are not transcribed here.)

Dr. L.: Well, I hear some moms who have really studied their children. The important thing is that you study your child, because in the special 30-minute playtimes once a week, beginning in one more week, I'll ask you to study your child with your eyes and notice everything about your child and everything they do for 30 minutes. Well, let's go back to the sheet, and do the second one. How about sadness? Did anybody see that this week?

Emily: Oh, yes.

Dr. L.: Emily, what did you see?

Emily: It's real important for me to prepare Chris for events that are going to happen, and I was trying to prepare him for the event that he's no longer going to have a caseworker. That lady will leave. It will be another loss and separation for him to experience, and when I told him that Cindy would no longer be his caseworker, he just immediately began to cry, and I said, "Chris, that makes you very, very sad," and he just cried, and he shook his head, yes, and I said, "Well, Cindy won't be your caseworker, but she will always be your friend. And, when you get lonely for Cindy, if you tell me, we'll call her, and see if we can do lunch together."

Dr. L.: I was listening to you and thinking, my, you really handled that well, because you touched on so many dimensions that he needed to know about. You recognized his feeling. You gave him the facts, and you also reassured him that she won't be gone forever. There can be contact later.

Sonya: I noticed from the film we watched of the kids, a lot of times when I think my kids are sad, they're angry. That squared-off mouth look. We were getting ready for preschool, and she didn't want to go. She had started crying, and I said, "Oh, Jenny, you look so sad," and she said, "I'm not sad, I'm angry." I thought, oh, she's sad because we're going, and she was very clear that she was not sad, she was angry. I have been noticing since then with my little one, I think she's sad and I try to comfort her, and she's mad as hell. She pushes away from me, like, "Let me be angry," and when she really is sad, she'll allow me to comfort her.

Debbie: Well, our big dilemma is really bedtime. We're talking 2 and 3 hours of this debating and talking. You can talk about this until the cows come home, about her feelings and how she feels about going to bed, but the fact is, Rachel still has to go to bed.

Dr. L.: Exactly.

Debbie: But, that didn't change this week. That is one of the hard-core problems. Saying "I know you're not happy about going to bed" didn't change anything.

Dr. L.: And it's not expected to in one or two times. These responses work even when they seem not to be working. Let me explain. Have you ever cut your finger? You put medicine on it, a bandage, and 30 minutes later you take the bandage off. The cut is still almost exactly like it was; so you wipe the medicine off, throw the bandage away. You ever do that?

Emily and
Sonya: No.

Dr. L.: You leave the medicine on. Why?

Sonya: Because it will slowly heal the cut.

Dr. L.: You assume it will eventually begin to be helpful. Have you ever gone to the doctor because you have a really sore throat or head stuff and he says, "Take this twice a day for 7 days." You take it for 1 day, you wake up the next morning and your throat's still sore, so you throw the pills away. No, you don't do that. Why?

Kim: You know you have to give it time.

Dr. L.: You assume that it's going to work, and it is working. You just don't see an immediate result. And with these responses, you won't always see immediate results. Some of you will see quick results, like with your daughter, Sonya. She even corrected you because you were trying to understand. It doesn't change the circumstances that it is bedtime, but, over time, Rachel will come to realize you understand, and she won't have to push so hard to get her message over to you, Debbie. We will work on the bedtime routine later. I'm going to make a note, and we will come back to that.

Sonya: Good, because I have problems with that, too.

Kathy: Good, good.

(All parent reports of their responses to emotions are not transcribed here.)

Dr. L.: Let's move on to something else. One of the things that we need to work on today is getting ready for your play sessions, which will happen not this coming week, but the next week. So I have several assignments for you. The first assignment is to put together a play kit similar to what I have here. This is a list of toys for the play sessions. (Hands out *Toy Checklist for Filial Play Sessions.*) I want you to go home and tell your child, "I'm taking a special class to learn how to play with you, and I go to class every Monday afternoon. My teacher is teaching us how to play with our children, and he gave us this special list of toys for our special playtime. We're going to have a special play-time once a week."

Then, you get a box, it can be about this size (points to box), and ask your child to help you collect these toys. Some of them, your child already has in his or her room. If you select toys your child has, you will need to explain the toys will be placed in a special box and can only be played with during the special playtime. Other toys, you can borrow from a neighbor or a friend whose children have outgrown them. A few of these, you may need to buy, and I suggest you take your child shopping with you. Get the list and say, "We're going to Wal-Mart or Kmart and we're going to go buy some of these items on this list for our special playtime." It will be like Christmastime for your child. You might find some of these toys in a garage sale. Let's go over the items. I want you to get Play-Doh, and, you'll probably find it in little containers of four, but you only need to put one of these out at a time. Put the other three somewhere else. Your child doesn't need to play with all four of them at the same time.

Sonya: You can't make your own?

Dr. L.: Oh, yes, that would be great. Make your own. How do you feel about your child playing with Play-Doh in your house? Does that bother any of you?

(Brief reactions)

Dr. L.: If the place you choose in your home for the special playtime is carpeted, you'll need a towel, or a cookie sheet, and when your child pulls the Play-Doh out, you say, "The Play-Doh is for playing on top of the towel." You just set a limit. Your child can't take this can of Play-Doh and run into the front room and play on your carpet in there. It can only be played with in the place you designate. Put some crayons together, and your child probably already has some.

Debbie: Like, how many?

Dr. L.: Just a few, 6 or 8, that's all you need. Sixty-eight crayons are too many choices. If your child has a bunch of crayons, choose some colors and break the crayons in two pieces, peel the paper off so the sides show, and break the points off the crayons. This will give your child a message that says, "You don't have to be careful." Points say, "Be very careful, be neat," and in this special time, your child can color with the side of the crayon. He can be messy. He doesn't have to color between the lines. You need some paper, and it can be like paper in your notebook there, or the backs of computer sheets, or some newsprint. Find a pair of blunt scissors. I want you to get a nursing bottle. If you have some tucked away somewhere, just pull one out of the closet. Laura, you're reacting.

Laura: Yeah, because Dawson was never a bottle baby, but last fall, I guess just because of different stressors, he wanted to suck on a bottle.

Dr. L.: And that will be okay for your child to do for this special 30 minutes.

Debbie: Really? Are you serious?

Laura: Yeah, he's serious.

Dr. L.: Some children, even 8 or 10 years of age, wonder what that used to feel like, and so they'll suck on the bottle. It is a quick way for them to find out how patient you will be with sucking on the bottle and how accepting you are during these 30 minutes. So, I really do want you to get a nursing bottle with a regular nipple on it. Your child may look at the nursing bottle and say, "There's nothing in there." What's your child really saying? "I want..."

Emily: A drink?

Dr. L.: Yes, "I want something in here to suck on," and you could say, "Well, we can go to the kitchen and get juice or water. Which would you like to have?"

Dr. L.: If your child wants to suck on the bottle for the whole 30 minutes, he can. This is the child's time to choose. But, no other time.

Kim: That's what I was gonna ask.

Dr. L.: Whatever goes in this box stays in the box, and after the session, the box is put in the closet, or if you really have trouble, and you can't keep your child from getting into the box, lock the box in the trunk of your car. They can play with these toys only during the special 30-minute playtime. The reason for this rule is that it makes the playtime really special. The second reason is, and this may be more important, you're going to help your child learn how to delay their need for gratification. They want to play with it now, but your playtime is on Wednesday afternoon and it's Monday afternoon, and so they have to wait until when? Wednesday afternoon. When will the ability to control their need for gratification be the most important in their life? When they get to what age?

Debbie: Isn't it 3?

Dr. L.: Teenagers.

Sonya: Jenny still takes a bottle when we're reading a story. We worked on her giving the bottle up about 6 months ago, and it was 2 weeks of hell. I decided I didn't have the energy, and I know I'm not going to wean her at this point. My question is, should I have a special bottle?

Dr. L.: Yes, a special bottle for the playtime.

Sonya: Okay, I'll do that.

Dr. L.: I also want you to get a dart gun, something like this. It doesn't have to look exactly like this one, but these are probably easiest to find.

Emily: They've got those at the dollar store for a dollar.

Dr. L.: You all have small children, so your child may have trouble pulling this plunger on the gun back, that is hard to pull back, and it would be okay for you to help your child. In fact, you may even have to show your child how to pull that back. Kim, how do you feel about having a dart gun?

Kim: I just know Toby's gonna go for my 2-month-old with that.

Dr. L.: It can only be used in this 30-minute playtime, and the other children won't be around. Just you and your child, so you won't have to worry about another child getting shot with it.

Nita: Could it be one of those that shoots the little Ping-Pong balls, or do they need to be darts?

Dr. L.: It could be the Ping-Pong ball gun, except that the Ping-Pong ball is more likely to knock something over because it's bigger. This dart is so soft and rubbery that, if it hits anything, it won't hurt. There's not enough force to knock anything over. So this gun may be better. With this toy gun, you get a chance to teach your child that people are not for shooting. Your child may start to shoot you with it, and you get a chance to say, "I'm not for shooting," and then your child learns something really important.

This toy gun also gives you the opportunity to work on setting limits: "I'm not for shooting. The lamp is not for shooting." If you will practice that response ahead of time, you will be ready. "I'm not for shooting. You can pretend the Bobo is me and shoot the Bobo, or the plastic thing is for shooting," and you point to that. And they can shoot that.

Emily: Can you set the limit that, "I'm not for shooting," and if the child persists, say, "If you insist on shooting me, then

I will have to remove the gun from the playroom." Can you set that kind of limit?

Dr. L.: Sounds great. We'll work more on limit setting later. You will need some toy soldiers, about 20 will be enough. Even 10 is enough. Fifty toy soldiers is too many, and the reason is, that's too many for you to pick up.

Laura: For us to pick up?

Dr. L.: I see you got the message, Laura. At the end of the session, you will pick up, because this is a special time, and your child uses the toys to express himself. The toys are like your child's words. Children use toys like words, and their play is like their language. And so, during this special 30-minute playtime, they play out messages or express themselves through play. If you say, "Now you have to clean up," then next time your child will play carefully so he doesn't have to clean up as much.

Your child may want to help you clean up, and that will be okay. If they don't want to help you clean up, that's okay, too. Helping clean up does not mean more playtime. A small cardboard box like this will serve as a place to store all the toys. Cut a door in one side and a window in another side. I haven't done that to this box, but just cut a door in one side and a window in another side. Draw some marks across the bottom like this and that becomes your dollhouse.

(All the other toys were shown and discussed but are not transcribed here.)

Dr. L.: Those are the toys for your special playtime. Now, let's talk about two other things. One, when you come next Monday, I want you to tell me the place in your house where you're going to have your special 30-minute playtime. It should be a place that's private, that will not be interrupted by other people in the house. If there are other people at home when you have your session, it will need to be a place where you can close the door. If everybody else is gone, it could be your kitchen. I do not recommend your living room. Use the kitchen or a den. Do not select your child's room, because all their other possessions are in there, and they will play with all that other stuff. The third assignment is to pick a time and a day for your special playtime and tell me next Monday.

Debbie: Can we ask you this? We both have the same problem, we have tiny little babies, and their schedules are very demanding.

Dr. L.: Try to pick a time when they usually are taking their nap.

Debbie: So it's going to be the very same time every week?

Dr. L.: Yes. If at all possible. This builds in consistency. "Every Tuesday at 4:00, I get to have my special playtime." And your child will look forward to that time. A wonderful time that happens without fail—nothing interferes with this special playtime. It happens every week. That helps your child feel secure. Routines help children feel secure. We want to build in predictability for your child. Okay, you have a lot to do this week. Any questions about that?

Emily: We have to get all this—the toys and everything—this week?

Dr. L.: I'd like for you to have it ready by next Monday, when you come.

Kathy: I can do that.

Sonya: That will be kind of fun, buying all that stuff.

Dr. L.: I hope you'll be able to get most of the toys without buying new stuff. Used toys are better. So, if you can get toys in garage sales or borrow some from the neighbors, or pull some out of your attic that you've stored away, great—use that. Now, can we shift focus?

Sonya: Sure.

Dr. L.: All right, I want to show you a videotape of one of my play sessions. You will see me doing what I would like for you all to do. Let's watch the video, and then we'll talk about it. The child is 4 years old, and this is our first time together.

(Dr. L. plays a segment of a video that clearly illustrates the concept of allowing the child to lead, while he follows the child's lead.)

Dr. L.: (Stops video.) Now, let's talk about what you saw me do.

Debbie: You gave him space when he came in the room. You weren't crowding him, which gave him his freedom, or space.

Dr. L.: Yes, I let the child move away and settle in, and then I went over to be close to him. What else did you see me do?

Kim: You let him pick what he wanted to do.

Dr. L.: I let him choose. He's in the lead. This is his time to play with any of the toys that he chooses to play with.

Sonya: You got down to his level.

Dr. L.: Yes, I got down to his level. Don't stand. You will say to your child, "It's time for our special playtime," walk your child back to your bedroom, close the door, and say, "This is our special playtime, and this is a time when you can play with these toys in a lot of the ways you would like to." Sit down, sit on the floor. If you'd rather sit in a chair, sit in a chair. But then when your child settles in, show interest in what they're doing by moving to be close to your child. Lie on the floor and prop your chin on your hand, and fiddle with the things that your child is fiddling with, but don't take over. Your child is to be in the lead. Now, I'd like for you to listen to who leads the conversation.

(Dr. L. plays more of the video.)

Dr. L.: (Stops video.) For 30 minutes, you are not your child's answer source.

Nita: Oh, my child will just start saying "Why?" to everything.

Dr. L.: For 30 minutes, you are dumb.

Kathy: Just for 30 minutes? (Group laughs.)

Sonya: You use a lot of paraphrasing. When he asked you a question, you just said, "Gee, I don't know why." I've used that a lot with Jenny, and I'm real surprised at her answers and the joy of the answers.

Dr. L.: They'll figure it out. He's asking, "Why don't these rocks go through here?" I'm not sure I have a good answer for that.

Debbie: You wondered it yourself. You said, "Hmm, wonder why those rocks won't go through that."

Dr. L.: You caught it.

Emily: That was interesting.

Dr. L.: When your child wonders about something, you just wonder about it, too. You're studying your child so intently, and you're so caught up in what your child is doing, it's almost as if you are doing it, too. And when your child is puzzling about something, you're puzzling about that, too. He says, "Wonder why these rocks won't go through there." "Hmm, wonder why those won't go through there." As if, I'm trying to figure that out, too, and I am.

Sonya: Well, how about throwing the ball back in their court and say, "Do you know why?" or, "What do you think?"

Dr. L.: Questions will usually result in your child saying, "I don't know, why?" So, just make a statement or, often, if you'll delay your response a little bit, your child will go ahead and answer you.

Debbie: Don't use the words "I don't know."

Dr. L.: Sometimes, I think that would be okay. Your child may ask, "Why is the sky blue?" "I don't know."

Debbie: Tell me.

Dr. L.: "Oh, you think I do know, but for 30 minutes in this special playtime, you can figure it out."

(Plays more of video.)

Dr. L.: (Stops video.) Who is leading this conversation?

(Everyone): He is.

Dr. L.: For 30 minutes, your child is in the lead. For 30 minutes, you follow.

Nita: When you describe what he's doing, is that to serve some purpose?

Dr. L.: Yes. Laura, you're reacting. Go ahead.

Laura: Well, when you acknowledge what he is doing, you're being a part of what he's doing.

Dr. L.: Yes, the message is to say, "I'm here. I understand what you're doing." Describing what your child does validates your child and the importance of what your child is doing.

Sonya: Isn't part of it, also, to say that "You're important to me." The things in my life that get my attention are obviously something I value that is important to me. And I would start showing my child that I value her and she's important to me.

Dr. L.: Sure, this is like the 30-second burst of attention. For that 30 seconds, you looked at your child and listened to your child. Now, I'm going to ask you to do that for 30 minutes. Describing or tracking what your child does says everything your child does is important to you, so that your child then feels important. You can't feel important, folks, until you're important to somebody. You must be important to somebody first. Nita?

Nita: I am a little confused. What if my son says, "You build such and such," or, "You draw a picture of baby."

Dr. L.: You stop, and you say, "Show me what you want done."

Nita: Mmm.

Dr. L.: Or, "Tell me what I am to do next." If you just start building, then you've taken over. The child may say, "You play with the toy soldiers." And I would say, "Show me what you want done with them." "Well, you take these, and

I'll take these, and you line them up." "Okay, show me where you want them lined up, and I'll line mine up." "Well, you line yours up right there. I'll line mine up right here." Now you know exactly what he wants done. So you start lining the soldiers up, and he starts lining his up. But you keep getting your direction from the child.

Debbie: Um-hmm. It's almost like role reversal, isn't it? From what we're accustomed to.

Dr. L.: Yes, we're usually in control, we're in charge, and we tell children what to do.

Nita: I'm so used to taking over his play.

Dr. L.: Usually, we tell our children what to do and how to do it, but for 30 minutes, they get to find out what it is like to lead. That's called self-responsibility. Do you see what you're teaching your child? Something important.

Laura: So we expect them to do it.

Dr. L.: Yes, you expect them to be able to take the lead and be responsible. And I believe they can figure it out, to be the way they want it to be.

(Plays more of video.)

Dr. L.: (Stops video.) Just tell your child what you see with your eyes. You are to communicate four messages: "I'm here." I'm fully here. I don't wish I were somewhere else. I'm here. "I hear you." I hear you with my ears, I hear you with my eyes. He's sitting there in the sandbox flipping sand, and I want to hear the flipping of the sand with my eyes. "I'm here. I hear you." Third message, "I understand." And we let our children know that we understand them by what we say. What your child hears back says, "I understand." And, then, the fourth message is "I care." If I communicate those first three messages, "I'm here, I hear you, I understand," then the fourth one comes along naturally. The child knows "I care."

(Plays more of video.)

Dr. L.: (Stops video.) Let's suppose that you're the parent, and I'm the child (picks up handcuffs), and I say, "What is this?" Now, we haven't worked on this, so let me give you a standard response. The standard response in these 30-minute play sessions is, "That can be whatever you want it to be." You are to free your child. If your child says, "What is this?," don't say back, "What do you think that is?" because your child will say, "I don't know. What do you think it is?" If your child says, "What is this?" and you say, "That can be whatever you want it to be," your child is free to say, "Oh, it's a space ship, and this is where you drop the bombs through." And you think, "Well, I would never have thought of that." You are to free your children's creativity. "That can be whatever you want it to be." "Can I play with this stuff?" (Dr. L. picks up a can of Play-Doh.)

Debbie: "On the towel."

Emily: "If that's what you choose, if that's what you choose to play with right now."

Dr. L.: Yes, "If you want to, that's for you to decide, on the towel." Your child will begin to realize for 30 minutes, I get to make decisions. "That's for you to decide." "I'm gonna take this guy and this guy falls right in the bucket." (Drops toy soldier into sand pail.)

Emily: "Did you hear how loud it hit the bucket?"

Dr. L.: Or, if it made no sound at all, you'd still say what?

Sonya: "I see you dropped that in the bucket."

Dr. L.: You just state what you see. That's called tracking. You could drop the words "I see."

Kathy: "He fell in the bucket."

Sonya: "He's in the bucket."

Dr. L.: Let's practice tracking and responding. Pair up with someone. One of you is the parent and the other is the child. What I'd like for you to do, children, is try to get your parent involved. Ask them some questions and give them a chance to practice giving the leadership back to you. And, other times, just play with the toys and let them practice reflecting what they see.

(Group role-plays.)

Dr. L.: Okay, folks, you can stop, and children, tell your parents something you heard from them that you thought, "That sounds like a neat response. That's what we've been talking about here." Don't just say, "That was great," or, "You did a good job." That's generic praise, and it doesn't help. State something you heard, be specific. "When you said_____, that felt good," or, "That's the kind of response we've been working on." OK, kids, give your parents some feedback.

(Discussion)

Dr. L.: All right, everybody stop, and children, you're now the parents. We're gonna reverse roles now, and parents, you're now the children.

(Role-playing)

Dr. L.: Okay, children, give your parents some feedback. Tell them something specific you heard that you thought, "That's a neat response."

(Discussion)

Dr. L.: Okay, folks, anyone have something happen in the role-playing you'd like to know how I might respond?

Sonya: "It's broken, you do it."

Dr. L.: "Oh, let's see, show me how you want it to work."

Sonya: "Well, make it shoot. It won't shoot."

Dr. L.: "Hmm, this is supposed to be pulled back right here."

Sonya: "You do it."

Dr. L.: "I'll help you do it."

Sonya: "I don't want to do it. You do it."

Dr. L.: "Oh, so, if I won't do it for you, you just don't want to do it. I'll help you do it."

Sonya: "Well, what do I do?"

Dr. L.: "See this, right here, if you put your fingers right there. That was hard. If you put your fingers right there, we can pull together. There, you got it." How was I able to end this? Did you hear what I said? I gave you credit in the end. "There, you got it." And that's the way we build our children's self-esteem. If I do it, then I get credit. If the child does it, or if I help the child, then the child gets credit. But, if I just take over and do it, then the child gets no credit.

You have a lot to do this week. Next week, I'll show you some more of this play session, and we'll talk about where you're going to have your session, when you're going to have it, and do you have the kit ready. I have a list of Dos and Don'ts for your special play time, and we'll go over that next week. Then, the next week, you'll have your first play session with your child.

Nita: It's just too hard.

Sonya: I know you can do it.

Dr. L.: It's different.

Nita: I'm just so used to directing his play, and he's just so used to, "Well, Mom, you show me."

Dr. L.: What you're saying is, it's hard to change, and that's okay. It's hard for all of us to change. Well, I'll see you next Monday.

References

Bratton, S., Landreth, G., Kellam, T., & Blackard, S. (2006). Child Parent Relationship Therapy (CPRT) Treatment Manual: A 10-Session Filial Therapy Model for Training Parents. NY: Routledge.

CHAPTER 9

CPRT TRAINING SESSION 3: PARENT–CHILD PLAY SESSION SKILLS AND PROCEDURES

Overview

The major focus for this session is preparing parents to be successful in their first 30-minute home play session, including specifics on what to tell their child and procedures for setting up and conducting play sessions. Basic "skill" guidelines for the play sessions, which includes eight "Dos" and "Don'ts" for parents to focus on during play sessions, are introduced and illustrated through demonstration and role-play. Play therapy skills of structuring/setting the stage, allowing the child to lead, and reflective responding are reviewed and practiced. Limit setting is briefly introduced and demonstrated. The partial transcript included at the end of this chapter illustrates many of the same therapist skills focused on in Session 2, including immediacy in presenting teaching points and the use of humor. Session 3 is unique in the amount of content that must be covered; therefore, of primary note is the therapist's careful balance between encouraging and supporting parents and covering the didactic content that is essential in order for parents to be prepared to conduct their first home play sessions.

Materials

Suggested materials include: *CPRT Session 3–Treatment Outline;* parent information form with pertinent notes on each parent; homework assigned in Session 2, including extra copies of any homework worksheets; and Session 3 handouts and homework including: *Session 3 Parent Notes & Homework, Play Sessions Dos and Don'ts (print on yellow), and Play Session Procedures Checklist (print on blue).*

> Note: because these two handouts are the most used and referred to, it is helpful to run them on colored paper for easy reference.

Additional materials include: *Special Playtime Appointment Cards,* demonstration video of play session skills (helpful, but optional), one fully equipped filial play kit (and additional toys as needed to facilitate role-play and demonstration of skills), and a photograph of filial play kit set up for a play session.

> Note: It is helpful for the therapist to make a demonstration video that specifically demonstrates basic CPRT (filial therapy) skills that parents need to learn in preparation for their first play session. We do not recommend using a play therapy demonstration tape, and it goes without saying that a play therapy client tape would never be used for demonstration purposes. Alternatively, for therapists without a training video, the last 5 minutes of the video *Child-Centered Play Therapy* by Dr. Garry Landreth *(see CPRT Treatment Manual for source)* can be utilized for this purpose or arrangements can be made ahead of time to demonstrate with a child of one of the parents.

> *Note: All handouts listed above, as well as a training session outline for the therapist, additional supplemental parent handouts, and resources for this training session are found in the* CPRT Treatment Manual *and accompanying CD-ROM, available from the publisher, Routledge.*

Content and Procedure

This session begins, as all sessions, with the therapist facilitating approximately 10 minutes of general discussion of how each parent's week has been, with a continued goal of building rapport with parents, providing support, and facilitating connections between parents. This informal group discussion time also allows a few minutes for latecomers to arrive before reviewing weekly homework assignments. This informal sharing time in the group provides an opportunity to check in with each parent's progress on collecting toys for their filial play kits and facilitate sharing of ideas for toys that parents had difficulty finding.

Continue to utilize the strategy of saying, "That's something we'll work on later. I'm going to make a note, so I won't forget," when parents get off topic and want the therapist to give them a quick solution to a problem. Avoid suggesting that parents try any of the play session skills in response to reported child behavior problems. **Remember that the problem is not the problem—keep the focus on the relationship!**

Review Homework and Skill Training from Session 2

The therapist begins the session with a discussion of homework assignments and review of CPRT skills, focusing on reflective responding. Most parents have difficulty making appropriate empathic, understanding, reflective responses; providing parents with examples that list multiple-choice responses is a strategy we have found helpful.

> Reminder: Asking parents to first identify the feeling, and then to make an empathic or reflective response using that feeling word, is a highly effective strategy. *Again, a primary aim in CPRT training is structuring activities that facilitate parents feeling encouraged and successful in their efforts.*

Next, parents are asked to report on arrangements for their special play sessions—when and where they will be held—and report on their progress in collecting the toys provided on the checklist. The success of the first home play session depends on the parents obtaining a majority of the toys on the checklist and carefully selecting a day, time, and place that is free of distractions for both the parent and child. In our experience, some parents will not have given serious thought to when and where they will hold their play sessions. We cannot overstate the importance of spending time ensuring that parents have carefully thought out a time and a place to hold their weekly play sessions! Parents are reminded of the importance of consistency in children's lives and asked to choose a day and time that they can commit to without fail, a time when they are rested and have the emotional energy to fully focus on their children—and a time when their children are rested and not missing out on activities that are especially important to them.

Generally, we recommend that special playtimes not be scheduled until at least 30 minutes after the child comes home from school, so that the child has time to unwind and have a snack. As parents share the locations they have chosen for their play sessions, listen carefully for potential problem areas, such as rooms where making a mess or breaking fragile items might be a concern for the parent or a place where interruptions by others in the household is likely. If necessary, review the guidelines for selecting a play session location covered in training Session 2. The therapist must anticipate any other potential problems that would interfere in the parents' successes and address these before reviewing basic procedures and practicing skills to be utilized in the play sessions.

Filial Play Sessions Dos and Don'ts

Parents are given the handout, *Filial Play Sessions Dos and Don'ts*, for conducting special play sessions. This handout includes the overall goal of the play session for parents, basic "Dos" and "Don'ts," and reminders about the four messages that parents should convey to their children during special play sessions. This handout is the most used of all training materials; therefore, we suggest reproducing it on bright yellow paper that parents can easily locate and refer to. As suggested in the Materials section, making a poster of the *Filial Play Sessions Dos and Don'ts* is a helpful visual aid in teaching these essential skills.

Goal of Filial Play Session for Parent

Parents' major tasks are to keenly observe their children's play and to communicate their understanding of their children's thoughts, feelings, and behavior, through their words, actions, and presence. The following "Dos" and "Don'ts" are considered essential to parents learning to successfully conduct home play sessions. Briefly cover each, but focus most on the following: do set the stage, do let the child lead, and do join in the child's play as a follower. It is imperative that the therapist briefly cover how to state a simple limit.

- **Dos:**
  - **Do set the stage.**
    - Prepare the play area ahead of time. (An old blanket can be used to establish a visual boundary of the play area, as well as to provide protection for flooring; a cookie sheet under the arts/crafts materials provides a hard surface for Play-Doh, drawing, and gluing, and provides ease of cleanup.)
    - Display the toys in a consistent manner around the perimeter of the play area.
    - Convey freedom of the special playtime through your words: *"During our special playtime, you can play with the toys in lots of the ways you'd like to."*
    - Allow your child to lead by *returning responsibility* to your child by responding, *"That's up to you, "You can decide," or "That can be whatever you want it to be."*
  - **Do let the child lead.**
    - Allowing the child to lead during the playtime helps you to better understand your child's world and what your child needs from you during this special playtime. Convey your willingness to follow your child's lead through your responses: *"Show me what you want me to do," "You want me to put that on,"* "Hmmm...," "I wonder...." Use whisper technique (coconspirators) when the child wants you to play a role: *"What should I say?" or "What happens next?"* (modify responses for older kids: use conspiratorial tone, "What happens now?," "What kind of teacher am I?," etc.)
  - **Do join in the child's play actively, as a follower.**
    - Convey your willingness to follow your child's lead through your responses and your actions by actively joining in the play (child is the director, parent is the actor): "So I'm supposed to be the teacher," "*You* want me to be

the robber and I'm supposed to wear the black mask," "Now I'm supposed to pretend I'm locked up in jail until you say I can get out," "*You* want me to stack these just as high as yours." Use whisper technique in role-play: "What should I say?," "What happens next?"

- **Do verbally track the child's play** (describe what you see).
  - Verbally tracking your child's play is a way of letting your child know that you are paying close attention and that you are interested and involved: *"You're filling that all the way to the top," "You've decided you want to paint next," "You've got 'em all lined up just how you want them."*
- **Do reflect the child's feelings.**
  - Verbally reflecting children's feelings helps them feel understood and communicates your acceptance of their feelings and needs: *"You're proud of your picture," "That kinda surprised you," "You really like how that feels on your hands," "You really wish that we could play longer," "You don't like the way that turned out," "You sound disappointed." Hint: Look closely at your child's face to better identify how your child is feeling.*
- **Do set firm and consistent limits.**
  - Consistent limits create a structure for a safe and predictable environment for children. Children should never be permitted to hurt themselves or you. Limit setting provides an opportunity for your child to develop self-control and self-responsibility. Using a calm, patient, yet firm voice: *"The floor's not for putting Play-Doh on. You can play with it on the tray." Or "I know you'd like to shoot the gun at me, but I'm not for shooting. You can choose to shoot at that" (point to something acceptable).*
- **Do salute the child's power and encourage effort.**
  - Verbally recognizing and encouraging your child's effort builds self-esteem and confidence and promotes self-motivation: "You worked hard on that," "You did it," "You figured it out," *"You've got a plan for how you're gonna set those up," "You know just how you want that to be," "Sounds like you know lots about how to take care of babies."*
- **Do be verbally active.**
  - Being verbally active communicates to your child that you are interested and involved in her play. If you are silent, your child will feel watched.

Note: Empathic grunts, "Hmm...," etc. also convey interest and involvement when you are unsure of how to respond.

- **Don'ts:**
  - Don't criticize any behavior.
  - Don't praise the child.
  - Don't ask leading questions.
  - Don't allow interruptions of the session.
  - Don't give information or teach.
  - Don't preach.
  - Don't initiate new activities.[1]
  - Don't be passive, quiet.

Remind parents that it is their attitude and intent in their responses that is most important. The therapist emphasizes that these play sessions (and the new skills they are learning to apply) are relatively meaningless if applied mechanically and not as an attempt to be genuinely empathic and to truly understand their child. Review the "Be-With" Attitudes by asking parents to list them:

- I am here.
- I hear/see you.
- I understand.
- I care.

Video/Demonstration of Filial Play Session Skills and Role-Play

After reviewing the basic guidelines for the play session, parents view a videotaped demonstration play session or a live play session conducted by the therapist in order to observe play session skills in action. If a video is used, stop the video frequently to point out the "Dos" by pointing to the poster and asking which "Do" have they seen you demonstrate. If a coleader is utilized and you have access to a two-way mirror, learning is enhanced by the coleader pointing out the "Dos" while parents observe a live demonstration play session. A child of one of the parents in the group can be used for the demonstration if on-site child care is provided during the

[1] "Don'ts" 1–7 are taken from Guerney, 1972.

CPRT training. In either case, parents are encouraged to verbally note when they hear the therapist using any of the "Dos" listed on the handout (or optional poster). Parents are encouraged to share their observations and ask questions and then to immediately put their knowledge into action by role-playing, taking turns being parent and child. In cases where space permits and the parents' children are in child care at the site of the CPRT training, parents can role-play with their children.

Filial Play Session Procedures Checklist

Parents are given the handout, *Filial Play Session Procedures Checklist*, with additional tips for ensuring a successful play session. This is a handout that parents will refer to often; therefore, we have found it helpful to reproduce it on colored paper. The following information is presented by the therapist (most of which is included in the parent handout, but with less detail):

- Plan ahead to avoid interruptions: encourage the child to use the bathroom prior to the play session, put pets outside or in another room, arrange for other children to spend special time with other parent or relative, **take the phone off the hook**, and **don't answer the door** during the special playtime. These actions convey the importance of the playtime to the child and communicate that the child is special.
- Tell the child 1 to 2 days ahead about the upcoming play session and explain that you will be having these "special" play sessions because "Mom (or Dad) is going to class to learn some special ways to play with you." Reinforce the "specialness" of this time together by assisting your child in making a **"Special Playtime—Do Not Disturb"** sign to be put on the front door during the playtimes. Marking the day and time on the family calendar and giving the child a *Special Playtime Appointment Card* are other activities that communicate the importance of this time with your child. Explain to parents about filling out the appointment card and giving it to the child the same day they make the "Do Not Disturb" sign with their child, suggesting the child tape the appointment card in a place the child will see it, such as the bathroom mirror or refrigerator door.

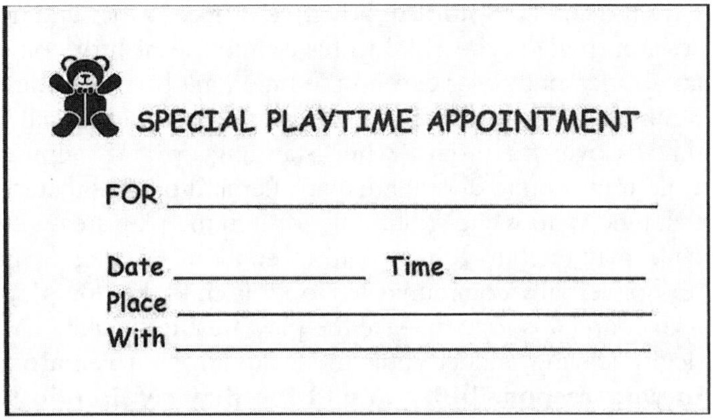

SPECIAL PLAYTIME APPOINTMENT

FOR ____________________

Date __________ Time __________
Place ____________________
With ____________________

Figure 9.1 Special playtime appointment card.

Note: Reproducible appointment cards are included on the CD that accompanies the CPRT Treatment Manual and depicted in Figure 9.1.

- Allow sufficient time to set up for your first play session so that you are not rushed and can begin on time. Follow the suggestions in "Do set the stage" and check video equipment to insure that the entire play area is in view and that the camera is operating. Parents are encouraged to videotape every week to become comfortable with the process.
- Begin the session by telling the child, "This is our special playtime for 30 minutes. You can play with the toys in a lot of the ways you would like to," and let the child lead from this point.

Reminder: **For 30 minutes, your child is your teacher and you are the student;** your child is the director, and you are the actor who hasn't seen the script and must look to the director for what your "role" is. For 30 minutes, pretend you don't know the answers to any questions. **For 30 minutes, you are dumb!**

- Set limits on behaviors that make you feel uncomfortable. If you don't set limits, your child will sense your discomfort and think you are upset with him.
- Avoid identifying toys by name because this can limit your child's expression and creativity—instead, refer to the toys as "it," "that," "them," "her," "him."

- Give the child a **5-minute advance notice** before ending the session to allow the child to have time to finish or complete an activity, but never exceed the time limit by more than 2 to 3 minutes. When time is up, verbally state, "Our special playtime is over for today," while standing up and helping the child transition to another activity. Remind parents that stating that time is up while continuing to sit in the play area with the child may encourage the child to continue playing. Standing up nonverbally communicates to your child that the playtime is over and it is time to leave the play area. If the child has difficulty leaving, reflect your understanding, but **remain firm in your responsibility to end the play session on time:** "Billy, I know that you wish you could play longer, but our special playtime is over for today." In some cases where the child has had previous experiences (pre-CPRT training) of the parent giving in with repeated pleas or whining, the child may be persistent in pleading to play longer. However, stand firm—and never give in! The child learns that the parent will follow through on stated limits, and that no amount of pleading and whining will work.

  Note: Parent is responsible for keeping track of time, so no timers allowed!

- Cleanup after the sessions is the task of the parent. Children may assist if they choose but may not continue to play after the time has ended. Generally, parents should have an activity or snack for the child to transition to immediately after the play session to provide an alternative to the child wanting to continue to play: "Billy, I know that you wish you could play longer, but our special playtime is over for today; we can play outside together after you have your snack." Or parents can provide a choice after stating that time is up: "You can choose to go outside and play with Sam or you can choose to have a snack. Which do you choose?"

Homework Assignments

- Play sessions begin at home this week—remind parents to arrange to videotape their sessions.
- Parents are reminded of the importance of conducting their first home play session at the same time and same place.

Confirm that the time and place they chose will work and that they have made arrangements for their other children, etc.

- Ask parents to take a few minutes to review *Filial Play Sessions Dos and Don'ts (yellow handout)* and *Filial Play Session Procedures Checklists (blue handout)* prior to their play sessions.
- Parents are reminded to complete their filial play kit—get old blanket/quilt, etc.
- Parents are reminded to make **"Special Playtime—Do Not Disturb"** signs with their children 1–3 days ahead (depending on children's ages) and give children the *Special Playtime Appointment Card* 1–3 days ahead.
- Remind parents of the Rule of Thumb for this week.
- Parents are instructed to make notes immediately following the play sessions about specific happenings in the play sessions, noting what their children did or said, their responses, and their emotional reactions. Parents are reminded that **the new skills they are learning are to be practiced only during the once-per-week special playtimes**. In addition, the first parent—or two (depends on the size of your group)—is scheduled to come to the clinic/office to be videotaped or to videotape his/her play session at home. Our preference is to have the first volunteer parent(s) come to the office/clinic playroom to be videotaped after having one home play session. For the parent's convenience, the parent can conduct the first play session at home during the prearranged time and then video a play session to be shown during group immediately prior to training Session 4. This practice allows the first parent(s) to be videotaped to have extra practice and support from the therapist.
- **Remember, structure all aspects of CPRT training to ensure maximum parent success!** In very rare cases where videotaping is not available, parents can conduct play sessions during CPRT training with the rest of the group watching from behind a chair or table, something to form a barrier of separation. *Note: The filial therapist should select the first parent to be videotaped, rather than asking for volunteers.* Select a parent in the group who seems to readily pick up on the skills being taught and seems open to feedback. Most parents are apprehensive about being videotaped knowing that their video will be viewed by the entire group of parents

at the next week's session; therefore, much encouragement and support is needed throughout the process. Again, having the parent come to your office/clinic to be videotaped allows you to provide extra support and encouragement for the novice parent. In rare cases, there may not be a parent ready to demonstrate his/her new skills on videotape this early in the training process; therefore, videotaping can be delayed one week. *Some flexibility in the structure of training is necessary to ensure that parents experience success.*

- End the session by emphasizing the importance of this first home play session and asking parents to make a commitment to keep this appointment with their children, as if it were a very important business meeting or doctor appointment. The therapist emphasizes that play sessions must never be used as a reward or punishment for the child's behavior. Close with the reminder about the rule of thumb for the week. Although this rule of thumb was covered in Session 1 as a teaching point, it is useful in helping parents focus on their goal for the first play session—to establish a different kind of environment for their children; that for 30 minutes this week, they are going to be like a thermostat, responding to their children's thoughts, feelings, and needs.

Partial Transcript of CPRT Session 3

(Parents began by discussing toys and reporting on times and places they had chosen for their playtimes.)

Dr. L.: This week I want you to make a sign with your child's help that says "Special Playtime—Do Not Disturb." You can use a piece of paper like you are writing on and tape a string to it to hang on the door knob when you go into the room for your playtime. If you are home alone, hang the sign on the front door. Tell your child, "Our special playtime is really important. If the phone rings, I'm not going to answer the phone." You could even disconnect the phone. If someone rings the doorbell during your playtime, say to your child, "They will come back." You can only answer the doorbell if you hear someone yell, "Fire!" The message you are communicating is your child and the special playtime are so important you won't allow anything to interrupt.

Debbie: How large does the area for the playtime need to be?

Dr. L.: The space does not have to be a big area. If you did not have any other place, the playtime could be in your bathroom.

Laura: The bathroom is the smallest place in the house.

Dr. L.: Yes, it does not have to be a big area. What were you thinking about, Debbie?

Debbie: I was thinking about having my playtime in my bedroom, because I can close the door and have more privacy.

Dr. L.: What's going to happen if you have to miss one of your playtimes?

Emily: We'll have to pay for it. (group laughter)

Dr. L.: What are you going to do?

Sonya: Reschedule as soon as possible.

Dr. L.: Yes, reschedule. The playtime is just as important as an appointment with your doctor. If he cancels, you reschedule as soon as possible. If you miss a playtime, you say to your child, "Oops, I forgot or I had a meeting. Let's pick another time for our special playtime."

(Parents fill out *Special Playtime Appointment Card* to be given to their child.)

Dr. L.: Prior to your special playtime, display the toys, and then go get your child and the sign and say, "Let's hang this on the door." Then you walk into the room where your session is going to be and you say to your child, "This is our special playtime. This is a time when you can play with these toys in a lot of the ways you would like to." Please do not say to your child, "You can play with these toys any way you want to." They can't, right?

Kathy: Right. (laughs)

Dr. L.: They can't do anything with these toys they want to do. They can't throw the toys into the lamp. They can't try to break something. They can't mark on the walls with the crayons. So, you will avoid saying to your child, "You can play with these toys anyway you want to." What will you say to your child?

Sonya: "Many of the ways you would like to."

Dr. L.: Or "a lot." The child's word is "a lot." "You can play with these toys in a lot of the ways you would like to." And then you sit down (gestures toward the floor) on the floor, or if that's not comfortable, you can sit in a chair, but do not remain standing. You sit down. And then once you have done that, there are rules for your sessions. (Hands out *Filial Play Sessions Dos and Don'ts* for play sessions to parents.)

Kathy: What if he's not ready to come in and start playing at 7:15? What if he's doing something else or says, "I don't want to right now?"

Dr. L.: Then you negotiate.

Debbie: Don't you think that after the first session this would be something they would be excited about?

Dr. L.: Yes, they will look forward to it. But if your child resists, and they may have something special that is just developing, then you say to your child, "Let's do this: Let's have 10 minutes of our 30-minute special playtime. At the end of that 10 minutes, you can decide whether you want to have the rest of the special playtime or stop." So you let the child continue to choose and make a decision. But you compromise, "We'll have 10 minutes and then you can decide." Your child may resist at first, but begin playing and have a good time. When you say, "Well, our 10 minutes are up. You can decide if you want to have the rest of our special playtime or stop," your child will probably choose to continue the special playtime. Look over the list of "Don'ts" and pick the one you think you're going to have the most trouble with. (Group discusses principles they will have difficulty implementing and Dr. L. gives suggestions.)

Sonya: I'm going to have trouble with the "Don't praise your child."

Dr. L.: Give your child credit for what he does rather than praise him. When we praise, we don't intend it to be hurtful, but it doesn't build the child's self-esteem. Praise causes your child to want to please you and doesn't teach your child to be creative. You want your child to grow up feeling good about what she has done. Let's work on this for just a minute. (Walks over to sandbox and bends down.) If I pick up the sand scoop, and I scoop a bunch of sand over into one place, how can you give me credit for doing that?

Debbie: Say, "You're piling up the sand."

Dr. L.: You just track what you see me do.

Debbie: "I see you're making a pile in the sand."

Dr. L.: Or maybe the first thing you said, "You're piling the sand up just as high as you want it to be." That gives me credit, "as high as you want it to be." If I stack this up (stacks cans on edge of sandbox), and it's kind of hard to make it stack, and it falls off, and I stack it again, you can now say what to me? "There, you…"

Sonya: "You did it. There, you did it."

Dr. L.: "There, you did it." Or there might be three or four blocks. "There you stacked those blocks way up high."

Sonya: It feels good just hearing you say that. I mean, if I was a little kid doing that, I would feel brave enough to do something else. I'd want to do something else.

Dr. L.: It builds up your child's self-esteem. And you don't have to say, "What a wonderful job you did." (returns to chair)

Sonya: I always say that. Now I feel terrible. "That was a good job, Katie, that was such a good job." But I can see now where there's more.

Dr. L.: Yes, there's more to it, and you're going to learn a different way to respond. This new way of responding is not going to feel very comfortable at first, but that's okay. What else are you going to have trouble with?

Debbie: Don't give information.

Dr. L.: Most parents want to teach their children.

Kathy: That will be a hard one.

Dr. L.: For 30 minutes, you may not tell the child how to work the Tinkertoys, or how it's supposed to be done, or "That doesn't look like this picture so you need to put this one here and make it look better." That's giving information.

Debbie: Okay.

Dr. L.: For 30 minutes, you're kind of dumb. For 30 minutes, you're not an information source. You don't have any answers. Ever get tired of giving information?

Sonya: Yeah.

Dr. L.: For 30 minutes, I give you permission not to give information.

Sonya: That'll work.

Dr. L.: It can be the way your child wants it to be. That's a phrase I'd like for you all to use a lot. Your child picks up an object you have in your toy box (picks up a dragon puppet) and says, "What is this?" And you can say, "That can be..."

Parents: "Whatever you want it to be."

Dr. L.: (puts puppet on hand) And then I can say, "Oh goody! It's a frog!" Well, if you had identified the puppet, you probably would have said it's a dragon. Or I might say, "Oh goody! It's a space man!" It can be whatever I want it to be for this 30 minutes. That way you help me to be creative.

Kathy: Can you say something like, "I don't know, what would you like to use it for?" or "What do you think it is?"

Dr. L.: If you respond to your child, "What do you think it is?" he will say, "I don't know." We avoid asking questions. Instead, we make statements because statements are much more freeing.

Kathy: I see.

Dr. L.: So you just make a statement. We almost never ask questions. When he asks, "What do you think it is?," just say, "It can be whatever you want it to be."

Kathy: Oh, I see (looking at list). "Don't ask leading questions," right there.

Dr. L.: Let's see. (picks up plastic Coke bottle) (to Kathy) What's this?

Kathy: I don't know.

Dr. L.: Begin with "that."

Kathy: That...

Dr. L.: Can be...

Sonya: Anything you want it to be.

Dr. L.: And it doesn't have to be a Coke bottle. It can be scrambled eggs if I want it to be. I may throw it in the pot here and say, "I'm scrambling this; I'm going to make eggs out of this." Or it could be a bowling pin. It could be a rocket ship. It can be whatever I want it to be. (Puts Coke bottle down and picks up plastic elephant.) What is this?

Parents: It can be anything you want it to be.

Dr. L.: I want you all to say that enough times that if you were sleeping and I suddenly whispered in your ear, "What is this?" you would say, "That can be whatever you want it to be." (laughter) The idea of what we're trying to do is free your child, to free their creativity so they can learn what it's like to make their own decisions. When you tell me it can be whatever I want it to be, you give the decision making back to me, and you put me in the lead.

(Parents continue to discuss items on "Don't" list that they believe will be hardest for them to avoid and Dr. Landreth responds by providing a rationale for the "Don't" and demonstrating what to do instead.)

Dr. L.: If you say the wrong thing, you can recover. **Rule of Thumb: The most important thing may not be what you do, but what you do after what you have done.**

Any of you ever do something and realize, "That wasn't the way I really wanted to do that?"

Parents: (agreement)

Laura: You feel stuck.

Dr. L.: You can recover. It's okay if you make mistakes. I have really worked hard at trying to live by that **Rule of Thumb: The most important thing may not be what I do, but what I do after what I have done.** Let's see, what else is on the list? Number seven; nobody mentioned that one, "Don't initiate new behavior."

Sonya: What do you mean by number seven, "Don't initiate any new behavior?"

Dr. L.: Initiating new behavior would be like saying, "Well, you haven't played with the Tinkertoys yet. Maybe you'd like to play with them." That would be to initiate new behavior. You are a follower for 30 minutes. You don't suggest, "We've had four special playtimes, and you still haven't colored anything. Maybe you'd like to draw a picture." You don't do that. For 30 minutes, you can't suggest anything for your child to do. They have to figure it out. In the process, what will your child learn?

Sonya: Problem solving.

Dr. L.: Yes, problem-solving skills. How to figure things out for themselves. What it feels like to make decisions. Let's take a look at the "Dos". Would you pick the one that you think you're going to have the most trouble with?

Several Parents: Tracking behavior, be a follower.

Dr. L.: Do you realize you can't learn what it is like to be a leader until somebody follows? And you'd all like for your children to be leaders probably in some things.

Emily: I know we'd like for them to follow us most of the time. (laughter)

Dr. L.: Yes, but for 30 minutes, you are the follower, and they are the leader. So that means if the child picks up this can, hands it to me, and says, "Go put that stuff over there," I'll say, "Show me where you want it put." And he may say, "In the sandbox." If the child says, "Go to the store and buy some groceries," I'll say, "What do you want me to get?" "Well, you get some eggs, some bacon, and some potatoes." You might have thought "hamburgers, bananas, and oranges." You always ask the child, "What do you want me to do?" The child says, "Here, take these Tinkertoys and make this." You say, "Show me how you want me to make it. There's a bunch of holes here. Which hole do you want me to put it in?"

Debbie: Does the child know that you're supposed to be an interactive part of the playtime?

Dr. L.: They find out whether you're going to interact with them as they go along. You don't say you will or won't up front. You just wait until they ask you to participate. And don't be disappointed if your child does not ask you to participate. Some children do and some don't. Some children need you to be a part of their play and some don't need you to be a part of it. You let your child ask you to play. If she says, "Hand me some of that stuff off the shelf," what are you going to say?

Laura: What would you like me to get you from the shelf?

Dr. L.: Yes, you don't do anything until the child tells you what to do specifically. If the child says, "Here, Mom, draw a picture on here," you're going to say…

Emily: "What kind of picture would you like me to draw?"

Dr. L.: Or, "What do you want me to draw a picture of?" And he says, "Draw a picture of a tree." "What color would you like the tree to be? Do you want it on this side or this side?" Do you realize what fun this is going to be for your child, to direct everything that you do for 30 minutes?

Sonya: Now that I think about it, my daughter is always telling me, "I can do that myself." If we're brushing teeth, it has really taken a lot for me to let her go ahead and squeeze the toothpaste out on the toothbrush, or in the bedroom when she's struggling to get ballerina leg warmers up and she says, "I can do it myself," and I say, "Okay." I can take that message, but she usually waits until I think I've overstepped my boundaries with her, and then she finally says, "I can do that."

Dr. L.: We want our children growing up to be independent. And there's only one way you can learn to be independent, and that's by doing what?

Laura: By being allowed to be independent.

Dr. L.: Yes, by being allowed to be independent and practice being independent. Then you know what independence feels like.

(Parents discuss "Dos" on list.)

Dr. L.: When your child is doing something, you track what they do. In this 30 minutes, you are to reflect what you hear with your eyes. Let me quickly give you a caution, though. I don't want you tracking this closely: (stands up and walks to sandbox) "You're getting up out of your chair, you took one, two, three steps. You're bending down, your hand is reaching, you picked up the can, you dropped the can in the sandbox, you're bending down…" That would drive you crazy. But if the child were to do the same thing, you would sit there and watch (picks up the can and drops it in the sandbox): "Oh, you just dropped that right there in the sandbox." (Dr. L. scoops up sand.) "Looks like you scooped some sand in it." Those would be your tracking responses. So that your child then knows you saw, took in, and recorded what they did. So what are the four messages we're working on? **I hear you with my ears, I hear you with my eyes—in this example it was hearing with eyes. I'm here with you, I understand, and I care.** And how does the child know we understand? Because of what you give back to them. (walks over to the sandbox) "You just dropped that in the sandbox there, and you scooped up some sand in it." Then the child knows you understood what they did. If your child is banging on the Bobo and saying not one word and you see anger, you would say, "You look angry," then the child knows you understand.

Kathy: What if my child wants to go get another toy to bring into the playtime?

Dr. L.: You can say, "I know you would like to play with the army truck in your room, but the army truck is for staying in your room. You can choose to play with it after our special playtime."

Kim: How do you handle the time? Do you have a timer?

Dr. L.: I am so glad you asked that. I almost forgot that. You will need a watch or clock, no timers. Why not set a timer for 30 minutes?

Laura: Because it makes a ticking sound and would be distracting.

Dr. L.: Yes, and the tendency is to attribute the cause for stopping to the timer. "Oh, shucks, the timer went off. We have to stop." Ending is your responsibility. Your child has been in the lead during the playtime, and now you're in charge. You will help your child get ready to end the playtime by giving a 5-minute warning 25 minutes into every playtime. "We have 5 more minutes in the playtime and then it will be time to stop." And then your child can get ready to bring the playtime to a close. The ending of the session returns control and responsibility to you all.

Kim: What if the child is not ready to end the session?

Dr. L.: We're going to make that a bit easier by doing three things: When time is up, you say, "Our special playtime is up for today," and you stand up, giving a second message that time is up. If you stay seated, the message to your child is time really isn't up. So you stand up, move towards the door and say, "It's time to go to the kitchen for cookies and milk." Then your child has something desirable to move toward. You may not have to do that every time, but it might be helpful the first couple of times. As you walk out of the room, you say to your child, "I'll come back and clean up." If your child says, "I want to help," that's OK, but no more playing. The rule of thumb at ending time is patience. If it takes several minutes for your child to walk away from the special playtime, that's OK. You walk towards the door, stop, and say, "I know you would like to play longer, but our time is up for today." Any more questions about your playtimes? Well, I have given you a lot to do today. I feel as though I have given you the whole course in one session.

(Group views a video segment of one of Dr. L.'s play sessions, and he explains what he does in the playtime.)

Dr. L.: Now, let's practice. You two are partners, you two are partners, and you two are partners. One of you is the child and one is the parent. (Group role-plays a play session, and Dr. L. moves from pair to pair listening and giving suggestions.) Next week when you come back, I will ask you, "How did your special playtime go? What happened in your special playtime? Did you have any problems?" So you will need to make notes after each one of your playtimes. I'd like to know what your child plays with or stories they play out. I need a volunteer to come here to the Center this week and be video-taped in your play session before we meet next time. (Dr. Landreth briefly scans the group and makes eye contact with Emily.) Emily, would you be willing to come to the Center with Chris this week? Then the group will watch part of your playtime next week.

Emily: I can do that.

Dr. L.: Thanks, Emily, I'll meet with you briefly after group to set up a time for you. Each week I will ask for a volunteer, and the playtime here will be your session for that week. I'll see you next week. I think your special playtimes are going to be fun for you.

References

Guerney, L. (1972). *Filial therapy: A training manual for parents.* Unpublished manuscript.

Bratton, S., Landreth, G., Kellam, T., & Blackard, S. (2006). Child Parent Relationship Therapy (CPRT) Treatment Manual: A 10-Session Filial Therapy Model for Training Parents. NY: Routledge.

CHAPTER 10

CPRT TRAINING SESSION 4: SUPERVISION FORMAT AND LIMIT SETTING

Overview

The major focus in this session is for parents to report on their first special playtime with their children, with the most time spent reviewing the video of the parent who volunteered to be videotaped. All skills introduced in training Session 3, as well as underlying principles of CPRT therapy, are continually reinforced by the therapist as parents report on their play sessions, but the major strategy is to encourage parents as they share their play session experiences, finding something positive to comment on in each parent's report. The partial transcript of CPRT training Session 4 found at the end of this chapter provides the reader with a glimpse into this process of balancing didactic instruction and dynamic support and encouragement of parents as they struggle to learn these new skills. Limit-setting skills are taught and demonstrated, and play session skills are reviewed and practiced, based on the needs of the group.

Materials

Suggested materials include: *CPRT Session 4–Treatment Outline;* parent information form with pertinent notes; homework assigned in Session 3, including extra copies of any homework worksheets; Session 4 handouts and homework, including: *Session 4 Parent Notes & Homework, Limit Setting: A-C-T Before It's To Late!, Limit Setting: A-C-T Practice Worksheet*, and *Parent Play Session Notes*. Additional materials include: display posters for both *Play Session Dos and Don'ts* and *Play Session Procedure Checklist (or laminated color copies of each can be used in lieu of poster)*, video clip of limit setting (optional), and video clip or live demo of play session skills.

> *Note: All handouts listed above, as well as a training session outline for the filial therapist, additional supplemental parent handouts, and resources for this training session are found in the* CPRT Treatment Manual *and accompanying CD-ROM, available from the publisher, Routledge.*

Content and Procedure

This session begins, as all sessions, with 10 minutes of parents sharing how their week went as they arrive. By this fourth session, parents generally feel more comfortable openly and honestly sharing their parenting struggles and the therapist utilizes this time to support and encourage parents. Resistant parents often share behavioral problems they are having with their children, often citing examples of how they tried to use a skill and it didn't work—"Nothing works with my child." Remind parents of the Band-Aid—that it's working even when they don't see it working. Ask them to trust the process, and not to take the Band-Aid off yet! The therapist can also use a resistant parent's reports of frustration with her child's behavior as an opportunity to reflect that what she is doing doesn't seem to be getting the desired results. Ask the parent to consider that her child may have special needs that require a different response, and that the 30-minute special playtime will teach her a new way to respond to her child's needs. This is a good time to introduce the **Rule of Thumb: When a child is drowning, don't try to teach**

her to swim. Ask parents what they would do if their child *were* drowning. Do you look into the pool and try and tell them what to do and try to give them a crash course in how to swim? Of course not! You would jump in and save your child. Liken the 30-minute special playtime to the parent jumping in to save the child (hence the name of the course: CPR). The special playtime is a time for parents to respond to their children's needs, without trying to teach a lesson, change behavior, etc. Reflective responding is the tool that parents use to respond to their children's needs. When a child is feeling upset or out of control, that is not the moment to teach, preach, or impart a rule.

The facilitator must be sensitive to the difficulty parents have with the concept of focusing only on the special playtimes, when they are having significant behavior problems that they want solved, and NOW! Continue to affirm their frustrations and struggles, writing down their concerns, and assuring them that you will come back to those issues in a few weeks. An exception to the rule regarding the use of skills outside of play sessions is the introduction of the concept of choice giving to address a relevant problem expressed by a parent. Choice giving is a skill that is relatively easy to learn and often produces immediate results. Although we typically teach the skill of choice giving in depth in Session 6, this skill can be covered briefly as early as Session 4, depending on the needs of the group. Choice giving is one skill that parents are encouraged to use outside of their play sessions and, as with many teaching points, this skill is more powerfully learned when introduced or reinforced in response to a parent's expressed concern, as illustrated in the partial transcript at the end of this chapter. **Some flexibility in presentation of content is often necessary in order to most effectively respond to parents' needs.**

Filial Play Session Reports

The majority of this session is focused on parents' reporting on their first special playtimes with their children. Parents are asked to report on such things as making their "Do Not Disturb" sign with their children, and their children's responses to parents' explanation of the specialness of the playtimes, etc. Each parent is asked to briefly describe the first play session with her child, with the "parent of focus" (parent who videotaped a play session) going last. The therapist carefully listens for parent strengths, finding something positive to comment on in each parent's report. Remember that the **Donut Analogy** applies to parents, too. They will have lots of "holes" at this point in the training, but the therapist's job in this session is to focus completely on "the good stuff."

Look for every opportunity to use parents' comments to forge connections and help them see that they are not alone in their struggles to try out these new skills. Find a part of a parent's report to respond to and build on in order to reinforce the Filial Play Session "Dos." For example, Debbie reported that during her first play session, her daughter climbed up on the bed close to her with the doctor kit, and that she (Debbie) responded, "I don't know what to do." Her daughter then responded, "Well, you lie down here, and I'll tell you." Although Debbie's response was not a perfect example of "*Do* let the child lead," the leader used this opportunity to encourage Debbie and reinforce a teaching point by responding, "So, you let Rachel know that it was up to her to decide what to do, and she let you know that she knew just what she wanted you to do!" Then, the therapist turned to the group and pointed to the poster of "Dos" and said, "That was an example of…," and two of the parents responded in unison, "*Do* let the child lead."

During the reporting of happenings in their first play session, parents typically ask for help with how to respond to specific situations. **The emphasis of CPRT training is on learning by experience and observation.** Therefore, role-play is utilized to address specific questions, with the therapist playing the role of the parent who presented the question and the parent playing the role of the child. The filial therapist may also introduce new teaching material that is relevant to parents' questions. For example, in the Session 4 transcription given at the end of this chapter, choice giving was introduced in response to Debbie's power struggle with her daughter about her clothes. Debbie was so frustrated with Rachel's behavior throughout the week that she could not keep her focus on her play session report. In response, the therapist reflected how frustrated Debbie seemed and suggested that Debbie try giving Rachel two choices of clothes to wear. After much discussion from Debbie about why choice giving will not work with Rachel, the therapist asked Debbie to work on choice giving, adding that he will check in with her next week *(and made a note to himself to do so).*

Following through on promises made to parents, such as this one, is important and models the value of parents following through on their promises to their children. This strategy also serves the purpose of ending the discussion and brings the topic back to Debbie's special playtime. Writing down parents' unsuccessfully resolved problems and other concerns helps them feel heard, conveys that their concerns are important, but most importantly, allows the therapist to refocus on the task at hand. Our experience is that successfully conducting a CPRT group is a continual and delicate balance between providing didactic instruction and supervision that helps parents learn the skills necessary for success, and facilitating a dynamic process so that parents feel supported and understood.

Filial Play Session Video Critique

The next and most important training element in this session is viewing the videotaped parent play session. An advantage of videotaping is that parents get to observe themselves, an experience that can produce tremendous insight. Other benefits of videotaped supervision are enhanced opportunities for vicarious learning for all group members and the opportunity for parents to give, as well as receive, help from each other. The experience of watching themselves on videotape usually produces considerable anxiety for parents, but the other parents in the group are always extremely supportive and the anxiety quickly dissipates. A major objective of therapist feedback is to provide support and encouragement and to be sensitive to the feelings parents experience. Correction is kept to a minimum. **Encouragement is the order of the day.** As mentioned earlier, while viewing the parent video the therapist carefully listens and watches for parent strengths and opportunities to offer encouragement and to reinforce the Dos and Don'ts listed on the poster.

In the viewing of the first videotaped play session, the therapist often has to work hard to find strengths to reflect. For example, Emily was the first parent to show her videotape, and after watching her video for several minutes, commented that she was much quieter than usual, because she wasn't sure what to say. The therapist stopped the video and encouraged Emily's periods of silence between her brief responses by commenting, "Emily, that shows me you were thinking about how you should respond, instead of responding how you typically would—that's the first step! Just now, as you watched your child playing with the Play-Doh, what were you aware of?" Emily quickly responds, "He's having fun rolling it and squishing it! [pause] Probably because I never let him have Play-Doh at home." The therapist uses that opportunity to encourage Emily's understanding of her child's play and suggests that as Emily begins to trust her instincts, she will be able to respond more quickly, with understanding, to her child's play.

Group Dynamics and Support

The therapist also uses every opportunity to link parents' shared experiences, by noting and commenting on verbal and nonverbal messages that convey "Me, too." For example, in the segment described above, Laura smiled, and Kathy nodded, when Emily revealed that she wasn't sure how to respond, prompting the therapist to reflect, "Laura, seems like you understand what Emily's struggling with…and, Kathy, I noticed you nodding your head, too." This led to a discussion about how all the parents felt awkward with practicing this new way of responding to their children's play and, more importantly, helped them feel that they were not alone in their struggles.

An issue that is usually brought up following the parents' first play session is that a child is enjoying the play session and doesn't want to stop when the time is up. Parents are reminded that it is their responsibility to end the sessions even though children may want to continue playing, and that this happening provides a perfect opportunity to demonstrate an example of limit setting. "Rachel, I know you would like to play with the doctor kit longer, but our special playtime is over for today. You can choose to play with the doctor kit next week." For the younger child, who may need a more immediate alternative, "Rachel, I know you want to play longer, but our special playtime is over for today. We can go to the kitchen and have a snack." This example of how to end a play sessions with a reluctant child leads into instruction of the skill of limit setting.

Limit Setting

The importance of parents establishing consistent limits with their children is briefly discussed: **consistent limits provide a predictable, safe environment and a sense of security**. The A-C-T model of limit setting is taught and demonstrated

(Chapter 5 includes more information and strategies for teaching this important skill). Parents are given the handout, *Limit Setting: A-C-T Before It's Too Late,* to refer to as the therapist teaches the 3-step process of the A-C-T Method of limit setting.

3-Step A-C-T Method

Begin by providing parents with a limit-setting scenario that might occur *during* a play session. Do not give a scenario that would take place outside of a play session; parents have enough difficulty resisting the urge to try this new skill to deal with problematic child behaviors. Example scenario: *Billy has been pretending that the bop bag is a bad guy and shooting him with the dart gun; he looks over at you and aims the dart gun at you, then laughs and says, "Now, you're one of the bad guys, too!"*

1. ***A***cknowledge your child's feeling or desire *(your voice must convey empathy and understanding).* **"Billy, I know that you think that it would be fun to shoot me, too."** *The child learns that his feelings, desires, and wishes are valid and accepted by his parent (but not all behavior);* simply empathically reflecting your child's feeling often defuses the intensity of the feeling or need.
2. ***C***ommunicate the limit (be specific and clear—and brief). **"But, I'm not for shooting."**
3. ***T***arget acceptable alternatives; provide one or more choices (depending on age of child). **"You can pretend that the doll is me [pointing at the doll] and shoot at it."**

The goal is to provide your child with an acceptable outlet for expressing the feeling or the original action, while giving him an opportunity to exercise self-control.

Why Establish Consistent Limits

Providing children with consistent limits helps them feel safe and secure. This method of limiting children's behavior teaches them self-control and responsibility for their own behavior by allowing them to experience the consequences for their choices and decisions. Limits set in play sessions help children practice self-control and begin to learn to stop themselves in the real world.

When to Set Limits

During play sessions, limits are set only when the need arises, and for four basic reasons:

1. To protect the child from hurting himself or his parent.
2. To protect valuable property.
3. To maintain the parent's acceptance of the child.
4. To provide consistency in the play session by limiting child and toys to play area and ending on time.

Before setting a limit in a play session, ask yourself

- "Is this limit necessary?"
- "Can I consistently enforce this limit?"
- "If I don't set a limit on this behavior, can I consistently allow this behavior and accept my child?"

Avoid conducting play sessions in areas of the house that require too many limits. Limits set during play sessions should allow for greater freedom of expression than would normally be allowed. The fewer the limits, the easier it is for you to be consistent—**consistency is very important**. Determine a few limits ahead of time (practice A-C-T): no hitting or shooting at parent, no Play-Doh on the carpet, no purposefully breaking toys, etc. Hint: Children really do understand that playtimes are "special" and that the rules are different—they will *not* expect the same level of permissiveness during the rest of the week.

How to Set Limits

Limits are not punitive and should be stated firmly, but calmly and matter-of-factly. After empathically acknowledging your child's feeling or desire (very important step), you state, "The Play-Doh is not for throwing at the table," just like you would state, "The sky is blue." Don't try to force your child to obey the limit. Remember to provide an acceptable alternative. In this method, it really is up to the child to decide to accept or break the limit; however, **it is your job, as the parent, to consistently enforce the limit**.

Limit-Setting Demonstration, Practice and Role Play

Provide parents with three to four written or oral examples of limit-setting scenarios and how to respond using A-C-T. Time may not permit a thorough review of the rationale for limit setting and when and how to set limits. Limit setting generally is an area of concern for parents and will continue to be a topic of focus for several weeks. Parents are asked to reread the handout for homework and note any limit they think they might need to set with their child. The therapist demonstrates limit setting through role-play, as with every skill that is introduced, and if time permits, a short video clip of limit setting is shown. Parents are typically very interested in limit setting and generate many questions about the use of this skill in everyday struggles with their child. However, the therapist uses humor to explain to parents that under no circumstances are they to try this outside of the play session! On a more serious note, remind parents that the goal is for them to be successful in learning to apply these new skills during their 30-mintue special playtimes with their children.

In some cases, the experienced CPRT therapist may introduce the limit-setting skill earlier in this session in response to a parent's concern, rather than wait until the end of the training session. Opportunities to teach and reinforce limit setting arise on a regular basis. There is no need to try to teach all limit-setting concepts all at one time in one session. Again, using relevant moments to teach skills enhances parents' learning, as illustrated in the transcription that follows. Debbie was expressing frustration with her daughter's screaming when she doesn't get her way. The therapist suggested that when that happens again, Debbie respond to Rachel by saying, "Sounds like you need to scream, but the kitchen is not a place for screaming. It hurts my ears. You can scream in your room." A very brief overview of the A-C-T model of limit setting is provided at that time, but the therapist continues to focus the process on parents' reporting of play sessions, letting parents know that limit setting will be taught in more detail later. Again, some flexibility of content delivery is allowed in order to respond to the unique needs of a particular group of parents.

Allow at least 15 minutes for parent pairs to role-play, each parent taking a turn being the child playing with toys and responding as the child to limit-setting situations. Since this week has been the parents' first opportunity to practice their new skills, they usually have so much they want to share about the experience that the time for specific training is minimal. Time constraints may require that the therapist provide more detailed instructions, practice, and role-play of limit setting during Session 5.

Homework Assignments

1. Parents are reminded of the importance of conducting their play sessions at the same time and same place (no excuses!), likening the play session to a weekly staff meeting with the boss (a meeting that no one would dare miss!), and parents are reminded to videotape their sessions.
2. Parents are reminded to take a few minutes to review the following handouts prior to play session: *Filial Play Sessions Dos and Don'ts (yellow)*, *Filial Play Sessions Procedures Checklist (blue)*, and *Limit Setting: A-C-T Before It's Too Late! (Optional assignment: Provide parents with a handout with several scenarios of children's behaviors in play sessions requiring limit setting, which they are to respond to in writing and bring the following week—this can be done in class the following week or given as homework after Session 5).*
3. Remind parents to notice one intense feeling in themselves this week; also, if they needed to set a limit during their playtimes, describe what happened and what they said or did, and think about what limits they think they might need to set for their child.
4. Parents are reminded after conducting the play session to complete the *Parent Play Session Notes* and bring to group the following week.
5. One to two parents are scheduled to videotape their play sessions to be shown in class the following week.
6. Remind parents of the Rule of Thumb for that week.
7. Close with a motivational poem or story (optional).

Partial Transcript of CPRT Session 4

(Informal group sharing and the first part of parents' reporting on home play sessions are not included.)

Debbie: How is Nita, the pregnant mom?

Dr. L.: Nita called and wanted everyone to know she's fine. She has an appointment with her doctor, but she's fine. Let's continue talking about your sessions. I'd like to hear from each one of you about how your sessions went, how you got started, what your child played with, what the playtime was like for you. We're going to see your video, Emily, so we'll skip you for now. Debbie, what was your session like?

Debbie: Rachel was bouncing off the walls. I set the playtime for 10:00 in the morning because my husband's schedule is so flexible, and I like him out of the house. But she was so excited about the playtime; she started bouncing off the walls at about 8:30. It was just horrible. I finally set the timer on the microwave and said, "Now, when it beeps, you can go in the room, and we can get started." I took the baby next door and I said, "Now, I'm going to be in the bedroom, and when it beeps, you come in there." Well, I heard it beep twice. She was at the microwave turning it off, so it would be time. (laughter)

Dr. L.: Good for her. She's eager, and I would suggest next time, don't set the timer ahead like that with a beeper to go off. You just decide when you are ready to start at a time close to the prearranged time. Display the toys, and then bring her into the room, or allow her to help you get the playtime ready.

Debbie: I don't have to start it at 10:00?

Dr. L.: You can be flexible. If she is eager to start, and you're ready to start, you may want to start 10 minutes early. We don't want to make an issue out of the time.

Debbie: I want to go back and listen to the tape. I taped it, and it was pretty good. Except, she wanted to play doctor, and she decided the thing you give shots with is for sticking in my nose. So here she is on the bed next to me close up, and I said, "I don't know what to do." She said, "Well, you lie down here, and I'll tell you." It was pretty interesting. She only played with two things. She had all these toys, but only played with two. Another real interesting thing was she took everything out of the dollhouse, but then she put everything back in the dollhouse before she went on to play.

Dr. L.: She put things away. That was unexpected by you.

Debbie: Yeah, it was. She put them all back in there and closed the door.

Dr. L.: So, what did you learn about your child?

Debbie: Nothing new, that I thought of. It was surprising that she put things away.

Dr. L.: And what does that mean?

Debbie: That she likes to be organized.

Dr. L.: That's a possibility. It also means she's capable of putting things away.

Sonya: She can put her things away before she moves on to something else.

Dr. L.: And without being told to do it. You learned that about her. That might be an important learning.

Debbie: But she doesn't put her toys away at other times.

Dr. L.: But now you know she's capable.

Sonya: Having that information, it's like oh, yeah, she can do that, but she chooses not to.

Debbie: I go through a lot of things with Rachel, like choice of dresses and stuff.

Dr. L.: It's a dressing problem in the morning.

Debbie: All the time; all throughout the day.

Dr. L.: All day?

Debbie: She goes through about five outfits a day.

Dr. L.: Because?

Debbie: She doesn't want to wear this, she wants to wear that, and when she's tired of that, then she wants to wear this, etc. It's always got to be a dress and all her pantyhose and her leotards are all ripped because that's the only thing she wants to wear.

Laura: I know what that's like, kids go through certain phases where that's what they want to wear. My nieces go through a spell where they don't want to wear anything but dresses, and that's what they wear.

Debbie: Well, the basic question really is: She wants something, and she can't have it, and you want her to know that you understand, that you know what she wants, but she can't have it. So you say, "I understand," but how do you say the other half of it? "But it can't be that way" or "But you can't have it?"

Sonya: I have something I just want to interject: the first thing that I do, if I feel like I'm having a "struggle of wills" with Jenny, she's almost 3, the first thing I do is check on, "How important is this?" Sometimes I just have to stop and think, "Is this worth arguing over?" If it is something that is important, then I will tell her. I'm going to give this example because" (to Dr. L.) "you mentioned it last week. If she starts crying over the smallest little thing and says, "I want my daddy," or "You're not my friend any more!" I stopped feeling guilty and playing the game with her like you said. I just said, "It sounds like you're very angry with me," and she just stopped in her tracks as soon as I acknowledged what her feeling was, and she didn't go on and on about "You're not my friend any more, I miss my daddy." Then I asked, "Are you going to call your daddy?" and she said, "Maybe later."

Debbie: Yeah, but what about the times when it is "No"? When she's not getting a candy bar before bedtime.

Sonya: And she's still throwing the fit? Yeah, "You look like you're very angry about this, and you still can't have a candy bar." And if she keeps pushing that, I'll offer her some choices on what she can do: "You can either lie down on your bed with the book now," or something else that's appropriate.

Debbie: Is it OK for her to…

Emily: To pitch a fit?

Debbie: Well, yeah!

Emily: Yes.

Dr. L.: Emily, you have experienced that, and Debbie, it sounds like you're really frustrated with Rachel. Perhaps you could try choice giving by giving her two choices of clothes to wear, and then how is she likely to react?

Debbie: She will scream.

Dr. L.: And you show understanding by saying, "You're really angry about your choices."

Debbie: I don't keep talking her through the screaming, do I? Is there a point where I withdraw?

Dr. L.: You can say, "Sounds like you need to scream, and your room is the place for screaming. I'm going to the kitchen, and you can have 5 minutes to scream in your room." And if she follows you into the kitchen, you can say, "The kitchen is not a place for screaming. It hurts my ears. My kitchen is not for screaming in. Your room is for screaming in." And you take her back to her room. It's OK if she screams back there. The important thing is that you are allowing her to get rid of some of her feelings, and she learns you're not too bothered by that.

Debbie: I won't do anything to reinforce her behavior.

Dr. L.: You got it. One of the things I keep hearing from you, Debbie, is you know what needs to be done. I didn't say anything about reinforcing. You know you're reinforcing some things you shouldn't be reinforcing.

Debbie: Maybe I need reinforcement. (group laughs)

Dr. L.: You're on the right track, Debbie. You just can't change the whole world. Right now you just need to work on choice giving. I have written that down (points to notebook), and I'll check on that next week. Let's go back to your special playtime.

(Focus on an issue unrelated to the special playtimes is typically not done until the last couple of sessions unless the parent has intense feelings about the issue. If that is the case, hearing the parent and suggesting something the parent can try provides a measure of relief. The parent can then focus on the task of learning skills for the playtimes.)

Debbie: (Describes more of her child's play behavior.)

Dr. L.: Did the time seem to go slow or fast for you?

Debbie: Very fast.

Dr. L.: That's a good sign. A caution, folks, the playtimes may not always go fast. There may be some special playtimes when the 30 minutes seems like an hour, and that's OK. What that says is you may not have been very interested in what was going on, but your child probably was. The playtime can also seem long if your child is giving you a hard time. The important thing is you are together. Debbie, tell us how your playtime ended.

Debbie: I said, "We have 5 more minutes and then our playtime will be over," and she said, "Oh, I want to play some more." I didn't respond, and then when time was up, I said, "Our time is up, we can go get some cookies."

Dr. L.: Who was in charge of the ending?

Debbie: I was.

Dr. L.: Yes, as you needed to be. I would add to one thing you said. When Rachel said at the end, "Oh, I want more time," reflect her feelings. "It would be fun to have a lot more time, but you have 5 more minutes." The time is not going to change. You just show understanding, but the time is not going to change. "I know you would like to have a lot more time."

Debbie: Later she was looking at the calendar and said, "Mom, when is our next special playtime?"

Dr. L.: So the playtime is important to her already. And I can see in your face, Debbie, that you enjoyed the playtime also. Kim, tell us about your playtime.

Kim: He had a hard time settling down to one thing. He has that problem anyway, he has attention deficit, and so he has a hard time.

Dr. L.: He played with everything?

Kim: Yeah, he's never seen any of the toys before, they're all brand new. So he was just bouncing off the walls.

So I put some of the toys away, and we just sat on the floor for a while with what was left.

Dr. L.: I'm not sure what you did there. What do you mean you put the toys away?

Kim: I put them back in the box. I had stuff on the table and stuff in a chair and on the floor. I left the chair stuff alone and put the table stuff away.

Dr. L.: Why did you put the table stuff way?

Kim: Because he wouldn't calm down or anything. He was overwhelmed by everything new. He couldn't concentrate on one toy.

Dr. L.: In this special playtime, it doesn't matter.

Kim: I was afraid he was going to get the hyperactivity type thing, where he won't settle down at all. But I brought them back out once he started playing on the floor.

Dr. L.: OK. I'd like to suggest that next time you leave all the toys out, and let's see what happens. Even if he gets really hyper, it will be an opportunity for him to act that out; it will also give you an opportunity to reflect a lot more. You will have more behaviors to respond to. In the rest of his world, nobody puts things away. Right?

Kim: Oh, you mean, when he's usually playing?

Dr. L.: Yeah, out there in the other parts of his world—on the playground, nobody tries to hide stuff, to put it away. He learns to cope with it. So in the special playtime, you can allow him to cope.

Kim: Yeah, I noticed he was talking about the toys. He didn't get to play with all of them, and he wanted to. For several days, he kept talking about the toys and trying to get to the top of my closet where I put the toys. I moved the box so he wouldn't know where it was, but he really wants to get to that stuff because it's all new, it's all his.

Dr. L.: The toys must be very special to him. Was there any one toy that he spent any more time with than the other toys?

Kim: The people, he likes the people a lot.

Dr. L.: What did he do with the people?

Kim: He wanted them to eat and sleep and go up the stairs. David, my husband, made stairs in our house. There's no upstairs, but there's stairs, like there was an upstairs. And Toby's very interested in stairs.

Dr. L.: So that's important to him.

Kim: For some reason. I guess it's new. I didn't try to make him go on to the next thing; I just let him play with the people for a while. They bend and so he'd try to make them lie down and sit down.

Dr. L.: One of the things I heard you say there was you let him choose. You could have tried to encourage him to go to something else…

Kim: Because he spent so much time on that one thing.

Dr. L.: And that kind of bothered you a little bit.

Kim: Well, there's all the other stuff there.

Dr. L.: "There's all this other stuff I got for you, show your appreciation and play with all of it!"

Kim: I didn't say it though. (laughing)

Dr. L.: (to the group) But whose time is this?

Kathy: The child's.

Dr. L.: And if your child came into this room (points to toys on shelves), how many of these toys could they play with in 30 minutes? Well, some of them, but probably not all of them very much, and that would be OK. It would be OK if they tried to touch everything in here. It would be OK if they played with this one thing (picks dinosaur up) for the whole 30 minutes and didn't bother with any of the rest of this neat stuff. It's their time. I appreciate your honesty, Kim, about it bothering you a little because he didn't play with the other stuff. Your reaction is typical. We want our children to play with lots of toys and maybe our children can sense that from us sometimes: "She really does want me to play with the rest of this." But in the playtime for 30 minutes, you restrained yourself and let him…

Kim: Yeah.

Dr. L.: Did the time seem to go fast?

Kim: Oh yeah, in fact we went over the time, and I didn't know it. I let him put the sign on the door with me; he was real excited about that.

Dr. L.: That makes the playtime really important.

Kim: Yeah, because everybody else was gone.

Dr. L.: How did it end?

Kim: He didn't want to stop. I had to bribe him to do something else, so I said, "You can go out and play."

Dr. L.: Well, you can just start putting things away. We haven't talked about that, but if you have some problem with your child wanting to continue to play, and your child won't walk out of the room with you, you can just start putting things away and end it. Sonya, what was your playtime like?

Sonya: It went pretty good. When I first told her we'd be having the special playtime, as soon as we got home, she taped the appointment card to the refrigerator by herself; so we have this little crooked appointment card taped on the refrigerator. The rough part about the playtime was that about 5 minutes into it, the baby started crying, but I let her cry. She cried for about 20 minutes and went back to sleep; so that was new information to me. I usually comfort her so she will go back to sleep. I started our playtime by telling Jenny to put her stuff up in her room, and while you do that, I'll fix up for our special playtime, and she did. So I quickly got everything out, and I sat on the floor in the living room. She walked in and said, "Are these all for me?"

Dr. L.: Like Christmas Day.

Sonya: Oh yes, just like it. She was real excited, and I made a comment about that and watched her get more excited as

I said it. And then, strangely enough, she started moving all the toys to the middle of the floor, where I was. She grabbed the Play-Doh first, took it out and checked it. She mostly played with the Tinkertoys, and they weren't quite what I thought they were; they're real complicated. She would say, "Ok, Mommy, let's build." I would say, "Ok, what do you want me to do?" And she would say, "Ok, these are for you, and these are for me." But every time I asked her, "What do you want me to do?" or "Show me what you want me to do," she wouldn't tell me. She moved on to something else. The message I got was, "I like you to sit here with me and watch me play, but don't get into any of that," and that was hard. I really wanted to get into it.

Dr. L.: Playing with the toys would have been more fun for you. Let's look more closely at your child's behavior. When she said, "Do this mommy," and you said, "Show me what you want done," and then she went on to something else, wonder why a child would do that? Why wouldn't she then go on with that play?

Sonya: I don't know, just trying to get the initial contact, or wondering "Are you really paying attention to me?" or "Are you really wanting to do this?"

Dr. L.: Could it be that was an old behavior of asking you to do something, and in the past you have automatically taken over and done it? Could it be that all the time your child has wanted to go on to something else?

Sonya: Yeah. And she's started saying a lot more, "I can do it myself," and I'm thinking, "Yeah, OK, well I just wanted to help you." Like with the potty thing, "I can do it myself." I've started clicking to the fact that she really wants more independence. I really thought that I had given her that, and I saw through the play session that I do too much for her. It was hard to hold back. And then she put the Tinkertoys back in the canister one at a time! *One at a time*, and I was thinking, I'm not going to say 200 times, "I see you put another one in, and another...." The time went real fast, and when I told her, "We have 5 minutes left for special playtime, and then I'll need to put the toys away," she started putting the toys away. I wanted to tell her, "Well, no, you have 5 more minutes." I felt a little sad, like maybe she didn't want to play anymore or be with me. She started putting all the toys away, and then she told me that I needed to help her, and even though it wasn't the end of our playtime, I helped her put things away at the end. I said, "Let's go pick out a bedtime book," because our playtime is at 8:30 at night. She went off, picked her bedtime book, and after we read the story, she said, "I want to see my special playthings again." I said, "And you will, next Monday. We'll bring them out again." And she didn't say anything after that, the whole week! She didn't try to get to them. That really surprised me. I thought we'd really wrestle with that.

Dr. L.: Sounds like a really active time, and there were some things that happened that were surprising to you. As with each of you, some of the things your children do are a little surprising. And you're learning some new things about your children.

(Other parents report on their play sessions and receive feedback.)

Dr. L.: Emily, let's see the video of your session.

Emily: Oh, let's not! (group laughs)

Dr. L.: Emily, tell us what it was like to come in here and be videotaped. You're the first one to do that, and I'm sure the group would like to know what it was like for you.

Emily: I was very self-conscious for the first 5 minutes or so, and then I forgot someone was behind that two-way mirror, and that I was being videotaped.

Dr. L.: So you forgot about being videotaped, and then how did it go?

Emily: Very fast, because I walked in there thinking, "Gosh, this is going to be the longest 30 minutes of my life!" (Group laughs.) The next thing I knew, I was thinking it's time to give him a 5-minute warning.

Dr. L.: Emily, I really appreciate your courage. It takes courage to be first and courage to come in here and be videotaped. I appreciate you're doing that. Let's watch your session.

(Group watches part of Emily's videotape. Dr. Landreth stops the video frequently to point out the skills Emily is demonstrating and to give Emily encouragement.)

Dr. L.: (Stops video.) That's the second time he has put a toy back on the shelf after he played with it. Is that typical of him at home, to put things away?

Emily: His bicycle was stolen this weekend, so he's very much into putting things back where they belong. (Group laughs.)

Dr. L.: There is a reason why children do the things they do in their play. So that's really on his mind—putting things back.

(Group watches more of Emily's video.)

Dr. L.: (Stops video.) Little comments like that may not seem to be very important, but they convey a powerful message. When you said, "You're pushing that car right on top of the sand," what did that say to the child about him?

Kim: He has the ability to do it.

Sonya: You're important to me. I noticed exactly what you did. I think my Mommy is watching me, now I know for sure. I must be important.

Dr. L.: Yes, I'm important and what I'm doing is important enough for her to pay attention to it. A child cannot feel important until he is important to someone. So, Emily, you helped your child to feel important because he is important to you. And what your child is doing becomes more important because it is important to you. There is a lot to a little statement like, "You're pushing that car right on top of the sand." Emily, you look natural in this playtime and your tracking responses are well spaced. They communicate your involvement.

Kathy: It's not natural for me. I'm an overfunctioning person. I have to take responsibility for how my child feels and what he does. I kept wanting to ask questions in our playtime.

Dr. L.: So it takes effort to track what he does.

Kathy: It's very, very difficult for me.

Dr. L.: The important thing is that you did it.

Kathy: Not very well.

Dr. L.: You think you should have done it better, but the important thing is that you followed through on your commitment, and you were with your child.

Kathy: Does practice help?

Debbie: That's what I did during the week. I really did my homework before my playtime. Since we started this training, I've been practicing making tracking responses and reflective statements before the playtime.

Kim: What we're doing in here kinda seeps into everything I'm doing even though I know we're only supposed to do it in the playtime. Like with my little girl, she nags, and I've noticed when I answer the first time, she doesn't go on. I used to think she was such a nag. Now if I look at her in the face and answer her, even if I tell her what she doesn't want to hear, she will leave me alone.

Dr. L.: It's enough for her.

Sonya: Just like with the telephone and the 30-second burst of attention. I've been doing that more often. I'll say, "Excuse me, let me give Jenny about 30 seconds." My friends will say, "Oh, OK," and as soon as I give Jenny attention, she leaves. My girlfriend has started doing the same thing with her son—so it's being passed on to others.

Emily: That also works when you're not on the phone. When my husband comes home from work, he helps me in the kitchen get ready for dinner. The kids are not supposed to bother us because that is our time. Chris came in one night, and my husband and I were trying to talk, and

I said, "Let me try something." I turned around to Chris, and I said, "Ok, Chris, I can give you 30 seconds, what do you need?" I didn't take my eyes off him. He said what he needed to say, I responded to him, I said, "Your 30 seconds are up," I turned back to my husband, and Chris ran off.

Dr. L.: It worked. He got what he needed. You all give Emily some feedback on her play session. Tell her what you saw.

Sonya: You gave him your undivided attention. You were like radar. You tracked him with your total body.

Kim: I would have a hard time not suggesting he go on to something else. You allowed him to focus on just one thing, and you were great with the limit setting.

Kathy: Yes, you handled shooting with the gun really well.

Laura: Your tracking was right with him. I was bothered by my tracking because I sounded so repetitive.

Debbie: You allowed him to lead the whole time.

Laura: And he seemed comfortable leading.

Dr. L.: Good job practicing what we've been working on. Now, let's work on limit setting. There are three steps to limit setting: Step 1: A—Acknowledge your child's feeling or want; Step 2: C—Communicate the limit; and Step 3: T—Target acceptable alternatives. The limit-setting process begins when your child starts to do something that shouldn't be done, or you sense your child is about to do it, or you see it coming. Your child has a ball, and he's looking at the light. You know what he's thinking. Here's the ball and there's the light.

Sonya: So you picture what can happen.

Dr. L.: Yes, and you start by letting your child know you understand, you acknowledge your child's feeling or want or need. Maybe there's not a feeling evident. Your child has a crayon in hand and heads toward the wall, and you know he's going to mark on the wall. You would say, "I know you'd like to mark on the wall." You don't know if he's angry or sad or happy or disappointed. You just know at that moment he would like to mark on the wall. Your child has the dart gun, looks angry, points the gun toward you, and you say, "You're angry at me." You identify or acknowledge the feeling.

The second step in limit setting is to communicate the limit. Your child is headed toward the wall with a crayon and you say, "You would like to mark on the wall. The wall is not for marking on." This is what I call the educational approach. You just state what things are for or not for. "The wall is not for marking on." "You're angry at me. I'm not for shooting." You identify the feeling and then communicate the limit. The child picks up a scoop of sand and here comes the sand across the sand box. You can see what's going to happen next, the sand is about to go over the side out on the floor. You say, "Looks like you'd like to pour that out on the floor. The sand is for staying in the sandbox." Just communicate the limit.

Then the third step is something we almost never do for children. We usually set out to stop their behavior. "Stop that. Don't do that." And we stop right there, but children still have an unexpressed feeling, want, or need. The third step is to target choices. "You'd like to mark on the wall. The wall is not for marking on." Now, what would be acceptable to mark on?

Kathy: You can mark on the chalkboard.

Dr. L.: The chalkboard is for writing on or if your child has a crayon, the paper is for marking on with the crayon. Or, "I can see you are angry at me. I'm not for shooting." And then what would be acceptable?

Kathy: The stuffed animals are for shooting.

Dr. L.: When you target an acceptable alternative, it is important to point toward the acceptable choice. "You can shoot the stuffed animals," or if there's a Bobo in the play sessions, "You can pretend the Bobo is me and shoot the Bobo," and point. Or, "I'm not for shooting. The door is for shooting." You might give a couple of choices. "The sand is not for pouring on the floor. The sand is for pouring in the sandbox or in the pail or in the funnel," and point. You can remember the steps to follow by remembering to act. The three steps are: A: acknowledge the feeling, C: communicate the limit, and T: target some choices. You just act. The light's not for shooting. Now, you give me a choice.

Kim: The bean bag is for shooting.

Dr. L.: For this 30-minute playtime, we want to give children an acceptable alternative, which means we don't stop the behavior or block the expression. We let them go ahead and express it, but they learn to do it in an acceptable manner. In your kitchen, you might say, "My cabinet door is not for kicking. You can tell me you're angry." Thus, children learn to express their anger in an acceptable way.

Kathy: Is that the same as when my child says, "Shut up"?

Dr. L.: "I'm not for telling to shut up. You can tell me you don't like what I'm saying. But I'm not for saying shut up to. Those are not acceptable words to use. You can tell me you don't like what I'm saying, or you can tell me you wish you didn't have to go to school." So we always get the three steps in. Now suppose the child has the dart gun and suddenly points it at you. You may not have time to start with the first step and reflect the feeling. First, you state the limit. "I'm not for shooting." Then you can go back to, "I know you would like to shoot me. But I'm not for shooting." So you may not always be able to start with the first step and acknowledge the feeling. You may have to start with step two. Your assignment for the week is to write down one time you set a limit during your playtime with your child, if a limit was needed. Sometimes the only limit you will need to set is ending the session. Also, I want you to notice one intense feeling you experience during your play session and share that with us next week.

(Dr. L. summarizes feedback and teaching points, parents do brief role-playing, and Dr. L. makes arrangements for videotaping 1–2 parents for the following week.)

References

Bratton, S., Landreth, G., Kellam, T., & Blackard, S. (2006). Child Parent Relationship Therapy (CPRT) Treatment Manual: A 10-Session Filial Therapy Model for Training Parents. NY: Routledge.

CHAPTER 11

CPRT TRAINING SESSION 5: PLAY SESSION SKILLS REVIEW

Overview

The major focus of this session is supporting and encouraging parents as they learn and practice their new play session skills. No new material is introduced to avoid overwhelming parents. As in each of the remaining training sessions, the majority of the session is spent on parents' reports of home play sessions, with the most time allocated to reviewing the video(s) of the 1–2 parents who volunteered to be videotaped for this week's focused supervision. A specific focus during group supervision is on increasing parents' self-awareness of their own feelings, particularly in relation to their children. The therapist also uses supervision and feedback to review and reinforce previously taught CPRT principles and skills, with an emphasis on the filial play session "Dos." The partial transcript of CPRT training Session 5 included at the end of this chapter provides the reader with an illustration of how the experienced filial therapist facilitates and utilizes group dynamics to spontaneously review and reinforce basic filial play session skills, including limit setting, while providing dynamic support and encouragement to parents.

Materials

Suggested materials include: *CPRT Session 5–Treatment Outline:* parent information form with pertinent notes; homework assigned in Session 4, including extra copies of any homework worksheets; and Session 5 handouts and homework, including: *Session 5 Parent Notes & Homework, Limit Setting: A-C-T Practice Worksheet, Limit Setting: Why Use the Three Step A-C-T Method, Parent Play Session Notes*, and *Play Session Skills Checklist*. Additional materials include: display posters for both Filial Play Session Dos and Don'ts, Play Session Procedure Checklist, and optional demonstration video clips to review and reinforce basic CPRT skills.

> *Note: All handouts listed above, as well as a training session outline for the therapist, additional supplemental parent handouts, and resources for this training session are found in the* CPRT Treatment Manual *and accompanying CD-ROM, available from the publisher, Routledge.*

Content and Procedure

The therapist begins the session by asking parents to briefly share how their week has been. With so much information and activity packed into each CPRT training session, therapists may be inclined to dispense with this informal sharing time. This activity is not to be underestimated. It is an important time for establishing rapport, building trust and safety in the group, fostering connections between the parents, and, most importantly, a time for the therapist to offer support and encouragement as parents share their struggles and failures as parents. The therapist helps parents to see that they are not alone in their child rearing by referring to or linking experiences shared by several parents. Parents who feel supported and not alone in their struggles are more likely to share openly and honestly, thus enhancing group dynamics.

Again, the therapist is encouraged to limit advice giving and to avoid suggesting that parents use the CPRT skills outside of play sessions. Although parents are generally eager to try the skills, they simply are not ready. The crucial element in parents' readiness to generalize CPRT skills to problems they are having with their child not only requires mastery of the skill, but more importantly for most parents, requires a significant shift in attitude toward their children and how they view their children's behaviors. Most parents are not ready to begin generalizing skills until around Session 8 or 9. As suggested in earlier sessions, the need to provide parents with answers, as well as parents' sidetracking on discussions of minor child-related problems, is avoided by briefly acknowledging parents, writing down their concerns, and letting parents know their concerns will be discussed later in the training. Use parents' sharing and "stories" about the week to transition to review of homework.

Review Homework

Parents were asked to be aware of one intense feeling they experienced during their play sessions with their children. Most parents have difficulty focusing on their feelings and initially may not be able to share an intense feeling. The therapist can use parents' reports of their home play sessions to reflect and point out feelings as they describe what happened. Focusing on parents' feelings is an important part of the overall strategy in CPRT training; parents who are not aware of their own feelings will not be able to identify and acknowledge their children's feelings. **The success of filial therapy training hinges on parents' ability to embrace and apply the skill of reflection of feeling.** The development of this skill also facilitates parents' beginning to trust their own instincts—a prerequisite for effective parenting. Parents are asked to share a time they used limit setting in their play sessions (if one was needed) and how it worked out. Remind parents that because they have carefully structured the time and place so that their children can have more freedom of expression, parents may need to set few limits during their play sessions. The limit of ending the play session on time is generally the most used. Be careful in presenting limit setting so that parents don't get the idea that they should be setting many limits during play sessions. Structuring play sessions so that limit setting is kept to a minimum is what is most important!

Filial Play Session Reports and Video Critique

As is true for all remaining sessions, the majority of this session is spent on supporting and encouraging parents as they report on their play sessions, with the greatest focus on giving feedback to the 1–2 parents who videotaped their play sessions. The specific goal for this session is to review and reinforce all CPRT skills taught in Sessions 1–4. **No new skills are introduced during Session 5**—parents need time to focus on the basic skills introduced in the first four sessions without being overwhelmed with new information. The therapist listens carefully for opportunities to point out parents' strengths and examples of when parents are using the basic CPRT skills taught thus far. Remember to model **"Focus on the donut, not the hole."** The focus in this session is on what parents are doing right, not what they should do differently.

Displaying the Filial Play Session Dos and Don'ts on a poster for parents and therapist to refer to as parents report on their home play sessions aids in the review and reinforcement of CPRT skills. After each parent briefly reports on the home play session, the therapist can ask other parents to point out one "Do" they heard used. Allow plenty of time for viewing the videotaped play sessions. This activity provides the richest learning experience for all parents and greater opportunities for vicarious learning than when parents report orally on their home play sessions. The therapist can use the supervision of videotaped play sessions to introduce the *Play Session Skills Checklist* that parents are asked to complete at home the next week after their play sessions. Pass out extra copies, briefly explain how to use them, and ask parents to use the form to note their observations of CPRT skills demonstrated during the viewing of videotaped play sessions. Stop the video frequently and facilitate a discussion of play session skills demonstrated, showing parents how you would use the checklist to note your observations.

Insuring that at least one parent brings a video to class is imperative; therefore, we suggest that parents scheduled for videotaping come to the therapist's playroom to do so. The therapist can keep the videotape to cue up for the next CPRT training session. Again, it cannot be overstated that **weekly supervision of the videotaped sessions, along with the dynamics of group interaction, are crucial elements in the success of the CPRT training**.

Limit Setting Review, Video, and Role-Play

Although all CPRT skills are reviewed in Session 5, typically the concept and application of limit setting is an area that most parents struggle with; therefore, review and demonstration of this skill is crucial. The therapist can show another video clip demonstration of limit setting and then ask parents to role-play, following up with a homework assignment to complete a limit-setting worksheet in which parents are given limit-setting scenarios to respond to. Parents often struggle with stating limits in a concise way. This can be a good time to introduce a new **Rule of Thumb: If you can't say it in 10 words or less, don't say it** (although when the therapist teaches the skill of choice giving, this rule is broken). Parents have a tendency to overexplain to children, with the result that their message gets lost in the words. "The doll's head is not for pulling off" can be understood by a child, but adding a long explanation about the cost of the doll can distract a child from hearing the limit. Parents are also asked to write down one limit set during their next play sessions (again, if one was needed), noting what happened, what they said, and how their children responded. Of all skills taught, parents are most eager to try limit setting outside of play sessions before they have mastered it. Remind parents again that, at this point in their training, **they are only to practice these skills during the 30-minute special play session**. The therapist's primary training strategy throughout the 10 sessions is to structure training and experiences to maximize parents' successes. Allow 10-15 minutes for role-play to practice limit setting before reviewing homework for the next week.

Homework Assignments

1. Parents are reminded of the importance of conducting their play sessions at the same time and same place.
2. Remind parents to take a few minutes to review the *Play Session Dos & Don'ts* and *Play Session Procedures Checklist* prior to their play sessions.
3. Remind parents to practice setting a limit during their play sessions, if needed, and to write down what happened and what they said. They are also reminded to complete the limit-setting practice worksheet.
4. Parents are reminded after conducting the play session to complete the *Parent Play Session Notes* and *Play Session Skills Checklist* and bring to group the next week.
5. One to two parents are scheduled for videotaping.
6. Remind parents about the Rule of Thumb for the week.

7. Close by introducing Sandwich Hugs and Sandwich Kisses (explained in the partial transcript at the end of this chapter) and ask parents to give each of their children a Sandwich Hug and Sandwich Kiss during the week (not during the special playtime). This type of assignment is designed to meet the CPRT training goals of helping parents rediscover the joys of parenting and helping families build warm, happy memories. The authors can both attest to the effectiveness of Sandwich Hugs and Kisses, as both have grown children who still get Sandwich Hugs and Kisses on occasion and who are now passing this practice to the next generation.

Partial Transcript of CPRT Session 5

Dr. L.: What has the week been like for you?

Sonya: My kids are really good kids, but my problem is trying to do everything by myself. Taking kids to school, fixing meals, baths, running errands, putting kids to bed. My youngest is still at home, and tomorrow it starts all over again. My children are still at the age that they're still pretty needy. Beth and Jenny can feed themselves, but they can't give themselves a bath. Sometimes I get overwhelmed.

Dr. L.: So if something's going to be done, it's up to you. That sounds pretty stressful.

Sonya: I think I handle it pretty well.

Dr. L.: You're always on call even when you're overwhelmed.

Sonya: And if any emergency comes up or one of the kids is sick, I'm the one who stays up with the kid at night. I'm the one who has to make it through the next day. It's hard even when things go smoothly.

Dr. L.: Even at the best of times it's stressful and overwhelming when things go wrong.

Sonya: Yes.

(Other parents report on their week.)

Dr. L.: One of your assignments was to be aware of one intense feeling you experienced in your playtime this week. What were you aware of feeling during your playtime?

Sonya: I felt really irritated and kind of rejected because my daughter played and played and didn't once invite me to play with her.

Dr. L.: So you were a little angry with her for not including you. Anyone react to that?

Laura: I'm learning to hold myself back so I won't interfere with my son's play to make it be what I want it to be.

Sonya: Yeah, I know I have a problem needing to be included in everything so I will feel better about myself.

Dr. L.: Laura, sounds like you and Sonya are both beginning to become aware of some of your own needs. That's great progress. Sonya, for 30 minutes you are giving your daughter a very special gift: your attention, your understanding, your caring. Anyone else experience an intense feeling during your playtime?

Kim: When my son pointed the dart gun at the two-way mirror, I was really afraid he was going to shoot it even though I set the limit. I was thinking, "Oh, gosh, now what am I going to do?"

Dr. L.: So you were anxious about what might happen, that he would do something he wasn't suppose to do. What did happen?

Kim: He didn't shoot the mirror. He just aimed the gun at the mirror for the longest time and then shot one of the dolls even though I had told him he could shoot the Bobo like you told us to do.

Dr. L.: He stopped himself. That's called self-control. Your response helped him to control himself.

(Other parents describe an intense feeling.)

Dr. L.: Nita, what was your special playtime like this week?

Nita: Jeff was *real* sick. And when he's real sick, he's very aggressive, very unhappy. I felt terrible, too, that day. In the evenings, I have lots of pain (she is pregnant), unless I have more control of my day, but I hadn't had any control of my day; so I was feeling lousy. He was *really* feeling lousy. He was just totally disorganized.

Dr. L.: You did the session anyway, even though you felt crummy.

Nita: Yeah, because I just knew there really wasn't another time. We had so much trouble the past 2 weeks with him coming down with this for a week, and then getting over it for a week. We ended up averaging maybe 5-6 hours of sleep out of 24 for 2 weeks.

Dr. L.: (to group) I want to tell all of you that one of the things I am reacting to is your commitment. Laura, you didn't want to have your playtime, but you did it anyway. Kathy, you had that terrible no-good happening, but you had your playtime anyway. Nita, you felt crummy, you didn't want to, but you did it anyway. That says commitment! I am really impressed with your commitment; I don't know if you would use that word to describe yourselves, but I hear commitment from each one of you. So, Nita, how'd it work out?

Nita: At the time, I didn't think it was working out at all because he kept trying to do things that he obviously knew he wasn't supposed to do.

Dr. L.: So he did some testing.

Nita: Oh yes, but he didn't just throw terrific fits or anything, like he usually does. He was too sick and too tired. He was pretty quiet and disorganized, but then he said what he's been saying for the past 2 weeks, "Mommy, I *need* you." I said, "Well what do you need me to do?" He climbed into my lap, and we just sat there. He didn't want me to say anything; he didn't want me to touch his hair; he just wanted to sit.

Dr. L.: He just wanted to be there, sitting in your lap. Sounds like a contented time in your lap.

Nita: And then finally he did get up and play.

Dr. L.: Let's talk about that just a minute. Whose time is this?

Sonya: His.

Dr. L.: He did what he wanted to do. You bought all these special toys, and your child chose to sit in your lap, that's what's important to him. It says that's more important right now than playing with a whole lot of new toys.

Sonya: Wow.

Dr. L.: What are you reacting to?

Sonya: Well, that's pretty special. To think that your kid would want to be with you a lot more than play with all these new things. He would rather just lie on you.

Dr. L.: It's also special that he got to sit in your lap and have all of you right then, even though you started out feeling crummy and would rather not have done this.

Nita: Definitely. That's really how we spent most of our time, him sitting in my lap. He did say, "I'm going to go get a book." I said, "No, we're playing with our special play toys," and then he just settled back down and just sat some more. And then he played with the Band-Aids. He'd go though a box of Band-Aids an hour if I let him. He had a lot of boo-boos, and he knew mommy had a lot of boo-boos, so he went through a box of Band-Aids.

Dr. L.: Folks, I'm sorry I didn't think to tell you ahead of time: when you buy a box of Band-Aids, take all the Band-Aids out of the box except five. Then your child can use *all of them!* There's something about using all of something that is satisfying to a child, and they're just as satisfied to use 5 Band-Aids as to use 50!

Debbie: What is the deal about Band-Aids?

Dr. L.: They are wonderful cures! It's a way to make things well, and your child evidently used a bunch on you, Nita.

Nita: Oh, yes. Well I'd been talking to him lately, in the evenings, about how I can't do a three-ring circus every evening.

I haven't been able to since before Christmas. So I tell him that Mommy has pains, doesn't feel good, and that it will soon be over. So he's aware, and he plasters both of us with Band-Aids.

Dr. L.: He was sensitive to your pain and nurtured you. (addresses group) Could I suggest that in the 30-minute playtime, you all change the "Mommy" to "me," to "I"? "I don't feel good," instead of "Mommy doesn't feel good." I've heard two or three of you say, "Mommy." Change that during the playtime to "I." Let's personalize it, "I."

Debbie: I know you think I keep picking, but why can't you say, "Mommy?"

Dr. L.: It's like you're talking about someone else.

Debbie: So, it personalizes it more, makes it more real.

Dr. L.: Debbie, I continue to be struck by the fact that you have the answers. You just don't trust them.

Debbie: No, I don't.

Dr. L.: I wish I had a magic wand. I would walk over, touch you on the head and say, "Now, trust the answers you have."

Sonya: I like your questions because it always feels good when you get clarification. It confirms things for me, too.

Dr. L.: Behind your questions, you have the answers.

Debbie: I just want to know if I have the answers.

Dr. L.: And I would like to give you permission with this magic wand to trust yourself. I don't have all the answers for you all. I can help you structure your special playtimes, but you're the real key, and the most important thing is that you trust what you are doing. Your child will sense when you trust yourself, and when you trust yourself, then you can trust your child more. Nita, how did your playtime end?

Nita: I told him we had 3 minutes left, and he totally and completely fell apart, screaming.

Dr. L.: Because he wanted more?

Nita: Because he wanted me, and he thought once it was over he wouldn't have me at all. Finally, I had to pick him up and carry him into his room and start telling him a story.

Dr. L.: You handled it. Did it work out, did he calm down?

Nita: Yes, once I told him his favorite story, he settled down. Somehow, I knew it was just the issue of needing me.

Dr. L.: He's very vulnerable right now. Someone else is about to take his place and that can be scary to a child. The important thing is that you are understanding of how he feels.

Nita: It just occurred to me that Jeff's wanting to sit on my lap so much lately is because I can't get down on the floor and be close to him like I used to do. Actually, I have been concerned about him wanting to sit on my lap so much.

Laura: He wants to be close to you, especially when he is crying. He feels closer, more secure.

Dr. L.: So, Nita, you learned something about Jeff.

(Parents report on their play sessions and receive feedback.)

Kathy: Cody put the handcuffs on me and I told him I hoped we got the handcuffs off. He was wanting to take them off and I didn't know he could. So I took them off.

Dr. L.: I heard you say also, "I don't think you can."

Kathy: Maybe I shouldn't have done that.

Dr. L.: Did you know he couldn't?

Kathy: No, I didn't know for sure that he couldn't, but…

Dr. L.: Therefore, you let your child try. And then it's his decision about whether or not he figures out that he can't take them off. You give him credit. In that way, he gets to feel powerful in a more positive way, because it seems to me he's wanting to feel powerful, to push you around, make you say things. Maybe that's not so good. He can feel powerful by doing something constructive. He figures out how to take the handcuffs off, and then he hears a self-esteem–building response from you, and he feels powerful in a more positive way. Kim, you videotaped your play session. Tell us what it was like for you before we see it.

Kim: It was kinda tense, but okay. I didn't know what to do. I just tried to do what we've been doing here. My son really enjoyed himself, but he did stuff we haven't talked about yet, and my reaction was "What do I do now?" I didn't want to stifle his play; so he did a lot of things he wouldn't normally do.

Dr. L.: Okay. Let's see your play session.

(Group watches video.)

Dr. L.: (Stops video.) Kim, I noticed that you said a lot with your eyes. You are so in tune with your child. As your child looked up on the top of that shelf, his eyes went up, and I saw your eyes go up. You were looking at what your child was looking at. A parent cannot be any more involved than that, to notice what your child notices. The message there is that you are completely involved with your child. Children know when you are that involved. Just as you said earlier, Debbie, your child senses when you're sure and senses when you're not sure. Our children sense when we're with them and understanding them, and they sense when we're not paying attention. Kim, that was a very powerful message you communicated with your eyes.

(Group watches video.)

Dr. L.: (Stops video.)

Sonya: That's exactly what Jenny does in our special playtime. She will say, "Mommy, I want you to do this or that," and as soon as I say, "What do you want me to do?" she goes on to something else.

Kim: Yes, he drops it and plays with something else every time.

Dr. L.: What does that mean?

Sonya: He's saying, "I just want you to sit there and watch me."

Dr. L.: Yes, that's enough.

Sonya: It kinda hurt my feelings when she first started doing that, because I really wanted to play.

Dr. L.: You felt left out, as though your child didn't want to include or didn't care about you.

Sonya: Yes, but I know she really does.

Dr. L.: So you have to watch out for your need to be needed.

(Group watches video.)

Dr. L.: (Stops video.) Kim, before we started watching your session, you said there were some parts that didn't seem to go very well, and I'm sitting here hearing some great responses.

Kim: I'm really nervous.

Dr. L.: Even though you're nervous, I was thinking that you're doing so well. I wondered if there might be a message in that for all of us.

Kathy: You don't give yourself enough credit.

Dr. L.: You got it. You don't give yourself enough credit for what you are doing. Debbie, you said that earlier, too, that you're smarter than you give yourself credit for. And you all do a better job than you give yourselves credit for. It's just that sometimes it doesn't feel very easy, or very comfortable, but you're doing a really great job, Kim, responding to your child in this session.

Sonya: I think there's something else going on there, too, Kim. You put what was going on inside you aside so you could be there for him. And you came across as being genuinely interested in him.

Kim: Yes, I knew he was having fun.

(Group watches video.)

Dr. L.: (Stops video.) Kim, you look comfortable. You might make one change there. You turned a great statement into a question, "You're taking the doll's clothes off?" The tone of voice turns it into a question and implies you don't understand. That really makes a difference. We want to let our children know that we understand, and you do that by making statements.

(Replays segment so group hears the question. Group watches video.)

Dr. L.: (Stops video.)

Kathy: Now I got it.

Dr. L.: What do you all see right there?

Debbie: I see he's happy.

Dr. L.: Yes, "You look happy." "You sounded happy." You can begin to add to your reflection of what your child does and what your child says by stating some of your observations. "You really look happy." "Wow, you sound happy," because of the joyful noises you hear. He really does look happy.

Dr. L.: Kim, let's see more of your session.

(Group watches video.)

Dr. L.: (Stops video.) What just happened there, Kim?

(Group laughs.)

Kim: I just reached out and fixed his shirt.

Dr. L.: It's an unconscious thing. Parents reach out and do things for their children. Things should be in their place, and a shirt should be pulled down. Perhaps more than we realize, we reach out and do things for children, and the message is "You're supposed to be neat."

Sonya: Kim looked so interested in everything.

Dr. L.: What feedback do you want to give, Debbie?

Debbie: You tracked him not only physically, but verbally and with your eyes. What impressed me the most was the look on your face as you watched him. If I were your child, I would know that you cared about me, that you love me. You looked like you cared, and it was genuine.

Dr. L.: Yes, having someone focus entirely on you, for even a few minutes, can be powerful. Well, let's shift focus and do some review of last week. Last week we worked on limit setting. If those of you who were here last week will tell what you remember about limit setting, that will help the parents who were absent last week to learn it.

Sonya: ACT—he gave us an acronym, and A means acknowledging the feeling or the want of the child. Like, I know you want to hit your sister. C was communicate the limit. Your sister's not for hitting. T is target the choices. You may hit your stuffed animals.

(Parents continue to discuss what they learned last week about limit setting, but it is obvious they are struggling with understanding and believing in the concept.)

Dr. L.: Why don't we watch a parent playtime as a way to review the A-C-T method. The child in the video is 2 ½. Most of you are probably thinking, no way a 2 ½ year-old can understand and respond to this way of limit setting.

(Parents laugh, then Dr.L. starts video. A partial transcript of the video is included here because it provides such a dramatic example of a child's inner struggle and the effectiveness of the A-C-T model, even with a child this young.)

Child: (Gets a cup from the kitchen and walks to the sink.)

Mom: Kristin, we have 5 more minutes in the playtime today and then it will be time to go.

Child: (Fills the cup with water from the sink faucet.) Five?

Mom: We have 5 more minutes, and then we need to go.

Child: (Walks to sandbox and pours water from the cup into sand.)

Mom: (While child is pouring water in the sandbox) One cup of water…

Child: (Child walks back to sink and fills cup with water, walks to sandbox and pours water in the box.) Two…

Mom: Two…you're counting…you poured that slowly. I heard it make a noise.

Child: (Goes back to sink again and fills cup a third time, then walks back to sandbox and pours water into sandbox. She looks very absorbed in her play.)

Mom: Three… you poured three cups of water in the sand.

Child: Just one more. (Child walks back to sink and fills cup with water.)

Mom: I know you would like to pour more water in the sandbox, but you have already put three in and that is all. (Standard rule in the playroom: only three containers of water allowed to be poured in the sandbox.)

Child: (Walks to sandbox with a cup full of water and starts to pour water in the box.)

Mom: Kristin, in here the sandbox can only have three cups of water, and you have already put three. No more water can go into the sandbox. (Mother leans toward the child and shows "three" with her fingers. She gives lots of nonverbal signs to Kristin. Her voice is firmer. Child stands in front of sandbox. She is about to pour more water, but listens to her mother.) I know you really want to put more water in.

Child: OK. (She stops herself.)

Mom: But you can pretend.

Child: I just…

Mom: You can pour that water into the sink. That water can't go in the sandbox 'cause you already put three in. You can pour that water into the sink.

Child: (Seems to be struggling with the idea of pouring more water in the sandbox. She tilts the cup a little bit, trying to pour water in the sandbox.)

Mom: Kristin, I know you really want to pour that water in the sandbox, but it is not for pouring in the sandbox. You may pour that water into the sink. You already put three cups of water, and that's all the sand can have.

Child: (Is still struggling. She tilts the cup forward more and some water dribbles into the sandbox.)

Mom: I see you pouring water. (Child pours a bit more.) Kristin, that water is not for pouring into the sandbox (said in a patient, but firm tone).

Child: I just put little bit…

Mom: I know you just really want to put a little bit in the sandbox.

Child: (Walks back to sink and dumps rest of water into sink.)

Mom: Now, you poured it into the sink.

Child: No more….

Mom: The sink is the place where you can pour that water.

Child: (Plays with water in sink.) I just pour out…cup…so I can…put this in it.

Mom: So you are getting more water in the cup and pouring it in the sink.

Child: Right there!!!

Mom: Right there!!!

Child: (Continues playing at the sink with water running.) Look at me. (She turns to her mother.)

Mom: I heard that! It went right down that drain. Oh…you're being careful…put it right in the drain….

Child: Some of it out.

Mom: Some of it out. That's where you want it to go.

Child: Two…

Mom: Mm-hmm.

Child: Three…

Mom: Three…

Child: Four…Five!

Mom: You counted to five!

Child: I want to put sand in it…(Stated in an unclear way. Child walks to sandbox and looks at mother to tell what she wants)…I want to put sand in…the sink…(Points toward sink.)

Mom: You want to do what?

Child: Put sand in the sink. (Child begins to scoop sand into cup.)

Mom: Oh, you want to put the sand in the sink. The sand is not for putting in the sink. The sand is for staying in the sandbox. You can play with the sand in the sandbox. You can put it in the pail or in the container…there are lots of places you can put the sand.

Child: (Grabs two hands full of sand and heads for the sink.)

Mom: Kristin, I know you really want to put the sand in the sink, but it's not for putting in the sink.

Child: I only…(Mumbling…Child turns, walks to sandbox, and puts most of sand back into sandbox.)

Mom: The sand is for staying in the sandbox. (The mother stands up to give a sign of ending the session.) Our time is up for today.

Child: I wash my hands…

Mom: You decided to wash your hands.

(Dr. L. stops tape—end of viewing mother/child play session.)

Dr. L: You see this child struggle with wanting to pour more water into the sand. She hears her mom's calm statements indicating the rule of three containers of water in the sandbox, but she still wants to pour more water. The result is a graphic example of the age-old inner battle between doing what the child wants to do and knowing that is not appropriate. This 2 ½-year-old's struggle demonstrates the effectiveness of the A-C-T model of therapeutic limit setting in returning responsibility to the child to bring self under control and to say "No" to self. Yes, the child did dribble a bit of extra water into the sand, but did control her inner urge, walked to the sink and poured the remaining water into the sink. If a 2 ½-year-old child can bring herself under control in response to the A-C-T model of therapeutic limit setting, then surely older children will even more easily respond in like manner. I'm not saying it's easy or always works, but with patience and persistence in using A-C-T, children can learn to control themselves.

Kim: So it's really not discipline during the playtime, it's just about putting limits on your child's behavior.

Dr. L.: Well, it actually is discipline. It's a different way of disciplining. In this kind of limit setting, you're teaching your child to say "No" to self. If I say, "The wall is not for marking on, the paper is for marking on," and the child stops himself or herself, who made the child stop?

Sonya: The child did.

Debbie: And it would work later when they get angry, instead of abusing someone.

Sonya: Yeah, you can't keep spanking them forever.

Dr. L.: At some point they have to learn to stop themselves, and now is the time to teach them that. It's called self-control.

Sonya: I got spanked until I was 15, and it didn't work. I left home and never went back. I don't believe in any type of physical discipline at all. I remember when I was a kid, I was mad. I was hurt. I didn't learn anything except that you shouldn't get caught. I seemed to spend my whole childhood trying to figure out "What do you want me to do? What is okay to do?" because nobody said what was okay. I just knew I couldn't get caught doing that.

Dr. L.: When we take responsibility for stopping our children from doing something, then we deprive them of the experience of learning how to stop themselves. So when we set a limit by saying, "I'm not for shooting, that's for shooting," the child is responsible because he is in a position to choose.

Kim: So does discipline follow if it doesn't work, or do you start all over again with acknowledging the feeling?

Dr. L.: That's a good question. There is a Step 4, but you go through the A-C-T steps several times first. Let's review those steps. What is the first step?

Sonya: Acknowledge the feeling.

Dr. L.: Yes. We always start by reflecting the child's feeling or want. "You're angry at me." And the second step?

Laura: Communicate the limit.

Dr. L.: Yes, set the limit. "You're angry at me. I'm not for shooting." And the third step?

Nita: That's the hard one; target an alternative.

Dr. L.: Yes, target an acceptable alternative, something the child can do. "You're angry at me. I'm not for shooting. You can shoot the Bobo." If you go through these three steps several times, and your child continues to try to shoot you with the dart gun, Step 4 is: "If you choose to keep trying to shoot me, you choose not to play with the gun for the rest of our playtime. If you choose not to shoot me, you choose to get to play with the gun." Or, "If you choose to keep trying to mark on the table, then you choose not to play with the crayons for the rest of our playtime. If you choose not to mark on the table, you choose to get to play with the crayons."

Kim: Then they made the decision.

Dr. L.: Yes. We'll work more on giving choices next week. Now, let's work some more on limit setting. Turn to the person next to you. One of you can be the child first. Use the toys and do something children might do to break the limit. Pretend you're going to break the toys, or pretend you're going to splash paint and let your parent practice setting limits.

(Parents role-play.)

Dr. L.: Okay, folks. Everybody stop. It is really important when targeting a choice to always point toward the choice. Sonya, role-play with me. You're the child and you start banging with that wood hammer. "I know you'd like to bang on that, but that's not for banging on. The wood over there," and you point, "is for banging on with that."

Sonya: And inside I'm feeling, "Oh, okay, I do get to do it."

Debbie: But there's a delay time, because I'm not sure what to say.

Dr. L.: That's okay. The words will come to you faster later. This is like learning a foreign language. The first few times you do this, you're going to feel tongue-tied. You may blurt out some old commands.

Sonya: Don't do that!

Dr. L.: Yes. You will sometimes go back to the old behaviors. But in this special 30-minute playtime, you try to contain that urge and go through the steps of limit setting. Now, let's switch roles.

(Parents role-play.)

Dr. L.: Okay, folks, time to stop for today. You have an assignment for next Monday to come back and report on one limit you set during your play session. Write down what happened, and what you said, and how your child responded. Next Monday, I'll share with you my Oreo Cookie Theory about choice giving. There are other ways to give choices. Who can come to the center this week and videotape your play session?

Sonya: I can.

Dr. L.: Thanks. Okay. I have one more really important homework assignment for all of you to do with your child and another family member. You do this sometime other than your play session—and you do this with all your children. It's called a **Sandwich Hug**. It looks like this. (Dr. L. gets up to demonstrate.) You and your husband get on either side of your child (pick your child up if she is little), and you say (playfully), "We're going to make a sandwich hug, you're going to be the peanut butter (or whatever sandwich child likes best) and we're going to be the bread." Then you give your child a big physical, noisy hug, "ummm—ummm!" (The noise is very important—children love that!) Be sure and give each of your children one. Older children may be a little resistant; adapt how you present it to fit their age. Then another time in the week, let your child know that you learned another funny assignment in this class that you are taking and it is called a **Sandwich Kiss**. (Dr L. demonstrates a sandwich kiss by taking his fists and putting them up to his own cheeks and pushing in while making a big kissing noise) "Ummm—smack!" (He reminds the parents again that making a really loud kissing noise is very important, and that parents are to do this with each child in the family.)

References

Bratton, S., Landreth, G., Kellam, T., & Blackard, S. (2006). Child Parent Relationship Therapy (CPRT) Treatment Manual: A 10-Session Filial Therapy Model for Training Parents. NY: Routledge.

CHAPTER 12

CPRT TRAINING SESSION 6: SUPERVISION AND CHOICE GIVING

Overview

Sessions 6 through 9 follow the same general format, with the main focus on supervision of home play sessions; therefore, this section provides a comprehensive overview of the critical elements shared by these four sessions. Each session begins with 10 to 15 minutes of parents' informal sharing about their week, followed by a discussion of homework assignments and brief reporting by all parents about their play sessions. The therapist provides suggestions and points out CPRT skills demonstrated as parents describe play session happenings, attending carefully to feelings expressed by parents. Greater attention is given to common problems parents are experiencing. The partial transcript included with each training session provides the reader with a dynamic example of group process.

As parents report on their play sessions, the therapist has two primary tasks: to find something to encourage in each parent, and to use parents' comments to reinforce the basic CPRT therapy principles and guidelines covered thus far. The therapist may find it helpful to continue to display a poster with the *Filial Play Session*

Dos and Don'ts for parents to refer to during play session reporting. For example, the therapist can ask the parent to talk about one "Do" they felt they did well and pick one "Do" they want to work on in their next play session.

An essential element in Sessions 6 through 9 is the weekly viewing and critique of 1–2 parent videos; therefore, it is imperative that the therapist take necessary measures to ensure that at least 1 parent comes to class with a videotaped play session. (In rare cases where a parent cannot or has not taped a session, a live parent–child session can be observed by the therapist and group, with the parent receiving immediate feedback.) An objective is that each parent will be videotaped and receive focused feedback at least once, and hopefully twice, during the 10 sessions of training. Weekly supervision of videotaped sessions, along with the accompanying dynamics of group interaction and various learning experiences that naturally occur, is a powerful process and the cornerstone to the success of CPRT training. An invaluable part of the learning process occurs when parents begin to recognize the basic "Dos" and "Don'ts" demonstrated and/or reported during supervision and are able to give constructive feedback to each other.

Taking the time to process parents' feelings as they arise is especially important and models for parents what you are asking them to do with their children: focus on feelings. Again, the therapist's skillful balance between the teaching content and supporting parents is critical to the success of CPRT training—this skill cannot be overemphasized. The therapist helps parents to see that they are not alone in their child-rearing struggles by linking experiences shared by several parents. Reviewing and role-playing of play session principles and skills are continued each session. As parents spontaneously begin to share happenings outside the play session that in any small way indicate generalization of CPRT skills, the therapist quickly acknowledges the newly developed coping strategy, with the aim of encouraging, empowering, and enhancing parental confidence. Enhancing feelings of parental efficacy, along with building self-esteem and self-confidence, is a primary aim for the therapist, just as a primary aim for parents in Sessions 6 through 9 is to actively respond to their children in ways that encourage and build their children's self-esteem.

As successful use of CPRT skills outside the play sessions naturally occurs (around Session 8 to 9), the therapist can begin to add homework assignments that encourage generalization of skills; for example, by giving parents an assignment to practice making a therapeutic limit-setting response to a typical happening outside the play session. As is true for all homework assignments, be specific in what you want parents to *write down* and report on the next week; and then, make sure to take a few minutes at the beginning of the next session for parents to share homework results.

Parents' growing confidence in themselves and the use of their newly acquired skills becomes evident in their interactions during the group supervision and feedback time in each session. Generally by the eighth session, parents begin to volunteer comments on changes they see in themselves, in their children, and in other parents in the group. The therapist takes this cue as an opportunity to facilitate parents' growth and learning to a higher level by asking them to give each other feedback as they watch and listen to each other's play sessions. Essentially, the therapist is moving parents into the role of peer-supervisors and helping them become more self-aware, with a goal of moving toward self-monitoring skills by Session 10.

In Sessions 6 though 8, the therapist continues to acknowledge parental concerns about long-term and crisis-related child problems not related to the special playtimes by listening and writing down concerns as they are expressed, but typically these issues aren't addressed until Sessions 9 and 10. As is true in all sessions, the inevitable sidetracking on discussions of minor child-related problems is carefully avoided by the therapist acknowledging the parent briefly with a word, but refocusing the discussion to the point at hand. In limited cases of some minor child-related problems, a brief suggestion might be offered but is not explained in a prolonged discussion.

The importance of consistency is emphasized over and over: consistency in holding play sessions, consistency in limit setting, consistency in daily routines, etc. The importance of consistency in conducting home play sessions at the same time and place each week is emphasized throughout, even if the child asks for changes and/or it would be more convenient for the parent to change the time. Parents often have great difficulty grasping the importance of consistency and predictability in children's lives. Continually remind parents that for children, **parental consistency → predictability → security → child feeling safe and loved!** At the end of each session, the therapist gives reminders about homework for the next week and schedules 1–2 more parents to be videotaped for the following week's focused supervision.

Although all essential teaching points and skills needed to conduct successful play sessions are covered in Sessions 1 through 5, new, but related, topics and homework are introduced in Sessions 6 through 9 to help solidify parents' learning and generalize their new skills to everyday happenings. The therapist can be flexible in introducing new topics and assigning homework according to the needs of the group. Specific to training Session 6, choice giving is the only new topic introduced.

> Reminder: As is true for all sessions, **avoid overwhelming parents with too much information or homework. Rule of Thumb for the successful filial therapist leader: Leave parents with no more than three or four main points or assignments to focus on between sessions**.

Materials

Suggested materials include: *CPRT Session 6–Treatment Outline;* parent information form with pertinent notes; homework assigned in Session 5, including extra copies of any homework worksheets; and Session 6 handouts and homework, including: *Session 6 Parent Notes & Homework*; *Choice Giving 101: Teaching Responsibility and Advanced Choice Giving: Providing Choices as Consequences, Practice Choice-Giving Worksheet*; *Parent Play Session Notes*; and *Play Session Skills Checklist.* Additional materials include: a display poster of *Play Session Dos & Don'ts, Choices, Cookies, and Kids* video by Garry Landreth *(see CPRT Treatment Manual)* to demonstrate choice-giving method of discipline, and optional video clip demonstrating filial play session skills focused on self-esteem–building responses and responses that return responsibility to the child. The therapist may also find it helpful to make a list of common problems often experienced by parents during play sessions to facilitate a discussion on challenging issues (refer to Chapter 18).

Note: All handouts listed above, as well as a training session outline for the filial therapist, additional supplemental parent handouts, and resources for this training session are found in the CPRT Treatment Manual *and accompanying CD-ROM, available from the publisher, Routledge.*

Content and Procedure

As explained in the overview, the major focus of training Session 6, as well as all remaining sessions, is supporting and encouraging parents' skill development and confidence through group supervision and feedback as parents report on their play sessions; thus, the majority of the allotted time is devoted to this activity. As in all previous sessions, the initial informal sharing time is used to support parents and forge connections, while shifting the focus to a review of homework. Parents are first asked to share their experiences with giving their children Sandwich Hugs and Sandwiches Kisses, followed by a discussion and practice of limit setting using either oral or written examples (use homework practice worksheet, if assigned). As parents report on their play session experiences, they are each asked to describe any limits set during play sessions. In addition, parents are each asked to discuss one thing they thought they did well and one skill they want to focus on in their next play sessions.

The **Rule of Thumb, "Grant in fantasy what you cannot grant in reality,"** is introduced to help parents understand the value of children's role-playing of behaviors during play sessions that would be unacceptable outside of the play sessions. For example, 3-year-old Margaret has a new baby sister and is naturally feeling a little jealous. During her play session, she takes the baby doll and throws her out of the play area. A helpful parent response would be, "You just didn't want the baby to be in here," or "You decided to just throw the baby over there." However, parents are generally disturbed by this kind of behavior, believing that if they accept this behavior during the session that their child will think it is permissible outside of session. The same is true of any aggressive or regressive play behaviors; therefore, the therapist must be careful to explain this concept in a way that parents can understand. The only new concept/skill introduced in this session is choice giving.

Choice Giving

The concept of giving children choices is introduced to build on the principles of limit setting focused on in Sessions 4 and 5 and as a strategy for empowering children to make decisions and avoid power struggles outside of play sessions. Emphasize to parents that choices given must be commensurate with a child's developmental stage.

RULE OF THUMB:

Big choices for big kids, little choices for little kids.

The skill of choice giving is most easily grasped by parents through demonstration and providing opportunities for practice. The *Choices, Cookies, and Kids* video by Garry Landreth is shown to clearly illustrate both the concept and the skill of choice giving. The video is approximately 30 minutes in length and should be previewed prior to use. Because of time constraints, the therapist may want to show part of the video during Session 6 and the remainder during Session 7. The Oreo Cookie Theory of choice giving is covered approximately 6 minutes into the video and should be covered during Session 6, even if time restricts a viewing of the full tape. Parents are provided with the handouts, *Choice Giving 101: Teaching Responsibility, & Decision Making* and *Advanced Choice-Giving: Providing Choices as Consequences*. The therapist reviews the following information from the handouts, clarifying the difference between choice giving to empower children and choice giving as a method of discipline. It is important to cover all the information in Choice Giving 101. Advanced Choice-Giving can be covered as time allows in Session 6, and completed in Session 7.

Choice Giving 101: Teaching Self-Control, Responsibility, and Decision Making

Providing children with age-appropriate choices empowers children by allowing them a measure of control over their circumstances. Children who feel more empowered and "in control" are more capable of regulating their own behavior, a prerequisite for self-control. Choices require that children tap into their inner resources, rather than relying on parents (external resource) to stop their behavior or solve the problem for them. If parents always intervene, children learn that "Mom or Dad will stop me if I get out of hand" or "Mom or Dad will figure out a solution if I get in a jam."

Presenting children with choices provides opportunities for decision making and problem solving. Through practice with choice making, children learn to accept responsibility for their choices and actions and learn that they are competent and capable. Choice giving facilitates the development of the child's conscience; as children are allowed to learn from their mistakes, they learn to weigh decisions based on possible consequences.

Providing children with choices reduces power struggles between parent and child—and importantly, preserves the child–parent relationship. Both parent and child are empowered; the parent is responsible for, or in control of, providing parameters for choices, and the child is responsible for, or in control of, his decision (within parent-determined parameters).

Choice Giving Strategies

Provide age-appropriate choices that are *equally acceptable to the child and to you.* Remember that you must be willing to live with the choice the child makes. In this instance of choice giving, do not use choices to try to manipulate the child to do what you want by presenting one choice that you want the child to choose and a second choice that you know the child won't like.

Provide little choices to little kids; big choices to big kids.
Example: Toddlers can only handle choosing between two shirts or two food items. Examples for 3-year-old: ***"Sarah, do you want to wear your red dress or your pink dress to school?" "Sarah, do you want an apple or an orange with your lunch?"***

Choice-Giving to Avoid Potential Problem Behavior and Power Struggles

Choices can also be used to avoid a potential problem. Similar to the example above, choices given are equally acceptable to parent and child. The difference is that choices are planned in advance by the parent to avoid problems that the child has a history of struggling with. In the example above, if Sarah is not a morning person and has trouble getting dressed in the morning, provide a choice of what to wear the evening before (to avoid a struggle the next morning); after she has made the choice, take the dress out of the closet, ready for morning.

In selecting choices to prevent problems, it is very important that parents understand what the real problem is that their child is struggling with. If your child always comes home hungry and wants something sweet, but you want him to have a healthy snack, plan ahead by having on hand at least two choices of healthy snacks that *your child likes*. Before he heads for the ice cream, say, **"Billy, I bought grapes and cherries for snack, which would you like?"**

Or, if you made your child's favorite cookies and it is acceptable for your 5-year-old to have 1 or 2 cookies for a snack, say **"Billy, I made your favorite cookies today. Would you like 1 cookie or 2?"**

> Hint: This is another place where "structuring for success" can be applied by eliminating the majority of unacceptable snack items and stocking up on healthy snack items! Structuring your home environment to minimize conflict allows both you and your child to feel more "in control." Remember: **Be a thermostat!**

Advanced Choice Giving: Providing Choices as Consequences

There are many instances when parents must make decisions for children—decisions that children are not mature enough to take responsibility for, such as bedtime and other matters of health and safety. However, parents can provide their children with some measure of control in the situation by providing simple choices.

Oreo Cookie Method of Choice-Giving

Example 1: Three-year-old Sarah is clutching a handful of Oreo cookies and is ready to eat them all (it is right before bedtime, and the parent knows it would not be healthy for Sarah to have all the cookies; but Sarah does not know that—she just knows that she wants cookies!): **"Sarah, you can choose to keep one of the cookies to eat and put the rest back, or you can put all of the cookies back—which do you choose?"** Or, if it is permissible to the parent for Sarah to have two cookies: **"Sarah, you can have one cookie or two—which do you choose?"**

Example 2: Three-year-old Sarah does not want to take her medicine and adamantly tells you so! Taking the medicine is not a choice, it is a given. But the parent can provide the child with some control over the situation by saying, **"Sarah, you can choose to have apple juice or orange juice with your medicine—which do you choose?"**

Example 3: Seven-year-old Billy is tired and cranky and refuses to get in the car to go home from Grandma and Grandpa's house. **"Billy, you can choose to sit in the front seat with Daddy or you can choose to sit in the back seat with Sarah—which do you choose?"**

Choice-Giving to Enforce Household Policies and Rules

Choice giving can be used to enforce household policies/rules. *Begin by working on one at a time.* In general, provide two choices: one is phrased positively (consequence for complying with policy), the other is stated negatively (consequence for not complying with policy). Consequence for noncompliance should be relevant and logical, rather than punitive, and must be enforceable.

Example: A household rule has been established that toys in the family room must be picked up off the floor before dinner (children cannot seem to remember without being told repeatedly and the parent is feeling frustrated with constant reminders and power struggles). **"We are about to institute a new and significant policy within the confines of this domicile"** (big words get children's attention!). **"When *you choose to* pick up your toys before dinner, *you choose to* watch 30 minutes of television after dinner. When *you choose not to* pick up your toys before dinner, *you choose not to* watch television after dinner."**

Note: Be sure to let children know when there are 10–15 minutes before dinner, so they can have time to pick up their toys.

Children may be able to comply the first time you announce this new policy, because you have just informed them. But it is important that you begin to allow your children to use their internal resources and self-control to *remember* the new policy without constant reminders (remember, the new policy was implemented because you were frustrated and tired of nagging!). So the second night, the parent says, **"Billy and Sarah, dinner will be ready in 10 minutes, it is time to pick up your toys,"** and walks out. When it is time for dinner, the parent goes back into room to announce dinner:

1. The toys have not been picked up: *say nothing at that moment.* After dinner, go back into family room and announce to children, **"Looks like you decided to not watch television tonight."** Even if children get busy picking up the toys, they have already chosen not to watch TV for this night. **"Oh, you're thinking that if you pick your toys up now that you can watch TV, but the policy is that toys have to be put away before dinner."** After children plead for another chance, *follow through on the consequence*, calmly and empathically stating: **"I know that you wish you would have *chosen* to put your toys away before dinner, so you could *choose* to watch TV now—tomorrow night you can *choose* to put your toys away before dinner and *choose* to watch TV."** *Some children will choose not to watch TV for several nights in a row!*
2. The children are busy picking up toys and have put *most* of them away: parent says (as she helps with the *few* remaining toys, which demonstrates spirit of cooperation and prevents delay of dinner), **"It's time for dinner—looks like you've chosen to watch TV after dinner tonight."**

Guidelines for Choice Giving in Relation to Limit Setting and Consequences

- Enforce consequence without fail and without anger.
- Consequence is for "today" only—each day (or play session) should be a chance for a fresh start; a chance to have learned from the previous decision and resulting consequence; a chance to use internal resources to control self and make a different decision.
- Reflect child's choice with empathy, but remain firm. Consistency and follow-through are critical!
- Communicate choices in a matter-of-fact voice. Power struggles are likely to result if the child hears frustration or anger

in the parent's voice and believes the parent is invested in one choice over another. The child must be free to choose the consequence for noncompliance.

Caution: Once your child has reached the stage of "out-of-control," your child may not be able to hear and process a choice. Take a step back and focus on your child's feelings, reflecting her feelings empathically, while limiting unacceptable behavior and holding her if necessary to prevent her from hurting herself or you.

Suggested reading for parents: "Teaching Your Child to Choose," *Parenting*, October, 2002. For more information on teaching choice-giving skill, refer to Chapter 5.

Common Problems in Filial Play Session

We have found that there are certain common problems that parents often struggle with during special playtimes with their children or that they have questions about. Some of these are:

"My child notices that I talk differently in the play sessions and wants me to talk normally. What should I do?"

"My child asks many questions during the play sessions and resents my not answering them. What should I do?"

"My child just plays and has fun. What am I doing wrong?"

"I'm bored. What's the value of this?"

"My child doesn't respond to my comments. How do I know I'm on target?"

"When is it okay for me to ask questions, and when is it not okay?"

"My child hates the play sessions. Should I discontinue them?"

"My child wants the playtime to be longer. Should I extend the session?"

> "My child wants to play with the toys at other times during the week. Is it OK?"
>
> "My child wants me to shoot at him during the play session. What should I do?"

We have found it helpful to make a list of these common concerns to hand out to parents in Session 6 to facilitate a discussion of challenging issues. Chapter 18 provides information regarding how to respond to these common problems, as well as others.

Limit-Setting Review

The skill of limit setting is an ongoing challenge for most parents and typically continues to be a major focus in Session 6. The therapist uses parents' spontaneous sharing of limit-setting struggles to review and practice the skill. The majority of parents struggle with following through once they have set a limit, especially when faced with their children's pleading, whining, and other behaviors that they have learned to use to manipulate and wear down their parents. Remind parents about the importance of follow-through: **When they don't follow through on limits set or promises made, they lose credibility with their child**—and ultimately, damage their relationship with their child. Trust is the foundation of a healthy relationship. When parents fail to follow through and provide consistency, the message to the child is "You really can't count on me to do what I say." Humor can be used to get this very serious point across; for example, by having parents repeat after you three times, **"When setting limits, I WILL Follow Through—I am Tough as Nails!"**

Self-Esteem–Building Responses and Video

If time permits at the end of the session, the therapist can briefly introduce self-esteem–building responses and the concept of giving the child credit as a way of enhancing the child's sense of personal power, assigning parents to practice making one self-esteem–building response in their upcoming play sessions. A brief videotaped demonstration of the use of self-esteem–building responses in a play session provides parents with concrete examples of this skill. A brief demonstration with a parent, or, even better, with one of the parents' children, can be used in place of a video.

Homework Assignments

1. Parents are reminded of the importance of conducting their play session at the same time and same place and to videotape their session.
2. Remind parents to take a few minutes to read over *Play Session Dos & Don'ts* and *Play Session Procedures Checklist* prior to their play sessions.
3. Remind parents to practice giving one self-esteem–building response during their next play sessions (if time permitted the brief introduction of the self-esteem–building skill).
4. Parents are reminded after conducting the play session to complete the *Parent Play Session Notes* and *Play Session Skills Checklist* and bring to the group the following week.
5. Ask parents to read *Common Problems in Play Sessions* for the following week and mark the top two to three issues they have questions about or write in an issue they are challenged by that is not on the worksheet prior to their play session, and to read *Choice Giving 101* and *Advanced Choice Giving* and practice giving at least one choice outside of the play session *(this is the first assignment to practice a skill outside of the session).*
6. One to two parents are scheduled to be videotaped.
7. Parents are reminded of the Rule of Thumb for this week.

Partial Transcript of CPRT Session 6

(Dr. L. notices that Kathy seems unusually quiet as she sits and waits for group to start.)

Dr. L.: How's your week been, Kathy?

Kathy: Last night Cody kicked me and I told him I wasn't for kicking, and then I didn't know what to say. It made me furious because he was mad when he kicked me. It was a bad time.

Dr. L.: So when he gets to the point of actually doing something, then you're not quite sure of what to do next, because you're so angry.

Kathy: Right, I told him I'm not for kicking, and then I was just furious. I figured, so I tell him to go kick something else, but then what's going to stop him from coming back and kicking me again, and again, and again?

Dr. L.: Seems like you're just not sure if it will work, especially when Cody is already so mad.

Kathy: That's right.

Dr. L.: And it may not work every time, especially if Cody knows you're furious with him. The reason that I want you to practice these skills only during your 30-minute play session is because it is a time when you are more in control of the situation. You purposefully chose a time for your play sessions when you would be less stressed and more relaxed, and this is a special time for Cody to play with all those neat toys. So you're more likely to be successful applying these skills during your play sessions. Kathy, I bet you are not the only one who has questions about limit setting. *(Several parents nod.)*

Dr. L.: *(Refocuses on group.)* Let's talk some more about limit setting during your play sessions. A-C-T can be used at other times, but we are really most concerned about applying it in the special playtime. When your child picks up the crayon and looks at the wall, you know what's in his mind. He's thinking, "I wonder what it would look like on the wall," and you simply go through A-C-T. "Looks like you'd like to mark on the wall, but the wall's not for marking on." Then the third step is to communicate some choices, which is to tell children what they can do. In this approach, we don't set out to stop the behavior. We set out to help the child complete what they started, but in a way that is acceptable. So, "The wall is not for marking on. The paper is for marking on." We always give a choice, so children can express their need. *(Dr. L. looks over at Kathy.)* "I'm not for kicking. You can tell me you're angry." Or the trash can could be for kicking.

Kathy: OK.

Dr. L.: In limit setting, it's really important that you point to what the acceptable item is. The wall is not for marking on. The paper (pointing) is for marking on. I'm not for kicking. The Bobo (pointing) is for kicking. You point to what is acceptable, and that diverts the child's attention toward what is acceptable. In this approach, the objective is to help the child to learn to say "No" to self. Where we're headed with this approach is when your child is 13 or 15, and he is across town, not under your thumb, and he needs to stop himself when peers suggest he do something he should not do. He will need to say "No" to himself. Kim, did you have an opportunity to use A-C-T?

Kim: Yes, a little too late. My daughter decided my solid lean-back chairs needed designs painted on them, but it worked when I told her that she could color on the coloring book, but not on my chairs.

Sonya: There was something you said last week that really left an impression on me. When you were talking about our children being angry, and that doesn't just go away. It stays with them until they're able to get it out in some form or another. I noticed that a lot this week with Jenny. Until she had a chance to resolve her anger, she would act out in tiny little ways all over the place. It was a powerful little piece of information, and it's true with her.

Dr. L.: In this new approach, you give your children a chance to express the need or feeling.

Sonya: And, one more thing.

Dr. L.: Yes.

Sonya: Just in the tools you've given us so far, I was able to make a decision after watching some of this work. I had the courage to wean both of the girls off of their bottles. It was like parenting from hell, though. Before coming here, I didn't know how to redirect their behaviors or just say, it's not okay to scream and holler and throw your body all over the house. I feel a lot more confident in being able to handle the repercussions of no crutch and perhaps replacing it with something appropriate like a special doll or something.

Laura: These playtimes have allowed me to appreciate my son more than anything else.

Dr. L.: Can you add to that?

Laura: We were having a real hard time, and I didn't really like a lot of his behavior. I associated a lot of his behavior with him, and didn't like him, and the playtimes have brought a new love feeling for Dawson, especially a closeness. Just learning to play and enjoy him, 'cause being a single parent I'm always the one who has to discipline him, and I forgot to just enjoy and play with my children. The playtime allowed me to do that, and I have found a new joy.

Dr. L.: It's almost as though you're saying, "I've rediscovered how to be a loving mother," instead of having to always keep things straightened out and take care of things.

Laura: Yes, everything has to be in control, and perfect, and that makes for a perfect life. Now, I've found that I can leave everything scattered around me, and I can take care of myself, too.

Dr. L.: So, your life is different. You know, as I listen to you, Laura, one of the things that keeps occurring to me is you're saying "I'm more free now."

Laura: Yes, I was a neurotic mom.

Dr. L.: That is a difficult place to be.

Laura: Yes, but the thing I'm still having trouble with is being in the middle of a crisis and being able to step back out of the crisis.

Dr. L.: And be objective.

Laura: And be objective from it and know that I don't have to react, that I can step back and get in control of my own emotions, and then decide what to do.

Dr. L.: Nita, you were reacting to that, when Laura said step back.

Nita: When Jeff does those things, the first thing I do now is just tell myself, he is not really doing this just to get to me. Because I used to feel that way, and that's how I would react: "You are doing this on purpose to get me." When I take myself out of it, then I handle the whole situation a lot better. I'm a lot happier, and he's a lot happier, but if I've got myself in there, my own ego or something, then it's just get focused on that!

Dr. L.: Then it's a real struggle, and self-defeating.

Nita: Oh, yeah!

Dr. L.: I think I hear you all saying that you're becoming more understanding. When you talk about stepping back, and being more objective, you're taking yourself out of the situation and working a bit harder at understanding your child at that moment.

Nita: Yes.

Sonya: And when we get together in these meetings every week and go over new skills or new techniques or whatever, it's easier than when I'm in the middle of some sort of struggle with Jenny because I'm taking this training. If I wasn't coming here, I wouldn't be keeping track of any of my behaviors, and each situation would just be more frustrating. Now, I feel a lot more comfortable in stepping back a little bit. Last night Jenny was yelling "I want my tootsie pop!" and I was thinking, I did promise it to her after dinner, but it's already almost bedtime. Finally, I said, "I need to think about this for a second." She was real quiet standing there watching me, and then I told her, I think it would be okay for you to have juice instead, and then you need to brush your teeth again. She said okay, the compromise was okay, and it was okay for me. I felt empowered.

Dr. L.: So you're starting to think about what you're doing, and that's giving you self-control.

Sonya: Knowing actions, instead of just reacting, that feels good.

Kathy: Cody keeps telling me to shut up. I tell him I'm not for telling to shut up, and that he can tell me he doesn't want to listen to me, but I'm not for telling to shut up, and he still does it quite a bit. He did it a lot last night, over and over and over again. He was with his dad this weekend. Maybe his dad told him to shut up a lot.

Dr. L.: Would it help if we saw some of your session right now, and that might give us a better picture of what you're having to deal with?

Kathy: It might.

(Parents view video.)

Dr. L.: (Stops video.) Right there, you need to set a limit. He's asking you to do something that you really don't want to do.

Kathy: That's right.

Dr. L.: He's asking you to use a word that you don't want to use. So, what would you like to say to him?

Kathy: "I don't want to say that."

Dr. L.: Sounds great to me.

Kathy: Okay, but I thought I was supposed to do what he wants me to do in his whole playtime.

Dr. L.: There are limits. For some reason, setting limits firmly is difficult for you.

Emily: Kathy, if he wants to mark on the wall, you're not going to let him mark on the wall.

Kathy: No, that's true. I'm not.

Dr. L.: There are limits. This is not a completely free or permissive relationship.

Kathy: He can say what he wants. Well, not exactly what he wants.

Dr. L.: Within limits.

Kathy: But I have the choice of saying what I want also, or something like that.

Dr. L.: You're the adult.

Kathy: Yeah.

Dr. L.: You're the authority, and you're the person responsible for setting limits. Your child is not. We set the boundaries, and the child is free within those boundaries, but they're not free to go outside those boundaries, and marking on the wall would be going outside those boundaries. Hitting you would be going outside those boundaries. Having you say words that you don't want to say is going outside those boundaries. The key to limit setting is responding quickly, firmly, and decisively. When you start hesitating, how does a child read that, Emily?

Emily: That he will get what he wants. That she's going to give in, and if I beg or throw a big fit, I'll get it.

Dr. L.: I would guess that some of what we just saw on the video is pretty typical of Cody.

Kathy: Oh, yes.

Dr. L.: When Cody tells you to say words you don't want to say, you could say…?

Kathy: "I don't want to say that, Cody."

Dr. L.: And then what's the choice you could give Cody since you're not going to say that?

Emily: "Is there something else you would like me to say?"

Dr. L.: Instead of asking the question, you could say, "You can choose some other words for me to say."

(Continue viewing video.)

Dr. L.: (Stops video.) You gave him credit. You made a self-esteem building response. He can feel powerful by doing something constructive, taking the handcuffs off you, and then when he hears, "There, you figured out how to get them off," he feels powerful in a positive way instead of feeling powerful by pushing you around.

(Continue viewing video.)

Dr. L.: (Stops video.) How do you feel about Cody pretending it's your birthday and spanking you?

Kathy: Well, he wasn't really doing it out of anger. He was doing it like a birthday, and it really didn't hurt.

Dr. L.: Does he do things like that at other times?

Kathy: When he spanks me out of anger and it hurts, then that makes me really angry. That is what I'd like to correct, but here he was just playing birthday.

Dr. L.: There may be some times when he doesn't know the difference between hitting you hard and hitting you easy.

Kathy: Yeah.

Dr. L.: Does he play this birthday game often?

Kathy: Yes, some.

Dr. L.: Maybe it would be a good idea to set a limit on spanking you during the special playtime. You could say, "I'm not for spanking. You can pretend the Bobo is me and spank the Bobo."

(Continue viewing video.)

Dr. L.: (Stops video.) It's really important that we not give our children mixed messages such as setting a limit on something in one playtime but not setting a limit on the same thing in the next playtime.

Emily: In this particular instance, Kathy, you allowed Cody to give you a birthday spanking. Well, the next time he gets angry at you, slaps you on the butt, and you discipline him, he can say it was just a birthday spanking. He looks like he's a manipulative child, like he's real good at what he does.

Kathy: He really is.

Laura: That's true of all kids, they learn manipulation. I've gotten manipulated, and children are very good at doing that, and they sense my uncertainty too, and boy!

Kathy: You're uncertain of what to do?

Laura: If I'm not firm, they sense it, but I've watched their reactions when I'm firm, and if I say "No," they know I mean "No."

Dr. L.: Laura, do you think Kathy's capable of being firm?

Laura: Yeah.

Dr. L.: I do.

Kathy: I don't know if I can.

Nita: Yes, yes.

Laura: Because I've been mush, too.

Dr. L.: And?

Laura: And I'm stronger now, and the more that I set a limit, then the easier it is.

Emily: Kathy, I was mush with my first born. He is now 13, and I pay the price on a daily basis, with his mouth, with his attitude, with his lack of respect, because I did not correct it at a much earlier age. I thought, "Oh, another fit, give him what he wants." But it's not any easier later—it's not.

Dr. L.: During your special 30-minute playtime, you get a chance to work on those issues, and for 30 minutes it can be easier. It doesn't mean you must do it for 24 hours, but you work on it for 30 minutes, with a commitment to stick this out for 30 minutes.

Nita: Since you're not trying to do laundry or something else, it's easier to stand back and assess and understand what's going on during that 30 minutes than when you're also trying to do something else and interact with your child and address issues.

Sonya: And that 30 minutes is great because it gives me enough practice time, and I try it a couple of more times during the week without thinking. If I had to do this every single moment of my life, I probably would give in too many times. Any time I try it outside of special playtime, I figure that's gravy on the potatoes.

(Continue to view video.)

Dr. L.: (Stops video.) Kathy, would you have preferred not to taste that sand?

Kathy: Probably.

Dr. L.: Then, you can say, "I choose not to taste it."

Kathy: Okay, but it seems to me if I didn't taste it, I wouldn't be doing what he wanted to do for that 30 minutes.

Dr. L.: That's not the rule. The rule is not that you have to do everything that he wants you to do. The rule is that he can do a lot of things he would like to do, and you will let him lead. That doesn't mean you do everything he wants.

Kathy: Okay.

Dr. L.: You do some of the things he wants if it's appropriate, but if there are some things you don't want to do, you don't do them.

(Group gives Kathy supportive feedback. It is obvious she has serious personal boundary issues that require more help than a filial group can provide. This is a classic example of a parent who needs private counseling sessions with the filial therapist.)

Dr. L.: Let me share with you my Oreo Cookie Theory about choice giving. The Oreo Cookie Theory of choice giving requires a shift in attitude, creative thinking, and spontaneous reaction. The shift in attitude is a change from making decisions for the child to allowing the child to decide. For example, if a child doesn't want to take her medicine, taking the medicine is not a choice—that is a given. So the parent can say, "You may choose to have orange juice with your medicine or you may choose to have apple juice with your medicine. Which do you choose?" The question calls for a commitment on the part of the child, and once the child has made a choice, the child is more willing to follow through. Allowing the child to be a part of the decision-making process usually results in cooperation or willingness to compromise. Keep in mind that you must be willing to live with either choice the child makes.

The Oreo Cookie Theory is also a new approach to discipline—not punishment, but discipline, helping a child to learn how to engage in making appropriate choices and learning self-responsibility. "If you choose to finish your homework by 4:00, you choose to get to play your computer game. If you choose not to finish you homework by 4:00, you choose not to play your computer game." This method of choice giving can be used in the special playtime to help your child learn self-discipline and self-control as the fourth step in the A-C-T model. You set the limit that walls are not for marking on, but your child keeps trying to mark on the wall. Now, what do you do? You've gone through the three steps three or four times, and your child is still trying to mark on the wall. (Parents brainstorm ideas of possible choices). Now, let's watch the video on choice giving.

(Parents watch Dr. Landreth's *Choices, Cookies, and Kids* video. This video can be obtained from the Center for Play Therapy, University of North Texas, P.O. Box 310829, Denton, TX 76203, or by visiting *www.centerforplaytherapy.com*)

Dr. L.: (After facilitating discussion regarding video.) Let's practice generating some choices. You three are in a group and you three are in a group. Your assignment is to think of at least three things your children have done or might do and develop a choice for each of those situations. Then you can share your situations and choices with the rest of us.

Dr. L.: (After parents have a chance to share the above assignment.) This week I would like for you all to give your child a choice. It may be during a special playtime or at some other time. "If you choose to continue to try to shoot me with the dart gun, you choose not to play with it for the rest of our playtime together today." "If you choose to try to mark on the wall, and the wall is not for marking on, you choose not to play with the crayon for the rest of the time today." That sets the item off-limits for the rest of the time—not forever, just for that time.

Kim: Do you think children understand the word "choice"?

Dr. L.: Yes, even at 2 years of age, they understand.

Kathy: But then when they do choose to give up the television or give up Mr. Rogers, how do you handle their anger towards that?

Dr. L.: You say, "I know you're angry." You reflect their anger and accept it.

Laura: We can't accept the guilt of it, because it's something they chose.

Dr. L.: Yes, parents have a hard time accepting their children's pain.

Dr. L.: Emily, we didn't get to hear about your play session. What was it like?

Emily: It was interesting.

Dr. L.: What does that mean, "interesting"?

Emily: He had all the little doll furniture and the dolls, and the plastic knife. He picked the knife up and said, "I'm going to stab the baby." He didn't wait for me to respond. He stabbed the baby, and then he went down the line, stabbed everyone, all five. That caught me off guard. I said, "Gee, you look real angry, why are you doing that?"

Dr. L.: You reflected his feeling. He knew you understood; so the question wasn't needed.

Emily: And he kept doing it. He took the plastic knife and started slashing furniture.

Dr. L.: Acting out his anger.

Emily: And then he threw the knife in the box, got on his hands and knees, started goo-goo and gaa-gaaing, got the bottle that was full of water, crawled into my lap, lay down like a baby, and said, "Rock me." So for the last 10 minutes of our special time, I rocked him.

Dr. L.: What a tender moment.

Emily: Yes, I think that time was significant in his life.

(The remaining parents report on their special playtimes.)

Dr. L.: I want to show you all a few minutes of one of my play sessions emphasizing the use of self-esteem–building responses. As your child is doing something, you can build their self-esteem by giving your child credit. A self-esteem–building response is when you see your child doing something, and you give your child credit for it. I'd like for you to specifically work on building your child's self-esteem in your 30-minute playtime this week. That will be one of your assignments.

(Parents view video.)

Dr. L.: (Stops video.) Okay, got the idea?

Kim: You didn't tell her what that number was.

Dr. L.: It can be whatever she wants it to be for 30 minutes. Later, in the kitchen tonight, it may need to be 5, but for this 30 minutes it can be whatever number she wants it to be. Give your child credit. You stacked those blocks as high as you wanted them to be. The child is counting, one, two, three: "Sounds like you can count all the way to three." You just give your child credit for all the little things they do in your 30-minute session. That's one assignment, self-esteem–building responses; your second assignment is to give your child a choice this week. Have a good week. I'll see you next Monday.

References

Bratton, S., Landreth, G., Kellam, T., & Blackard, S. (2006). Child Parent Relationship Therapy (CPRT) Treatment Manual: A 10-Session Filial Therapy Model for Training Parents. NY: Routledge.

CHAPTER 13

CPRT TRAINING SESSION 7: SUPERVISION AND SELF-ESTEEM-BUILDING RESPONSES

Overview

Refer to the Overview section at the beginning of Chapter 12 as a thorough review of the overall supervision process and important reminders that apply for Sessions 6 through 9. As in training Sessions 6 and 7, the major focus of this session is supporting and encouraging parents' skill development and confidence through group supervision and feedback; thus, the majority of the allotted time is devoted to this activity. Self-esteem building is the only new skill introduced this week.

Materials

Suggested materials include: *CPRT Session 7–Treatment Outline;* parent information form with pertinent notes; homework assigned in Session 6, including extra copies of any homework worksheets; and Session 7 handouts and homework, including: *Session 7 Parent Notes & Homework*, *Esteem Building Responses*, *Parent Play Session Notes*, and *Play Session Skills Checklist*. Additional materials include: a display poster with *Play Sessions Dos and Don'ts*; *Choices, Cookies, and Kids* video by Garry Landreth (if used in Session 6 and time didn't allow viewing the entire video), and optional video clip demonstrating self-esteem-building responses.

> *Note: All handouts listed above, as well as a training session outline for the therapist, additional supplemental parent handouts, and resources for this training session are found in the* CPRT Treatment Manual *and accompanying CD-ROM, available from the publisher, Routledge.*

Content and Procedure

As in Session 6, the major focus of this session is supporting and encouraging parents' skill development and confidence through group supervision and feedback; thus, the majority of allotted time is devoted to this activity. The only new skill introduced in Session 7 is esteem-building responses.

Review Homework

The session begins with parents sharing how their week has been. The therapist uses this time to ask parents to briefly report on their homework assignment to practice giving a choice outside the play session and to review the handouts, *Choice Giving 101* and *Advanced Choice Giving*, and finish viewing the *Choices, Cookies, and Kids* video by Garry Landreth, if necessary. The skill of choice giving is an important tool for parents; therefore, allotting plenty of time to review and practice this skill is a priority. Continuing to review homework assignments, the therapist asks parents to get out the *Common Problems in Play Sessions* worksheet and addresses parent concerns (suggested answers to these common problems can be found in Chapter 15).

Filial Play Session Reports

Parents report briefly on their home play sessions and their homework assignment to practice choice giving during a play session, if the occasion arose. The therapist listens for opportunities to reinforce the skill of choice giving in the parents' sharing of play session happenings, providing additional strategies for successful choice giving, as needed. The skill of limit setting remains a challenge for most parents; therefore, allowing time to reinforce and practice this skill continues as a training priority. Role-play and worksheets that provide limit-setting scenarios for parents to respond to are helpful supplemental strategies for helping parents master this skill.

Esteem-Building Responses

Self-esteem building is the only new skill focus for training Session 7. Introduce the **Rule of Thumb: Never do for a child that which he can do for himself.** *When you do, you rob your child of the joy of discovery and the opportunity to feel competent. You will never know what your child is capable of unless you allow him to try!*

Parents help their children develop a positive view of self not only by providing their children with love and unconditional acceptance, but also by helping their children feel competent and capable. Parents help their children feel competent and capable by first allowing them to **experience** what it is like to discover, figure out, and problem solve. Parents show faith in their children and their children's capabilities by allowing them to struggle with problems, all the while providing encouragement (encouragement vs. praise is covered in detail in Session 8). For most parents, allowing children to struggle is hard, but it is a necessary process for children to truly feel capable. The next step in helping children develop a positive view of self as competent and capable is learning to respond in ways that give children credit for ideas, efforts, and accomplishments without praising.

Esteem-Building Responses to Use in Filial Play Sessions:

"You did it!"

"You decided that was the way that was supposed to fit together."

"You figured it out."

"You know just how you want that to look."

"You like the way that turned out."

"You're not giving up—you're determined to figure that out."

"You decided…"

"You've got a plan for how…"

Example 1: Child works and works to get the lid off the Play-Doh and finally gets it off. Parent response: **"You did it."**
Example 2: Child works and works to get the lid off the Play-Doh, but can't get it off. Parent response: **"You're determined to figure that out."**
Example 3: Child struggles to get the dart to fit into the gun and pushed in all the way. Parent response: **"You figured it out."**
Example 4: Child spends time drawing, cutting, and gluing a nondescript piece of "art" and shows you with a smile when he is finished. Parent response: **"You really like the way that turned out."**
Example 5: Child is carefully setting up army soldiers and telling you all about a battle that is going to take place and what is going to happen and how one side is going to sneak up, etc. Parent response: **"You've got a plan for how that side is…"** or **"You've got that all planned out."**

Many parents and children have difficulty with this concept. Most parents do too much for their children, and in response their children have learned to depend on their parents to solve their problems, believing they cannot do it by themselves. The therapist needs to take time to role-play how parents respond when children say, "Here mommy," (handing the Play-Doh to mom) "take the lid off for me." Or, "Daddy, help me set the soldiers up." Parents need lots of practice in how to return responsibility to their children to do things they are capable of figuring out for themselves. Parents benefit from seeing a video demonstration illustrating the use of esteem-building responses or a brief live demo in which that skill is focused on.

Filial Play Session Video Critique

This portion of the training session continues to hold the most importance for parents learning and integrating the skills. The therapist uses the focused supervision time of the videotaped parents to not only emphasize the Filial Play Session "Dos," but to also to point out examples and missed opportunities for making self-esteem–building responses. Emphasize to parents that **simply noticing and showing interest in their children's play is a powerful builder of self esteem—that their actions can speak as loud as words!**

Role-Play

Allow 10–15 minutes at end of session for role-playing self-esteem–building responses, limit setting, and reflective responding.

Homework Assignments

1. Parents are reminded of the importance of conducting their play session at the same time and same place and to videotape their sessions.
2. Remind parents to take a few minutes to review *Filial Play Session Dos & Don'ts* and *Esteem-Building Responses* prior to their play session.
3. Remind parents to practice giving at least one self-esteem–building response during their play sessions and one self-esteem–building response outside of the play sessions. They are to write down what their children did and how they responded.
4. Parents are reminded after conducting the play session to complete the *Parent Play Session Notes* and *Filial Play Session Skills Checklist* and bring it to the group the following week.
5. Each parent is asked to write a note to their child of focus, as well as to other children in the family, pointing out a positive characteristic or a quality the parent appreciates about the child. Ask parents to write down the following sentence: "Dear ____, I was just thinking about you and what I was thinking is you are so ___________," (thoughtful, responsible, considerate, loving, etc.) "I love you, ______ [Mom, Dad]." If time permits, the therapist can help parents generate some ideas. Providing parents with a list of positive character qualities is beneficial. Suggest that parents mail their notes; children

seldom get mail, so this makes the note an extra special treat. If the child cannot read, arrange for someone else in the home to read the note to the child when it arrives in the mail, if possible; if not, the parent would read the note. Parents are to continue this assignment each week, identifying a different character quality for the remainder of the CPRT training, varying how the note is delivered; for example, placing in child's lunchbox, taped to the mirror in the bathroom, on the child's pillow, under the child's dinner plate, etc.

6. One to two parents are scheduled to be videotaped.
7. Parents are reminded of the Rule of Thumb for the week.
8. Close by reading *The Struggle to Become a Butterfly: A True Story (see Session 7 handout in the CPRT Treatment Manual.)*

Partial Transcript of CPRT Session 7

(After parents shared how their week had been, including briefly reporting on their homework assignment to make two self-esteem–building responses in the play sessions and to practice giving a choice outside of the play sessions, Dr. L. went over the handout on Common Problems in Filial Play Sessions. This part of the transcript was omitted, because the answers to the questions contained in that worksheet can be found in Chapter 15. The transcript begins with parents reporting on how their play sessions went, with the therapist using parents' reports to look for opportunities to review and reinforce skills, particularly focusing on the skill of choice giving.)

Dr. L.: Emily, what was your play session like this week?

Emily: Pretty normal. I haven't seen any aggressive behavior since that one time with the knife when he stabbed and cut everything. Actually, that one time was enough for me, because it was pretty scary.

Dr. L.: So maybe he needed to get some anger out, and he did.

Emily: Yeah, I guess. (pause) But he still likes playing with the dart gun, shooting the darts and asking me to get them for him.

Dr. L.: How do you feel about having to retrieve the darts for him?

Emily: I think it's fun.

Dr. L.: So it doesn't bother you.

Emily: No, not at all. As a matter of fact, I'm not sure he has ever asked me to get the darts. It's just something I started doing. He shoots them and I go get them. That's just the way it is.

Dr. L.: And for 30 minutes, he's in charge. Maybe then he doesn't have to get angry or be aggressive to try to be in charge at other times. You have already met that need.

Emily: That's true. He has been angry a lot less lately. He still likes the Band-Aids. He uses every one I put in the box every week. He puts them in a criss-cross pattern one on top of the other and makes a big patch out of them on my hand. He thinks that's lots of fun. He played with the Play-Doh a bunch, just rolling it into balls and stuff and made some pretty creative things. Our playtime is in my bedroom, and he got some things out of the bathroom like a comb and a brush, and a bottle of lotion. He pushed them down into the Play-Doh and made different imprints. Then he would feel the different imprints. He spent a lot of time doing that.

Dr. L.: His play this time seems to have been a bit different: calmer, quieter, more subdued, and a fun time for both of you. You followed his lead. I do have one suggestion. The special playtime is just for the part of the room where you set the toys. The rest of the room and other items in the room are off-limits so this can be a consistent and predictable time for Chris. He might want to play with some items in your bedroom that you wouldn't want him to play with, like a lamp or clock. He might have taken the top off the lotion bottle and poured some out, and that would make a huge mess. During the special playtime, he is to play only with the toys you have in the play kit. You can practice reflective responding and set a limit by saying, "I know you would like to play with stuff from the bathroom, but this is our special play area right here in this part of the room, and these toys are the only things that are to be played with during our special playtime." How do you react to that, Emily?

Emily: I can do that—makes sense to me. But what do I do next time if he wants to play with those same things, and he says, "Last time you let me?"

Dr. L.: You can say, "I know I didn't say anything last time, but I should have said, 'Those things are not for playing with during our special playtime.'"

Dr. L.: Nita, what was your play session like? Describe it to us.

Nita: Jeff keeps up a running monologue. I just sit there and watch him, and he keeps up this running monologue. I have very little opportunity to say anything. He's very, very pleased with the playtimes.

Dr. L.: So he's doing what he wants to do for that 30 minutes, a lot of talking.

Nita: He says things like, "I'm doing this like this, and then you see I put this like this. You see this, Mom." I say, "Yes, I see that."

Dr. L.: That's his way of including you. When children talk about their play, "Now, this guy is going to do this, then he's going to jump in here," that's the child's way of including you in his play, without you actually being a physical participant.

Nita: Sometimes Jeff wants me to go outside and play and I tell him, I just can't. I am just so tired. I just really don't feel good, and he'll say that's okay, because I know at special playtime it'll be just you and me, anyway.

Dr. L.: So the playtime is a very special time for him and a place where he gets his needs met.

Nita: And he will tell me things like, "Wesley and I do this at Nanny's house." But when I ask him, "What did you do at Nanny's house?," he just says, "I played." But during the playtime, he'll say, "Wesley did it like this at Nanny's house." He tells me about things I could never get out of him otherwise.

Dr. L.: Sounds like some important things are happening. He's sharing his life with you.

Nita: I just thought of something. We're still having trouble when it's over. He understands it's over. He says, "That's okay, Mommy, you go wash your face," or whatever. I just go ahead, put the toys in the box, and put the box away. Then, sometimes he hits me and kicks me because he wants to play more.

Dr. L.: You're not for kicking. So, give him a choice. If you choose to kick me, you choose to—what choice could you give?

Nita: Go to bed without a story.

Dr. L.: I'd rather not take a bedtime story away from him. That's important sharing time.

Nita: He likes using the telephone a lot.

Dr. L.: Okay, if you choose to kick me, you choose not to use the phone for the rest of the day. If you choose not to kick me, you choose to get to use the phone.

Nita: That's what I'll do.

Dr. L.: How about the rest of you—what kind of choice would you give your child in a similar situation? Remember that the consequence you establish needs to be something your child will not like giving up, but just like the example of not using forfeiting a bedtime story, in general, the consequence should not take something away that is a special time in your relationship or in your child's relationship with other important people, like grandparents.

(Parents discuss choice-giving ideas and continue to report on play sessions).

Dr. L.: Debbie, tell us a bit about your session before you show your video.

Debbie: It was OK, but Rachel didn't want to leave. She started screaming, and I had to carry her out of the playroom. It was awful!

Dr. L: Let's see what happened.

(Note: Debbie is the parent we are following more closely from intake through follow-up; see Dr L. uses Debbie's play session happenings to focus the training on self-esteem–building responses, limit setting, and reflective responding.)

Dr. L: We're going to use Debbie's play session with Rachel to work on self-esteem–building responses. I want all of you to notice when you think Debbie uses a self-esteem-building–response—when she gives Rachel credit for deciding, figuring out, knowing, etc.

(Group watches video.)

Child: (Looks at Debbie, laughs, runs to Bobo, hits it, and then runs to kitchen cabinets.) What is this? A kitchen. (Opens cabinet doors and then runs back to easel.)

Child: (Looks at Debbie, moves to toy shelves, and plays with cash register on floor by the sandbox.)

Debbie: You're making those numbers go up. (Sits in chair next to the table.)

Dr. L.: (Stops video.) What kind of response did Debbie just make?

Sonya: She gave Rachel credit.

Kim: A self-esteem–building response.

Dr. L.: Yes, Debbie's statement "You're making those numbers go up" empowers her child.

(Starts video.)

Child: Look Mommy!

Debbie: Wow!

Child: (Sits next to sandbox.) I'm going to take my shoes off.

Debbie: You're going to take your shoes off?

Dr. L.: (Stops video.) Debbie, that was an accurate reflection of content, but what did your tone of voice say?

Debbie: I didn't hear anything.

Dr. L.: (Replays last comment.) What did you hear that time?

Debbie: My tone of voice turned it into a question.

Dr. L.: Yes, that says you don't understand.

(Starts video.)

Child: Yeah, and socks and stuff before I go in there.

Debbie: You take your shoes and socks off before you go in the sand.

Child: Yeah. Look what I can do, Momma (jumps in sandbox).

Debbie: You're making your fingers go right through that…your toes go right through that sand.

Dr. L.: (Stops video.) Your tracking comment shows you are noticing what Rachel does.

(Starts video.)

Child: (Sits down in sandbox.) Look what I can make, Momma. I can make something. I just need these. (Puts pebbles in Debbie's hand.) I don't think…(silently stares at bottom of the sandbox.) Why do they put that much in here?

Debbie: Hmm…why do they?

Dr. L.: (Stops video.) Debbie, you are being very empathic. Rachel is wondering, and you are wondering with her.

(Starts video.)

Child: (Pours sand into a bucket.) I'm getting it all over my new outfit.

Debbie: You're getting it all over your new outfit.

Dr. L.: (Stops video.) Group, what did Debbie just communicate to Rachel?

Emily: That being messy is OK.

Sonya: She's being very accepting.

Dr. L.: And understanding.

(Starts video.)

Child: (Takes pebbles from Debbie's hand and puts them on top of the sand mold.)

Debbie: Oh…you're putting these on top.

Child: Ah!

Debbie: (Laughs.)

Child: (Holds her hands toward Debbie, nonverbally suggesting Debbie should put the pebbles back in child's hands. Child puts the pebbles on top of the bucket which is full of sand.) Ahhh! (Child picks up bucket and tosses it in the air. Sand flies up at Debbie.)

Debbie: I'm not for throwing sand at.

Dr. L.: (Stops video.) Group, what kind of response did Debbie just make?

Group in unison: Limit setting.

(Starts video.)

Child: But Momma! (Walks away from sandbox, looks at other toys, then picks up machine gun and points it in Debbie's direction.)

Debbie: I'm not for pointing the gun at. You can point it at the Bobo or you can point it at the wall. (Debbie points at alternative targets.)

Dr. L.: (Stops video.) Excellent job setting a limit, and you pointed toward an acceptable alternative.

(Starts video.)

Child: (Starts shooting in the air. Child is excited by the sound the gun makes and puts the gun closer to her ears while shooting, then puts the gun back on the shelf, touches a knife and two dart guns, but does not play with them. Child finds a box on the shelf and shows it to Debbie, mumbling excitedly. Debbie smiles and walks to Child and kneels down next to her. Child picks up doctor kit and brings it to the art table.). I got a doctor bag, Momma. Let's play doctor.

Debbie: You want to play doctor.

Child: Yeah, over there, we'll play it. (Points to chalkboard, is busy checking the doctor kit and clearing space.) Lay down over there. Lay down, Momma.

Debbie: Where?

Dr. L.: (Stops video.) What does that one word "where" do for Rachel?

Laura: It keeps her in the lead.

Dr. L.: Yes.

(Starts video.)

Child: (Points to floor.) That place…you know, where you are standing. Lay down. (Child sits on a chair facing Debbie, then starts looking inside the doctor kit.)

Debbie: Oh…lay down here? (Sits on the floor.)

Child: Yes. (Glances at Debbie.) Lay down.

Child: (Goes through doctor kit, picks up stethoscope, and turns to Debbie.) Let's play doctor, Momma.

Debbie: Are you taking those out of there?

(Debbie catches herself before anyone in the room can respond—blurts out. "Oops, asked another question." Others laugh; video is not stopped.)

Child: (Takes out a second stethoscope.) This is a special one. (Puts it on her head.)

Debbie: A special one…

Child: (Offers two boxes of bandages to Debbie.) Do you want the little ones or the big ones?

Debbie: I don't know…hmmm…what do you think?

Child: (Looks at box of little ones.) Oh… that's for fingers.

Debbie: That's for fingers.

Child: Lay down, Momma.

Debbie: Where? Show me.

Child: Just lay.

Debbie: Oh, okay. (Lies down on floor.)

Dr. L.: (Stops video.) Rachel obviously knows what she wants.

Debbie: Yeah, she always does.

(Starts video.)

Child: (Goes to Debbie with stethoscope on her ears. Child tries to lift up bottom of Debbie's shirt.)

Debbie: (Holds her shirt down.) No! My clothes are for staying on right now. You can check my ears...my nose...my mouth…*(Blurts out "No" then makes quick recovery to set limit and provide alternative choices.)*

Child: But this is for looking into you.

Debbie: (Sits up and looks into Rachel's face.) I know, but my clothes are for staying down right now. I know you want to, but…*(Shows understanding.)*

Dr. L.: (Stops video.) Great job recovering; your first impulse was an old behavior—"No"—but you quickly recovered, set a limit, and provided an acceptable alternative of several choices. Then you came back to the first step in A-C-T by saying, "I know you want to."

(Starts video.)

Child: (Pushes Debbie down.) Lay down, Mommy! (Said with frustration.)

Debbie: You can check my eyes and my nose and my mouth. (Lies down.) Okay?

Child: (Checks Debbie's eye with stethoscope, runs to the doctor kit on the art table, puts the stethoscope down, and picks up syringe.)

Debbie: (Sits up.)

Child: Lay down, Mommy! ***(Pushes Debbie down.)***

Debbie: Oh...Oh...OK...(Lies down.)

Child: Let me give you a shot. (Gives shot to Debbie and opens bandage box.)

Dr. L.: (Stops video.) Debbie, or some of the rest of you, how do you think Rachel is feeling right now?

Emily: Like she's in charge—that she gets to boss her mom around.

Dr. L.: Yes, she looks like she's really enjoying being charge for these 30 minutes. She can't be the rest of the week, but Debbie, during these 30 minutes, you can grant Rachel in fantasy something she can't do the rest of the week: boss you around. Remember the Rule of Thumb we talked about last week—this is a perfect example of "Grant in fantasy what you cannot grant in reality." Rachel can't smack her baby brother at home, but she can pretend the baby doll is her brother and smack it during her special playtime.

Emily: So, that's like when Chris was angry and was going around stabbing all the toys with the play knife? He certainly couldn't do that in real life.

Dr. L.: Exactly, You were granting him in fantasy to do something to get his anger out that he couldn't do in reality.

(Starts video.)

Child: (Places bandage on Debbie's arm where she gave the shot.)

Debbie: You're putting that right there on my arm. (Sits up.)

Child: (Gets blood pressure instrument from the doctor kit and puts on Debbie's arm.)

Debbie: You're putting that right there on my arm.

Child: Lay down Mommy! Why do you keep getting up?

Debbie: (Lies back down.)

Dr. L.: (Stops video.) How's Rachel feeling right now?

Debbie: I think she's frustrated with me because I keep getting up.

Dr. L.: So you could say…

Debbie: You're frustrated with Mommy. You want me to stay laying down.

(Starts video.)

Child: (Takes Debbie's blood pressure and goes back to the table, takes a plastic reflex hammer from the doctor kit and taps Debbie's arm hard with it.)

Debbie: Ouch! (Gently reaches out in an attempt to grab the reflex hammer.)

Child: I know what it's for, Mom.

Debbie: I know that's what it is for, but Mommy is not for hitting. (This time she realizes she did not personalize her response and corrects.) I'm not for hitting.

Child: But this one's just for a little bit, this is for a little bit…(Goes back to the doctor kit and gets eye examiner.) Lay down, Mom. (Looks into Debbie's eyes with examiner, goes back to the table.) And okay, Mom, you're all good. You can't do it because you don't know how. (Puts all the doctor instruments back in the kit.)

Dr. L.: (Stops video.) Rachel sure seems to know a lot about what doctors do—how could you give her credit for that?

Nita: When she says that at the end, "You don't know how," could you say something like, "But you do, you know how to doctor"?

Dr. L.: Sounds good to me, gives Rachel credit, builds her self-esteem.

(Rachel goes over to dollhouse and picks up doll.)

Child: How do you take this off Momma? (Trying to undress doll.)

Debbie: Hmm…you got it, it was kind of hard, but you did it.

(Kathy starts to say something, so the video is stopped.)

Kathy: I would have probably reached over and taken the clothes off for her—the doll is so small, and I didn't think she could get it off. But, Debbie, you waited, and she did it. You could tell she was happy that she got it off by herself.

Dr. L.: Yes. Debbie, that was a good example of not doing for a child that which she can do for herself—another Rule of Thumb to remember. We never know for sure what children can do, unless we let them try. Every time you do something for children that they could figure out for themselves, you rob them of the opportunity to feel good about themselves, to feel competent. So remember the **Rule of Thumb: "Never do for a child that which she can do for herself."** So what kind of response did Debbie make when she said, "You got it—you did it."

Sonya: (Smiling.) A self-esteem–building response. (Others responded almost at the same time.)

(Dr. L. nods and starts the video.)

Child: (Concentrates on trying to put clothes back on.) Hey! Momma!

Debbie: Oh! You're putting them there. You should be putting them right on there…put them on right…right there…(Mom departs from role and instructs. Child corrects her.)

Child: I don't like for you to tell me what I can do. So I want you to stop. I know what I can do, I know…hey Momma!

They're taking a bath. Take this off. How do you take this off? (Child walks away and finds a hammer and nails.) I have something else I want to play. Stay there, Momma. Stay there.

Debbie: (Stands up and tries to walk with child.) Stay right here. (Debbie sits on the floor.)

Debbie: Oh! You're hitting that right there. Putting that right into that. You're hammering. You're hammering all by yourself.

Child: You know...I need a chair. (Drags chair over, sits on it, and continues to hammer.)

Debbie: You're hammering it right into that.

(Stops video.)

Dr. L.: That's a good place to stop, another good example of a self-esteem–building response. You were giving Rachel credit for figuring out how do that all by herself. And you could tell she was proud of herself.

Debbie: I was really surprised that she could that. I would never have let her have a big hammer like that. I would have been afraid that she would hurt herself.

Dr. L.: So what did you learn about Rachel?

Debbie: That she was capable of hammering a nail without hurting herself. She was being careful. I really wasn't afraid, because she was being careful.

Dr. L.: You wouldn't let her have a hammer unsupervised. That wouldn't be appropriate. But during this 30-minute special time, you can allow her more freedom, and you know you're right there to keep her safe.

Emily: I think that Rachel knew that you thought she could do it. You could tell. That was really empowering.

Dr. L.: Any other feedback for Debbie?

Nita: Debbie really did well at allowing Rachel to play with what she wanted and just following along.

Kathy: And she did a great job of setting limits—something I have a lot of trouble with! (Smiles.) Especially when Rachel wanted to pull her sweater up to doctor her. I wouldn't have known what to say. I'd probably let her and then remember I was on video and yank it down. (Everyone laughs.)

Dr. L.: Since, we're talking about limit setting, let's shift focus and work on the Limit Setting worksheet we didn't get to last week. We'll work some more on self-esteem–building response a little later. Did everyone find it? It looks like this. OK. Susan picks up the dart gun. Aims it at your head. How did you respond?

Kathy: I'm not for hitting.

Dr. L.: I'm not for shooting.

Kim: Susan, I'm not for shooting.

Dr. L.: Kim, you added something different there, a really important word.

All: Her name.

Dr. L.: What's important about that?

Sonya: I'm talking to you.

Dr. L.: Exactly. You get your child's attention in a hurry when you say their name.

Kim: Susan, I'm not for shooting. If you choose to shoot at me, you choose time out for 5 or 10 minutes.

Dr. L.: Sounds a little long, Kim. How about if you take the middle part of that out and read it. "Susan, I'm not for shooting."

Kim: "You can shoot at the Bobo."

Dr. L.: The choice does not need to be given until you have gone through the limit setting three or four times. And then you can say, "If you choose to shoot me with the gun, you choose not to play with the gun." But that's not needed until later. Give your child a chance to comply first. Emily, what did you put down?

Emily: I don't have anything written down.

Dr. L.: In your mind, what do you say?

Emily: "Susan, I'm not for shooting."

Dr. L.: Uh-hum. And then we want to give an alternative. "You can shoot the Bobo." And what do you do with your hands?

Kathy: You point to it.

Dr. L.: So the child's eyes follow to what is an acceptable alternative. Look at number four on the sheet. Paul is very angry with you, calls you names, and tries to kick you. What did you say?

Emily: The first thing that popped into my mind when I read this was to slap him across the head.

Dr. L.: Giving up your initial reaction and responding more calmly, Emily, you'd say…

Emily: Paul, I can understand that you're very angry right now, but I'm not for calling names or kicking.

Dr. L.: Yes, you're not for calling names. There is no choice on that. Go through the whole thing again.

Emily: Paul, I can understand that you're very angry with me right now, but I'm not for calling names or kicking.

Dr. L.: And, then, we still need to help him do what he needs to do. And that is?

Emily: Hit the bop bag.

Dr. L.: The Bobo is for kicking. The important thing is that you end your statement by telling your child what he can do. I might even offer this, "You can tell me you're angry. You can say, 'I'm angry at you.'"

Laura: It's interesting that we adults go through life trying to find out what our choices are in buying a car, in doing lots of things. The more choices we have, the more freedom we feel like we have to choose what is best for us.

Dr. L.: Yes, and it's important for children to find out what their choices are and to learn how to make decisions. When you make a decision, you are then responsible. So you're helping your child learn what it feels like to be responsible. I want to show you a short videotape of a child with me in the playroom. I want you to count how many times you hear me make a self-esteem–building response. A self-esteem–building response is when you give your child credit for knowing or doing. "You made that stay together."

(Parents view video.)

Dr. L.: (Stops video.) How many did you hear?

Kathy: I got eight.

Emily: I got 12.

Dr. L.: When children feel better about themselves, what difference does that make in their life? They do better. They're more self-confident, they follow through. Lots of important things happen. Now, let's do some role-playing. Let's work on two things. Limit setting: children, you all do some things that will cause your parent to set limits. "I'm going to paint on the wall," or "I'm going to cut this," or "I'm going to break this." And let your parents set a limit. Also, parents, you practice making self-esteem–building responses.

(Group pairs up to practice responses.)

Dr. L.: That's all for today. Your homework is to practice giving a self-esteem–building response outside of the play session and at least one during your play session. Write down what your child did and how you responded and bring it next week. Who will volunteer to come to the clinic to video your play sessions? OK, Laura and Emily. See you all next Monday.

References

Bratton, S., Landreth, G., Kellam, T., & Blackard, S. (2006). Child Parent Relationship Therapy (CPRT) Treatment Manual: A 10-Session Filial Therapy Model for Training Parents. NY: Routledge.

CHAPTER 14

CPRT TRAINING SESSION 8: SUPERVISION AND ENCOURAGEMENT VS. PRAISE

Overview

Refer to the Overview section at the beginning of Chapter 12 as a thorough review of the overall supervision process and important reminders that apply for Sessions 6 through 9. As in training Sessions 6 and 7, the major focus of this session is supporting and encouraging parents' skill development and confidence through group supervision and feedback; thus, the majority of the allotted time is devoted to this activity. Encouragement is the only new skill introduced this week and builds on the training on esteem-building responses covered in Session 7.

Materials

Suggested materials include: *CPRT Session 8–Treatment Outline;* parent information form with pertinent notes; homework assigned in Session 7, including extra copies of any homework worksheets; and Session 8 handouts and homework, including: *Session 8 Parent Notes & Homework*, *Encouragement vs. Praise*, *Parent Play Session Notes*, and *Play Session Skills Checklist*. Additional materials include: a display poster with *Play Sessions Dos and Don'ts* and optional video clip demonstrating play session skills, specifically self-esteem-building responses and encouragement.

> *Note: All handouts listed above, as well as a training session outline for the therapist, additional supplemental parent handouts, and resources for this training session are found in the* CPRT Treatment Manual *and accompanying CD-ROM, available from the publisher, Routledge.*

Content and Procedure

Review Homework

The session begins with parents informally sharing about how their week has been. The therapist uses this time to ask parents to briefly report on their character quality note-writing activity, remembering to caution parents not to expect an overt response from their children. Parents are reminded to continue the note-writing activity over the next few weeks. This time is also used to ask parents to report on their homework assignment to practice giving a self-esteem–building response outside the play session (if parents bring up during session responses, ask them to share those responses when they report on play sessions in a few minutes).

Filial Play Session Reports and Video Critique

Parents report briefly on their home play sessions and their homework assignment to practice self-esteem–building responses during their play sessions. The therapist listens for opportunities to reinforce this skill in the parents' sharing of play session happenings, providing additional strategies as needed. Review of self-esteem–building responses continues to be a focus during focused supervision of the videotaped parent. The therapist encourages parents to give each other feedback (parents are generally ready by Session 8 to move into peer supervision). As the videotaped parent's session is reviewed, the therapist stops the video after an obvious CPRT skill has been demonstrated and asks parents if they have any feedback for that parent. This strategy encourages parents' sharing of feedback and keeps the focus on parents' strengths.

Caution parents that the newness of the special playtime and the toys may begin to wear off and their children may seem uninterested or bored. The playtime is still important. Continue to insist on having the playtime.

Encouragement vs. Praise

The concept of encouragement, and how it differs from praise, is introduced in training Session 8. When possible, the therapist uses the focused supervision time to spontaneously introduce the concept by pointing out examples of encouragement in play session happenings of the videotaped parent. The therapist introduces the **Rule of Thumb: Encourage the effort, rather than praise the product**, either in response to a play session happening that fits this rule of thumb (as demonstrated in the transcript below) or when reviewing the skill. Parents are given a handout, *Encouragement vs. Praise*, that explains the rationale for using encouragement over praise and delineates how to use encouragement in different situations, both during and outside of play sessions. This handout is used during the session as a visual aid to helping parents understand encouragement and how to use the skill, and later as a review for homework. Most parents have difficulty grasping the concept of encouragement and how it differs from praise. Society, particularly schools, places a strong emphasis on praise as the preferred way to motivate children to do what authorities want them to do.

Praise: Although praise and encouragement both focus on positive behaviors and appear to be the same process, praise actually fosters dependence in children by teaching them to rely on an external source of control and motivation rather than on self-control and self-motivation. Praise is an attempt to motivate children with external rewards. In effect, the parent who praises is saying, "If you do something I consider good, you will have the reward of being recognized and valued by me." Overreliance on praise can produce crippling effects. Children come to believe that their worth depends upon the opinions of others. Praise employs words that place value judgments on children and focuses on external evaluation. For example:

Parent response: "You're such a good boy/girl." *The child may wonder, "Am I accepted only when I'm good?"*

Parent response: "You got an A. That's great!" *Are children to infer that they are worthwhile only when they make As?*

Parent response: "You did a good job." "I'm so proud of you." *The message sent is that the parent's evaluation is more important than the child's.*

Encouragement: Focuses on internal evaluation and the contributions children make; facilitates development of self-motivation and self-control. Encouraging parents teach their children to accept their own inadequacies, learn from mistakes (mistakes are wonderful opportunities for learning), have confidence in themselves, and to feel useful through contribution. When commenting on children's efforts, be careful not to place value judgments on what they have done. Be alert to eliminating value-laden words (good, great, excellent, etc.) from your vocabulary at these times. Instead, substitute words of encouragement that help children believe in themselves. Encouragement focuses on effort and can always be given; children who feel their efforts are encouraged, valued, and appreciated develop qualities of persistence and determination and tend to be good problem solvers.

Note: The parent's voice should match the child's level of affect; if the child is excited about getting an A on a test, the parent responds likewise, with excitement in her voice, "You're really proud of that!" Use celebrations (after the event, based on the child's pride in achievement) instead of rewards (an external motivator to get the child to achieve) to recognize achievement. In the above example, the parent could add, "Sounds like something to celebrate—let's make a cake!," or "Sounds like something to celebrate—you choose the restaurant!"

- ***Encouraging phrases that recognize effort and improvement:***
  - "You did it!" "You got it!"
  - "You really worked hard on that."
  - "You didn't give up until you figured it out."
  - "Look at the progress you've made..." (Be specific)
  - "You've finished half of your worksheet and it's only 4 o'clock."
- ***Encouraging phrases that show confidence:***
  - "I have confidence in you...you'll figure it out."
  - "That's a rough one, but I bet you'll figure it out."
  - "Sounds like you have a plan."
  - "Knowing you, I'm sure you will do fine."
  - "Sounds like you know a lot about..."
- ***Encouraging phrases that focus on contributions, assets, and appreciation:***
  - "Thanks, that was a big help."
  - "It was thoughtful of you to..." or "I appreciate that you..."
  - "You have a knack for __________. Can you give me a hand with that?"

In summary, encouragement is (a) valuing and accepting children as they are (not putting conditions on acceptance), (b) pointing out the positive aspects of behavior, (c) showing faith in children so that they can come to believe in themselves, (d) recognizing effort and improvement (rather than requiring achievement), and (e) showing appreciation for contributions. The therapist emphasizes that encouragement shows faith in children and fosters self-esteem, self-motivation, confidence, and creativity in children by focusing on effort, improvement, and contributions. On the other hand, praise limits children's creativity, self-confidence, and self-motivation by teaching them to depend on others' views and opinions to determine their own self-worth *(refer to Chapter 5 for additional discussion and strategies for teaching encouragement).*

Homework Assignments

1. Parents are reminded of the importance of conducting their play session at the same time and same place and to videotape their sessions.

2. Remind parents to take a few minutes to review *Filial Play Session Dos & Don'ts* prior to their play sessions.
3. Parents are reminded after conducting the play sessions to complete the *Parent Play Session Notes* and *Play Session Skills Checklist.*
4. Remind parents to practice giving children a choice outside of play session and report back.
5. Ask them to write down one thing in play session that didn't go well and write down one thing they did in play session that went really well.
6. Write down one issue they are struggling with most outside of play session time. It may be one they have brought up before, or they may have already solved that one on their own and have a new issue they want help with.
7. Read over handout, Encouragement vs. Praise, and practice giving child encouragement one time outside play session, reporting back on how that went.
8. One to two parents are scheduled to be videotaped.
9. Remind parents of the Rule of Thumb for the week.

Partial Transcript of CPRT Session 8

(Parents shared about their week, reported on making self-esteem–building responses, described their character quality note writing, and reported on giving a choice outside the playtime.)

Dr. L.: Well, how have your playtimes gone? Laura, we'll see your videotape in a few minutes, so we'll hear from you then.

Kathy: We had a pretty good one.

Dr. L.: Tell us some specifics. What happened in the playtime?

Kathy: He wanted to play with some different things this time. He has usually been playing with the punching bag and that kind of stuff, but this time he got the furniture out and started arranging that. He didn't ask me to do anything with him. Sometimes when I tell him I see what he's doing, he says, "Mom, quit talking," or "Mom, I know that already. I know what I'm doing already."

Debbie: Yeah, Rachel said, "I don't want you telling me what I'm doing." She got real agitated with me for making tracking comments.

Dr. L.: Such responses may mean your children feel that you're tracking a little too closely. Sometimes, that may be your child's way of pushing you a little bit to find out "Can I get away with this? Can I tell you I don't like that?" It may not really bother them so much at all. It's just a way of pushing you to find out how you're going to react. If you sense that is going on you can say, "Oh, the way I'm talking now bothers you." It doesn't mean you're going to change, it just says, "I have recorded what you said." The other possibility is maybe your child doesn't want you to change. They would like for you to be the way you used to be. Why?

Debbie: It's comfortable.

Kathy: Change is uncomfortable for them.

Dr. L.: Do you experience any of that, Emily?

Emily: No, I haven't gotten anything so far but real positive results from the playtimes. As a matter of fact, my child is really different since we started doing this.

Dr. L.: Tell us about that.

Emily: He's not nearly as demanding. The temper tantrums are gone. He's just different. He doesn't argue as much. I usually tell him, "These are your choices." He never picked the right one. He doesn't do that anymore. It may be because I follow through in the sessions now.

Dr. L.: So you're more consistent now.

Emily: Probably. He doesn't test me as much now.

Dr. L.: So, he doesn't have a need to test you as much.

Emily: Maybe he feels he doesn't have to kick me or bite me to get my attention anymore because we have the special playtime.

Dr. L.: So, you're meeting his needs, and you're doing it, not someone else.

(Emily describes playtime.)

Dr. L.: Listening to you, I can tell it's fun for you, too.

Emily: It is. I love that time together. I really do.

Dr. L.: Then Chris surely must know that you like being with him, that you enjoy the time. If you put yourself in Chris's spot, and your mom likes being in the play session with you, looks forward to it, and has fun while you're together, how would Chris feel?

Emily: Pretty special. Loved.

Dr. L.: Loved, and that he's important. That's a special gift you're giving. Sounds like a real active time, too. Sonya, tell us about your session.

Sonya: They're getting more and more interesting. Now, she wants to help set up the toys before time to start. She takes everything out of the box and sets it where she wants it, and then pretends like she's starting: "Oh, here's some toys," and then she comes in and plays. She's exploring the more aggressive toys now. I get the feeling that maybe she feels like it's safe to do that now. Before, she never touched the gun or the knife, or the oven mitt that looks like a dragon. Now, that's her pet. She gives it a different name every week. She feeds it Tinkertoys. And even though it's scary looking, she says, "He's nice."

Dr. L.: He's a nice dragon, and she is experiencing being in charge of the playtime.

Sonya: Uh-huh. She likes the Band-Aids, too. She always Band-Aids the dolls. I'm amazed watching her. She's 3 years old, and she takes the Band-Aid out of the wrapper, and it will be sticking to her fingers, but she can get it all undone by herself. It's so frustrating for me to sit there. I want to say, "Honey, let me do that for you."

Dr. L.: You want to take control.

Sonya: Yes, but once I see her achieve, it feels so good. I say, "You did that all by yourself." And she says, "I know." (Sonya smiles.) You could tell she felt good about it.

Dr. L.: So you knew that your response was heard, that Jenny felt empowered. By being patient and allowing her a chance to figure things out for herself, you gave her the opportunity to feel good about "doing all by herself." And your response let her know that. Folks, one of the best things we can communicate to our children is that they are competent. Tell a child she is capable and she will believe she is capable. Tell her or show her enough times she can't do it, and sure enough, she can't.

Emily: So, if we do it for them, we're telling them they can't do it.

Dr. L.: You got it! Sonya, tell us some more about your play session.

Sonya: The big deal for her the past couple of times is she ties the bop bag up. Last week she put the Lone Ranger mask on the bop bag and said that was the mean daddy. She spent most of the session tying up the mean daddy. She took pieces of tape, taped him all up, and shot him. She wanted me to stick him with the knife and I told her I wouldn't like to do that. And she said, "Okay, I will."

Dr. L.: So you were able to convey your feeling in such a way that she still felt free to go ahead and do what she wanted to do. She didn't feel, "Oh, I'm not supposed to do this."

Sonya: Yeah.

Emily: That kind of surprised me when you said, "So she took the knife and did it." I expected her to say, "Why don't you want to do that, Mamma?"

Sonya: I just told her I wouldn't like to do that. It didn't feel good. That's the first time she brought up her dad in the playtime, and I really wanted to find out more about this mean daddy, so I stepped out of the nondirective play role and asked her about the mean daddy. She didn't respond and I went, "Oops," that's not going to work.

Dr. L.: You learned something important about playtime. Questioning doesn't work.

Sonya: Um-hum. She just went on with something else. It's a real important time for her and me, and it's getting more fun as we do it. I can't wait to see what she explores next. She's starting to use the toys in different ways. Now when it's time to pick up, she says, "I'm going to help you." And she starts picking up the toys, and I'm thinking, "What is this?" I have to negotiate deals with her all the time to get her to pick up.

Dr. L.: So, what have you learned about her?

Sonya: Well, she is capable of picking up her toys.

Dr. L.: She is capable of being helpful. Isn't that amazing that she will volunteer to pick up in the playtime but not where you would like for her to?

Sonya: It's just absolutely amazing. I have found in using the A-C-T limit setting a lot of times all I have to do is say, "You look very angry," or "I understand that you want to do that," and that's all I have to do for her to decide that it's not a big deal anymore.

Dr. L.: That's the end of it. She stops herself because you allow her to stop herself.

Sonya: I don't have to count one, two, three, or four anymore. And another thing, now, when she says, "I don't like you. You're not my friend anymore," I haven't been feeding into that. I just check, is she angry or frustrated? Usually she's angry. I just say, "Sounds like you're very angry because I won't do what you want me to do," and it works great.

Dr. L.: At that moment, your child knows that her message has been received by you and that you understand. She doesn't have to escalate to get her message across.

Sonya: She seems to really cherish the fact that this is a special time just for me and her.

Dr. L.: So, she feels important.

Sonya: Uh-hum. I think I'll probably just keep doing the playtimes way after the training.

Dr. L.: So, they have become important to you, also. Debbie, did you have a playtime this past week?

Debbie: A short one. Rachel really wasn't interested. I think she's really angry with me. She's not really saying it, but she's demonstrating it really heavily, and she doesn't want playtime to be very long.

Dr. L.: Tell us what happened.

Debbie: We got into the playtime, and she wanted to play. She seemed very distracted. Even outside playtime, she won't pay attention to me because she's angry with me. She really is. There's other things going on.

Dr. L.: All the more reason for you to have the playtime even though she's not quite sure she wants to be there with you.

Debbie: So, make her stay in the playtime?

Dr. L.: You can take a compromise position when she wants to leave after just a few minutes. You can say, "We have 20 more minutes, and then it will be time to stop." If that doesn't work, and in a minute or two she says, "But I want to leave now," then try compromising. "We have 20 more minutes, let's do this. Let's take 10 more minutes to be together in our special playtime, and at the end of the 10 minutes, you can decide if you want to have the rest of the playtime, or if you want to end it." So, she still gets to feel in control. When things are not going well in your child's life, or in your life, that may be all the more reason to have the special playtime and to stick it out even if she's angry at you. Can you try that?

Debbie: Sure.

Dr. L.: Kim, how was your session?

Kim: It was great.

Dr. L.: What made it great?

Kim: He played with toys he had never even picked up before. I want to ask you something. If he names things wrong during playtime, I can't correct him, right?

Dr. L.: What do you think my answer is?

Kim: No. But I can't let him get away with thinking incorrect labels are correct.

Sonya: Like what?

Kim: Like the house. He knows what's right. But it's like he's waiting for me to tell him he's wrong. I just sat there and didn't correct him.

Dr. L.: So you passed the test. Maybe he's wondering, "Can it be what I want it to be, or will Mom tell me, "No, it's got to be a house"? You passed the test.

Kim: But outside the playtime, I should tell him that's not what that is.

Dr. L.: Outside the 30-minute playtime, you can be his teacher and give the right answers.

Emily: But inside that 30-minute playtime, you're stupid.

Dr. L.: And it can be whatever they want it to be.

Kathy: It's hard to stop yourself.

Sonya: Or to say, "It looks like you want that to be the refrigerator or you want that to be the stove."

Dr. L.: Yes, change is difficult. Kim, what else did he do?

Kim: He just played. He talked a lot. He doesn't usually talk. We've been trying to stimulate his verbal ability, and in the playtime, he was just rattling on and on. I told my husband when he got home, I didn't talk hardly at all in the playtime because Toby was just rambling on.

Dr. L.: Sounds like he surprised you in a lot of ways, and you're really pleased.

Kim: Oh, yeah. He's come a long way from not wanting to play at all.

Dr. L.: And it was a fun time.

Kim: Oh, yeah. It was great.

Dr. L.: Well, we've heard from everybody. Laura, let's see the video of your playtime. Do you want to tell us anything about your session ahead of time?

Laura: It was different than what I expected as far as what his interests were. (She describes different toys her son played with.)

Dr. L.: Well, let's see what happened.

(Parents watch video.)

Dr. L.: (Stops video.) Dawson quickly got involved. You made the kind of nonevaluative response that we've talked about. Instead of saying, "That's a pretty picture," you responded to his effort, "Working real hard on that." That's an example of another important Rule of Thumb we are going to talk more about today, "Encourage the effort instead of praising the product." You can always find something to encourage in your children, but praise can only be given to your child when he does something that meets some external standard. In this case, Laura, you gave Dawson credit for working hard on his picture. This kind of encouragement fosters creativity—praise limits creativity and freedom of expression.

Kathy: So we're not supposed to tell our children that their drawings are pretty?

Dr. L.: Not during this 30-minute playtime. We'll come back to this later. Let's watch more of Laura and Dawson.

(Parents watch video.)

Laura: (Stops video.) I put a limit on him there, right? By stopping him from mixing the colors.

Dr. L.: It would be okay to mix the colors. If you could redo what we saw right here, physically, not what you said, what would you do differently? Did you see yourself?

Laura: I leaned toward him with my hands to stop him.

Dr. L.: Yes, and you'd do what next time?

Laura: I won't try to touch him physically to stop him. I'll just tell him.

Dr. L.: Because the message is, if you start to reach out, "I don't believe you will stop yourself."

Laura: I didn't touch him or grab him. But I started to reach.

Dr. L.: And we want our children to stop themselves without any kind of threat. Here comes Mom's hand. I'd better…

(Parents view video.)

Dr. L.: (Stops video.) Dawson has your full attention. I haven't seen you even look away from him. He has your absolute attention.

Debbie: And he's taking care of himself.

Dr. L.: Yes, he is.

Laura: He washed each brush. He cleaned the sink afterward, and he cleaned the play dishes that were in the sink.

Dr. L.: Such responsibility. I gather from your reaction that's pretty unusual for him.

Laura: Yeah. I was shocked to see him clean each brush and put it back, and he even cleaned the whole sink after all that.

Dr. L.: You're discovering some new attributes of Dawson. Why is it that your children will take this kind of responsibility in this 30 minutes?

Laura: Because it is their choice. It wasn't because Momma was standing there telling him to do it. And him standing there saying, "I'm not going to do it."

Debbie: No battles.

Dr. L.: And when your children are free to make some of these kinds of decisions, they naturally move toward taking care of themselves and the situation without a lot of hassle.

Laura: Yeah, boy, do we know that.

Dr. L.: What an important discovery that in the playtime when you're not the teacher, you're not the boss, and you're not correcting, your child's self-direction comes forth. The only way you could have discovered that is in this kind of free playtime.

(Parents view videotape.)

Dr. L.: (Stops video.) Laura, that was an esteem-building response. You gave him credit for remembering.

(Videotape continues.)

Dr. L.: (Stops video.) This segment of your video is an example of your facial expression saying a lot more than any words can ever say. You reflect his feelings with your face. Watch your face. No words. Everything about your face says, "I'm here with you, I hear you. I understand. I care." I hear your message in your face. "You're excited about that. It's fun for you." You say no words, and yet you conveyed everything you needed to convey to him.

Laura: I don't think he ever looked at me.

Sonya: I think so. Yes, he's checking.

Dr. L.: Watch this. (Plays video.) He did see you—right there. (Stops video.) Children don't miss a thing. This is a delightful scene right here, clearly enjoyed by both of you.

(Video continues.)

Dr. L.: (Stops video.) My, such patience, Laura. Not once did I hear you say, "Now hurry up. You've been washing your hands there a long time now. Now hurry up." You all give Laura some feedback. What did you see, and what did you hear?

Kim: You stayed right with him. He knew you were interested.

Sonya: I agree. You didn't overtrack what he did. You let him lead. And you reflected what he was feeling.

Emily: You were so patient and relaxed, real comfortable, real calm. Looked like you've done this for years.

Kathy: I liked your facial expressions. Your response built up his self-esteem.

Debbie: Your reflections were so good. You didn't take over, and you allowed him to struggle to figure things out.

Dr. L.: Were you feeling as relaxed inside as you looked?

Laura: Well, if you look at body posture and if you look at signals, really, you know…

Dr. L.: You looked pretty relaxed to me.

Laura: Well, my hands are usually clutched, which would indicate to me that I wasn't as relaxed.

Dr. L.: Well, maybe you're more sensitive to that than you need to be. You looked pretty relaxed for a videotaping session here. He's obviously very comfortable in this setting. Good interaction, good tracking.

Laura: I've really been working on noticing his feelings, saying, "I can see that you're really angry." A lot of times he doesn't know what he is angry about. But at least just to label his feelings seems to help.

Dr. L.: Yes, he knows you understand.

(Dr. L. passes out handout, Encouragement vs. Praise, and reviews the similarities and differences between the two. Examples of encouraging responses for use in different situations are reviewed and parents are given a homework assignment to practice encouragement with their children.)

Dr. L.: Okay, let's stop, and I want to remind you we have two more sessions. For homework, I'd like for you to reread the handout I just gave you and work on the use of encouragement. Write down one time you made an encouraging response to your child this week. Come back next week and report on what your child did or said and how you responded. I also want you to practice choice giving again this week, so write down one time you gave your child a choice and what happened. Also, would you make a note right after your session this week on anything that happens in your special playtime that doesn't go very well for you or a time when you're not quite sure what to do or say, and also write down one thing that went really well.

Next week we will be discussing how to use some of these skills outside of play session—so think of an issue that you'd like help with and write that down. So, you have a lot to do this week—four assignments: 1) practice encouragement, 2) practice choice giving again, 3) write down something in your play session you'd like to have some help with and one thing you're really proud of, and 4) one issue outside of your play session that you'd like some help on. See you next Monday.

References

Dinkmeyer, D., & McKay, G.D. (1982). *The parent's handbook.* Circle Pines, MN: American Guidance Service.

Bratton, S., Landreth, G., Kellam, T., & Blackard, S. (2006). Child Parent Relationship Therapy (CPRT) Treatment Manual: A 10-Session Filial Therapy Model for Training Parents. NY: Routledge.

CHAPTER 15

CPRT TRAINING SESSION 9: SUPERVISION AND GENERALIZING SKILLS

Overview

Refer to the Overview section at the beginning of Chapter 12 as a thorough review of the overall supervision process and important reminders that apply for Sessions 6 through 9. Supporting and encouraging parents' skill development and confidence, as well as their struggles, through group supervision and feedback continues as the chief aim, with the majority of training Session 9 spent in group supervision and support, rather then didactic instruction.

No new skills are introduced; rather, the focus is on advanced application of CPRT skills and on generalizing the play skills to happenings outside of the play session, specifically those concerns that parents have introduced over the past 8 weeks. The use of the A-C-T model of limit setting outside of play sessions receives extra emphasis, as this is the hardest skill for parents to master in everyday happenings.

Materials

Suggested materials include: *CPRT Session 9–Treatment Outline;* parent information form with pertinent notes; homework assigned in Session 8, including extra copies of any homework worksheets; and Session 9 handouts and homework including: *Session 9 Parent Notes & Homework, Advanced Limit Setting: Giving Choices as Consequences for Non-Compliance, Generalizing Limit Setting to Outside the Play Session, Structured Doll Play for Parents, Parent Play Session Notes,* and *Play Session Skills Checklist.* Additional materials include: a display poster of *Filial Play Session Dos and Don'ts,* an optional video clip demonstrating specific play session skills parents are most struggling with, and, most importantly, **the written list of concerns that parents have expressed over the past 8 weeks**.

> *Note: All handouts listed above, as well as a training session outline for the therapist, additional supplemental parent handouts, and resources for this training session are found in the* CPRT Treatment Manual *and accompanying CD-ROM, available from the publisher, Routledge.*

Content and Procedure

Although training Session 9 follows a similar format to Sessions 6 through 8—sharing how the week went, reporting on home play sessions, and focused supervision of the videotaped parent(s)—this session differs in the amount of time spent in group processing of the parents' week. The majority of homework assignments from last week focused on the use of skills outside of the play sessions; therefore, focusing more time and energy into the sharing of happenings outside of playtimes is warranted. The amount of time spent will vary depending on the needs of the group. The more advanced the group, generally the more they will generalize skills outside the play sessions; therefore, more time is spent on applying skills to everyday activities. Typically by Session 9, parents are demonstrating greater awareness of their own feelings and reporting greater sensitivity to their children's feelings; therefore, the therapist uses the parents' discussion of happenings outside of play sessions to facilitate parents' sharing of their feelings, as well as their recognition of their children's feelings. This informal sharing provides many opportunities for parents to continue to practice how to more effectively respond to their children's feelings, wants, and needs, without accepting all behavior.

Review Homework

Homework assignments to practice encouragement and choice giving are reviewed and reinforced as parents share how their week has been. The therapist should be prepared for a lively debate and discussion about encouragement vs. the use of praise. The concept of praise, along with reward and punishment, is so ingrained in parents' thinking that they typically challenge the suggestion that praise should be limited in their interactions with their children.

Filial Play Session Reports and Video Critiques

Parents report briefly on their home play sessions and their homework assignment to write down one thing that went well and one thing they need help with. The therapist listens for opportunities to facilitate peer feedback to reinforce CPRT skills in the parents' sharing of play session happenings, following the strategy employed in training Session 8, to stop the video after **an obvious skill has been demonstrated** and ask parents if they have any feedback for that parent. The therapist's goal is to facilitate parents' growth and learning to a higher level of awareness. The ability to recognize demonstrated skills and give accurate feedback to others is not only empowering, it requires a higher level of learning for parents than simply being able to demonstrate the skills in their play sessions.

Parents are reminded of the importance of being consistent in their interactions with their children while allowing their children to struggle with responsibility for their own behaviors. It is not the parent's responsibility to make the playtime fun or interesting for the child or to entertain the child. The child is in the lead and is responsible for what she does for 30 minutes. Most parents have difficulty with this. As seen in the following interaction between the therapist and a parent during training Session 9, parents often believe they are responsible for their children's happiness—and unhappiness.

Dr. L.: Kim, I heard you say something I want to check on. I think I heard you say that you have a hard time keeping Toby interested.

Kim: Yes, he has a short attention span, and when we first started, the toys were new.

Dr. L.: For 30 minutes, it is not your responsibility to keep Toby interested.

Kim: But, I wait all week for the playtime, and then he doesn't have fun.

Dr. L.: So *you're* disappointed—

The therapist uses these kinds of sharings to generalize CPRT play session skills to outside the playtime, in this case, to emphasize that the parents are not responsible for their children's happiness. It is not their job to make sure their children are always occupied, interested, busy, or happy. Remind parents that if they take responsibility for their children's happiness, their children will never learn to do that for themselves. Although no new play session skills are introduced, the therapist may introduce strategies that will help parents with specific problems. An example shown in the transcript below is the therapist introducing the use of "Structured Doll Play" as a way of helping a parent who is struggling with her child not wanting to go to play therapy, a new happening in this child's life. Additional strategies can be introduced, as needed, as long as the strategy is consistent with the basic child-centered philosophy that CPRT training is based on.

Because limit-setting continues to challenge most parents, it is helpful to briefly cover limit-setting strategies for non-compliance.

Advanced Limit Setting: Giving Choices as Consequences for Non-Compliance

Play Session Example: After the parent has stated that the Play-Doh is for playing with on the tray, 5 year-old Billy dumps it on the floor. Next, the parent follows the A-C-T method of limit setting: **"Billy, I know that you want to play with the Play-Doh over there, but the floor (carpet, etc.) is not for putting Play-Doh on." (pointing to tray) "The tray is for putting the Play-Doh on."** Billy continues to ignore the parent and begins to smash the Play-Doh on the floor. The parent may patiently restate the limit up to three times before beginning the next step of stating *"If–Then"* choices (consequences) for following or not following the limit.

> Note: This example assumes that the parent has chosen a location for the play session where the floor surface can be easily cleaned after the session.

Next step: Begin "If–Then" choice-giving method to provide consequence for unacceptable behavior. Note the number of times the word choose *or* choice *is used! Remember that your intent is for your child to bring himself under control; therefore, patience is the order for the day. Children need time and practice to learn self-control.*

"Billy, *if you choose* to play with the Play-Doh on the tray" (pointing to tray), "*then you choose* to play with the Play-Doh today. *If you choose* to continue to play with the Play-Doh on the floor, *then you choose* not to play with the Play-Doh for the rest of today." (pause) Patiently restate this if the child does not make the choice to comply with the limit (if no answer and Billy continues to play with Play-Doh on floor, then he has made his choice). **"Billy, looks like you've *chosen* to put the Play-Doh up for today. You can *choose* to give me the Play-Doh or you can choose for me to put the Play-Doh up for you—which do you *choose*?"** If the child begins to cry and beg for the Play-Doh, the parent must be tough and follow through, acknowledging the child's feelings and giving him hope that he will have a chance to make a different choice in the next play session. **"Billy, I understand that you're unhappy that you *chose* to have the Play-Doh put up for today, but you can *choose* to play with it in our next play session."**

In the above example, if at any point the child took the Play-Doh and put it on the tray to play with, the parent must be careful to respond matter-of-factly, **"Looks like you decided you wanted to play with it some more today."**

Generalizing Skills to Outside the Play Session

Although by this point in this session the therapist has already addressed some parent concerns and how the CPRT play session skills can be used to respond more effectively, be sure to allow time to go over your written list of parents' concerns from the past

8 weeks. Begin by checking to see which ones are still troublesome. It is our experience that many of the "problems" are not problems anymore! Prioritize concerns to address by those shared by the most parents. When discussing the generalization of play session skills to problem areas, tell parents the **Rule of Thumb is "Don't try to change everything at once!"** The therapist should allow time to go over generalizing limit setting to outside the play session and what to do when limit setting isn't working outside of play sessions. Begin by reviewing the 3-step A-C-T model:

1. ***A***cknowledge the feeling.
2. ***C***ommunicate the limit.
3. ***T***arget alternatives.

Next, go over an outside-of-play session example of the A-C-T method of limit setting, followed by "If–Then" Choice Giving, to establish consequences for noncompliance of the limit.

3-Step A-C-T Method of Limit Setting, Followed by "If–Then" Choice Giving

Scenario: Your child found your hidden stash of candy, has a piece in his hand, and is starting to unwrap it (it is 30 minutes before dinner).

1. ***A***cknowledge your child's feeling or desire *(your voice must convey empathy and understanding):* **"Billy, I know you'd really like to have the candy."** *He learns that his feelings, desires, and wishes are valid and accepted by parent (but not all behavior); just empathically reflecting your child's feeling often defuses the intensity of the feeling or need.*
2. ***C***ommunicate the limit (be specific and clear—and brief): **"...but candy is not for eating before dinner."**
3. ***T***arget acceptable alternatives; provide one or more choices (depending on age of child). **"You can *choose* to have a piece of fruit now** *(pointing to bowl of fruit)* **and *choose* to have the piece of candy after dinner."** (If you do not want your children to ever have candy, don't keep it around.) *The goal is to provide your child with acceptable alternatives—ones that are acceptable to you, the parent, and ones that you believe will allow your child to get his need met (in this case, to have a*

piece of candy, but not until after dinner—and if he is hungry, to meet that need with an acceptable before-dinner snack).

Note: Pointing helps redirect your child's attention. *If* your *child chooses fruit, stop here. Patiently restate the limit up to 3 times, depending on the age of the child, to allow* the *child to struggle with self-control before proceeding to the next step.*

4. "If–Then" choice giving (consequences) as next step, after noncompliance (examples of possible responses): *Billy continues to say that he doesn't want fruit, he wants the candy.* **"Billy, having candy now is not one of the *choices.*" If you *choose* to give me the candy now, *then you choose* to eat it after dinner; *if you choose* for me to put the candy up, *then you choose* not to have the candy after dinner. Which do you *choose?*"** *(pause; Billy says nothing).* **"*If you choose* not to *choose, then you choose* for me to *choose* for you"** *(pause).*

- *(Billy gives you the candy.)* **"I can tell that was a hard decision—I'll put it up here for you for after dinner."**
- *(Billy continues to hold on to candy.)* **"I see that you've *chosen* not to have the candy after dinner"** *(state empathically as you reach for the candy to put it up). After dinner, if Billy comes to you and says, "Now can I have the candy?," your response is,* **"Remember when you *chose* not to give me the candy before dinner—at that very moment, you *chose* not to have candy after dinner."** *He may continue to plead and cry (because it has worked in the past); BE FIRM—don't give in!*

Provide parents with a practice worksheet with additional examples. This is a difficult skill to learn. Parents feel foolish using *choice* and *choose* so frequently. Follow with a discussion of how to modify choice giving and establishing consequences with older children. Remind parents of the **Rule of Thumb: Give big choices for big kids and little choices for little kids.**

No matter how skilled the parent is at using limit setting, it will not always work. Parents need to know that! Allow time to discuss what to do when the A-C-T method of limit setting doesn't work (a supplemental worksheet is provided in the *CPRT Treatment Manual*).

1. Look for natural causes for rebellion.
2. Remain in control, respecting yourself and the child.
3. Set reasonable consequences for disobedience.
4. Never tolerate violence.
5. If the child refuses to choose, you choose for him.
6. Enforce the consequences: Don't state consequences that you cannot enforce. If you crumble under your child's anger or tears, you have abdicated your role as parent and lost your power. **GET TOUGH!** Introduce the **Rule of Thumb: Where there are no limits, there is no security. Consistent Limits = Security in the Relationship.** When you don't follow through, you lose credibility and harm your relationship with your child.
7. Recognize signs of more serious problems: As parents feel more confident in their newfound skills, they are typically eager to tackle every problem they are having with their children. Help parents **choose one issue to focus on**—for example, bedtime problem, aggressive behavior, hitting, getting ready for school, etc.—and report back the following week on which issue they have selected to focus on.

Homework Assignments

1. Parents are reminded of the importance of conducting their play sessions at the same time and same place.
2. Remind parents to take a few minutes to review *Play Session Dos & Don'ts* prior to their play session.
3. Parents are reminded after conducting the play session to complete the *Parent Play Session Notes* and *Play Session Skills Checklist*.
4. Parents are asked to notice the number of times they touch their children in interactions outside the special playtime (hugging, patting on the head, a touch on the arm, etc.). Ask them to actually try to keep count during the week.
5. A related assignment is to play-wrestle with your children. Research shows that when asked what activity they remembered most in playing with their parents when they were children, both male and female adults in their late 20s identified

wrestling as the activity they remembered and had the most fun doing. (Example: In a two-parent family with small children, mom and kids can sneak up on dad and try to get him down on the floor—accompanied by lots of fun and laughter.)

6. Parents are asked to choose one issue they are struggling with (outside of the play session) to focus on and report back the following week on how they can use their play session skills to respond to the issue.
7. One to two parents are scheduled to be videotaped.
8. Remind parents of the Rules of Thumb for the week.

Partial Transcript of CPRT Session 9

Dr. L.: How has the week gone for you?

Laura: I tried to bring David, my 6-year-old, to the clinic here for play therapy this week, and he refused to stay; it was a really bad time. I was real angry at him when we left. But I didn't vent a lot of things on him that I would have at other times in the past. On the way home in the car, he said, "Well, Mommy, you were a kid once too, and I just didn't want to go into the room with that lady." I blew it for a moment by saying, "Yes, I was a kid too, but I didn't have parents that cared enough about me to try to help." I was still angry at him, but I didn't say some things that I usually would have said.

Dr. L.: So you didn't dump on him.

Laura: No, except for that one statement.

Dr. L.: That's progress. You controlled your emotions.

Laura: Yes, that is progress for me.

Dr. L.: Laura, if you could go back through that episode of bringing him here, and he didn't want to stay, what would you do differently?

Laura: I guess it has to be OK, but it's hard to believe a 6-year-old should be allowed to make a decision about whether or not he, uh…

Dr. L.: Needs help or not.

Laura: Yeah, but I don't know what to do except let him decide.

Dr. L.: For some reason, he's anxious about going into the playroom with the therapist, or he's anxious about you leaving him. Let's try something.

Laura: OK. Tell me what. We're supposed to go back Wednesday at 6:00.

Dr. L.: Today is Monday. Before he goes to bed tonight, and again tomorrow, I would like for you to try a procedure I call structured doll play. (To the group) This is a procedure all of you can use when your child is anxious about something or your child is worried about something, like being left with a babysitter, going to the dentist, going to school, or going to a birthday party for the first time. Laura, sit down with David, and say to him, "I want to tell you a special story. For this story, we need a toy or stuffed animal that can be you and one that can be me." Let David choose the items. "We also need a car." David chooses, and the story begins. "You're playing in your room, and I say, 'Dinner is ready.'" You use the chosen characters to act out the story as you tell it. "You sit down at the table, and we eat. Then I wash the dishes. OK, it's time to get in the car and go to the university. Here I go and here you go," as you show the characters going to the car. "You buckle your seatbelt, click, and I buckle mine, click." Be sure to use lots of noise props in telling the story. Make motor noises, brrrmmm brrrmmm, as you drive. "Here we are at the university. Click, I lock the car and we walk across the parking lot to the special center where they have a playroom, and we go in. Oh, we need something that will be Mrs. Brown, who will be in the playroom with you. David, choose something to be the lady. We go in, and Mrs. Brown says, 'Hi!", and you start a conversation between David and the lady back and forth. "You go down the hall with Mrs. Brown to the playroom," show the figures walking down the hall, "and I wait right here in the waiting room. I read a book while you're in the playroom, and the playroom has lots of neat stuff to play with.

I'm sitting here wondering what you're playing with in the playroom and think, you're going to be in the playroom for 30 minutes." Look at your watch. "And then I hear you coming down the hall; so I get up and look down the hall and sure enough there you are coming down the hall. I say, 'Hi, we can go home now.' We get into the car, put seatbelts on, click, and drive home, brrrmmm, brrrmmm. We go in the kitchen and we have chocolate chip cookies and milk. Yum, yum, these are good cookies." And the story ends with a big kiss (smaaaack) as you show the characters kissing. Be sure the kiss is a loud smaaack. Children like that. And the story ends. The story should not take longer than 5 minutes to tell.

The reason this kind of story is important is because your child will remember what he has seen and how the story ended. If you just tell your child what to expect, he won't be able to visualize what is going to happen. Your child will remember what he has seen and that it ended OK. So, Laura, you will tell your son this story Monday night and Tuesday night. It would be great if you could also tell him the story Wednesday afternoon before you take him to the playroom. This will help him to get ready for the visit.

Some of you are having trouble with your child at bedtime. You can use the same kind of story to prepare for bedtime. You tell your child a story about what is going to happen in the process of going to bed and end the story with, "I give you a big kiss (smaaaack), I tuck you in bed, and I go to my room to work; so I'm in my room and you're in your bed. Before I go to bed, I come back and check on you. 'Yep, he's asleep,' and I give you a big kiss so you will know I came to check on you." That's reassuring to your child to know you will be there after he goes to sleep. Laura, your son may be afraid you aren't going to be there when he comes out of the playroom.

Kim: Yeah, that he would be there all by himself with a stranger.

Laura: When I got ready to leave for work Sunday, David went running out to the car, got in, and locked the doors because he didn't want me to leave.

Dr. L.: Let's work on getting him ready for his playtime Wednesday, and then we'll work on a story to help him get ready for you to leave for work. You had an assignment last week to use choice giving at least one time this week. Did anyone give a choice this week?

Kathy: I did at the movies. We went to a movie, and Cody kept flopping around in his seat, kicking the back of the seat in front of him, so I took him out in the lobby and told him, "If you choose to kick the seat and bother people, then you choose for us to leave the movie." It worked. He stopped kicking.

Dr. L.: You took charge, Kathy, and Cody brought himself under control. There is another half to the choice giving though.

Laura: If you choose not to kick the chair, you choose to get to stay and watch the movie

Kathy: Well, he was real good for most of the movie, but then he started kicking again, so I said, "I see you have chosen to leave the movie," and we left.

Dr. L.: So you followed through, and Cody experienced the consequence of his choice. Kim, did you give a choice this week?

Kim: Toby has a really low frustration level, and he will get hysterical about little things and that has gotten a lot better, but we're still working on that; so we used the choice giving a lot this week. He will throw things in anger, and I won't allow that, so I give him a choice. But it's sad, because I have to take toys away.

Dr. L.: (Interrupts.) Excuse me, I'm not sure I heard you accurately. I think I heard you say, "I have to take away his toys."

Kim: (Interrupts.) He chooses to get the toys taken away. (Laughs.)

Dr. L.: Oh! Do you hear the difference?

Kim: Yeah.

Dr. L.: Yes, that's his choice. So, Kim, you can sit there and tell us with great calmness, "Would you believe he chose to give up his favorite toys 3 days in a row?" (Group laughs.)

Kim: That's true. My two kids share toys, and the other day Toby was playing with his sister's doll, and he threw it. That was real hard taking it away from my daughter because it's hers, but I can't let her play with it if I have taken it away.

Dr. L.: She can play with it because it's hers.

Kim: That doesn't work because they share everything.

Dr. L.: What else does Toby like to do?

Kim: I can't take TV away because they both watch TV.

Dr. L.: Is there just one room in your home? (Group laughs.)

Kim: No, there are lots of rooms. (Laughs.)

Dr. L.: Oh, you have more than one room. (Group laughs.)

Kim: Yeah.

Dr. L.: (Long pause.) So…

Kim: What do I do?

Dr. L.: How old is Toby?

Kim: Four and a half. Oh, he chooses to stay in his room a lot.

Dr. L.: The doll is your daughter's and Toby chooses not to play with it; you use the next step, "If you choose to keep trying to play with the doll, you choose to go sit in your room for 5 minutes. If you choose not to try to play with her doll, you choose not to go to your room for 5 minutes."

Kim: So you think it's wrong to take the doll away.

Dr. L.: If the doll was his, then that would be an appropriate choice, but taking the doll away punishes her.

Kim: Oh, I see.

Dr. L.: OK. You had an opportunity to use choice giving.

Kim: And it works. It really does. Oh, I started having playtimes this week with my daughter, like we talked about. She is so different from Toby in the playtimes.

Dr. L.: How did it work out?

Kim: She really liked it. The problem has been that the baby gets a lot of attention, and because he has special needs, Toby gets lots of attention; she has felt left out. I could see a difference in her behavior this week because of the special playtime. Her behavior was better. It was neat to see how she is different from Toby in the way she plays with the toys.

Dr. L.: So you learned something about her.

Kim: Oh, yeah. Everything we learn here is seeping into real life outside the 30-minute playtimes, and the whole family is different now.

Dr. L.: Great report.

Debbie: I have a question about bedtime. At what point do I start the choice giving, after she gets up?

Emily: When you put her to bed tonight, because she has already been getting up a lot every night. If you choose to get out of bed, you choose to give up TV in the morning.

Dr. L.: There are two parts to choice giving. If you choose not to stay in bed, you choose not to watch TV in the morning. If you choose to stay in bed, you choose to watch TV in the morning. Be sure to use both sides of the choice. The word "choose" must be used four times.

Emily: I don't think I've been doing that.

Laura: I haven't either.

Kim: Yeah, me too.

Laura: I've been saying, "You choose this or you choose this."

Debbie: And then that's where the spanking comes in.

Laura: I've learned lately that I go to spanking when I don't know what else to do. I've lost total control, and I think

I can control my children by using physical strength and it doesn't work.

Debbie: My use of spanking has decreased by 99 percent since this class started. I use to spank her for everything because I didn't know what else to do.

Dr. L.: Great progress.

Debbie: But I still have this urge to clobber her sometimes.

Dr. L.: But you're controlling yourself.

Laura: I feel like I'm overcoming that, and it's a powerful feeling.

Debbie: It's just that bedtime is so exasperating. That's the only time now that I feel physically angry at her.

Dr. L.: Bedtime has been a problem for some time, and you get really angry at Rachel; you need to intervene in a different way. You have two things you're going to do. You're going to tell her the going to bed story first and then go through the choice giving.

Kathy: Cody was sleeping in my bed when I first started coming to this class, but now he's sleeping in his room.

Laura: When I come home on Saturday nights, my kids are usually in bed, and after 16 hours at work, I'm not a real happy person. (Group laughs.) Well, this past Saturday night when I came home, they weren't in bed, and they wanted my attention. I wasn't physically or emotionally ready to give them any attention.

Dr. L.: How did you handle that?

Laura: Because of what I have learned in my playtimes with Dawson about detaching and being objective, I was able to be calm, detach from my day, and reflect their feelings. "I know you want to spend some time with me, and you would like to stay up, but this is not the time for staying up longer. It's time to be in bed."

Dr. L.: And what happened?

Laura: They went to bed and didn't get back up, and I visited with the couple that was babysitting the kids.

Dr. L.: So you handled it.

Laura: Yeah, I thought, wow! (Group laughs.)

Dr. L.: You did it!

Laura: Yes, without getting angry. That's an awful feeling to be so angry at your child. I know what you feel, Debbie, and it's awful.

Dr. L.: So you're not alone with that, Debbie.

Laura: And it's hard not to hit sometimes, but I can learn a new way.

Dr. L.: It seems to me, Laura, you're saying, "I have learned a new way."

Laura: Yes, I think so. For such a long time I was afraid of my own feelings, even to touch my kids for hugs and kisses.

Dr. L.: And now?

Laura: Now, I'm not afraid, since I've been coming to this class.

(Other parents discuss issues they are struggling with outside the play sessions. Group shares what didn't go well in their play session and what went well. Dr. L. gives home assignments and reminds group next week will be the last training session.)

References

Bratton, S., Landreth, G., Kellam, T., & Blackard, S. (2006). Child Parent Relationship Therapy (CPRT) Treatment Manual: A 10-Session Filial Therapy Model for Training Parents. NY: Routledge.

CHAPTER 16

CPRT TRAINING SESSION 10: EVALUATION AND SUMMING UP

Overview

Parents briefly report on their play sessions and one or two parent play sessions are viewed. Basic CPRT principles are reviewed, and parents are asked to share what part of the training has been the most helpful and what parts they continue to have the most concerns about. The last part of the training time is spent with parents sharing their evaluation of the experience, how they and their children have changed. Parents share their perceptions of changes they have observed in other parents. Therapist shares notes of parents' original descriptions of their children as points of reference for parents to evaluate progress. The partial transcript at the end of this chapter vividly illustrates typical parent comments regarding their changes in perceptions of their children and themselves. Parents are encouraged to accept and own their part in contributing to changes in their children's lives. This is usually a very rewarding and empowering experience for the parents. Parents are encouraged to continue the special playtimes. Parents and/or children needing additional help are scheduled for such help.

Materials

Suggested materials include: *CPRT Session 10–Treatment Outline;* parent information sheet with notes **including parents' descriptions of their children from Session 1**; homework assigned in Session 9, including any homework worksheets; and Session 10 handout, *Rules of Thumb & Other Things to Remember.*

> *Note: All handouts listed above, as well as a training session outline for the therapist, additional supplemental parent handouts, and resources for this training session are found in the* CPRT Treatment Manual *and accompanying CD-ROM, available from the publisher, Routledge.*

Content and Procedure

As is true of the first 9 training sessions, Session 10 is a jam-packed time. Lingering concerns of parents need to be addressed and suggestions offered. Supervision of play sessions is continued. Basic skills may need to be reviewed. Parents need to debrief the experience and prepare to disengage from the group. Parents evaluate the experience and share their perceptions of how they and their children have changed. Time must be taken to emphasize the importance of the special playtimes and encourage parents to continue to have their special playtimes. Arrangements need to be made for those parents who want to begin having a special playtime with a child other than their child of focus. If older children are to be involved, appropriate toys and materials will need to be discussed. The specifics of plans for follow-up sessions will need to be presented.

Support and encouragement are the rule of the day throughout this last session. The cohesiveness of the group is usually fully evident in this last session through increased parent interaction, and the leader may often find it helpful to stay in the background as parents process their feelings and reactions. Typically, parents are generous with their support and encouragement for other parents and may playfully tease each other, modeling the type of humor exhibited by the leader in earlier sessions. This playful, accepting, fun attitude modeled by the leader throughout the training sessions reduces the threat of "There must be something wrong with me, or I wouldn't need to be here," and helps parents to relax, thus aiding the learning of a new parenting role.

Wrap-Up of Parent Concerns

Parents are asked if they have any lingering concerns about the special playtimes or other issues they would like to share. These questions project an attitude of continuing concern on the part of the leader for parents in the group. The following interaction in the CPRT group we have been following was facilitated by these questions:

Kathy: At what age can you tell a child that there's something serious going on, like my sister has breast cancer, and she could die? I don't know how much to tell Cody (6 years old) about why I'm so on edge.

Dr. L.: You're really worried about your sister, and all the facts aren't important for Cody to know. What is important is the general message: your concern, your worry, because she is very sick and is in the hospital. Those messages can be understood by Cody.

Kathy: He has found out stuff he wasn't ready for. I was on the phone telling a close friend when Cody found out his dad was in jail. He went around announcing to the world, "Daddy's in jail."

Laura: Yeah, I know. Dawson reacted kind of like that, and I told him we weren't with his dad because he hurts us. I didn't go into the details of how he hurt us. He just needed to know that because he hurts us, we're not with him.

Dr. L.: So you told him as much as he was ready for.

Laura: Yes. (To Kathy) So you could do the same and say your sister is really sick. You don't have to explain what's wrong with her.

Dr. L.: I have a feeling that by asking the question, you're beginning to feel Cody should be told something.

Kathy: Yeah, I know he should know something. I don't know how much to burden him with right now.

Dr. L.: I hear you saying almost the same thing Laura said last week when her concern was, "Gee, I don't think I should go home and burden my child with my feelings," when she was feeling stressed to the limit because her music teacher had really dumped on her.

Laura: Yeah, I'd still like to hit him over the head with my guitar. (Group laughs.)

Dr. L.: A safe place to start is with yourself, your own worry, that your sister is very sick and she is in the hospital. How does that sound to you?

Kathy: I get worried about Cody going into depression because he's a very moody child.

Dr. L.: As you handle your feelings by sharing some of them with him, perhaps that will help him learn to handle his. If he seems bothered, you could suggest he draw a picture for her.

Sonya: I have been thinking I need to have a playtime with my second daughter. I feel like I'm ignoring her.

Dr. L.: Your other daughter, Jenny, doesn't seem to be ready to stop her playtimes; so how do you feel about a special playtime once a week with each of your daughters? I think you are ready to take that on.

Sonya: That's what I was thinking of doing.

Dr. L.: Ok, you can let us know in our follow-up meeting how that works out.

(Since this interaction is included here, it is not repeated in the transcript at the end of this chapter.)

Depending on the size of the group, the discussion time on these topics will need to be limited. Avoid getting bogged down in new concerns of major significance that may not be of interest to the rest of the group. Keep the interaction moving and focused. Supervision, evaluation, and follow-up are the primary concerns of this session.

Review Homework

Parents give a very brief report on what they noticed about the number of times they touched their children and their reaction to the wrestling time. Parents also report on issues they are struggling with and CPRT skills they can use.

Supervision

As in previous sessions, parents report on their play sessions and a parent–child play session is viewed. Continuing supervision in the last session is important because parents need all the feedback they can get, and issues emerge in supervision that might not otherwise be explored. At this stage in the group process, parents are usually quite adept at modeling the leader's approach to supervision by overlooking mistakes and responding to positive behaviors and skills. Our experience is that at this point in the training, most parents do a very satisfactory job of demonstrating the skills that have been taught.

How Child Behaviors Have Changed

The therapist shares her notes of parents' original descriptions of their children as points of reference for parents to evaluate progress. This sharing usually facilitates accounts of dramatic changes and tremendous insight on the part of the parents as in the following interaction: *(This CPRT training group is not the group we have been following throughout this book. This interaction is included here because the parent–child play session results are so dramatic and unusual).*

Dr. L.: Ten weeks ago, as you were talking about your child of focus, I wrote down your descriptions. I'd like to read these descriptions, and then you give us an update on what your child is like now. Jan, in our first session, you said Jennifer does a lot of attention seeking, especially at bedtime. She has severe headaches and gets attention because of her medication and medical problem. She doesn't get along very well with other children. She's been like a little adult. She argues a lot. She has several seizures a day and the medication doesn't help. You said,

"I think she has learned to cause her own seizures to get attention." Has any of that changed?

Jan: Yes. She had only one seizure in the past 4 weeks and has complained of a headache only 3 or 4 times in the past 4 or 5 weeks.

(Group applauds.)

Dr. L.: What a dramatic change! That is a super report.

Jan: She was having as many as 10 seizures a day on some days.

Dr. L.: What has made the difference, Jan?

Jan: Well, I think a lot of it, ah…well, I've probably made some difference by the way I respond to her. I know the playtimes have really helped her.

Dr. L.: Yes, you have made a difference in your child's life.

Jan: She seems happier now. And there's a lot less stress at home.

This is a remarkable description of behavior change, especially when considering the short time span of only 10 weeks. However, this description is not atypical of descriptions given by parents when they report behavioral changes in the 10th session. In the first CPRT training session, Erin described her 2-year-old daughter as a strong-willed child. She reported that they often engaged in power struggles, and that from the moment that her daughter was born, she found it difficult to connect with her. In the 10th session, Erin stated, with tears in her eyes, that she finally love her daughter. She had stopped punishing her and was able to spend more quality time with her. *(This report and the following parent reports in this section are not from the CPRT training group we have been following in this book.)*

In Session 1, Michal reported that she rocked her 4-year-old daughter to sleep in her stroller every night in order to avoid bedtime arguments. In the 10th session, Michal reported that her daughter now went to sleep on her own and that their relationship was much more calm and loving. She also stated that her relationship with her two teenagers had improved and was now based on attitudes of understanding and respect.

In Session 1, Jeanie expressed fear of her 7-year-old son's anger and aggression. She wept as she described his behavior problems in school, her inability to control his behavior at home, and her shame. After two play sessions, she reported progress in her son's behavior and how excited he was that she was taking a class to learn how to play with him. In the 10th session, Jeanie beamed with excitement as she said her son was no longer angry or out of control, there were no behavioral problems at school, and she was no longer afraid of her son. She particularly benefited from the homework assignment in which she wrote her son a note saying she appreciated his honesty and mailed it to him. He was excited about the note and asked her hopefully, "Is it true?" The note had such an impact on her son that she decided to e-mail the exercise to all of her friends as well as the school counselor.

Tenth session parent reports from the group of parents we have been following through the previous nine sessions are described in the partial transcript of CPRT Session 10 at the end of this chapter.

How Parents Have Changed

Asking parents how they are different now, how they have changed, or how their feelings about their children have changed facilitates opportunities for insight and can result in parents feeling more empowered. Parents need an opportunity to formulate new descriptions of themselves. Succinctly summarizing parents' descriptions of themselves helps them to recognize their changes and their accomplishments. It can also be helpful to ask parents to compare and contrast what is currently occurring in their families to what was happening 10 weeks ago, and what is currently happening in the play sessions to what happened in the first special playtime. The objective is to send parents away feeling empowered.

Important changes in parental behavior and attitudes can be seen in the following excerpts:

Dr. L.: Group, how are you different now?

Kim: I believed that parents had to be in charge of every single thing that kids did. I expected my children to make decisions and to behave kind of like adults. Now I see my children as so much more. They're not an extension of me. They are different. They are unique. Now my son knows I'm going to love him for who he is, and that I still love him and trust him even if he doesn't make the right choices.

Sonya: I was a sergeant-of-arms with my daughter, and we usually got into power struggles. Our interactions were like open-heart surgery crisis-type. I mean, screaming and crying and slamming doors. My anger was abrupt and quick, and we yelled and hollered at each other at least four or five times a day. Now, I know a lot of her behavior is kinda normal, and I'm more accepting of her. Filial has taught me how to set limits without getting angry to make my point.

Debbie: I used to yell at my daughter all the time. I don't do that anymore, so there's less stress. I spend more time with her now. I feel more in control. Even when I make a mistake, and things go wrong, I know I can do it differently next time.

Laura: I had a lot of my self-worth tied up in trying to make my children happy. I tried real hard not to do things that would make them mad at me. I felt completely responsible for their happiness. My children had to obey me so other people wouldn't think I was a bad mother. I learned in the play sessions that I don't have to fix things for my child. This one principle has changed my thinking and attitude about parenting. I have learned to acknowledge my children's feelings without having to fix them or do things for them. I can be there and offer what I have to offer, and I don't have to fix it.

Kim: I've discovered I don't have to be the perfect mom. I've been trying to be the perfect mom and provide everything for my child, meet all his needs, and I don't have to do that.

Dr. L.: And that feels good to you.

Kim: Yes, it does! It's a relief.

Dr. L.: Debbie, you're shaking your head.

Debbie: Yeah, I feel less stressed and a lot better about myself and the way I am responding to my daughter. I know I can handle the problems now. Before I didn't think I could; so I wouldn't even try.

Kathy: I feel closer to my son. I don't love him any more, but I feel closer. I listen to him better now. I don't turn him off.

Emily: I'm more ready to be a parent now. I haven't had special playtimes with my other children, but I respond differently to them. I have realized that these situations with my children don't have to be resolved immediately, that it often takes time to work through the process.

(This interaction is not repeated in the transcript at the end of this chapter.)

It is also reinforcing to ask parents how they think other parents in the group have changed or how they are different. They often are aware of changes not recognized by the parent of focus. It is difficult to maintain positive changes in behavior and attitudes if there is no awareness of the changes that have occurred. Since behavior is a function of self-perception, helping parents' perceptions of themselves to "catch up" with where they are now is key to sustained behavioral change. It is important that parents go away from this last session with a reinforced new perception of themselves.

Parents Evaluate the Experience

Parents are asked to share their reactions to the CPRT training and what part of the training has been most helpful to them. Sharing on this topic provides opportunities for review of basic skills that can serve as a reminder to parents of skills they will need to continue to focus on and utilize with their children. Parents can also be asked to share how what they have learned has been transferred or generalized to other children in the family. A mom shared about her increased confidence in a note, "I never dreamed parenting could be so easy and so very rewarding!!!"

Increased confidence seems to be a key factor for parents, as is seen in the following reactions:

Sonya: I would do this training forever even if I was perfect doing the techniques, because of the support of everyone in this group. And not just that, but also because we have Dr. Landreth sitting here, who is supposed to know everything. And he takes the pressure off when he doesn't know the answer by just saying, "I don't know." I need to know if I'm going to screw my kid up. I'll really miss that.

Laura: It's just nice having an outlet, somebody you can talk to that knows what you're talking about. A person who knows and understands and touches on your feelings. Somebody who cares about you.

Debbie: The special playtimes started out being for my daughter, but now they are for me, too. I came from a really bad family background, and I don't have a good parenting role model; so you (Dr. Landreth) have become my parent role model figure. I need more of this.

Kim: I wish this could be a once a week session until the kids are all grown! The supporting atmosphere with positive suggestions, comments, and stories in a safe, caring, nonjudgmental atmosphere is so wonderful. We didn't analyze what we were doing wrong, so there was no guilt trip.

Emily: Recently, my family experienced some problems, and I was truly grateful for the skills I learned here because I think they helped keep some difficult times from going into disastrous times. When things got out of hand, I was aware of how automatically some of the new skills came to mind.

(This interaction is not included in the transcript at the end of this chapter.)

This last training session is typically characterized by an air of camaraderie, and telephone numbers are usually exchanged with parents offering to help each other with projects or babysitting.

Continuing the Special Playtimes

When CPRT groups complete their 10 sessions of training, about half of the parents tend to stop having special playtimes. The reasons vary. Parents become involved in other projects that they placed on hold while they were in CPRT training. They no longer have the group or the leader to answer to. Their children's behavior has improved, so they no longer feel a sense of urgency to get something done. The importance of encouraging parents to continue having their special playtimes cannot be overemphasized. The 10 sessions of CPRT training are considered to be minimal, and children who have more severe problems certainly necessitate more extensive training to equip parents with the skills required in such cases. However, in all cases, parents should be encouraged to continue having their special playtimes. Introduce the following **Rule of Thumb: Good things come in small packages.** *Explain to parents that they should not wait for big events to enter into their children's worlds—that entering into their children's lives in small ways is what really matters. Continuing to have a weekly 30-minute special playtime is one way for parents to enter into their children's lives and create special moments between them and their children in a relatively small amount of time.*

Dr. L.: Even though summer school is out and vacation is about to begin, I want to encourage you to continue your special playtimes. They are valuable, because what you do for 30 minutes in the special playtime usually doesn't occur at other times in your home.

You have no tasks to complete during that time.

You focus completely on your child.

You are a mirror for your child's emotions.

Your child is allowed to take the lead.

Your child directs himself and assumes responsibility.

For 30 minutes, you are not your child's teacher.

You are encouraging, supportive, and accepting.

You don't offer any suggestions or solve any problems.

You don't criticize any behavior.

Now that we have concluded the first training phase, it's important that you continue your play session each week, then when we meet in September, you can report on how the month has gone with your playtimes.

Kathy: Cody wants the playtimes to be longer and to have three playtimes each week.

Dr. L.: Thirty minutes is enough time. You all have busy schedules, and you may not be able to be consistent if you have longer sessions and more sessions each week. Also, your child doesn't need three playtimes each week. One will be enough. It is better to be consistent in having one play session each week than to be inconsistent in trying to have three.

The therapist discusses the importance of continuing the home play sessions, and parents are asked to sign a contract committing to continue the play sessions for x number of weeks. The therapist tells the parents, "If you stop the play sessions now, the message is that you were playing with your child because you had to, not because you wanted to." Parents will usually commit to continue the play sessions at least until the follow-up training session around 4 to 6 weeks later. Parents may also set up their own continuing support group with time for the children to play and the parents to talk. One of the parents should take responsibility for coordinating the group's meeting time and place. The filial therapist concludes the session by providing parents with the handout, *Rules of Thumb & Other Things to Remember*, as a reminder of main points covered over the past 10 sessions. We have also had this handout made into a refrigerator magnet to provide a handy resource for parents (or you can laminate the handout and add a stick-on magnet).

Follow-Up Session

We have had some success scheduling one-month follow-up sessions for updating, dealing with play session problems, answering questions, etc. The therapist sends parents a postcard reminding them of the follow-up training session. Providing child care at this session is important for the reasons described earlier, but also because the children like to revisit the clinic with "all those neat toys." The session begins with the parents sharing their experiences in their play sessions since the last meeting, focusing on changes in themselves and their children. The therapist uses their comments to reinforce the CPRT skills and principles taught earlier. The therapist affirms the parents' progress by asking them to give examples of their successful use of the skills. A primary focus of this session is on helping parents generalize their skills outside the play sessions. Parents are encouraged to give each other suggestions, a process that can be very empowering for them as they help each other with their difficulties. Parents may choose to continue to meet on their own for support. If there is enough interest, another follow-up training session can be scheduled to be held in about 3 months.

Updating of parent skills can also be provided for by scheduling an advanced CPRT training group for parents who have completed previous CPRT training. In advanced CPRT training, skills are reviewed, the play process is examined in more depth, parent–child issues are updated, and much more time is spent than in the previous training on applying skills outside the play sessions. The therapist sends a personal invitation to CPRT "alumni" spanning several years, inviting them to sign up for the advanced CPRT training. The importance of advanced CPRT training was described by a parent:

> I have been having some major problems with my child, and I knew things would get better if I would start having play sessions again. I just couldn't get started having them, though. Coming to these training sessions meant I had to make a commitment to have playtimes, and my child's behavior has improved dramatically.

Partial Transcript of CPRT Session 10

(Parents shared about their week, reported the number of times they touched their child, and excitedly described their play-wrestling experiences with their children.)

Dr. L.: Ten weeks ago, as you were talking about your child of focus, I wrote down your descriptions. I'd like to read these descriptions, and then you give us an update on what your child is like now. Debbie, you said Rachel was sensitive, strong-willed. I get angry. I totally reject her, I spank her, and it doesn't work. She's bossy and demanding. She throws temper tantrums. I'm wishy washy. What's that like now?

Debbie: She still throws her tantrums, but they are more controlled.

Dr. L.: What are your reactions to her now?

Debbie: My reactions are more calm. When I see her throw herself on the floor, my reactions are no longer, "What do I do?" Now they are, "OK, let's try something." It's OK. This is what I've got to do. Knowing what to do has helped me take all the undercurrent out of my reactions to her. Giving choices has been the key. She has direction now.

Dr. L.: Choices allow her to use her own resources.

Debbie: Giving choices places the responsibility back on her. She's more than capable of deciding what she wants to do.

Dr. L.: So you're a different person with her.

Debbie: I think so. It just makes it easier to put the responsibility back on her. Now, I know what to do, and that solved 90 percent of the problem, instead of spanking or doing something else that doesn't work.

Dr. L.: What is the spanking like now?

Debbie: I don't spank anymore. The only time I have spanked her is when she is in direct harm.

Dr. L.: So most of the behaviors you were concerned about have changed.

Debbie: Yes.

Dr. L.: How about your own reactions; you said, "I get angry and totally reject her."

Debbie: That is what I am really working on, not physically pushing her away. I realized that I constantly pushed her away rather than embrace her. Pushing her away makes her more and more hyper. Putting responsibility back on her keeps me from getting angry. I think the feeling of being out of control is where the anger comes from.

Dr. L.: So you feel in control now, and it seems to me that you are saying, "I am more loving with her."

Debbie: I am. And in turn, her loving attributes come out.

Dr. L.: Because of what you do.

Debbie: She's even mirroring choices. For so long I feared the terrible 2s and terrible 3s because I just didn't know what to do. I have really prayed for a class like this for a long time to teach me what I need to know, because I come from a highly dysfunctional family. I needed basic tools.

Dr. L.: You sound very satisfied with yourself now, and you do have some tools.

Debbie: Yes, but I have to choose to use them because there are times when I would like to throw her out with the trash. (Group laughs.) I have a relationship with her now, not a dictatorship.

Dr. L.: All because of what you are doing.

Debbie: But because of the tools I've been given.

Dr. L.: But you are the one that uses them.

Laura: Debbie, he's trying to give you a compliment, but you're not letting him.

Debbie: I think every one of us here wants to be good parents, but until this class, we didn't know how.

Sonya: We didn't know what to do.

Debbie: We've all been taught children are told what to do, and they have to do it.

Emily: "Be seen and not heard." That's how we were raised. I was scared not to do what my parents said to.

Laura: I don't think it was so much fear as it was respect.

Emily: I didn't have that respect. I did for my Dad. He only gave me one spanking in my whole life. He was always there to reason with me.

Kathy: I still don't have a close relationship with my parents.

Debbie: Haven't we grown up thinking, "My parents did this wrong and that wrong, and I don't want to do that to my children"?

Emily: I think for a really long time I blamed Mom, that was so wrong of her to do that, but then I had to resolve within myself that she probably did what she was taught, what she learned from her parents. And she did the best she knew how to do.

Sonya: Mom was so off the mark, but I know she meant well.

Debbie: Before this class, I could see Rachel being 14 and being messed up.

Dr. L.: What I hear all of you all saying is, your children are going to grow up, and they will say different things about you as parents, that you parented in a way they will want to parent. Sonya, you said of Jenny that she is trying to show me something, and I'm not sure what it is. I don't use physical discipline; you were already giving some choices and so forth. But your main concern was that you were sensitive to the fact that she was trying to show you something.

Sonya: She's angry, she's real angry. I thought a lot of it was sadness, and I found out through the things we did here in class that she was angry. And what I learned to do through these classes was to set up a safe situation for her. That poor bobo, he gets taped up and knifed. I think the first three or four playtimes she never even touched the knife, the gun, or any of the aggressive looking toys. I have learned how to read her face. When she cried, I thought she was sad, so I would say, "Oh, are you sad?," and she seemed so confused by what I was saying to her. Now, she will say, "I'm angry." So often I just didn't know what was going on with her, and I think that even though

I'm not comfortable with physical discipline, the verbal yelling and screaming I did hurt her emotionally as much as if I had spanked her. I'm glad I don't have to do that anymore. I do know what else to do. I feel empowered. She's even giving her little friends choices now. I can tell she is feeling more comfortable with being able to say what she needs, and the special playtimes made the difference. I really needed to set up a time for her to know that she can be and do and say whatever she needs to, and know that she is safe, and there never was that time. I'll continue to do the special playtime; it's really important. I feel a lot better, I do.

Dr. L.: Sonya, you have made a huge difference in your child's life, and you're really sold on the special playtimes. Laura, you said of Dawson: lots of anger. He has resented my times with the baby. He's very demanding. He wanders off, he's a real challenge. He pushes the limits. I have a real hard time following through. He demands my time. How are those behaviors now?

Laura: Kara is very independent, she doesn't need much of my time, so there's not that much competitiveness there. They seem to be better friends; his resentment toward her seems to be less. He doesn't wander off. I think there are other things that have helped that. He does have a physical boundary. He knows the limits and he has a choice; if he gets beyond the boundary, then he has to come back inside the house.

Dr. L.: How about his being very demanding of you?

Laura: I think it has been resolved. I don't feel as stressed about it as I did.

Dr. L.: How about this statement: you said, "I have a hard time following through."

Laura: We are doing better with that, too. He doesn't test the limit as much anymore, either. When he is in time out, he stays there now.

Dr. L.: So you are different in some ways, and he's different.

Laura: Yes, there are a lot of changes in our lives. I'm just excited about the depth of what we are really giving to our kids. I've done a lot of research on myself, and my inner child and where I came from. I know that allowing children to make choices, learn self-discipline, and allowing them to express themselves is wonderful.

Dr. L.: I'm aware of changes in you. You are more relaxed, open, more shows in your face now than when this training began.

Laura: Yeah, its not so frightening to talk about those skeletons in the closet anymore. Here, there is acceptance from other people who are having the same struggles.

Dr. L.: I hear you saying "Thank you" to these people in the group.

Laura: It just feels good. When I first came in here, I wanted you to make me feel better, but it's something much bigger than that.

Dr. L.: The bigness of it is what's in each of you.

Sonya: We feel better about ourselves.

Dr. L.: So you react differently to your children, and they like themselves better.

Laura: Yes, I think that has a lot to do with Dawson. He likes himself better. Our interactions are so much better now. Before, he was going to go out the window no matter what, and it was a struggle every time. Now we don't have exchanges like that anymore. He doesn't go out the window anymore. He realizes now he will get to go out later.

Dr. L.: And who has made the difference?

Laura: A lot of things.

Dr. L.: I'm not going to let you off the hook, Laura. Who has made the difference?

Laura: I have.

Dr. L.: You have, yes, you are doing things differently. I heard you say, "I've been working on myself, I'm learning about my child." You have made the difference. That's true of each one of you. You can't give someone else credit, Debbie. Each one of you did it.

Debbie: I'll accept that. (Group laughs.)

Dr. L.: Kim, you said of Toby, "He was premature, has ADD, delayed speech. He's in speech therapy, has low self-esteem. He's very affectionate, real sweet, easily frustrated, impatient with himself." Has any of that changed?

Kim: Oh, yeah. A lot. It's a result of what my husband and I have been doing and all the outside help. Even Toby's speech is getting better, so he's feeling more confident about himself. His interactions with his sister are just so much better. Yesterday, he told me Michelle hit him, and he told her, "I'm not for hitting." I know he got that from our playtimes. It's helped a lot.

Dr. L.: How are you feeling about him, now?

Kim: Oh, a lot better. I was the youngest and was spoiled rotten. I never had any limits. Setting limits was the hardest thing for me. I wanted my children to like me so much, to be their friend. I wanted my children to know that they were loved all the time, and it was hard to discipline them. But I've learned that disciplining them is loving them. Now I'm not afraid to go to restaurants. (laughter) Now, they are so much more in control. I came here to help my little boy, but the choice giving has helped my little girl, too. I felt frustrated. I felt like I was failing. I knew that my child wasn't where he needed to be developmentally, and now I've realized it wasn't my fault, but I can help him.

Dr. L.: It's pretty hard to do things the way they need to be done when you feel like you are already failing. Your creativity is stifled, and so the solutions and good things you're already capable of don't come out, because you are so frustrated. One important thing I hear you saying is your perception of yourself has changed.

Debbie: When I started coming here, I had Rachel in day care full time because that's where I wanted her to be. My reaction was, "Oh, good. She's going to school. I can't get her there fast enough." Now, I put her in school just one day a week because I want to be with her. This training has made a big difference in her.

Emily: When we started this class, you wanted us to concentrate on one child during this 10-week period, but everything you have taught us, we've been able to apply to all of our children, no matter their age. It works for all ages.

Kim: I've even caught myself using these skills at work when things are difficult.

Debbie: Yeah, it works with husbands too. "You can choose meatloaf or chicken, which do you want?" (laughter)

Dr. L.: I appreciate so much the eagerness with which you all have tried these skills. It's easy to suggest that you try this or this would be helpful, but you all are the ones who have to make it work. And you have made it work.

(Other parents report on changes. See instructions for Session 10 for continuing the play sessions and plans for follow-up.)

Dr. L.: My students, who have been watching these sessions from the observation room, would like to come in and ask you some questions, if that is OK with you all.

Group: Sure, we don't mind.

(Students enter. Introduces students and they ask questions.)

Student: How do you feel now that you have gone through this training?

Sonya: Relieved. I like the word empowered, that I am not going to permanently damage the psyche of my child. (laughter) I feel empowered to make the right choices. I have been given the ability to choose. I can do a little extra work and do it this way, or I can scream and yell at my kid. I can make choices today. I had pretty limited options before.

Kim: Now the children answer to me, rather than me answering to them. My days are much easier. Everything that goes wrong is not my fault.

Student: Do you feel like your philosophy of child rearing or ideas of what your child might need from you are any different now than when you started the course?

Debbie: Definitely. I used to be really scared of children in the beginning. Yesterday, I taught a 4-year-old Sunday school class, and I wasn't terrified sitting there. Now, I know more about what they want. I feel good about myself when I'm dealing with children.

Student: How has having the support of the whole group helped rather than just doing the training one on one with Dr. L.? What has it been like having each other to bounce ideas off of?

Emily: I think Dr. Landreth could sit there and tell us all day that there are other parents like you who are struggling, to try to make us feel better, but knowing that there are other people we can see, hear, and touch makes a big difference.

Dr. L.: It's a really frustrating and scary spot to be in when you think, "I'm the only one."

Kathy: And now we know we're not. At 8:30, thousands of parents all across the country are trying to get their child into bed just like me! (laughter) It has changed my attitude.

Student: What have you learned specifically about yourself?

Sonya: I'm capable. Before it was frustrating not knowing what the options were. I thought I had to know how to be a parent just because I had a baby. That's how it was for my mom, and I thought I should know, too. It has been nice to find out that I am capable, and that I can do all these things.

Emily: It's parent training, but it's also a support group here.

Student: What do you think was the most difficult concept or skill that was taught?

Emily: Tracking has got to be the most unnatural thing, because you can see what the child is doing, but to verbalize it was the most difficult thing. I just felt so stupid. It's very awkward. Now it's not, but it was 10 weeks ago.

Kim: For me, it was not being able to direct my child's play or tell him what to do or what things are. That was hard, to let it be what he wanted it to be. If the number is a three, it's hard to say, "That can be whatever you want it to be."

Sonya: Choices, but also sitting back and letting the child lead. I kept wanting to give directions. We covered how to give choices to problems, but when there is a unique situation, I have to stop and really think about a choice I could give that makes sense.

Student: Did any of you at any point think that this training was not working, and wanted to drop out?

Group: No.

Sonya: The first time I was here, I was thinking, this is not what I thought it was, especially when I came in here and saw all these toys. I wanted some more specific behavior things. But after the first assignment, I was hooked.

Debbie: Dr. Landreth started out restricting what we did to the 30-minute playtime knowing our use of these skills would spill over into the rest of our week. (laughter)

Student: Were there any skills or techniques that you didn't agree with?

Kim: At first I disagreed with the no praising, but then when I tried it in the 30 minutes, I saw and understood why I shouldn't praise him. Now, I don't say "Good job" anymore. I expand that and give my child more by saying, "You worked hard on that." Now he knows I see exactly what he is doing. It builds his self-esteem.

Debbie: Leaving off the praise makes you really focus on what the child is doing instead of just making a general praise statement. Now, Rachel will say, "Tell me what I am doing, Mama."

Sonya: I took an Active Parenting class, and it just didn't help me like this one did. This is really working. Jenny is 3 years old and she tracks herself: "I'm doing this all by myself," she says. She even tells me how I'm feeling.

Student: What was your favorite part of the training?

Laura: The special one-on-one playtime; I didn't know what I was missing.

Debbie: All of it, especially the sharing time. Each point made sense, and Dr. L. structured it so well, giving us a little at a time so that it all fell into place.

Kim: It was all so easy to understand. I always remember the stories or catch phrases when I'm trying to think of what to do.

Student: What about the videotaping of your playtimes? Do you see that as a positive part of your learning process?

Emily: I thought it was real helpful, and also that there were people here to critique you. Every time I watched the video, I heard myself saying, "Didn't you?" I knew I didn't need to be saying that. It was real helpful. Every week I watched my first session to see what I was doing differently in that week's session. Was I more relaxed or tracking better? The feedback here was wonderful. I was told all these great things I did and then there was one thing I needed to improve on.

Dr. L.: Is this a good place to stop? Again, I really appreciate your courage to allow all these people to watch our sessions, and your courage to go home and try all the things I asked you to do. It has been a very rewarding time for me to see you all get excited about what was working. I have had fun being with you, and it was because of you that I had fun. Thank you.

References

Bratton, S., Landreth, G., Kellam, T., & Blackard, S. (2006). Child Parent Relationship Therapy (CPRT) Treatment Manual: A 10-Session Filial Therapy Model for Training Parents. NY: Routledge.

CHAPTER 17

DEBBIE'S JOURNEY THROUGH CPRT TRAINING: A ONE-WEEK, 4-YEAR, AND 13-YEAR FOLLOW-UP

In previous chapters, we have followed Debbie's journey through 10 sessions of CPRT as she struggled with her own feelings of inadequacy and her relationship with her daughter. At this point, it might be helpful to revisit some of Debbie's reasons for wanting CPRT training. Debbie had been married for 5 years and had two children, Rachel, who was 4 years old, and Josh, who was 3 months. She was a stay-at-home mother and struggled with feelings of isolation from her husband, depression, and anger, and she was overwhelmed by the requirements of parenting.

Her relationship with her husband was characterized by a lack of communication and an inability to connect with each other on most matters of importance. Debbie felt as though she was parenting by herself with no support from her husband in efforts to parent: "I do all the parenting by myself. He undermines me. I put Rachel to bed at night, later she wakes up, he decides she is hungry and feeds her. Then she's wide awake and tearing around the house, and I'm supposed to take care of her." (Several years later, Debbie described this time as "the darkest period of my marriage.")

Debbie felt out of control and felt everything in the home was out of control. Many little factors seemed to create an explosive situation. Debbie felt powerless to create the kind of home and to be the kind of parent she would like to be because "I don't know what a home and family is supposed to look like. I don't know what is normal for a family. I have no role model." She wanted a sense of peace and calm in her home but didn't know how to make that happen. "I have no building blocks to create a home. I have no routine in my life." Debbie didn't have a sense of home; she didn't know how to stay home and create order and routine. "When Rachel was a tiny baby, I would put her in a car seat and be gone all day long. I would come home just before my husband came home from work. The house was always a disaster area." Debbie didn't know how to build routine into her life, her home, and her children. Yet, she wanted this desperately. "I want to figure things out, to make my home better, to be a better parent. I need skills so I won't feel so overwhelmed and angry toward my children. I need to know what I am supposed to do. I'm hungry for information."

As was evident in her interactions in the first few sessions, she questioned, challenged, and struggled with some of the basic concepts, but was still open to the process of attempting the new behaviors required in the special play sessions. Her questioning and challenging was not motivated by resistance, but was a function of her natural tendency to want details and facts and her long-standing history of doubting herself and feeling inadequate. Some of her interactions revealed remarkable insight and her experience in filial therapy was a time of tremendous personal growth as she incorporated, practiced, and internalized the child-centered play therapy philosophy, skills, and attitudes taught in the 10 sessions.

Parent Reactions to CPRT: a One-Week Follow-Up

Three parents in the CPRT group we followed in earlier chapters through their ten sessions of training were randomly selected and interviewed one week following the tenth session for their responses to the following questions. Debbie was one of the parents interviewed.

What did you like best about the training setting?

Debbie: I liked the fact that the training was done in a group. I now know that I am not the only one out there who has problems with her child. I don't feel as isolated. I enjoyed the shared experience and the bonding that took place between parents.

Kathy: I liked the fact that the group was small enough so we could have discussions. I also enjoyed learning about other parents' experiences and hearing their opinions.

Kim: I enjoyed the group setting, and I liked hearing the other mothers' opinions and feedback.

What was the most effective skill that you learned?

Debbie: I really like the choice giving skill. It has definitely helped me the most, especially when I am trying to get my daughter to stay in her bed. The choice giving has cut down on her getting out of bed at night by at least 50 percent.

Kathy: The choice giving; it really helps my son make decisions, and it gives him power and responsibility for his actions.

Kim: The reflective listening and the reflection of feelings. I think my child perceives me as being more understanding towards him now. I also liked the choice giving, and making him more responsible for his actions.

What was the most difficult skill to master?

Debbie: I have problems reflecting my daughter's feelings. I still feel very awkward when I do this, and it seems very unnatural to me.

Kathy: The limit setting. I have problems following through with the alternatives.

Kim: The tracking and reflecting what I see. I feel like I sound like Mr. Rogers.

Is there something new that you learned about yourself?

Debbie: I have learned that I can control my anger, and that it is okay to be angry with my daughter. I now have new alternatives to spanking and yelling, and I am not feeling as frustrated as I did before. I am feeling more like a parent now.

Kathy: I have learned that I don't have to be perfect, and that I am more capable than I once thought. I have learned that it's okay if I get angry, and it's okay if I am frustrated. I feel more in control.

Is there something new that you learned about your child?

Debbie: I learned that Rachel is especially bright and very perceptive. She has caught on to the choice giving very quickly, and she now has limits and boundaries. I also discovered that I like her. I have always loved her, but now I like her, too. It's a great feeling.

Kathy: I have learned that Cody is more capable than I thought. He can control himself if he wants to, especially when he has choices.

Kim: I have noticed Toby more in general. I notice that he needs attention, and I also noticed that he is very bright.

How has your child responded to the special playtimes and the skills you are using?

Debbie: Rachel really enjoys the time that I am spending with her. She seems to appreciate that I understand her more now, and that I don't spank her as much. She seems to respect me more, and I think she senses that I am being a better parent.

Kathy: Cody usually enjoys the play sessions. However, he sometimes wants to end them early. I think we get along better after the play sessions.

Kim: Toby loves the playtimes and looks forward to them every week. He is not getting into trouble as he used to. Now he has a place where he knows he will get one-on-one attention.

How is your child different as a result of the filial therapy training?

Debbie: She now has more freedom to be herself, and she seems to feel more secure now that she has limits and boundaries. She seems to be more free.

Kathy: Cody seems to have slowed down a lot. He seems happier and more in control of himself.

Kim: Toby seems to have more self-confidence. He is more secure, and he seems happier because he knows I am "there."

Have you taught your spouse any of the skills?

Debbie: Yes, I have taught my husband choice giving and limit setting, but I would like for us both to go to a filial group together. I think he would benefit more from that setting, rather than me trying to teach him.

Kathy: (Single parent, so she did not respond.)

Kim: Yes, he is now a better listener to Toby.

Was the videotaping beneficial to you?

Debbie: Yes, I videotaped every play session. I watched each one over and over with Rachel, and I corrected myself with her watching. If I forgot to give a self-esteem–building response, I would interject one while we were watching together. She loves it.

Kathy: I liked the videotaping, but I was very embarrassed for you all to see how Cody acts. He is far worse than any of the other children, and I was embarrassed about my video.

Kim: Yes, I still watch the first play session I recorded.

Was the supervision feedback you received beneficial?

Debbie: Yes, it was excellent. I learned something new about myself that I might not have ever known had it not been pointed out to me.

Kathy: Yes, it was. However, next time I would like for Dr. Landreth to have a play session with my child, so that I could see how someone else handles him.

Kim: Yes, it's just not possible to learn some things about yourself until someone points them out to you.

4-Year Follow-Up

As a part of the activities of the graduate level filial therapy class I was teaching one semester at the University of North Texas, I arranged for the class to observe the following interview with 3 parents from the CPRT therapy group whose transcribed sessions are provided as a part of the descriptions for the 10-session training model described in earlier chapters. This interview served as a 4-year follow-up to that training. Debbie was one of the parents interviewed.

Dr. L.: Well, I'm glad you all are here, Laura, Debbie, and Kim. I know the group appreciates you being here and sharing your experiences with us about what the filial therapy training was like for you 4 years ago. That's a long time in a person's life, and a long time in a child's life. I think we would all be interested in knowing what you remember most about the filial training.

Laura: Recently, when I got the call to come, I started thinking back about where we were at the time and what encouraged me to be a part of that group. With Dawson, in the beginning I remember the tracking and the play sessions. At that time, the kids' faces would just light up when they were being tracked, even in play. I could feel some of the joy seeing their faces light up. And choice giving, letting them know they could make choices was a big help.

Dr. L.: So the playtimes and the choice giving made a difference. Kim or Debbie, what do you remember most about the filial training?

Kim: Choices, and I've told a million people the Oreo Cookie Theory! That changed not only what I do with my kids, it has changed how I deal with other adults in my life by giving them choices. I don't know how I would have parented or made it through the last 4 years without the choice-giving approach, especially with my son. I mainly took the course for my son, and he has come such a long way. I can't imagine life without the discipline techniques that you taught me.

Dr. L.: Kim, I remember 4 years ago, one of the things you were concerned about was your son's poor self-esteem.

Kim: He has ADD and I wanted to take more of an active role in his development instead of just letting the school district do it. The choice giving has made a big difference in his learning self-control. And allowing him to make decisions by saying, "It's whatever you want it to be, Toby," empowered him. I don't know how I would have been able to answer his questions or deal with his problems if I didn't have those skills.

Dr. L.: You have been able to give some of the responsibility back to him instead of being the answer source.

Kim: Yes, and I had a 6-month-old when I first took the course. The difference in her discipline compared to the 8-year-old is dramatic, because she never knew any other way. The minute I say, "You can choose," she stops what she is doing and says, "OK Mom, I don't even want to hear it. I know what to do." It's helped a lot.

Dr. L.: Debbie, what do you remember?

Debbie: I can't say one specific thing, because everything in the training has changed my entire outlook on being a parent. When I began the training, I had a feeling that I wasn't really a parent. Somebody else was controlling things. I didn't feel like I was the grown-up. I acted just like my 4-year-old daughter did, short of throwing myself on the floor. During the training and seeing her responses in the special playtimes, I realized I was a parent. I felt like a parent inside of myself. And that is what I wanted. That awareness of being the parent has carried over to my son. He was only a couple of months old when we started the filial training. Now he is the age that my daughter was, 4 ½. I feel like an adult with him, I feel like the parent and that is a good feeling.

Dr. L.: I remember one of the things you said in reference to Rachel, who was 4 years old at the time, was that you were wishy-washy with her. You weren't really sure about yourself in that relationship and that you found yourself sometimes rejecting her.

Debbie: Yes, I felt like her playmate, because when she wanted cookies and milk, we had cookies and milk because she decided we would have cookies and milk. I didn't know anything better. Nobody told me, "It's 9:00 in the morning, you don't have that." In the filial training, I had a sense of growing up. I had a sense of taking my role, my position as a parent.

Dr. L.: So, what is it like now for you?

Debbie: I'm older inside. I'm in my place and I know who's in charge, so to speak. Not that I am in control, because you taught us that children can have control and choices. It's a relief to know I can be in control. I'm not caught up in a major struggle for position and for power. It's an automatic, it's a given now. I'm the parent.

Dr. L.: Laura, I saw you shaking your head in reference to that. What were you reacting to?

Laura: About being in charge and giving children choices when there are choices. And letting them know it's not negotiable.

Dr. L.: Standing firm.

Laura: Standing firm on the choices given.

Debbie: And knowing the difference.

Dr. L.: Kim, is taking a firm stand any different for you?

Kim: My kids get excellent reviews at school because they do what they are told immediately. All three of them go to different schools and I think their behavior at school has to do with what we do at home now.

Dr. L.: So you not only see a difference in your own home, but the differences carry over into your children's school activities.

Kim: They always get excellent reviews, not always in math, but always in behavior. When someone is older or in charge, like the babysitter tells them what to do, they do it because they know they choose to lose Nintendo or whatever if they don't. But they still test us.

Dr. L.: Sure. There are some things that don't change; children still try to do some of the things they have always done, but I hear you all saying you are different in the way you respond to what your children are doing. How have you changed personally as a result of the filial therapy training? Have you seen any differences in yourself?

Kim: I would say I have taken a more active role. You gave us the tools to express feelings. I didn't have the words to express myself, and you gave us the words. I really agreed with what you taught about how to discipline without spanking. All the sudden, that came home to me in one of our classes. You wouldn't hit your coworker if she did something you didn't like. So you are giving more respect to your coworker than your own children. I expressed that to my husband, and it was hard to get him to see things my way. I would take home my stuff every day and show him what we are doing. I would say, "This is what we are going to implement." (Laughter)

Dr. L.: So you were training him.

Kim: Yeah, I would come home and tell him, "Look, this is the deal." Every once in a while, I will tell him to count to 10 because I could tell he was going to spank. I would tell him, "Would you treat your boss this way?" No, so give the children the same respect. I guess it was the words. I needed the words and I got the words from you just telling me what I am feeling.

Dr. L.: So you are different in that you respond differently and have some tools to teach self-discipline.

Kim: Yeah, I can verbalize what I want, and I can describe the skills we learned. A lot of people I work with are a lot younger than I am and they will come to me and ask me questions about child rearing. Now I can actually put into words my theory of how I parent my children. I can even explain why physical punishment or spanking isn't right.

Dr. L.: So one of the additional changes is you have some reasons now for doing what you do. How about you, Debbie or Laura, have you changed in any way? Are you any different than you were 4 years ago because of the training?

Debbie: I think I'm stronger inside. I think I know what I believe. You encouraged me to trust that I had some correct answers and to believe in myself. Now, when my daughter is pushing me in the wrong direction, I can say, "This isn't right," and I don't have to do it just because she wants it done. I think that helped me to internalize what I was doing.

Dr. L.: So, one of the ways you are stronger is to stand up to your children now—not just give in to them.

Debbie: A 4-year-old's logic is impeccable. Unless you have something to counteract that with, you're lost. The battle is already over. Believing inside myself that "It is not right to do this," or "This is what you have to do," became more real to me.

Dr. L.: Laura, are you any different?

Laura: When I was in the filial group, I was a single parent and parenting was a real struggle. Trying to do things differently than the way I was raised was really hard. I had lost a lot of the joy of being with my children. That changed while I was in the filial group. I became aware of the consequences of having so much anger and strong feelings inside myself. I learned to be more objective about acknowledging my child's feelings.

Dr. L.: So, you have become more objective with your children when you need to be and more aware of your own feelings. Speaking of feelings, Debbie, I remember one of the things you shared with us was there were times when you didn't like your child.

Debbie: No. No I didn't.

Dr. L.: Can you get back in touch with what that was like and how it changed for you?

Debbie: She was and still is a very strong child. I don't like the term "strong-willed"—that kind of gives it a different connotation to me. She is very strong inside herself about what she wants to do and how it should be done. If she wanted to bake a cake, she wouldn't do it the way I asked her to do it. Any kind of interaction with her became a major struggle. I rejected not only what she wanted us to do, but her. And so she was taking in all those feelings. I hated her because she controlled me. It really helped me to learn how to separate her actions from her as a person. Learning how to give her choices and letting her suffer the consequences of her choices was a real turning point for me. I was able to see a little girl, a different little girl emerge.

Kim: We still have the 30-minute playtimes, even though on some Saturdays I just don't want to do it. I do it anyway, because I know the end result will be worth it.

Dr. L.: So, 4 years later you're still having the special playtimes with Toby. You sound really committed to the playtimes.

Kim: Yes, because it is very important. I also have special playtimes with my other two children. Magically, my son goes to my husband, and they spend a lot of time together, so our playtimes together are really special and he likes it. You can tell he waits for it. And he knows it will come every Saturday. On vacation, I don't have a playtime, but I take him on a walk for 30 minutes, just the 2 of us. It's an important time, because he is 8 and still real loving. He turns it off when his friends are around, but when there is no one else around, he turns back into my little boy.

Dr. L.: That sounds very satisfying. Laura and Debbie, would you bring us up to date on whether you are still having special playtimes or doing any of the things that you applied during the special playtime?

Laura: We bike ride together or walk together, and we spend time together reading. Dawson needs a lot more of my time than the other two children. He asks a lot of times about the play box, especially if he sees me open the closet where the toy box is kept. It still seems to be important to him even though we have not continued to do the playtimes.

Dr. L.: What's it like for you, Debbie?

Debbie: I still have the 30-minute playtime with Rachel. I incorporate story time with Mark and a quiet time where we have time together. We still do the sandwich hug. They like that. I do wish that I was still doing the playtimes, because it does something different than just your reading time and together time. It accomplishes something different.

Dr. L.: Have your children changed?

Kim: Well, it's hard to tell with my littlest one, because the filial approach is all she's ever had, but Toby has definitely changed. Before, he was such a handful, I would throw my hands up in exasperation and not deal with him. Now I deal with him immediately. I drop everything and deal with him because I have found out that it only gets worse. Ignoring bad behavior doesn't work. When I'm in the grocery store and my children start getting disruptive, they know we will walk out and go home. They know I'm serious. They know I'm serious about what I do now.

Dr. L.: So now you will follow through with what you say you are going to do, and they know it.

Kim: If I say we aren't going to do something because of their behavior, they know they are not going to get it. Before, I would have given in. If we had planned to go to the park and they did something they weren't supposed to do, I would still take them to the park because I wanted to go, too. I also learned not to give a choice about things I can't control. If it's not a realistic choice, then they know you won't enforce it. I have learned to limit that so they know whatever I say is definitely going to be done.

Dr. L.: Kim, you sound firm and committed. Laura, 4 years ago you were concerned because Dawson was so demanding. Is that any different?

Laura: Yes. At that time he used to just leave home. He and the dog would just stray off. The doors on our house had deadbolts, but Dawson would go out the window. He would hide underneath the other mobile homes. He could disappear in a minute. I would bolt the doors and he would find another way out. Now, he definitely knows the boundaries. When I call his name, he responds to me and answers me. Before, he wouldn't even answer me. That has definitely improved. He was very demanding and things had to be his way. If he asks for more time, and doesn't get it, he's no longer destructive. He is much more content now.

Dr. L.: It sounds as though he is calmer. Debbie, 4 years ago, one of the things you were concerned about was Rachel's temper tantrums. She was also very demanding. Is she any different in those areas?

Debbie: Yes. She has changed. She is calmer now. She might cry, but she doesn't throw herself on the floor and try to use guilt trips on me. Even at 4, she was real big on guilt trips. My son is now 4 and he is able to say, "I'm berry, berry, berry angry with you." He doesn't throw a tantrum.

Dr. L.: So, you have seen your children use your skills in identifying feelings.

Debbie: Oh yeah. It's interesting to hear them say it.

Dr. L.: Kim, I saw you shaking your head.

Kim: Yes, my middle child thinks she is the mother of the house. She disciplines her little sister the way I discipline by giving choices. I think it's funny.

Laura: All of my children are more in tune with their feelings and communicate more openly.

Dr. L.: Debbie and Kim, have you seen any differences in your relationships with your husbands because of the training? Are you aware of responding in that relationship any differently?

Debbie: I do. I felt like I grew up during the training. I felt like I took a role and I wasn't a kid anymore. I wasn't throwing tantrums anymore myself. I was able to respond to my husband differently because I was responding to the children differently. Four years ago, I felt like I was fighting with siblings all day long and when my husband came home at night, he was just another sibling to fight with. Everything in our relationship has shifted.

Kim: Some people say money is a sore spot in people's marriages, but I think our problems came from the children. The parenting techniques I learned in the filial training gave me a solid goal for what I wanted. The training also gave me something to back me up on what I wanted. "Excuse me, Dr. Garry Landreth taught me this." (Laughter)

Kim: I used to say that all the time. When we do the sandwich hugs, my husband becomes more emotional, giving kisses and actually showing his love and telling his love. He doesn't do the play sessions, but he sets aside a block of time for each child. I think that helps our relationship, because it makes me so proud to see him being an excellent father. I take pride in the fact that I taught it to him. I think those things have helped our relationship.

Debbie: The filial training has changed my entire life. There are only a handful of things that you can really pinpoint that have significantly changed your life, and the filial training is one of those for me. The 30-minute playtimes gave my daughter confidence and provided a place to work on all the things that I was able to work with her on. The training changed me inside. I keep saying that, but it's important to say that. Once you change in your heart, it spills onto your children. It's not a technique. It's not something you're teaching your children; they are not monkeys. They are not going to perform; change has to begin in their heart.

Dr. L.: It is obvious from listening to you all that parts of the training have become a part of you. And you and your children are different in some ways because of that. I'm sure some of the students in my class would like to ask you all some questions.

Student: It's been 4 years since the three of you had the filial training, and it has made a big impact on you that went from a level of learning a skill to a level that entered your heart. What was it about taking the filial training that made it different for you? How is it different than any other parenting class you may have taken 4 years ago? After the filial training, you all are able to identify tracking, reflecting feelings, and limit-setting skills that you remember 4 years later. I'm not sure you could be that specific about other parenting classes. What makes the difference? Why are you able to recall things from the filial training?

Debbie: Giving choices is probably a good example of what happens and why we can remember. When I began choice giving in the playtimes, choice giving was pretty much surface stuff and superficial, not really life issues as occurs outside the playtimes. Then when I transferred the choice giving to other times outside the playtimes, I began to realize there was a deeper meaning, because the choice giving put the responsibility back on the child and the child learned decision-making skills and morals at 4 years of age, something most of us didn't learn until we were adults. I began to realize I'm making choices and that what I was learning in the class also applied to me.

Dr. L.: So the choice giving had some real-life application immediately.

Debbie: Exactly.

Dr. L.: Kim and Laura, did either of you react to the question?

Kim: Yes, I work at night and don't put the kids to bed four nights a week. I realized that I needed to make a choice about which is more important, me working or putting my kids to bed. They're only going to be in the house another 10 years; so I chose to give up a night of work so I would be at home to put them to bed another night. I made the choice that my children were more important. The filial training infiltrates your mind and everything you do. I think the reason I learned the skills and this new approach to parenting so quickly, and took it on and kept it for 4 years, is because of the simplicity that Dr. Landreth adds to the training. It's easy to say give your children a sandwich hug, but just hugging isn't what is important. It's the whole idea of what's behind the hugging. Dr. Landreth just made it so easy by calling it a sandwich hug. It sinks into your life.

Dr. L.: Laura, you were reacting.

Laura: We were really active in participating in the training, too. We did the play sessions; we wrote notes to our children; we discussed our playtimes in class—so we were able to apply what we were learning to our lives where we were then. Two years ago I remarried, and I have used the rule of thumb: the most important thing may not be what you do but what you do after what you have done in my relationship with my husband when I get angry and say things I shouldn't have said. Another thing I use a lot is the 5-minute warning. When we are out somewhere, that helps my children to get ready to leave.

Kim: That is so funny, because I had forgotten that Dr. Landreth taught us that rule of thumb. I just thought that was something I had come up with. (Group laughter.) I was thinking about that principle the other day. So many of the things I use, I have forgotten the source, like the 5-minute warning you mentioned.

Debbie: And the 30-second burst of attention was fabulous.

Dr. L.: So these skills have become a part of you. You don't even think about where you got them. Other questions?

Student: What did you all look forward to each time you were preparing to go to class?

Debbie: The sharing. We would have this big huge problem and Dr. Landreth would say, "Here, try this." He was so soft and calm. The next week we would run back to class and say, "That worked!" The sharing was the greatest for me.

Kim: For me, it was empowerment. The more classes I went to, I got more and more power as a parent.

Dr. L.: We need to stop for today. I want to thank you for sharing so personally with us today.

The personal sharing of Debbie and the other parents makes it quite clear that the filial therapy training helped them gain a sense of personal adequacy and empowerment not only as a parent, but in other relationships in their lives.

13-Year Follow-Up with Debbie

In July 2004, I conducted a CPRT workshop in the Center for Play Therapy Summer Play Therapy Institute on the University of North Texas campus and invited Debbie to share her experience with the workshop participants. As a part of the training experience, I had shown video segments of Debbie's filial therapy group (with their permission) so the participants already had a limited acquaintance with Debbie.

Dr. L.: Group, this is Debbie, 13 years later. Debbie, I'm sure everyone is eager to hear what you remember about the filial therapy training and what impact it had on you.

Debbie: First of all, I would like to say thank you to Dr. Landreth because he empowered me as a parent to do what I needed to do with my child. Prior to the filial therapy lessons, I had a 4-year-old daughter who was pretty much running the household, and she would tell me what to do. To give you an example, we would be in my van driving, and I would start to sing a song. She would say, "No! We're not singing that song!" So I would say, "Ok, what song are we going to sing?" My thought was if Rachel was happy, I was happy. And she would say, "We are going to sing 'Jesus Loves Me.'" So I would start singing. Then she would tell me what part of the song I was going to sing, how long I was to sing, and when I was supposed to stop singing it.

This is what I lived with day in and day out, a child telling me what to do. I didn't know any better, so I would do what she told me to do. I was under the assumption that if she was happy, everything was OK. But I felt inside myself major frustration and anger. I can still remember the comment I made in the filial group saying the anger came out of frustration. My rejection of Rachel came from not knowing what to do with her. She was a bundle of energy and she was in control. At 18 months, she was telling me what she was going to wear. Her being in control started very young. I had no parent training. Most parents don't. I didn't have anywhere to go for the basic tools of child communication, so I pushed her away. I was so angry with her and tired of her. I put her in day care because I didn't know how to deal with her.

I don't know how I found out about Dr. Landreth's class, I was just told about it. I came to his class, and he began to teach us how to relate to our children. As you saw in the videos, I was really involved in the training because I was so eager to learn how to be a parent. I started the training with the idea of learning how to control my child. How can I make my child do what I want to do? How do I make her sing the songs I want to sing? I discovered in the training that as Dr. Landreth began to give me tools to use, I wanted to know more. I didn't miss any of the sessions. I was in his face every session asking him all my questions about parenting. He wrote my questions down saying, "We will work on that later." I was probably one of the parents he wanted to go to and say, "Will you please leave my group." (Laughter) "The other people need to talk."

Rachel was a very precious little girl, but she controlled our lives. She was very strong-willed and determined. I didn't see those as good personality traits, which she still exhibits today. But back then, she ruled the house. Logically, I could not understand going into a 30-minute play session and allowing her to control it. It didn't make any sense because she was already controlling my life. In the filial training, I realized the change needed to be in me, not in my daughter.

In the special playtimes, I could relax because most of what Rachel did there was OK. Actually, she learned very quickly where the boundaries were. I didn't have to explain the rules to her ahead of time. Those special playtimes began to change me and the way I viewed my daughter. I began to see her in a more positive way, that she wasn't really trying to make my life miserable all the time. The skills I learned to use in the special playtimes worked; they were wonderful and I began using them outside the playtimes. I sensed a change in Rachel. It was as though she knew there was a change in the atmosphere of our relationship. She had more freedom in her choices and she became less demanding of me.

The infant you all saw in the video of one of our filial therapy training sessions is my son. I saw things that came out in our play sessions that helped me to understand what Rachel was feeling about the new baby. Even though I had to set limits and boundaries on her behavior, our new relationship was so freeing to me that all my anger began to evaporate. Today, we have a wonderful sharing relationship, and Rachel wanted to come with me today to hear what I have to say to you all.

Dr. L.: Rachel, stand up so the group can see you.

(Applause)

Debbie: Rachel remembers our special playtimes and the different things we did together. The important thing about Rachel is that she is extremely self-sufficient today. She is very strong-willed but that is tempered with sensitivity to other people. She has a lot of confidence in herself. She tackles problems and goes after a lot of things I wouldn't dream of doing. And she is very successful doing the things she has chosen to do.

If I had not had the filial therapy training and learned the skills and tools I was taught, there's no telling what Rachel's personality traits would have become and what would have been manifested in them. There is just no doubt when I say that the filial therapy and the tools I received changed my life. It changed my home, it changed my family, it changed everything.

Dr. L.: Thank you Debbie. Would you all like to ask Debbie a question?

(Question asked by audience member.)

Dr. L.: The question is, Debbie, did you continue to do the play sessions after the training ended?

Debbie: Yes, I continued them for a little while. Then, as my son got older, it became a little more difficult to do. As Rachel got older, we changed the structure of the playtimes to doing special things together, like going shopping and allowing her to make decisions about where to shop and what we would do, but she didn't decide how much money to spend.

Rachel is now 17, my middle child is 13, and I have a 10-year-old. Instead of a playtime, I give each of them 20 dollars, and they decide what we are going to do for our special time together. It is a time where I let go. It's an internal letting go and the focus of the time is on them. Even though it isn't a playtime with toys, it is still basically the same thing because each child has all of my attention and none of my control during our special date time.

Dr. L.: Is there another question or two you would like to ask?

(Question asked by audience member.)

Dr. L.: Debbie, the question is what specific changes did you make after the training?

Debbie: Everything. The way I approached Rachel, the way I dealt with her, the way I even saw her. One of the first assignments Dr. Landreth gave us was to notice a physical characteristic about our child that we had not noticed before. I had to go home and look at Rachel in a wondering way and for a few minutes in that process I saw her differently. Another change was that, in the special playtimes, I stopped emotionally pushing her away from me. Before the training, I rejected her because I didn't know how to deal with her.

I recognized Rachel wasn't very happy having all of the control I allowed her to have. With that awareness, my attitude about myself began to change. It was amazing what happened when I began taking control of myself and began giving Rachel choices. I started using choices, setting boundaries, and setting limits in my interactions with Rachel. It was just amazing what wonderful things happened in our relationship. I think we both began to like each other better.

Dr. L.: Thank you so much for sharing with us, Debbie. I appreciate you being here.

(Applause)

Debbie was eager to share her experiences in these interviews and continues to be a strong advocate for filial therapy training. Perhaps I should point out that I had no contact with Debbie after the conclusion of the filial therapy training until I contacted her just prior to the 4-year follow-up interview. After that interview, I lost contact with her until 1 year prior to the 13-year follow-up session, when she happened to learn that I was teaching a family-focused training class and joined the group.

CHAPTER 18

QUESTIONS PARENTS AND CHILDREN ASK, AND PROBLEMS AND SOLUTIONS IN CPRT TRAINING

Therapists who plan to use filial therapy need to be prepared to answer questions parents may ask about filial therapy training. Anticipating many of these questions and responding to them in the intake interview or during the first filial therapy training session can help alleviate parents' confusion and anxiety, thus helping parents to relax, feel more secure about the training, make a commitment to the process, and more readily engage in the process of learning new skills.

Questions Parents Ask About CPRT

Question: **How will having playtimes with my child correct his behavior problems? He already plays with toys a lot.**

Response: That does seem unlikely, doesn't it, that a special playtime could help change behavior problems? Yes, most children play with toys a lot. However, they usually are not playing with a parent in the kind of relationship I am going to teach you to build with your child. The special playtime you will have with your child is a different kind of playtime, a time when you will work on building a different kind of relationship with your child. We have found that when children experience a play relationship in which they feel accepted, understood, and cared for, they play out many of their problems. They feel better about themselves, they develop self-control, and they assume greater self-responsibility. How children feel about themselves is what makes a significant difference in their behavior. In these special playtimes where parents learn to focus on the child rather than the problem, children learn to correct their own behavior because how children behave, how they think, and how they perform in school is directly related to how they feel about themselves. When children's needs are met in the special playtimes, their behavior problems diminish. When children feel better about themselves, they behave in more self-enhancing ways rather than self-defeating ways.

Question: **How do I explain to my child why we are having these special playtimes?**

Response: Tell your child, "I like to be with you, and I want to spend more time with you, so I am taking a special class to learn how to play with you." This helps to make the playtime really special. Your child can brag to his friends that his parent is taking a special class to learn how to play with him. How many other children can say that? That makes it a big deal. Your child doesn't need a lengthy explanation and facts are not necessary. Yes, you are experiencing some problems with your child, but the reason you are having the playtimes is to build a better relationship with your child, not to fix the problem.

Question: **We live in a really small apartment. There's just no place for a special playtime.**

Response: The special playtime should be scheduled for a time when other family members are out and could take place in your kitchen. Another possibility is to fold a blanket, place it on the floor in one of your rooms, and designate the blanket as the special place for the playtime each week. The borders of the blanket become the boundaries for the playtime. If you can only have the special playtime when other family members are home, you can use the bathroom as your private place. Although not ideal, this space can work quite well. It is important that your child have a private time and place where other family members will not watch or interrupt.

Question: **I am a single mom with 3kids, and I just can't keep the other two, ages 4 and 8, out of my special playtimes with my 6-year-old.**

Response: Their behavior is normal and may indicate they want to have their own special playtime with you. You could ask a friend or relative to take the 4- and 8-year-old for a special time at the park or to get a treat. You might be able to swap some time with another single parent. Be sure to explain to your children that you will be having a playtime with them in 5 weeks or 8 weeks (identify the number of play sessions left in the first child's sequence of 10 sessions). In the meantime, each child can choose to do something special each week with you: read a story, bake cookies together, go get an ice cream cone, or some other special time. You might swap babysitting with a friend or neighbor who could babysit your 4- and 8-year-old while you have your playtime. You could give the 8-year-old babysitting responsibility for the 4-year-old during the 30 minutes of the playtime and pay her to play with the 4-year-old and keep him out of your playtime. You might try having the playtime in the evening after the 4-year-old has gone to bed and elicit the 8-year-old's cooperation. If that doesn't work, you could use choice giving with the 8-year-old: "If you choose to stay out of the room while I am having a playtime, you choose to get to watch TV that day. If you choose to interrupt the playtime, you choose not to get to watch TV that day."

Question: **My son is 10 years old and probably isn't going to be interested in most of the toys on this list. How do I get him to play?**

Response: This is your child's time to decide what to do for 30 minutes. Whether or not he plays with the toys is his decision. He might decide to talk for 30 minutes. There is no requirement that your child play. However, our experience is that even 10-year-old children find very creative things to do with the toys on this list. Some of the things your child does with the toys may surprise you, or you may have difficulty accepting some of the ways your child chooses to play, such as ignoring you and playing silently for 30 minutes, or sucking on the baby bottle. One of the parents in our filial therapy training reported that her 9-year-old daughter chose to sit in the middle of the bed and talk for 30 minutes during her first play session. In succeeding play sessions, she played actively with the toys. Let's find out how your child reacts to the toys. If he chooses not to play with any of the toys, we will talk about adding some different toys.

Question: **What's wrong with asking questions if I am interested in my child's play?**

Response: Tracking statements that describe what you see and statements that reflect the content and feeling of what you hear convey your interest in a more positive and encouraging way. Questions imply you don't understand. Questions also put you in the lead in the relationship and can interfere with your child's creativity and decision making during the playtime. It is important that your child be allowed to stay in the lead and discover how it feels to make his own decisions for 30 minutes.

Question: **I don't see anything significant in my child's play. What can I do to help her begin to work on her problem during our playtime?**

Response: The relationship you are building with your child during the special playtimes is more important than whether or not your child is working on a problem. As your relationship with your child is strengthened, your child's problem will diminish. Your child may be working on issues through her play that you are not aware of. Remember the lesson of the Band-Aid (see transcript of CPRT Session 2 in Chapter 8). What you are doing in the playtimes is working even when you don't see any change. Children can change as a result of what they do in play sessions with parents or play therapists even though we are not aware of what they are working on. Your job during the special playtimes is to follow your child's lead and to be nonjudgmental, understanding, and accepting of your child. Your empathic responses will help your child to focus on the issues that are important to her.

Question: **My child really likes to play with these toys, and keeping them out of his hands is a major problem. Why can't I let him play with them at other times?**

Response: Allowing your child to play with these toys only during the 30-minute playtimes helps to convey the message that this is a special time, a time just for the two of you, a fun time. Setting the toys apart makes the playtime unique and more desirable. Another reason is that this time with your child is an emotional relationship time and the toys become a part of that emotional relationship during which your child expresses and explores emotional messages through the toys because of the kinds of empathic responses you make. This same kind of emotional exploration cannot occur during other playtimes because you are not there to communicate understanding of your child's play. Additionally, being allowed to play with these toys only during the special playtimes helps your child learn to delay his need for gratification. If you are having trouble keeping your child from playing with the special toy kit, try storing it out of sight on the top shelf of your closet. If that doesn't work, lock it in the trunk of your car.

Question: **I always thought it was good to praise my child. What's wrong with praising for doing a good job?**

Response: Praise is evaluative, judgmental, and leading. "Oh, that's such a beautiful picture you painted" communicates an evaluation of the picture and reinforces the child to paint similar pictures to obtain similar praise, thus stifling the child's creativity and self-direction. A person who makes such praise statements also has the power to evaluate the picture to be ugly, and that is what a child fears. A statement such as, "You worked hard on that picture," or You put a lot of colors in that picture," recognizes the child's effort or prizes what the child has done. How your child feels about herself is always more important than what your child does. Praising what a child does results in children becoming externally motivated to seek praise for what they produce by pleasing. Recognizing a child's effort results in children becoming internally motivated. Such children are more creative, have better self-concepts, and are self-motivated. Rule of Thumb: Recognize the child's effort rather than praising the product.

If your child is persistent about seeking praise—"Do you like my picture?"—and you have already responded with "You put lots of colors on your picture," "You're proud of your picture," "You worked hard on your picture," etc., you can say, "I know you want me to decide if I like your picture, but during our special playtime, the important thing is whether or not you like your picture."

Question: **I'm having trouble finding some of the items on the toy list. Is it really important that I have all of this stuff?**

Response: The toys are like words for your child, and play is your child's language, so it would be helpful for you to try to find as many of the items as possible. All of the items are on the list because we have found they help children act out a wide range of experiences and express a wide range of feelings about those experiences. You should go ahead and have your play sessions and add the missing items as soon as possible. Let's take a few minutes and find out what toys everyone had trouble finding and share information about where some of you found the toys that other parents are having trouble locating. The toys don't have to be new or best quality. Check out garage sales, dollar stores, and grocery store toy aisles.

Question: **I'm bored. What's the value of this if my child just plays with the same toy over and over? Am I doing something wrong?**

Response: Playing with the same toy or playing out the same theme repetitively is not unusual for some children and may indicate they are trying to master a new skill, solve a problem, or work through an intense emotion or something significant in their life. Play that is repeated within a session or across several sessions may be the result of a child trying to process and integrate a new experience or previous event into his life, or it may be the child's way of expressing a particular need in his life. The important consideration is whether or not the child seems interested and involved in the play. If the child is interested, then the play has meaning for the child and something important is happening. It is not necessary that you figure out the meaning.

Being bored in a playtime is not an unusual happening because parents have busy schedules, are on the go a lot, and are not used to sitting and interacting quietly for 30 minutes. You can increase your interest level and involvement in your child's play by responding to what you see in your child's face, asking yourself questions such as, "What is he feeling?"

"What is he trying to say in his play?," "What does he need from me?" "What is so interesting to him about the toy or the play?" and by making more tracking responses and reflective responses. The most important thing you can do is continue to be patient with the process of the play sessions. (Being bored may be an indication that the parent has not acquired the necessary skills or is not putting enough effort into using the new skills. In either case, additional training in the form of modeling and role-playing the skills of tracking and empathic responding is needed.)

Question: **My child asks lots of questions and gets mad when I don't answer all of them. What am I supposed to do?**

Response: We always begin by reflecting the child's feelings. "You're angry at me." Sometimes a child feels insecure when a parent changes typical ways of responding and is angry because he doesn't know how to react. Your child may feel insecure and be trying to get your attention the way he has done in the past. Your objective is to encourage your child's self-reliance and self-acceptance. "In our special playtime, the answer can be anything you want it to be." Your child asks, "What should I draw?" You want your child to know he's in charge of his drawing during the special playtime, so you respond, "You've decided to draw, and in this special playtime, you can draw whatever you decide." Our objective is to empower the child, to enable the child to discover his own strengths.

Question: **What do I do when my child wants my help?**

Response: This is a playtime, this is not a time to sit and observe your child. You are to be involved in and a part of your child's play as you might at other times, with one major difference—you are to get instructions from your child. You are not to assume you know what your child wants or how your child wants something done. Remember, for 30 minutes, you are dumb. Therefore, you will need to get instruction and direction from your child. "Show me where you want me to line up the soldiers." "Tell me what you want me to cook for breakfast." "We can go to the kitchen, and you can show me what you want in the baby bottle." "You can show me what kind of cat you want me to draw." Your objective is to keep your child in the lead so your child experiences making decisions and doing things for himself.

Question: My child wanted to leave after 10–15 minutes. What am I supposed to do?

Response: You always want to communicate your understanding, so you could say, "You would like to go do something else, but we have 15 more minutes in our special playtime. I would like to be with you longer. When could we have our whole playtime?" Another possible approach would be to reflect your child's desire to leave and add, "We have 15 more minutes in our special playtime. I will tell you when you have 10 more minutes, and then you can decide to stop or play for the last 10 minutes." This is a time to negotiate. Forcing your child to stay another 15 minutes might interfere with the reason for having the special playtime. On the other hand, the relationship can't be worked on if the child is not present. Patient understanding is needed. The important thing is that the special playtime occur this week sometime. That is more important than adhering to the scheduled time.

Question: When it was time for our special playtime, my child didn't want to participate at all. What can I do?

Response: Communicating understanding is always important. "You don't want to have the special playtime. You would rather do something else. Let's have the special playtime for 10 minutes, then you can decide if you want to have the rest of the special playtime or do something else." This response helps your child to feel understood and to feel in control. A child in that position in a relationship is much more likely to compromise. In most cases, a child will get started playing and will decide to have the rest of the playtime.

Question: **Why can't I have a special playtime with each of my children each week or rotate each week so each child gets a playtime with me?**

Response: You have three children, so that would mean three playtimes each week. My experience is that parents are very busy and being consistent in having just one playtime each week can often become a problem. I wish you had the time to have two or three playtimes each week with each of your children. It is crucial, though, that you be absolutely consistent in having the playtime each week so you and the playtime become predictable. This communicates a powerful message to your child that he is important, so important that nothing will interfere with your special playtime with him. Let's begin with a playtime each week with just one child and see how that works out with your schedule. We'll consider adding playtimes with the other children later.

You can learn best how to build this new kind of relationship by having the playtimes with the same child each week for 8 or 10 weeks. All of your children do not always need you equally at the same time in their lives. Which of your children needs you most at this time in their life, or which child are you having the most difficulty with now? That is the child who needs the special playtimes most right now. If all three of your children climb a tree in the back yard, and one child fall out of the tree and breaks a leg, which child will you take to the emergency room at the hospital? Yes, the one with the broken leg. Why not take all three children to the emergency room? Because two of them don't have a broken leg, so they don't need you as much at that time as does the child with the broken leg. In 8 or 10 weeks, we will talk about you adding playtimes with the other children or rotating playtimes so each child gets a playtime with you.

Questions Children Ask and Comments They Make About the Play Sessions

One of the most common concerns of parents in the early stages of CPRT training is how to respond to children's questions and unexpected comments. Parents frequently feel unprepared for the barrage of questions children have during the initial play sessions and the surprising comments they make. Therefore, the therapist will need to help parents anticipate some of the questions and comments children may spontaneously present and formulate short, standard responses parents will be able to readily call to mind when needed. This preparation will do a lot to ease parents' anxieties and help them to feel more in control in the new experience of a nondirected play relationship.

A common practice of children is to ask the parent a multitude of questions, which may be their way of making contact with the parent in this new playtime relationship. However, the parent should consider that children already know the answer to many of the questions they ask. Examined from this perspective, responding to children's questions becomes a matter of trying to understand the motivation behind the question rather than attempting to provide an answer. Providing answers to questions can inhibit children's use of items by binding children to the parents' world of reality. When 5-year-old Hershel holds up the handcuffs and asks, "What are these?," and his parent answers, "Handcuffs," they can no longer be the special new kind of spaceship he was thinking about. The parent could facilitate the coming forth of Hershel's creativity and imagination by responding, "That can be whatever you want it to be." Hershel is then free to proceed with what he already had in mind but had not verbalized. When Judy asks, "What happens if something gets broken in here?," a sensitive parent would respond, "Sometimes accidents happen in here." Judy then knows this is not a place of punishment, or a place where you must be careful. She then feels freer to express herself more spontaneously and completely.

RULE OF THUMB:

Don't answer questions that haven't been asked.

Answers to obvious questions can result in lengthy question-and-answer routines that increase children's dependency. When children ask questions during special playtimes, the parent would do well to consider what the underlying meanings are before responding to what seems to be the objective of their questions. Trying to anticipate what children are saying in their questions, rather than attempting to answer the questions, is usually much more facilitative of expression and exploration. What the parent senses at the moment would determine the kind of response to be made.

Question: **What do you want me to do?**

Response: In this special playtime, you can decide what you want to do. (This response clarifies the special nature of the playtime and returns responsibility to the child. We do not worry about the possibility that this response may result in the child deciding to do something that would not be allowed. The need to set a limit is not considered until the moment a limit is needed. The parent does not suggest any activities or offer any solutions for the duration of the 30-minute playtime.)

Question: **Can I play with my computer game?**

Response: It would be fun to play with your computer game, but these are the toys for playing with during our special playtime. You can play with your computer game later today if there's time. (The alternative should be truly an alternative. Don't say something you can't follow through on. Items that are not similar to the filial therapy items are not allowed in the special playtime because they are too structured, do not facilitate playing out personal experiences by the child, and do not allow the child to express a wide range of emotions. Note: The response recognizes the child's desire, gently sets a limit, and grants fulfillment at a later time, thus communicating understanding and conveying to the child that he will get to do what he wants. This elicits the child's cooperation and avoids an adversarial position. The words "later today" are deliberately chosen instead of "after our playtime is over" because computer games are so highly attractive to many children that saying, "after our playtime is over" might result in the child then insisting on ending the playtime.)

Question: **Can we go play outside?**

Response: You would like to play outside, but our special playtime is for this room. You can choose to play outside when our special playtime is over. (Reflects the child's desire and communicates that the child will get to go outside later. There are too many distractions outside and too many opportunities for unexpected happenings for the inexperienced parent to handle. The confined area inside the house helps promote the desired relationship. After the sixth or seventh play session, it would probably be okay to allow the playtime outside, but with all the playtime structure and requirements intact.)

Question: **Why can't we play longer?**

Response: You're really having fun and would like to play a lot longer, but our special playtime is over for today. We will have another special playtime next Tuesday. (Even though parent and child are having lots of fun, the time limit is adhered to because this promotes consistency, affords the parent an opportunity to be firm, and provides the child with an opportunity to bring himself under control and end a very desirable playtime. If your child persists, you could say, "Joey, I wish we had more time, too, but our 30 minutes are up for today. We'll get to have another playtime next Tuesday.")

Question: **Why do you keep saying what I say?**

Response: Sounds like what I am saying bothers you. I just want to let you know I understand what you are saying and what you are playing, so you will know I am interested. (There is the possibility the parent is reflecting word-for-word exactly what the child says too often, or the parent sounds too stilted and unnatural, and it is irritating to the child.)

Question: **You sound weird. Why are you talking like that?**

Response: I sound different to you. That's my way of letting you know I heard what you said. Remember, I'm going to that special class to learn how to play with you. (The child may be saying he notices the parent is different; having a surprise reaction to the verbal attention; annoyed by too much reflection of words; or saying he notices the difference in the parent's reflective-type responses. The child may also be saying he doesn't want the parent to change because that will mean he must then change and adjust to the parent's new way of responding.)

Comment: **Guess what I am going to do next.**

Response: You have something in mind you are going to do. You can tell me. (A variation might be "Sounds like you have something planned. You can tell me." This shows understanding and frees the child to continue to be in the lead. Guessing what the child will do next places the parent in the lead and is structuring because the child may then feel obligated to do what the parent guesses. Trying to guess what a child will do next could go on indefinitely. If the child is unusually insistent or demanding, as some older children might be, you might want to consider going along with the child's insistence and making a guess.)

Question: **Do you know what I am going to do next?**

Response: You have something planned. You can tell me. (This response says, "I heard your underlying message," and keeps the child in the lead. The child is really making a statement rather than asking a question. A response should be directed to what the child is saying rather than respond to the obvious question.)

Question: **What is this?**

Response: That can be whatever you want it to be. (This response keeps the child in the lead, returns responsibility to the child, and frees the child to label the item whatever the child wants it to be. There are several subtle possibilities in this child's question: She might be unfamiliar with the toy and unsure of how it is supposed to be used, trying to decide what she would like to do with the toy, testing the permissiveness of the special playtime, trying to engage the parent, seeking direction or approval from the parent, or wanting to use the item for something other than the apparent use. Labeling the item would prevent any of these possibilities from being expressed.)

Comment: **I'm bored.**

Response: You're not having any fun. This is a time when you can decide what you want us to do. You can decide to play with the toys, or talk, or create something. (This response shows understanding and returns responsibility to the child to decide how she wants to spend the time together. Such a comment by a child is often disconcerting to a parent, resulting in the parent feeling responsible to make the child happy, a behavior usually typical of the relationship outside the playtime. The parent is not responsible for the child's happiness in the special playtime. Conveying this principle to parents prior to their special playtimes can help prevent some of their anxiety.)

Problems and Solutions in CPRT Training

The unique dimensions of CPRT in training parents to be therapeutic agents in their children's lives creates a number of problems for the filial therapist that must be dealt with prior to initiating filial therapy training and during the process of training. A few of those potential problems and possible solutions are presented here to help the filial therapist anticipate and prepare for their occurrence.

Problem: Making the transition from being a therapist to being a teacher/trainer.

Solution: Mental health professionals who pursue training in filial therapy typically have had little or no training or experience as a teacher, educator, or supervisor. This issue is explored again in this section because many of the skills required of a filial therapist go counter to much of what a therapist does with clients. Since most mental health professionals do not have a background of training or experience as a teacher or educator, they may lack the basic skills required to involve individuals in a learning process. They have graduated from graduate programs that have emphasized broad philosophical and theoretical issues and conceptual skills. Many graduate classes in these programs encourage a learning-on-your-own approach. These approaches to learning, while appropriate for graduate students, are not effective in training parents to be therapeutic agents in their children's lives. The filial therapist must make the transition from therapist to the task of teaching specific skills, and these skills must be taught in small incremental steps—no exploration of broad conceptual issues here. In filial therapy, the focus is on developing specific skills and accepting attitudes.

Becoming a filial therapist requires a significant shift in the mental health professional's emphasis in a number of significant dimensions: the identified client, focus on what is deemed important, identified objectives in the therapist–client relationship, methodology utilized in working toward a solution of the problem, skills employed in facilitating behavioral change, and personal need fulfillment. Parents generally seek out filial therapy because they are having "problems" with their children, but in filial therapy, the therapist does not work directly with the identified children. The relationship between parents and children occupies the central focus of the filial therapist, yet the therapist is dependent on the parent to develop a therapeutic relationship with the child that will facilitate change.

Unlike counseling relationships, wherein the identified objective is the emotional growth of the clients, in filial therapy, the objective is facilitation of the acquisition of therapeutic skills by parents. The methodology utilized in working toward a solution of the problem is teaching and training, a procedure foreign to most mental health professionals because they do not have experiential backgrounds in teaching and training. Although some mental health professionals have natural teaching skills, most have not been attracted to teaching methodology because it does not meet their needs for close interpersonal relationships, or planning and organization have a low priority in their need fulfillment. Supervised experience in leading a filial therapy group is key to the beginning filial therapist in learning what the teaching process is like. This discovery is described in the self-critique of a graduate student:

> The most important thing that I learned in this session is that I know more information than I give myself credit for. I was really worried about teaching parents what I know about play therapy, but I found out that I could do it! I learned that I can teach this material! I thought that since I did not have teaching experience, I would not be able to teach parents very well. It is my interest and passion for working with children in play therapy that inspires me to teach everything that I know to parents. I believe that it is this love for what I am doing that helps make me a better teacher.

The skills employed by parents in interactions with their children in the special playtimes to facilitate behavioral change are basic child-centered play therapy skills, and the filial therapist must be able to train parents in how to incorporate those skills into their interactions with their children. Therefore, filial therapists must first be competent and experienced child-centered play therapists. Secondly, they must be able to skillfully train parents in the appropriate use of child-centered play therapy principles and skills, and in that process they must be able to draw on their own play therapy experiences to add sparkle to the learning process.

The solution to this problem can only be thorough training and experience in play therapy, and then in-depth filial therapy training and experience that has a strong component focused on how to be an effective trainer and supervisor. Just as parents do not automatically know how to parent effectively simply because they become parents, mental health professionals do not automatically know how to be effective trainers just because they decide to become filial therapists.

Problem: Covering all of the specified material for each filial therapy training session.

Solution: One of the problems that plagues inexperienced filial therapists and filial therapists who do not have a background of teaching experience is staying on track each session and covering the designated material for that session. Organizational experience, a sense of timing, and group facilitation skills are needed to keep the group moving toward the learning objectives for each session. Each session should begin on time. This may mean interrupting social conversations that are generated as parents wait for the session to begin. Beginning on time models for the parents what is expected of them in their play sessions and communicates to the parents that they are expected to be on time for the training sessions.

The therapist must be able to keep the group from getting bogged down in relating personal stories, child behaviors that are problematic, or issues that sidetrack the discussion from the learning topic at hand. The key is organization, organization, organization. The therapist should be well prepared prior to each session with the agenda well thought out, handouts ready, homework assignments prepared, and toys for role-playing and video equipment ready prior to the parents arrival. The prescribed material must be covered or parents won't be prepared to conduct play sessions, nor will they be successful in doing so.

The therapist may find it helpful to make an agenda outline for each training session showing topics to be covered and activities, such as viewing a video or role-playing, to be utilized, and assign specific clock times to each topic and activity. The therapist will then know, for example, that at 3:10 parent role-playing should begin. A brief time outline for CPRT training Session 2 might be

2:00 Review homework
2:15 Empathic responding, demonstrate with a parent playing role of her child
2:45 View video of therapist playtime
2:55 Explain basic principles and guidelines of 30-minute play sessions
3:10 Parents role-play in pairs
3:20 List of toys to be used in special playtimes; show toys and demonstrate responding
3:50 Select a time and place for special playtimes and assign empathic response sheet
4:00 Adjourn

At times it may be necessary to cut off discussion and say, "We need to move on to the next activity for today." Such structuring, although difficult for therapists because they are accustomed to following the client's lead and facilitating exploration, is essential because 2 hours with an active group of parents can zip by in a hurry. In early training sessions especially, parents often bring up problematic issues, such as bedtime problems, that are unrelated to the training at hand. These concerns are responded to respectfully, and the therapist tells the parent, "I am making a note about your concern," (writes note to self) "and we will come back to the bedtime problem in later sessions. Right now, we need to work on..." Writing a reminder note gives the parent a sense that she was heard and reassures the parent that the therapist recognizes the importance of the problem to the parent and that the problem is being dealt with. Many of these concerns are not an issue in filial therapy training for a couple or one parent.

Problem: Parents who do not complete homework assignments or have persistent difficulty applying the skills.

Solution: Not all parents enter CPRT with an equal commitment to developing a new approach to relating to their children. Some parents enter filial therapy training to get their children "fixed" by the therapist and may be reluctant to enter fully into the training regimen because they want a quick fix for their children's behavioral problems. Many parents in filial therapy training are stressed by the problems they experience with their children and may feel helpless. Given such circumstances, it is understandable that some parents may not think homework assignments are important. After all, it has been years since a teacher gave them a homework assignment, so they show up with nothing to report. As exasperating as this may be for the therapist, patience and an encouraging attitude from the therapist are the rules of the day. It may be necessary to clarify for parents that the problems they are concerned about will be worked on in their special play sessions as they utilize their skills as therapeutic agents in their children's lives. Helping parents understand how the homework assignments relate to their roles in the play sessions and their relationships with their children will be encouragement enough for most parents. The key to working with the reluctant parent is persistent encouragement and an attitude of expectancy.

Sitting down privately with the reluctant parent for tutoring on the homework and exploring the difficulty with the homework often will elicit cooperation. The therapist may discover during this one-on-one time that the content of the homework assignment reminded the parent of an unresolved emotional issue that resulted in the parent avoiding the homework assignment. Exploring such issues can be very releasing to the parent and free the parent to become more directly involved in the training.

Some of the skills taught in CPRT training may touch on a parent's difficulty in his or her life or relationships and may result in the parent persistently having unusual difficulty in applying some of the skills. Sometimes these issues can be worked through quickly in the group, as in the case of a mother who had difficulty applying limits effectively in her play sessions. As she struggled with the dynamics of trying to set limits, she fairly quickly gained insight into her own long-standing struggle with boundary issues. In the course of the training session discussions, she shared the following insight into her difficulty:

> I was the youngest and was spoiled rotten. I never had any limits. Setting limits has been the hardest thing for me. I wanted my children to like me so much, to be their friend. I wanted my children to know that they were loved all the time, and it was hard to discipline them. But I've learned that disciplining them is loving them. Now I'm not afraid to go to restaurants. Now, my children are so much more in control of their behavior.

Asking a parent who is having persistent difficulty in applying certain skills to make a video of her play session, and critiquing the video with the parent, will often produce quick insight on the part of the parent. This approach must be undertaken with much patience and sensitivity to the threatening nature of the experience. When a point of difficulty is observed in the video, it is sometimes helpful to stop the video and ask the parent if she is aware of what is needed at that point or how her response needs to be changed. The therapist will need to avoid providing a quick answer or solution. It is more important that the parent make the discovery and, in the process, achieve insight. If the parent is unaware of what needs to be done, replay the segment a couple of times if needed. When the parent is able to provide an acceptable response, the therapist can then offer a self-esteem–building response to the parent: "There, you figured it out," or "You knew how to respond all along. It just didn't come out." This could then be a good time to explore what was blocking the response. The therapist should role-play various scenarios of the situation several times with the parent to help the parent feel comfortable with the new "language."

Do not assume that the parent's difficulty is a result of a crisis the parent is experiencing. Although this may be a factor, our experiences with incarcerated parents, single parents, nonoffending parents of sexually abused children, and many other parents in crisis situations have shown that these parents can quickly learn the skills taught in CPRT training. Parents, as is true of children, are quite resilient and, given an understanding, supportive, encouraging, and safe environment, can and will learn, change, and draw upon their inner coping mechanisms.

Problem: Parents who are noncompliant or inconsistent in having parent–child play sessions at home.

Solution: A good starting place to process this problem is to ask the parent, "What do you think you need to do differently to solve the problem?" Any confrontation with parents who are having difficulty must always be done gently. The therapist is always attempting to understand the parent's viewpoint. Parents who are not compliant in having playtimes at home may have serious doubts about their ability to use the skills that have been taught even though they may have adequately demonstrated use of the skills in role-playing experiences with toys in training sessions. Patient encouragement, although highly recommended, seldom results in these parents changing their behavior because they are convinced they will "mess up." A personal interview with the parent may be necessary to clarify the underlying causes for the noncompliance. If the therapist determines that self-doubt is the central factor, one solution is to schedule the parent to bring his child of focus to the agency or therapist's office at a time other than the CPRT training time for supervision and videotaping of their play session. In the supervision feedback time, the therapist is especially sensitive and responsive to the parent's feelings of anxiety and apprehension and responds with encouragement and support by pointing out specific positive responses and skills the parent exhibited. A part of the videotape can then be shown in the next CPRT training session. The other parents are usually sensitive to the noncompliant parent's reluctance and are generous in their praise and support, thus breaking down defensive barriers.

If a deeper emotional issue of rejection or resentment of the child by the parent emerges in the personal interview as the basis for the noncompliant behavior, exploration of the issue can proceed rapidly because the filial therapist has already established a therapeutic relationship with the parent. This initial therapy session can be such a powerful insight-producing experience that the parent will decide to go home and have her first parent–child play session. If nothing seems to work with the noncompliant parent, the therapist may need to have a private session with the parent and suggest that in light of the difficulty the parent is having in following through with the special playtimes, this may not be a good time for the parent to be in filial therapy training.

Problem: Resistant parents.

Solution: When parents are resistant to the training, look for underlying causes. Some parents are threatened by the possibility of changing their typical reactions to their children because changing may mean having to accept the fact that what they have been doing has not worked. Other parents are resistant because they came to filial therapy with the expectation that the therapist would change their children, and then they discover there are some attitudes and behaviors they are expected to change.

Dealing with a resistant parent can be frustrating to the beginning filial therapist, as revealed in this self-critique:

> An area for improvement involves my discomfort in redirecting or keeping a parent on task. During the first part of this third training session, I divided the group into dyads to practice reflection. Mr. Smith was very hesitant to practice his reflection skills. He asked numerous questions which I believe he already knew the answers to and often changed the subject. It was quite clear to me that he was using these tactics to avoid practicing reflection. I knew he understood the skill, so his delay tactics were those of resistance to practicing them. I am really uncomfortable dealing with his resistance. It was very difficult for me to get him back on task. Since I often hate to be put on the

> spot when I am unsure about something, I found it too easy to let him "off the hook" when he strayed off task. I realize that it is important for me to help parents practice all the skills and not just the ones that are comfortable. Practice is the only thing that will increase Mr. Smith's comfort. Yet, I found myself going along with his resistance so I wouldn't offend him or make him uncomfortable. This issue isn't going to go away! I must become more skilled at dealing with parent resistance.

In the case of Mr. Smith, there are no techniques that will solve this problem, and trying to figure out just how to break through Mr. Smith's resistance is not the solution. The issue is not making Mr. Smith uncomfortable; the issue is the therapist's discomfort. The therapist feels intimidated and lacks confidence. The problem lies with the therapist, and this issue was dealt with in supervision. One helpful thing the therapist could do would be to share his concern with Mr. Smith about wanting to be helpful to him but feeling apprehensive about keeping him on track or correcting him because he might feel hurt in the process.

RULE OF THUMB:

The therapist should model what she teaches.
In CPRT, we hope parents will share their
feelings and reactions with us.

Problem: A parent who dominates the training time.

Solution: A highly verbal parent who dominates the discussion time can be a deadly element in a filial therapy group. Other parents may roll their eyes, look knowingly at each other, stare at the floor, and begin to "tune out" when the domineering parent begins talking. Domineering individuals are typically insensitive to other people's reactions and continue to plow ahead. The experience can be so frustrating to parents that some may decide to drop out of the training. A general principle of group work is that no member should be allowed to destroy a group.

There are several methods of intervention to be considered in dealing with a domineering parent. After listening empathically to several minutes of the domineering parent's story, gently inserting (interrupting if necessary) a response summarizing the parent's story, and then asking "Anyone else in the group ever have that kind of problem?" can take the domineering parent out of the lead. Another way to intervene at this point is to relate the domineering parent's point to a teaching point and push ahead with the training plan:

> Jan, sounds as though you are really frustrated with your husband's parents. Group, there may be times when you are frustrated with your child during a special playtime. At such moments, you will need to work hard to get back in touch with your child. Look through your child's eyes. Ask yourself, "What is my child feeling?" "What does my child need right now?" "What is my child trying to communicate?" and try to make an empathic response as quickly as possible. Getting frustrated with your child is natural, and we will talk about your frustration and other feelings here in our training sessions.

The filial therapist should always be sensitive to a parent's emotional needs and may determine that it is necessary to have a special counseling session with the parent. Sometimes, a one-on-one counseling session with the domineering parent will meet enough of the domineering parent's needs and result in less verbal activity in the filial therapy training sessions. If a counseling session does not seem necessary, another possibility would be to have a private session with the offending parent, explaining that other parents are having a difficult time entering into the discussion and eliciting the cooperation of the domineering parent to help other parents to participate.

Problem: The therapist is not a parent and is apprehensive about having anything of value to offer parents.

Solution: Being an effective filial therapist is not dependent on having experienced parenthood, although the experience can have some positive benefits for the filial therapist in helping parents feel they are understood and in helping the therapist to be sensitive to some parenting issues and struggles. The child-centered play therapy principles and skills the filial therapist has acquired from training and experience and can teach to parents are more important than the experience of being a parent. Feelings of inadequacy related to not being a parent are often related to other generalized feelings of inadequacy resulting from lack of experience. Supervision can be a significant help in this area. A part of the solution to feelings of doubt related to the absence of parenting is supervised experience as a filial therapist to discover that inexperience in parenting is not a deterrent to effectiveness as a filial therapist.

Many inexperienced filial therapists who are not parents feel inadequate about trying to teach parents how to relate to their children. These feelings of inadequacy and how they were worked through can be seen in the self-critiques of the following filial therapists who were enrolled in a graduate course in filial therapy that had a supervised practicum experience.

Judy: During the first two or three filial therapy sessions I led, I was extremely nervous because I thought I did not know enough because I have never been a parent. I now realize that just because I have never been a parent does not make me unknowledgeable about children.

Geri: I felt awkward during the first few training sessions because I do not have children. I questioned why these parents would listen to me. After our last filial therapy training session, one of the moms approached me and told me that at the beginning of the training group, she questioned how I would be able to understand or to help her, since I had told the parents that I had no children. She said that she had been skeptical of my ability and competency, but she had changed her mind over the past 10 weeks. She said that she now felt my responses to parents facilitated their thought and growth. I am now confident in my skills despite not having children of my own. I now realize I only need to be myself and to convey to parents the information I do know about children, play therapy, and filial therapy.

Megan: I was nervous at first because I am not a mother. I felt that the parents would question my experience and knowledge because I have never dealt with a child on a day-to-day basis like a mother does. I now realize that being a mother does not matter. In fact, not being a mother may even strengthen what I have to say. A mother will see things that I cannot even if I was a parent, and I will see things that a mother does not see. So if we work together, we get to see the whole picture, and this will benefit the child. I found that I was able to use examples from my own life, and the parents related to them.

Alisha: I felt uncertain about my ability to teach parents, since I have no parenting experience. I was surprised that the parents seemed to trust and respect me as a leader, without questioning my expertise or experience. Throughout the filial therapy training sessions, I began to feel more comfortable with the parents and more confident in my ability to instruct and guide them, despite our differences in parenting experience.

CHAPTER 19

A MOTHER'S PERSPECTIVE ON CPRT TRAINING: LEARNING ABOUT MY CHILD AND MYSELF

Theresa L. Taylor Kellam[1]

This chapter presents a case study of filial therapy sessions the author had with her son and the impact of the treatment on both of them. This unique perspective provides insight into the interrelationship between the parent, the child, and the healing process. Over the course of the sessions, the child progresses from overlapping symptoms of oppositional defiant disorder, depression, and Attention Deficit Disorder to alleviation of his initial symptoms.

Lacking in the literature are case studies describing an individual child's progress in filial therapy. In fact, only one case study examining the effects of filial therapy has been published (Packer, 1990) to date. While the importance of controlled experimental research is indisputable, case studies are also of paramount importance in adding depth and understanding to the process of therapy

[1] Theresa L. Taylor Kellam, PhD, is a licensed psychologist in private practice in Arlington, Texas. She is also an adjunct professor at Tarrant County College, South Campus, in Fort Worth, Texas.

that experimental research cannot, making them a good source for future experimental research with potentially more substantial research questions. In addition to describing the progress and success of an individual child, this chapter presents the author's personal experience in filial therapy with her son. By describing filial therapy from this unique perspective, the author attempts to bring depth and understanding to the process, touching on theoretical implications that hopefully will inspire future research topics.

Child's Presenting Problems

Dylan, age 8, had developed oppositional defiant disorder with symptoms becoming more and more severe. At the time I began filial therapy, his symptoms were the most severe. He was often disciplined for screaming at, hitting, and pushing his parents and his sister. He was angry much of the time at home and often would not cooperate with simple requests. He refused to do chores, yelled at his parents, and had angry outbursts. During one of these outbursts, he broke his closet door; in another, he punched a hole in the wall of his room. He argued frequently with his parents and could not seem to get along with his little sister. He did not respect others' boundaries, often intentionally getting in their personal space to annoy them or push or hit them. During the past year, Dylan had also become more and more hyperactive and unsociable to the point of being unable to make lasting friendships at school. He was not often invited over to children's houses to play and complained of not having any friends. He was so hyperactive and so difficult to socialize with that other children did not want to play with him. He was very critical of other children, complaining about them with vague descriptions—for example, saying he didn't want to play with a particular child because he was "stupid" or another because he was "not any fun." He came home from school many days crying, saying he hated school.

Dylan also seemed to be depressed. He was very sensitive about mistakes he made and often would not try something for fear he could not do it. He had a low frustration tolerance and would give up easily when trying to do something, often throwing it down in anger and yelling or crying. At bedtime, he would complain that he never got to see his mom and dad, was often afraid to go to sleep, and had occasional nightmares. Dylan also had difficulty taking responsibility for his mistakes, often blaming others for them. He berated himself, complaining that he was "stupid" at times and at other times claimed to have superpowers. He also seemed to be obsessed with aliens, often drawing, playing, or talking about them. There was a noticeable decrease in Dylan's frustration tolerance, scholastic abilities, self-esteem, and self-confidence. His drawings were regressed at times and reflected chaos and pain.

At school, Dylan was in trouble frequently for disrupting the class. He was described as the "class clown" by his teachers. He did not stay in his seat or follow directions and did not usually complete assignments he was supposed to at school. He had trouble paying attention. He had to be reminded several times to stay on task, often staring off into space or becoming interested in something other than the assignment he was supposed to be working on. He also had great difficulty completing homework assignments and was very sensitive about receiving any constructive criticism or instruction from others. He struggled for hours on assignments that should have taken minutes. At times, he seemed unable or unwilling to read, because of his angry, defiant behavior. The professionals at his school did not believe he had a learning disability and discouraged testing him for one. I also wondered if something had happened to him that we didn't know about, but when I questioned him, he assured me that no one had abused him in any way.

When Dylan was 8 years old, I went to a parents' night at his school just before I started filial training and saw a picture he had drawn (Figure 19.1) displayed on his classroom wall with pictures the other children had drawn of smiling faces. Dylan's picture stood out. I could see the pain and turmoil Dylan was feeling.

For example, the face of the central figure in the drawing is a profile, perhaps indicating Dylan's inability to face his problems. The expression on this figure's face seems to reflect intense fear—teeth clenched, eyes wide, and hair standing straight up—but Dylan described him as tough. This expression could also be interpreted as one of pain, considering the oozing wound drawn in the center of the figure's chest. The two faces in the top corners of the drawing are reminiscent of comedy and tragedy masks, but instead depict sadness and anger. The little figure standing beside the big one is perhaps the little bit that is left of Dylan, seeming to be numb, frightened, and overwhelmed.

Figure 19.2, also drawn just prior to filial therapy training, looks more like a 4-year-old's drawing. It is regressed and

Figure 19.1

Figure 19.2

chaotic, depicting a house and tree with pained expressions and antennae.

This drawing accurately illustrates the stress of the family environment at the time. The absence of a chimney is perhaps symbolic of Dylan's inability to express his feelings in the family due to my husband and I becoming more controlling and strict in reaction to Dylan's behavior problems. The leaning of the house could possibly indicate a loss of psychic equilibrium. The tree leaning in the direction of Dylan's drawing hand could be an indication of a longing for control over his self-being (Allan, 1988). While the trunk is not broken or wounded, the zig-zag through it may imply some sort of scar or damage to the trunk, indicating a past psychological trauma (Allan, 1988). I knew Dylan was in a lot of pain, but I didn't know how to help him.

Filial Therapy Training

I participated in a filial therapy training group led by Garry Landreth as part of a graduate course in filial therapy at the University of North Texas. The filial group was made up of 5 parent-graduate students in the class of 25 who volunteered to participate. We met each week in the middle of the room for part of the class time as a way for Dr. Landreth to demonstrate the principles of filial therapy. Members of the group were instructed to tell their children that they were taking a class to learn how to play with them. We were given a list of toys to gather, which included: dollhouse furniture (bathroom, bedroom, and kitchen); a doll, blanket, and baby bottle; army soldiers in two colors; a dart gun; a rubber knife; a Lone Ranger–type mask; six crayons and paper; a doctor's kit; a can of Play-Doh; a ring toss game; a deck of cards; Tinkertoys; a hand puppet; a bop bag; masking tape; a rope; and a plastic car or truck. These were kept in a cardboard box with a lid, and the rooms for a dollhouse were defined on the lid by strips of tape. The toys were to be used only during the special playtime. We were also instructed to choose 30 minutes during the week that we could commit to using for special playtime and decide on a place to have the special playtime that would allow for privacy. We were instructed to tell our children to unplug the phone and put up a "Do Not Disturb" sign on the door so that no one would interrupt ring our special playtime. During filial therapy group time, bers shared and discussed the special playtimes they had with r children, and the instructor based the material for the classes on what the members discussed.

Training Approach

The approach I used in my special play sessions followed the Landreth model of filial therapy: 10 sessions of training in which parents are trained to use client-centered play therapy skills with their own children. Parents are taught the principles of child-centered play therapy (reflective listening, therapeutic limit setting, choice giving, and how to allow the child to lead the session) through lecture, role-play, supervision of play sessions, and homework assignments using a group format. The emphasis of the training is to show parents how to be aware of, and sensitive to, children's emotional needs and how to respond to those needs therapeutically.

My Guarded Beginning

Even before I began sessions with Dylan, I gained a lot from being in the group training time. I was looking forward to participating in the group, but at the same time I felt very nervous about revealing the problems my son was having. I came to the first session somewhat guarded, minimizing the problems that Dylan and I were having to myself and to the group. I remember feeling somewhat judgmental of one mom as she began to describe her frustration with her daughter. These feelings were, of course, a defense mechanism against my own feelings of inadequacy, frustration, and helplessness about parenting and the shame and pain I carried for mistakes I had made as a parent.

I had no idea at the time how guilty I felt about the problems my son was having. My judgmental attitude quickly suited me up in arrogance and would have served to separate me from the group, but, fortunately, Dr. Landreth swiftly brought my dilemma to my attention. One mother mentioned that she had yelled at her child, and Dr. Landreth asked, "Anyone else here ever yell at your child?" His question felt like a blow at first. I was flooded with uncomfortable thoughts and feelings. I was not the perfect parent I was pretending to myself to be. I also was intensely aware of the fear I was feeling about being judged in the same way I had been judging others. I was afraid of being thought of as someone who needed help or needed to change.

The group was silent. We looked at our notepads and squirmed in our seats. My shield of arrogance had lost its power. I put my pen down and crossed my arms in front of me, trying to protect myself from exposure. Then Dr. Landreth asked me directly, "Theresa, what about you?" "I've gotten a lot better," I explained, still feeling defensive, "but yes, I've yelled at my kids." "Sure, we all have. Parents yell at their kids. Parents aren't perfect," Dr. Landreth explained. He continued to normalize all of the thoughts, behaviors, and feelings we thought had set us apart from the "good parents" we wanted to be, and conveyed acceptance for mistakes we had believed to be unforgivable. My arrogance was not stripped away to expose my incompetence, but transformed into confidence and an openness to myself and others. Now, instead of pretending to be perfect or better than the others in the group, I belonged. I was part of a group of parents who cared about their children and each other.

Our First Playtime

I expected that the first special playtime I had would have no real impact, because I had already used child-centered play therapy skills at home everyday. But my relationship with Dylan was changed forever during the first part of the session. The most poignant moment was when Dylan stated that he was going to play 52 pick-up with the deck of cards.

Dylan: (Looks at his mother before scattering the cards, as if to ask permission.)

Mother: Oh, you've decided what you want to do with those cards.

Dylan: I can do it?

Mother: You get to decide what to do.

Dylan: (Gleefully scatters the cards.) I'll pick them up.

Mother: Oh, you've decided to pick up the cards.

Dylan: (He picks up a couple more cards, nodding.) Uh–huh. (Suddenly stops, surprised and elated.) Oh, I decide not to pick them up! (Scatters those he had gathered.)

I had become very strict at home as a reaction to Dylan's hostile behavior. What he, in fact, needed was some way to express the turmoil he felt inside. I didn't realize it at the time, but the moment described above seemed to symbolize Dylan's need for permission to express the chaos he had been experiencing internally. It was difficult for me to even acknowledge Dylan's internal chaos at this point because I was still caught up in the belief that if my son experienced inner turmoil, it meant that I had been a bad parent and that I didn't have any business being a therapist. The significant thing that happened in the moment when Dylan threw the cards was that I was not focused on whom I needed to make him into or how I needed to shape him into a particular person I had in mind. I was focused on who he was at that moment, and I connected with him for the first time since he was a baby. In that moment, I just allowed myself to be with him, and that changed us forever.

Despite my needs to protect myself from Dylan's true feelings, he was able to express them and even have them acknowledged on some level, due to the structure of the responses I used during the play sessions. He was greatly freed and relieved by the experience. He was also grateful for it and began to express warm and affectionate feelings toward me for perhaps the first time in a very long time. Dylan began to improve dramatically after the first session. During the second playtime a week later, he tenderly held my wrist and designed a bracelet for me. I was deeply touched by the love I felt from him. I realized that the accepting environment I had created in our special playtime had been missing in our home. By allowing Dylan to experience his feelings fully, I became aware of how much pressure I had put on myself to make sure my child was always happy and secure. In turn, I had been pressuring Dylan to be perfect. I was saddened by this awareness, but I also was grateful for it, because it was the key to understanding Dylan's world.

My Own Chaos

By the third week, Dylan was exclusively expressing chaotic themes during our playtime. He scattered all the toys and acted out an earthquake in the dollhouse. I felt as though I was unable to make a connection with Dylan during these sessions, but I believe now that, on an unconscious level, I had been avoiding making that connection. I know now that I was experiencing boredom because of my resistance to descend into Dylan's pain with him. I have found it to be true that, whenever I experience boredom during a play therapy session in my private practice, it is due to my resistance to see the world through the child's eyes, because it reflects my own unresolved pain.

I had been experiencing a lot of grief over the changes that had taken place in my son, the loss of the relationship we once had, and feelings of helplessness I felt about not being able to take away the apparent pain he was experiencing. I became uncomfortable at the group meetings, afraid that my wounds and inadequacies would show. I felt distanced once again, this time with an intense awareness of the shame I carried. I soon found out, though, that my attempts to keep my feelings covered were useless in such an accepting environment. No matter how much I wanted to pretend that I felt happy and confident, my true feelings rose out of me as if they had been given a will of their own.

The unconditional love and acceptance that Dr. Landreth exuded and facilitated in the group were so powerful, it was as if I had no choice but to allow all of myself to be present. As I shared my feelings, I felt both ashamed for letting them out and blessed that I had been able to. Not only did my feelings about parenting and my son become manifest, but so much of me that I had hidden or denied was now a part of me again. The most wounded and vulnerable parts of me had been released, but so had the strength that contained them. My shame was transformed into grief by the acceptance offered in the group. Dr Landreth and the group comforted me as I wept, but I had much more grieving to do than group time would allow. The caring words, gestures, and expressions that Dr. Landreth and the group gave to me during this session became a powerful image that I kept with me to give me the support I needed to face my most painful feelings. These images helped me to continue to grieve once I left the session.

As my feelings surfaced, I thought, at the time, that I was going over ground I had traveled before. I've heard so many clients and therapists express this same frustration saying, "I thought I had already dealt with this." It seems to me now, though, that these familiar journeys are actually a deepening of experience. I will experience this pain and every feeling known to humankind over and over again, and each time I will have the opportunity to go deeper and deeper into that feeling. From this perspective, I am not continually reopening old wounds when I experience the pain that formed them; instead, I am passing through the doors they have made for me, traveling through their eternal pathways, each time finding a deeper level of understanding and a more meaningful connection with others.

Reconnecting

I began facing all the things I had done to my child, not meaning to, all the messages I had given him about how I needed him to be some other person than who he was. It was very difficult for me to face how I had hurt Dylan and to face how much he was hurting. I was experiencing such intense grief that I was having trouble connecting with Dylan during the special playtimes. I didn't want to know anymore, it was too painful. Dr. Landreth suggested that Dylan and I spend the time set aside for the special playtimes doing something that would be fun and enjoyable for both of us. For the next two weeks, the sessions were still nondirective and child-centered, but we played outside, spontaneously deciding where to go or what to do next.

Once we had stepped out into the world, the possibilities seemed endless to both of us. During the second of these two sessions, Dylan and I rode our bikes to his school playground to play. What emerged was highly symbolic play directed by Dylan. He asked me to bury all but his head and his hands in a pile of sand. Once I had buried him, he said that I should pretend that I came along and found him trapped there and I should rescue him by holding his hands and pull him slowly out of the sand. This reminded me of how I had experienced the unconditional love and acceptance offered by Dr. Landreth. Our barriers to understanding seemed to melt away as I pulled him up to me and we embraced for a long time. I knew that a part of Dylan that had been hidden in darkness was now free. Next, he asked me to stand on one side of the field while he stood at the other so we could run to each other. When he reached me, we hugged and he asked me to whirl him around in my arms. Dylan had given himself and me an abiding memory of the connection we had made to each other and ourselves. On our way home from the playground, he requested that, for our next session, we use the special playtime toys in the room where we had previously had the sessions. He was ready to bring the endless possibilities of the world inside with us and so was I. As I tucked him in that night he said, "Mom, I miss you." He had said it so many times before, but this time I didn't feel guilty when he said it. I reflected, "You're wishing we could be together." "Yeah," he said. I wondered if his feelings were connected to jealousy over his younger sister, Deva, being with me while he was in school. I explored the situation. "Maybe you wish you could stay home with me during the day like Deva does," I queried. "No," he said, "I like school and I need to go to it, because I'm going to be a scientist. I just miss you." "Oh," I said, "missing me is one of the feelings you feel as you make your way in the world." "Yeah," he said, "I want to decide what to do, but I miss you." "I know, I miss you too," I said as I hugged him, "but I feel so proud as I watch you make your own way." "It's tough out there, Mom," he said. "Yes, it is," I reflected, "and I'm here if you need me." "I know," he said, and whispered and looked at me as he said, "I love you, Mom." "I love you too, Dylan." There we were, connected, but now also allowed to be separate. By encouraging Dylan to be who he was and not who I needed him to be or thought he should be, he and I began to know and enjoy who he truly was.

Following this session, Dylan no longer complained about not being able to spend enough time with me, and his nightmares, fears, and obsession with aliens subsided. His drawings changed dramatically, becoming more organized and depicting peaceful scenes (Figure 19.3).

He described this drawing as a walk down a country lane and seemed satisfied, contented, and peaceful as he drew and described his work. The white clouds could be symbolic of spiritualism. The eggs in the basket seem to be symbols of promising things to come, or anticipation of transformation. The path's perspective upward and to the right seems to indicate positive movement, while the tree on one side of the path is strong, straight, and tall, indicating health and well-being. The trees on the other side of the path indicate strong needs, possibly for self-control or a return to the past to deal with past trauma. The tree that has fallen over the path seems to indicate an obstacle or past trauma that needs to be dealt with.

Themes of Struggle

The next few playtimes revealed themes of struggle. Dylan molded monsters out of the clay that would devour all the "good guys."

Figure 19.3

He also liked to have battles with the army men and with me, requesting to wrestle or shoot each other with the dart guns. For several sessions, his favorite thing to do was to tie me to a chair with masking tape. He would also tape odd things to me like diapers or toys, apparently wanting me to know what it was like for him to be humiliated.

At times I felt hurt by Dylan's desires to humiliate me, or guilty because Dylan was experiencing such turmoil. Many times, I had to fight off the urge to rescue Dylan, reminding myself that those feelings were related to my needs, not Dylan's. At other moments, though, I felt gratified by Dylan's play, because I realized that he trusted me enough to let me know how he really felt.

Disclosure

The theme of the sessions changed again when Dylan asked if we could talk instead of play. During the first of these "talking" sessions, he revealed to me the depths of his loneliness and disappointment and spent most of the session crying in my arms. During the next two talking sessions, he told me things he had done that he was ashamed of. Both of these sessions ended with him being held like a baby in my arms at his request.

I was able to descend into Dylan's sorrow and shame only because I had developed a deep faith in his emotional experience. It was, of course, painful, but comforting to be with him in it, knowing that he would not have to deal with these feelings alone anymore. Through our sessions together I came to know that the chaos, pain, confusion, shame, and sorrow that Dylan experienced were feelings that deepened him as they do all of us, and that trying to protect him from those feelings would limit him and our relationship. Facilitating the expression of Dylan's feelings taught me to trust in his ability to cope with life and heal his wounds.

As my trust in Dylan grew, so did his trust in me and our trust in ourselves. I began to enjoy being with Dylan again and looked forward to having playtime and other activities with him. We had a wonderful summer together, bike riding, exploring a nearby creek, and going to a nearby amusement park. Dylan worked very hard at his chores and was responsible for more than he ever had been. He and his sister also became close, and he began to be very nurturing toward her. Although he became angry occasionally and still yelled, he did not push or hit others anymore. He still showed no improvement in peer relationships, but seemed content to stay at home and spend time with me and his sister.

Once school started, he began immediately to berate himself, calling himself stupid and saying that nobody liked him. He also had a couple of angry outbursts, but more often cried and felt sad about his problems at school. This behavior was due, at least in part, to Dylan's struggle with learning disabilities. His disabilities became much more apparent in the third grade, not only because the material was more difficult than the previous year, but also because he had stopped masking his difficulties with hyperactive, defiant, or disruptive behavior. Dylan's third-grade teachers were also much more sensitive to his needs and behavior and recognized his problems immediately. They were extremely helpful in convincing the administration to have him tested. It was discovered during this process that Dylan had dyslexia. Although he was very frustrated by his disability, he experienced acceptance and understanding for the same behaviors he was humiliated for during the previous year. During our playtime, he began to reveal how he had been shamed and humiliated the previous year by his inability to do the work expected of him. He had believed that he was stupid and had devised elaborate cover-ups to hide his disability from the other children and the teachers. His behavior in the classroom changed dramatically as he began to feel accepted.

Recovery

Dylan began to thrive in ways my husband and I had hoped for. He began to make friends and was open to playing with children he had refused to play with before. Children started calling to see if he could come over or walk to school with them. They stopped by the house frequently and invited Dylan over to their homes. It seemed that several children liked Dylan and enjoyed his company, and vice versa. He also began to play again during his play sessions with me. His play centered around good winning over evil, depicting a good monster devouring the bad guys and transforming them into good guys. He began to be able to admit his weaknesses and rely on his strengths, in particular his creativity. He became flexible and willing to take risks appropriately. His soccer coach described him as the player who was willing to try every position and enjoyed participating and learning, even when he made mistakes.

Dylan also started sculpting beautiful abstract sculptures he imagined as "places for children." He described these places as fun and safe, pointing out the ways in which children would enjoy climbing, sliding, hiding, and playing with other children on them. The sculptures marked the beginning of Dylan's renewed enjoyment in pleasure activities completely of his own initiative and his first serious attempt at sculpting. He was very proud of his sculptures and imagined one day making them large enough so that children really could enjoy them the way he envisioned. The artwork in his play sessions also began to change. He drew a house with trees (Figure 19.4) that was dramatically different from the house he drew just before play sessions began (Figure 19.2).

The house has three chimneys, each one with a smaller puff of smoke than the last, seeming to imply a decrease in anger. The trees appear to be strong and healthy, unlike the scared trees of his previous drawings. Dylan also began to draw islands with palm trees (Figure 19.5), what Allan (1988) describes as symbolic of ego strength.

The following year in school, Dylan won third place in a photography contest he decided to enter, where he competed with children two grades ahead of him. He took a photograph of a tree branch curving upwards and titled it "The Curvy Line." In his artist's statement he wrote, "I walked all around the tree until I got to the point where it was just right and I got a very wonderful feeling. When you listen to your heart, anything can happen."

Figure 19.4

Figure 19.5

My Personal Journey: What I Learned

Experiencing the remarkable changes that took place in my son and in our relationship has been a transforming experience for me and has developed in me a deep belief in a child's ability to heal. What became quickly apparent through these sessions was how my expectations of my son and disappointments in him affected him and our relationship. Much of my parenting behavior that I thought was motivated by my child's needs was instead a result of my own needs. It was only by rendering my expectations, disappointments, and needs as powerless during our weekly play sessions that I was able to be aware of them. The play sessions provided my son with a consistently safe and healthy environment that he could use as he most needed. They also provided me with the opportunity not only to become more aware of behaviors that impeded my own and my son's growth, but also to function without those behaviors, thus breaking cycles, even generational cycles, of dysfunctional behavior. Because this is indeed a monumental task for any parent, I believe it is important that overly enthusiastic parents be required to restrict themselves to only one 30-minute session per week while in training.

Seeing the world through Dylan's eyes and giving him the support and freedom to express any of his feelings allowed me to once again experience the wonder of childhood, but it also brought me face to face with Dylan's most painful feelings, the ways in which I had prevented him from healing, and my own childhood wounds. Initially, these feelings were so overwhelming that I was unable to experience them and instead found myself feeling bored during sessions. It took time and support to move through my feelings of loss and sadness, and it was only after that I was ready to be with my son in his struggle. This experience was reminiscent of childbirth, where I experienced resistance to pain, then finally totally surrendered to it, giving birth to a miracle. In this way, it seems to be a natural process, creating a rebirth of the self for the parent and the child.

My experience with my son was, of course, in many ways a much different experience than that of being a play therapist, but it helped me to develop in ways that I feel will benefit any client I see. This experience has also helped me to better empathize with and understand the parents I work with. Although I had used these skills before with other clients, and in certain situations with my own children, I had used them as a therapist or as I needed them, but not always when my son needed me to. What I have learned from this experience has affected all areas of my life. In the group, I saw firsthand how feelings I reject in myself build a wall of shame internally and a wall of judgment and arrogance externally. I have learned to trust my feelings of rejection toward others as a guide to reclaiming that lost part of myself that they have brought to my attention. As I learned to allow Dylan and myself to express our true feelings, I learned to appreciate that our emotional experience is what guides us not just to a connection with each other, but to the depths of our being and a connection to all that has been created.

I know that my son will still struggle and sometimes fail. I will still make mistakes that will deeply hurt him, and we will both experience painful feelings, but I no longer believe that to be healed means to never feel insecure or ashamed. Instead, I will strive to honor these feelings as an important part of us. Through this experience I have learned to value wholeness more than healing, allowing myself to embrace that part of me that will always be wounded.

Dylan and I continued to have special playtime for many years. Sometimes we played, sometimes we talked. One special playtime, we spent the entire time howling and making strange noises. I was never sure what our time would be like. The world through my son's eyes unfolded and I just knew how lucky I was to be there with him.

Dylan is now 17 years old. In his early teens, whenever he needed to talk to me about something that was bothering him, he would say, "Mom, I need a special playtime." I would listen to his problems using the same skills I had in our playtime, practicing my faith in his ability to be guided by his own inner wisdom. Dylan is in high school now and is often complimented by his teachers for his intelligence, creativity, and ability to get along with others. Although he still struggles with dyslexia, he is enrolled this year in an advanced placement class for English and history. He is a gifted writer and wants to be an author and filmmaker.

References

Allan, J. (1988). *Inscapes to the child's world.* Dallas, TX: Spring Publications.

Packer, P. (1990). *The initial process of filial therapy: A case study of a four-year-old child and her parents.* Unpublished doctoral dissertation, Pennsylvania State University, University Park.

CHAPTER 20

VARIATIONS OF THE 10-SESSION CPRT MODEL

The model of once-a-week training sessions is considered ideal; however, the emotional needs, availability, or schedule of parents or children may necessitate consideration of other sequences of training sessions. The traditional concept of scheduling once-a-week sessions does not always match the dynamic needs of a family. A week between sessions can be a terribly long time in the life of a family in the midst of trauma or crisis. We have achieved positive results in adapting the 10-session CPRT model to meet the emotional and situational needs of families.

Although the frequency of CPRT training sessions may vary as suggested in this chapter, the content and structure of the training sessions remain virtually the same. The content of the 10-session model of training is considered to be the minimal amount of training needed to equip parents with the skills necessary to enable them to become therapeutic agents in their children's lives. A reduction in the content is likely to result in a corresponding reduction in effectiveness of the training. Although we do not have research findings to verify this assumption, our experience with a multitude of parent and child populations in a variety of settings supports this conclusion at this time. Research findings in the future may prove our assumptions to be incorrect, since the capacity of the human organism to assimilate experiences and adjust is not fully known or understood. We do have scientific studies that verify the effectiveness of condensing the time between training sessions while maintaining the content of the 10 sessions of training in the Landreth CPRT filial therapy model.

Once-a-Week Filial Therapy Schedule

Since the once-a-week CPRT model has already been thoroughly described, additional information is not needed here. The once-a-week CPRT model is mentioned here simply to provide a complete listing of the possible variations in scheduling the 10-session model of CPRT. The once-a-week structure does provide an opportunity for parents to take a more leisurely approach to scheduling the parent–child play sessions. When the time between training sessions is condensed, play sessions need to be scheduled more frequently during the week for supervision purposes. The parent should have a play session to report on in each training session after the first three training sessions. The parent–child play sessions are considered to be a key part of the 10-session model.

Twice-a-Week CPRT Schedule

The scheduling of once-a-week counseling or filial therapy sessions is generally done to meet the needs of the therapist—but what about the needs of clients? Could it be that clients are capable of assimilating and integrating experiences more rapidly and do not need a week between therapy sessions? This is an especially key consideration when families have been torn apart and their lives shattered by traumatic experiences that leave them feeling helpless with no relief in sight. These families may need short-term intensive CPRT training sessions twice-a-week for 5 weeks to help them get through the crisis more quickly.

Another consideration is parents who are not able to sustain continued focus for long periods of time. We found this to be the case in working with a group of teenage mothers. They seemed to lose interest and focus after about 50 minutes, so the format was changed from once-a-week 2-hour sessions to meeting twice weekly for 45 minutes. This shorter time frame seemed to be a much better learning experience. Some of the material also had to be adapted in very concrete ways to help this group learn. A lot of role-playing was added to the format, and initially the therapist had to assume the role of the child because the young mothers were uncomfortable playing the role of a child. These teenage mothers were dealing with huge personal issues that, if unaddressed, would hinder their ability to learn. Therefore, it was necessary to devote a larger amount of time to the process dimensions of the model and to be especially sensitive in determining when the group was ready to move on.

What is to be done for families who are not available for 10 weeks of therapy? This was the case for incarcerated mothers we wanted to involve in CPRT training before they were sent to another correctional facility. They were awaiting trial and/or sentencing or had been sentenced and were remanded to the county jail before being sent to a regional correctional facility in another part of the state. Since the majority of incarcerated female inmates are single mothers of dependent children, these children are usually placed with extended family members. Incarceration of the mother can be a terrifying experience for young children who can visit their mother only at designated times and in the frightening setting of a jail.

Arrangements were made with the county sheriff's department to provide 2-hour CPRT training sessions twice-a-week for 5 weeks for 4 groups of mothers. Almost 75% of these mothers had not completed high school and almost half of them had annual incomes of less than $5,000. Fifty percent of the mothers were Caucasian and 41% were African American. The CPRT training sessions were conducted in a small room in the county jail. After the third training session, parent–child play sessions were scheduled between each training session in a small space that could be supervised. CPRT toy kits were provided for the parents to use, and each play session was videotaped for supervision and research purposes.

We found that the mothers in the CPRT training groups significantly increased their empathic interactions with their children, significantly increased their attitude of acceptance of their children, and reported a significant reduction in the number of behavior problems with their children (Harris & Landreth, 1997). These are encouraging results, and they demonstrate the power of the 10-session CPRT training model as well as the efficacy of the intensive training. The results of this study are truly remarkable given the extreme conditions and stressful circumstances of a county jail setting and the restricted backgrounds of the mothers. We anticipate similar results using a twice-a-week format with other parent populations.

Every Day CPRT Schedule

Some families may be experiencing such intense situational circumstances and/or emotional and physical trauma that CPRT training sessions every day are warranted.

Mothers and children who reside in a domestic violence shelter or homeless shelter are often there for only 2 or 3 weeks and then are relocated to a halfway house, return to their homes, or find some other place of residence. Even twice-a-week CPRT training sessions would not be sufficient under these circumstances. Therefore, CPRT training sessions every day are necessary in such a setting. Smith and Landreth (2003) modified the structure of the 10-session filial therapy model to provided intensive CPRT training (12 sessions in 14 days) for mothers and children in a domestic violence shelter and a homeless shelter. In order to accommodate the mothers' hectic and stressful work schedules, shelter-assigned chores, and shelter training schedules, the training segment of the model and the parent–child play sessions were merged into 1 ½-hour training sessions 5 nights a week and during the day on weekends.

Smith and Landreth found that children in the CPRT group demonstrated a significant increase in self-concept; a significant decrease in overall behavior problems; a significant decrease in internalizing and externalizing behavior problems; and a significant decrease in aggression, anxiety, and depression, compared to children in a control group. Mothers who received CPRT training demonstrated a significant increase in empathic interactions with their children, based on analysis of pre- and post-videotapes of mother–child play sessions. These results are extraordinary considering the high levels of stress, anxiety, depression, and fatigue these mothers were experiencing on a daily basis. The results are also significant in view of the fact that children's relationships to their mothers have been identified as a key factor in how children are affected by witnessing domestic violence.

A comparative analysis of the results of this study with the Kot, Landreth, and Giordano (1998) intensive, short-term, child-centered individual play therapy study (12 sessions in 14 days) in the same domestic violence shelter and the Tyndall-Lind, Landreth, and Giordano (2001) intensive, short-term, child-centered, sibling group play therapy study (12 sessions in 14 days) in the same domestic violence shelter showed no significant differences on the dimensions identified above between the intensive CPRT training, the intensive short-term individual play therapy, and the intensive short-term sibling group play therapy groups. Intensive CPRT training was found to be as effective as intensive individual play therapy and intensive sibling group play therapy conducted by professional play therapists.

The significant results of scientific studies on the effect of collapsing the time between sessions attests to the robustness of the 10-session CPRT model.

Multiple Weekend CPRT Schedule

The weekday schedule for some families is so hectic and stressful that they have difficulty making a commitment to 10 weeks of training. For these parents, it may be necessary to lengthen training sessions and significantly reduce the number of training sessions. To assess the impact of collapsing the time between CPRT training sessions and reducing the number of sessions, parents were given the opportunity to enroll in CPRT training for 4 consecutive Saturdays or the traditional model of 10 weekly sessions. The parents in each group lived in a large city, and their children were displaying a wide spectrum of behavioral problems. Since there were fewer opportunities for parents in the four-session Saturday group to have home play sessions with their children and receive supervision from the therapist, parent–child play sessions were added to the training schedule and child care was provided on-site for the children. An advantage of this arrangement was that the therapist always had a child available for demonstration of the skills being taught, as well as providing an opportunity for parents to immediately practice those skills.

Test results showed that parents in the 4-session Saturday training group were initially much more stressed than parents in the 10-week training group. After training, no significant differences were found between the two training groups on parental stress, parental empathy, parental acceptance, and child behavior problems. Parents in the 10-week filial therapy training group demonstrated greater skill development in empathic responding. Parents in the 4-session Saturday group seemed to become a more cohesive group than parents in the 10-session group. This may have been a function of a smaller number of parents in the four-session Saturday groups (Ferrell, 2003).

Weekend CPRT Schedule

A couple called me about concerns for their 6-year-old son, James, who they described as bossy, manipulative, angry all the time, "wants to sleep in our bed every night," and a severe discipline problem. "We can't do anything with him. Spanking doesn't work anymore. Nothing works." I recommended play therapy, but the only play therapist I could locate in their rural area of west Texas was a 3-hour drive away. I called them back and described CPRT training to them. They were eager, excited, and said, "That sounds like just what we need!" Since they lived several hundred miles away, arrangements were made for them to come to the Center for Play Therapy for a weekend of filial therapy training.

I condensed the 10 sessions of CPRT training into 2 hours of training on Friday evening and 7 hours on Saturday. In the Friday evening session, I focused on parts of the first 3 sessions of the 10-session model: active listening, reflecting feelings, returning responsibility, and tracking. My primary objective was to help both parents acquire a few of the basic skills needed for a first 10-minute mini-play session with their son that evening. This decision was based on their high level of commitment, the intensity of the setting, and my thoughts that a mini-play session that evening would help reduce their anxiety about the experience. The schedule for the second hour was

- 10 minutes — Demonstration play session with James, which the parents observed through a two-way mirror.
- 15 minutes — Critique of the play session focused on what they saw (nonverbal behaviors: sat down quickly, smiled, nodded head, tracked James with my whole body) and what they heard (verbal responses: reflected content, reflected feelings, returned responsibility, made tracking responses), and answers to their questions.
- 10 minutes — Mother–child play session. As we observed, I pointed out to the father the positive responses the mother made.
- 5 minutes — Feedback to the mother.
- 10 minutes — Father–child play session. As we observed, I pointed out to the mother the positive responses the father made.
- 10 minutes — Feedback to the father and outline of what to expect the next day.

A babysitter was hired to take care of James when he was not in the playroom Friday evening and all day Saturday.

Saturday content schedule was determined by the immediate needs of the parents but was still content within the framework of the 10-session model (flexibility was the rule of the day):

- 1 hour — Therapeutic limit setting training, role-played in the playroom.
- 1 hour — Supervision: 15-minute parent–child play session with 15-minute feedback for each parent.
- 1 hour — Training, role-playing, viewing of video segments of my play sessions.
- 1 hour — Lunch.
- 1 hour — Supervision of parent play sessions.
- 1 hour — Training, role-playing, viewing segments of one parent play session.
- 1 hour — Supervision of parent play sessions.
- 1 hour — Training, viewing segments of one parent play session, wrap-up, and planning for at-home play sessions by both parents and telephone follow-up supervision.

At the 1-month and 2-month follow-up, both parents enthusiastically reported feeling empowered and described significant behavioral changes for James. By the end of the second week, he was sleeping in his own bed. By the end of the first month, the angry outbursts had disappeared and there were no discipline problems. They reported the Oreo Cookie Theory of choice giving was the most helpful tool they acquired.

Long-Distance CPRT Training

The number of mental health professionals and agencies that provide filial therapy training is minimal because the majority of existing play therapists have not been trained in filial therapy. Therefore, this highly effective procedure for improving the mental health of families is not readily available to the majority of parents. Entire regions of the United States and other countries do not have the services of a filial therapist. Indeed, some entire nations may not have a single filial therapist. One temporary solution to this dilemma is the provision of filial therapy training via the telephone. We have had several successful experiences using the telephone to provide long-distance CPRT training for parents. The following cases describe what happened in two families when CPRT training was conducted via the telephone.

A Traumatized Child in Israel

Nine-year-old Rachel, an Israeli, was riding in a bus that was attacked by 3 terrorists who shot and killed 11 of the adults and children aboard. Rachel was not physically injured, but after witnessing the brutal attack, she withdrew into herself and became very subdued and quiet although she had formerly been a playful, talkative child. She also developed severe mouth ulcers that were so painful she had to be placed on a liquid diet. She was taken to several physicians, but the ulcers seemed immune to medication.

Seven months after the attack, Rachel's mother was desperate for help and called her cousin, Suzi Kagan, one of my doctoral students in the play therapy program at the University of North Texas at that time. Suzi, who had completed filial therapy training and supervision, was faced with the dilemma of responding to the mother's concerns on the phone, hoping to help her find a mental health worker nearby in Israel or wait to provide help in person when she returned to Israel two months later. The mother was so distressed that Suzi concluded that immediate support was crucial to the family.

In the span of about 20 minutes, the significance of a special playtime was quickly explained, and examples of tracking and empathic listening were described. A few toys were recommended, and the mother was encouraged to sit on the floor and allow Rachel to decide how to spend the time together, playing or just sitting quietly in mom's lap if Rachel chose to do so. Suzi also suggested that the mother tell Rachel, "I know how scared you are and how hard it is to talk about what you saw on the bus."

Suzi made a commitment to call her cousin in a week. However, 24 hours later, Rachel's mother called again to report the play session had produced some immediate and startling results. Excitedly, she described the experience for Rachel as being like a huge, bulging ball of anxiety, pain, and fear that had finally been burst. Rachel, who had attempted to avoid crying since the terrorist attack, cried throughout the whole day after the playtime and into the night. She talked about how frightened she was and that every day she believed another terrorist attack would occur. That night Rachel slept through the whole night without waking up frightened, something she had not done since the attack.

Encouraged by the dramatic impact of the first play session, Suzi continued CPRT training once-a-week via the telephone for 10 weeks. During that time, she mailed the mother handout material typically used in the Landreth 10-session CPRT training. In the second telephone training session, the mother reported Rachel's mouth ulcers had begun to heal and Rachel had started eating solid food. As the play sessions progressed, she became more expressive and vocal in the special play sessions and in her daily life. By the 10th week, she had returned to her normal level of functioning and displayed no major trauma symptoms. The mother also described significant positive changes in her own relationship with her daughter and with other family members, as well as improvement in the overall atmosphere of the home. She was also able to generalize the new skills comfortably in her relationships outside the special play sessions.

An Isolated Family in a Rural Area

The parents and three children, ages 5, 3, and 4 months, lived in an isolated rural area of Minnesota, a 3-hour drive to the nearest airport. The mother was not employed outside the home, was taking graduate level correspondence courses, and often felt overwhelmed by the amount of time required to care for three small children, especially in the winter when they were confined to the house much of the time due to extreme cold and heavy snows.

David, the 5-year-old child of concern, was described as unmanageable, strong-willed, manipulative, exhibiting infantile behavior at times, with an extremely low threshold for frustration, and a physical threat to his 3-year-old brother. His kindergarten teacher reported no behavioral problems. The parents, who had not heard of play therapy or filial therapy, learned about these approaches to helping children from a relative who lived 1,000 miles away. Arrangements were made for a graduate student at the University of North Texas to provide long-distance CPRT training for the mother once-a-week under the close supervision of Dr. Garry Landreth.

The format of the 10-session training model was followed, information and homework assignments were faxed, and the mother was encouraged to e-mail pressing questions that occurred between the weekly phone sessions. Since the mother was so stressed, a part of the early training sessions was spent responding empathically to her feelings. Since she had not seen a demonstration play session, she seemed to have a great deal of difficulty in the early training sessions grasping the concept of empathic listening and acknowledging feelings, and had a hard time keeping evaluative and problem-solving statements out of her reflections, so the video *Child-Centered Play Therapy* by Garry Landreth was mailed to her. Viewing this video seemed to crystallize for the mother many of the concepts and skills she had difficulty understanding.

A major benefit of the CPRT training was that the mother gained insight into how she normally responded to David and did not allow him enough responsibility in his play. She was able to incorporate her new skills into her interactions outside the play sessions. David became less rigid, demanding, and aggressive, and his acting-out behavior diminished. His mother reported he had fewer serious "blow-ups." At conclusion of the 10 sessions of training, arrangements were made for the mother to continue to e-mail her questions to the graduate student and to videotape a play session once a month for more specific supervision.

Problematic Areas in Long-Distance Training

It is difficult to teach and practice reflective listening skills over the phone. For every emotion reflected, there must first be a verbal statement to communicate the emotion. The subtleties of facial expression and mood conveyed through the body are lost in this format. Scenarios that communicate particular emotions without using the feeling words themselves must be developed. The use of computers equipped with Webcast (video cameras) would alleviate some of this problem.

The use of toys to demonstrate a child's behavior in a play session and corresponding recommended responses is not possible via the telephone, nor can tracking skills be demonstrated. The absence of these concrete examples is a significant hindrance to training. Therefore, it is imperative that arrangements be made early in the training to send the parent a video demonstrating a play session with a child. It is essential that the parent be able to see what a play session is supposed to look like. Filial play sessions are so foreign to how parents typically react that it is almost impossible for parents to visualize the nature of the play sessions. Scheduling the viewing of a specified section of the video by the trainer and the parent at the same time during a CPRT training phone session enables the trainer to have the parent stop the video so the trainer can explain what is happening in the play session or call attention to specific responses. This procedure greatly enhances the learning experience for the parent. If the trainer does not have a video that can be mailed to the parent, we recommend the video *Child-Centered Play Therapy* by Garry Landreth. Again, the use of WebCast-equipped computers can alleviate some of these problems because the more technically advanced cameras, also more expensive, can be set to focus on a table containing toys for demonstration purposes.

The potential benefits of supervision are significantly diminished when the trainer is not able to observe a parent–child play session. Parents are simply not skilled enough to be aware of the subtle happenings in play sessions that make a huge difference in the impact of the sessions and then describe those happening to the trainer in a supervision session. Parents' interpretation of events in play sessions often do not match what is seen on videos. The graduate student's critique of one of her training sessions with the mother in the second case described above highlights this difficulty.

Some of the essential problems with the long-distance format were revealed in full force during this session. Audio messages without a visual component are less than reliable messages and so communication by phone makes it more difficult to give and receive accurate information about feelings or to communicate genuine support. The mother's report of the first play session had been encouraging. Based on what the mother said, it sounded like she had a good grasp of how to conduct the sessions. However, after viewing the video of her second play session, I was no longer sure that what she reported fully reflected what was really happening. She reported that the second session had also gone well, but the tension in her voice and happenings I saw on the video told another story. For example, the mother described a scene in which David was so frustrated with not being able to untie a knot in the rope that she decided to take the rope out of his hands and undo it for him. What I saw on the video was David picked up the rope, mentioned there was a knot in it, and then his mother immediately took the rope out of his hands to undo the knot.

This problem can be largely overcome by requiring the parent to videotape play sessions, make copies for herself, and mail the videos to the trainer for supervision. Skills the parent has difficulty utilizing can be focused on in the following training session through role-playing and modeling by the trainer. Segments of the videos can also be viewed at the same time by the trainer and parent during training sessions to reinforce positive parent behaviors and highlight areas that need to be improved. This simulcast or long-distance viewing of a videotaped session at the same time by the trainer and the parent facilitates a supervision process similar to face-to-face supervision when a video is being watched.

Based on our experiences, we encourage the limited use of CPRT training via the telephone with parents who live in areas where filial therapy training is not available. A caution: The filial therapist must have had extensive training and supervision in play therapy and filial therapy. One or two workshop experiences in filial therapy training are not sufficient.

Individual Parents and Couples

Having both parents attend CPRT training and learn the skills required for conducting special play sessions is highly desirable since these principles and skills will be generalized outside the play sessions. An important principle in child rearing is that both parents "be on the same page" in utilizing general child rearing principles, especially in areas such as discipline. When parents do not use a similar approach in child rearing, children become confused, feel insecure, and may compensate by acting out or becoming manipulative. Therefore, the therapist makes every effort possible to encourage and accommodate a reluctant spouse's schedule to make it possible for both parents to attend, even if the reluctant parent can only attend every other session or once a month. The therapist can also offer to schedule a special training session at the reluctant parent's convenience: an hour before reporting to work, during lunch, on the way home from work, a night session, etc. After obtaining permission from the child, a parent in training can invite their reluctant spouse to sit in on the at-home special playtimes to observe. This can be highly effective in helping to lower defensive barriers. When a parent is invited to sit in on the special playtime, a caution is in order: The invited parent is to sit on the floor and observe, and the parent in training will do all the talking for both parents. This requirement is necessary to prevent the nontrained parent from taking over the playtime, offering inappropriate suggestions to the child, asking leading questions, etc.

Our experience has been, however, that attendance at CPRT training sessions by both parents is not the norm. Fathers are notorious for being "too busy." In many cases, mothers have reported that they have taught fathers many of the skills they learned. One particularly "take charge," forceful mother said, "I just told my husband to listen up, this is the way we are going to start responding to our son." Many parents have reported teaching the skills they have learned to the absent parent and have been rewarded when they later observed the absent parent responding empathically or giving choices. Parents often jokingly relate stories about using the skills with the absent parent and how effective the skills were. A multitude of research studies have reported significant positive results in correcting children's behavioral problems even though only one parent received CPRT training. This is understandable since the parent is the child's therapeutic agent and is therefore somewhat similar to a play therapist in the child's life. In play therapy, significant positive results are often achieved even though the parents are not involved in therapy. This fact is demonstrated daily in elementary schools where elementary school counselors utilize play therapy and seldom have direct contact with the children's parents.

The 2-hour training format is usually not needed when working with one parent or a couple. One hour of training each week should be sufficient because so much more material can be covered. Skill development is speeded up because of the one-on-one mentoring, making it possible for the parent or couple to begin at-home play sessions the first week of training.

When training one parent or a couple, arrangements can be made for the child of focus to be brought to each CPRT training session for therapist demonstration play sessions and parent practice play sessions. A typical format for the first training session might be

- 25 minutes — Basic information, skill development, and role-play; the therapist points out what the parent is to look for in a demonstration play session.
- 10 minutes — The therapist demonstrates a play session with the child as the parent observes through a two-way mirror. Alternatively, a video camera could be set up in a corner of the playroom and the parent could watch on a TV monitor from another room. Less desirable, but workable, the parent could sit in the hall and observe through the partially open door or sit in the playroom and observe but not interact.
- 5 minutes — Critique: therapist directs parent's attention to what she did, explains the purpose of responses to the child, and answers parent questions.

- 10 minutes — Parent–child play session; therapist observes and makes notes.
- 10 minutes — Feedback to parent; therapist takes the role of the child to help the parent practice needed response changes.

The one potential problematic factor with this format is arranging for someone to babysit the child while the therapist is training the parent or couple. If a secretary is not available, an older sibling could fill the role of babysitter. Another possibility is to provide the child with toys to play with in the hall outside the office or playroom door, if the hall dead-ends on one side of the door and there are no office or exit doors in that part of the hall. The therapist can position her chair so she can see the child if the child walks past the open door of the playroom or therapist's office. This same arrangement could be utilized if the playroom or office door opens into a waiting room, and toys can be placed on one side of the waiting room with the open door of the playroom or therapist's office between the toys and the entrance door to the waiting room so the child would not be able to leave the area without being seen.

The format of the first filial therapy training session is recommended for the second and third training sessions. The format for the remaining filial therapy training sessions might be

- 30 minutes — Reviewing homework assignments, supervising at-home parent–child play sessions, and training.
- 15 minutes — Parent–child play session.
- 15 minutes — Therapist feedback and training.

This training format could be revised to meet the needs of a parent or couple, as in the case of a parent who is having difficulty in her play sessions and needs to observe the therapist more.

References

Ferrell, L. (2003). *A comparison of an intensive 4-week format of the Landreth 10-week filial therapy training model with the traditional Landreth 10-week model of filial therapy.* Unpublished doctoral dissertation, University of North Texas, Denton.

Harris, Z., & Landreth, G. (1997). Filial therapy with incarcerated mothers: A five-week model. *International Journal of Play Therapy*, *6*(2), 53–73.

Kot, S., Landreth, G., & Giordano, M. (1998). Intensive child-centered play therapy with child witnesses of domestic violence. *International Journal of Play Therapy*, *7*(2), 17–36.

Smith, N., & Landreth, G. (2003). Intensive filial therapy with child witnesses of domestic violence: A comparison with individual and sibling group play therapy. *International Journal of Play Therapy*, 12(1) 67–88.

Tyndall-Lind, A., Landreth, G., & Giordano, M. (2001). Intensive group play therapy with child witnesses of domestic violence. *International Journal of Play Therapy*. *10*(1), 53–83.

CHAPTER 21

RESEARCH EVIDENCE FOR CHILD PARENT RELATIONSHIP THERAPY (CPRT): A 10-SESSION FILIAL THERAPY MODEL

With a total of 33 studies involving over 800 subjects, Child Parent Relationship Therapy (CPRT) is one of the more well-researched treatment protocols in the field of child psychotherapy. The evidence for the efficacy of this treatment methodology is impressive, supporting its usefulness with a variety of presenting issues and with diverse populations. A summary of the research findings from all 33 studies is included in this chapter, preceded by an overview of the pioneering research efforts of Bernard and Louise Guerney. But first, we have included a brief summary of the meta-analytic research support for play therapy and filial therapy as a context for interpreting the research findings on the 10-session Child Parent Relationship Therapy model.

Meta-Analytic Findings for Play Therapy and Filial Therapy

A recent meta-analysis of 5 decades of play therapy research revealed that across the 93 treatment-control comparisons, the mean ES was 0.80 ± 0.04 (significantly greater than zero, $p < .001$), revealing a "large" treatment effect for play therapy interventions with children (Bratton, Ray, Rhine, & Jones, 2005). The authors used Cohen's (1988) guidelines for interpreting effect size, in which he proposed that 0.20 is considered a "small" treatment effect, 0.50 a "medium" effect, and 0.80 a "large" effect. On average, children receiving play therapy interventions performed more than three-fourths of a standard deviation better on given outcome measures when compared to children who did not receive play therapy. Of the 93 outcome studies included in the meta-analysis, 67 studies focused on play therapy conducted by a mental health professional and 26 measured the effects of play therapy conducted by paraprofessionals. A paraprofessional was defined as a parent, teacher, or mentor who was trained in play therapy procedures and directly supervised by a mental health professional who had specialized training in play therapy. All studies coded to this group used filial therapy methodology (Guerney, 1997; Landreth, 2002), with all but four studies using parents to provide treatment.

To further investigate the impact of involving parents (and other significant adults) fully in their children's therapy, the authors coded and statistically analyzed filial therapy as a treatment modality apart from play therapy conducted by a mental health professional. Bratton et al. (2005) found that filial therapy showed stronger evidence of treatment effectiveness than traditional play therapy, and in fewer sessions. Results indicated a large treatment effect (ES = 1.05) for play therapy conducted by a paraprofessional (filial therapy) and a moderate to large treatment effect (ES = 0.72) for play therapy provided by a professional. Because the majority of paraprofessional studies involved parents, the authors calculated an effect size for the parent-only filial studies, revealing an even stronger treatment effect of 1.15. Analysis of treatment provider group differences revealed that the mean effect size of parent-conducted filial therapy was significantly greater ($p < 0.01$) than the mean effect size of play therapy treatment provided by a mental health professional.

The present authors further analyzed meta-analytic data gathered by Bratton et al. (2005) to investigate the overall treatment effect for only those filial studies that employed Child Parent Relationship Therapy (CPRT) methodology (generally referred to in these research studies as the Landreth 10-Session Filial Therapy Model). To insure adherence to treatment protocol, we included only the studies in which individual researchers were trained and supervised directly by either of us. We included both unpublished (dissertation research) and published outcome studies. Statistical analysis indicated a very large treatment effect (ES = 1.25) for the 10-session model. These findings provide strong evidence for the overall efficacy of this model and, furthermore, support the importance of training and adherence to a well-developed treatment protocol.

Guerneys' Pioneering Research Support for Filial Therapy

We would be remiss if we failed to acknowledge the early, groundbreaking research of Bernard and Louise Guerney and their protégés. Their vision in establishing filial therapy as an innovative treatment for children, as well as their efforts to prove the efficacy of their model, provided the foundation for the development of the 10-Session Child Parent Relationship Therapy model. Therefore, a brief overview of their research is presented.

Stover and Guerney (1967) conducted the earliest filial study designed to examine parents' effectiveness in using child-centered play therapy skills with their children and found that parents were capable of learning the necessary skills to be effective. In what can be considered the landmark study on filial therapy, Guerney and Stover (1971) supported their earlier results with a more robust study of 51 mother/child pairs. Data obtained from live observations showed that after 12 to 18 months of treatment, the mothers demonstrated statistically significant gains in empathic interactions with their children who were diagnosed as emotionally disturbed. In addition, all 51 children, ages 3 to 10 years, demonstrated improvement in social adjustment and behavior problems, with improvement of 28 of the children rated statistically significant. Because the above study did not utilize a control group, Oxman (1972) studied a matched sample of 77 mother/child pairs who received no treatment and found that, in comparison, the filial-trained mothers from the Guerney and Stover study reported a statistically significant improvement in their children's behavior over the matched sample, as well as significantly more satisfaction with their children. A longitudinal investigation of the Guerney and Stover study was conducted by Guerney (1975), with 42 of the original 51 mothers responding. Results indicated that 76% of respondents reported continued improvement in their children 1 to 3 years after treatment, while 86% reported that their children's improvements had been maintained.

Utilizing a research design in which 32 parents (19 mothers and 13 fathers) of 19 clinic-referred children acted as their own control group, Sywulak (1978) used the Guerneys' methodology to train and supervise parents to conduct filial play sessions with their children. Results gathered after 2 months and 4 months of treatment showed a statistically significant improvement in parental acceptance as well as in child adjustment, with withdrawn children evidencing faster changes than aggressive children. In a follow-up of Sywulak's study, Sensue (1981) formed a matched no-treatment comparison group of parents whose children had not been referred for therapy and found that the filial-trained parents reported statistically significant gains in parental acceptance and in their perceptions of their children's adjustment over the comparison group at 6-month and 3-year follow-ups. At the time of follow-up, the filial-trained parents' children who had formerly been diagnosed as maladjusted were found to be as well adjusted as the comparison group parents' children who had never been referred for therapy. Following the Guerneys' lead, other early researchers investigated the effects of this approach with positive results (Payton, 1981; Wall, 1979; Dematatis, 1982; Boll, 1973; Kezur, 1981). Research findings from these early outcome studies assessing the effectiveness of training parents to conduct child-centered play therapy with their own children provided convincing evidence that filial therapy was an effective intervention for children and set the stage for continued research.

Research Support for Child Parent Relationship Therapy

Of the 33 research studies examining this model, the vast majority have focused on treatment effects. The following 27 outcome studies investigated the efficacy of training paraprofessionals (primarily parents) to conduct play therapy with children, utilizing the 10-session filial therapy model first proposed by Landreth (1991) and formally named Child Parent Relationship Therapy (CPRT) in this text. Collectively, these studies involved over 800 participants from a variety of populations. Each of these studies utilized a pretest–posttest control group design, with the exception of Glazer-Waldman, Zimmerman, Landreth, and Norton's (1992) pilot study with chronically ill children, in which they used a pre-post treatment group only design. "Statistical significance" and "significance" are used interchangeably to report results in which the significance of change between the groups due to treatment was $p < .05$ or better.

Unless otherwise specified, in each of the studies, parents attended weekly 2-hour filial therapy training sessions for 10 weeks and conducted weekly 30-minute child-centered play therapy sessions with their children after the third week of filial training. In the majority of the studies ($n = 23$), the researchers and treatment providers were directly trained and supervised by one or both of the present authors and are clearly denoted in the listing of Child Parent Relationship Therapy studies at the end of this chapter. *Note: Because this model was not formally termed Child Parent Relationship Therapy (CPRT) prior to this text, the research studies that follow refer to the 10-session filial training model developed by Landreth. However, the treatment protocol followed in each study is the protocol presented in this text.* The summaries that follow highlight only the major findings in each study and are not meant to provide the reader with a critical review of research methodology. As with most research in the field of child psychotherapy, small sample sizes limit the generalizability of results.

Research Support for Child Parent Relationship Therapy: Parent Studies

Using a pretest–posttest, randomized control group design, Bratton and Landreth (1995) examined the efficacy of the 10-session filial therapy model with 43 single-parent families whose children, ages 3 to 7 years, were identified by their parents as having behavioral problems. When compared to a no-treatment control group, the 22 experimental group parents evidenced a statistically significant increase in empathic interactions with their children when directly observed in play sessions by trained raters. The filial-trained parents also reported statistically significant change on all other measures, including increase in parental acceptance, decrease in stress related to parenting, and decrease in their children's behavior problems. Glass (1987) obtained similar results in a controlled study of 27 parents of 5- to 10-year-olds. Parents in the filial group (n = 14) reported statistically significant increases in feelings of unconditional love for their children and significant decreases in perception of expressed conflict in their families compared to parents in a no-treatment control group. In addition, increases in both parent and child self-esteem were noted, although gains were not statistically significant. Control group parents (n = 13) and children showed no positive change on any measure.

Several recent studies examined the effects of the 10-week filial training model with parents of children with specific presenting issues. Glazer-Waldman et al. (1992) conducted an uncontrolled pilot study investigating filial therapy as an intervention with families of chronically ill children. Filial therapy was used with mothers (n = 5) of children between the ages of 4.5 and 8.0 years with chronic illnesses. Results showed that parents were able to judge more accurately their children's level of anxiety and reported differentiation between themselves and their children. Qualitative reports of outcomes indicated that the parents believed that the course had a positive impact on their relationships with their children. Tew, Landreth, Joiner, & Solt (2002) expanded on Glazer-Waldman's research, using a pre-post, randomized control group design to investigate the effectiveness of the 10-week filial therapy training model with 23 parents of chronically ill, hospitalized children. Compared to a no-treatment control group, the 12 parents who received the filial training reported statistically significant change on all measures, including a decrease in stress related to parenting, an increase in parental acceptance, and a reduction in their children's behavior problems.

Kale and Landreth (1999) trained 22 parents of elementary school–age children diagnosed with learning difficulties. The 11 parents randomly assigned to the filial group reported statistically significant increases in parental acceptance and statistically significant decreases in parenting stress compared to a no-treatment control group. Beckloff (1998) studied the effectiveness of filial therapy as a method of intervention for 23 parents with children diagnosed with pervasive developmental disorder. The 23 parents were randomly assigned to the experimental treatment group (n = 12) or the no-treatment control group (n = 11). Parents in the experimental group reported statistically significant increases in their parental acceptance related to their children's needs for autonomy and independence and made positive, though not significant, gains on their overall attitude of acceptance toward their children. Children also showed improvement in the areas of aggressive problems, externalizing problems, and depressive/anxiety symptoms, although not at a statistically significant level.

In a pre-post comparison group study, Smith and Landreth (2003) explored the effectiveness of utilizing filial therapy as an intensive treatment intervention with mothers residing in a domestic violence shelter with their children who were believed to be witnesses of the violence. The researchers adapted the model to accommodate the shelter setting by extending treatment to 12 sessions condensed into a 2–3 week time period. The 11 mothers in the filial treatment group reported statistically significant reductions in their children's behavior problems, while their children, ages 4 to 10 years, reported statistically significant increases in their self-concept compared to child witnesses in a no-treatment comparison group. In addition, the filial-trained mothers demonstrated statistically significant increases in their parental acceptance and in their empathic interactions with their children (as assessed by trained raters). Smith and Landreth further examined the effectiveness of this model by comparing the findings to two earlier studies with matched populations and settings (Kot, Landreth, & Giordano, 1998; Tyndall-Lind, Landreth, & Giordano, 2001). They concluded that intensive filial therapy conducted in a shelter with child witnesses of domestic violence was equally effective as intensive individual or group play therapy conducted by professional therapists when measured against a no-treatment comparison group.

Costas and Landreth (1999) examined the effects of filial therapy with 26 nonoffending parents of sexually abused children, ages 5 to 9 years. Group assignment was nonrandom, with parents assigned to treatment or control based on geographic location. Results indicated that the 14 parents assigned to the filial treatment group demonstrated statistically significant gains in their empathic interactions with their children compared to parents assigned to a no-treatment control group, also assigned based on location. They also reported a significant increase in acceptance of their children and a significant reduction in parental stress. Although not statistically significant, marked improvement was reported in children's behavior problems, anxiety, emotional adjustment, and self-concept for the children of the filial group. Using a pretest–posttest, control group design, Ray (2003) reported the use of the 10-session filial therapy methodology proposed by Landreth (1991) to study the effect of filial therapy on parental acceptance and child adjustment with 50 parent–child dyads identified "at-risk" due to history of potential attachment problems or parents who were identified as having emotional problems. Results indicated that the 25 filial-trained parents reported a significant increase in parental acceptance over the 25 no-treatment control group parents. Although not statistically significant, findings also showed a reduction in parenting stress and children's problematic behavior as a result of filial training.

Landreth and Lobaugh (1998) and Harris and Landreth (1997) investigated the effectiveness of the Landreth (1991) filial model with incarcerated parents and found statistically significant results on all measures. Utilizing randomized group assignment, Lobaugh studied the effects of filial training with 32 incarcerated fathers of 4- to 9-year-olds. Parent–child filial play sessions were held in a medium-security federal prison during children's weekly scheduled visitation with their fathers. Compared to the no-treatment control group, the 16 filial-trained fathers significantly increased their acceptance of their children and reported significant decreases in their children's behavior problems and in their own stress related to parenting. In addition, the children in the experimental group showed a significant increase in self-esteem. Harris & Landreth studied 22 incarcerated mothers with children ages 3 to 10 years. The filial training model was adapted to accommodate the women's average length of stay at the county jail (5 weeks); therefore, the 12 mothers assigned to treatment received 2-hour filial therapy training sessions twice per week for 5 weeks (for a total of 10 sessions) and conducted biweekly 30-minute play sessions with one of their children during scheduled visitation times at the jail. Compared to a matched no-treatment control group of 10 mothers, filial-trained mothers significantly increased their empathic interaction with their children and reported significant gains in parental acceptance and a significant decrease in their children's behavior problems.

The effectiveness of the 10-week model has also been researched with diverse populations, including Native American,

Korean, Israeli, and immigrant Chinese and immigrant Korean parents living in the United States. Although this model has been used with Hispanic parents and African American parents, no outcome data has been collected to date. Current outcome research at the University of North Texas is studying the impact of Child Parent Relationship Therapy on Hispanic parents and their children. For more information on specific adaptations to accommodate for cultural needs, refer to individual studies.

Glover and Landreth (2000) utilized filial therapy training as an intervention for 21 Native American parents and their children, ages 3 to 10 years, residing on the Flathead Reservation in Montana. The 11 parents assigned to the filial treatment group demonstrated significant gains in empathic interactions with their children compared to the 10 no-treatment control group parents. Their children also demonstrated significant increases in desirable play behaviors with their parents compared to the control group children. Although the measures of parental acceptance, parental stress, and children's self-concepts did not show statistically significant change, improvements were shown on all measures. The researchers noted concerns regarding the compatibility of the instruments with the Native American culture.

Using random group assignment, Chau and Landreth (1997) investigated the use of this model with 34 immigrant Chinese parents of children ages 2 to 10 years residing in the United States. Compared to the no-treatment control group of 16 parents, the 18 filial-trained parents demonstrated statistically significant change on all measures. Replicating Chau and Landreth's study, Yuen, Landreth, and Baggerly (2002) investigated the effects of 10 sessions of filial therapy training with immigrant Chinese parents in Canada, obtaining similar results. The 18 filial-trained parents demonstrated significant change over the control group on all measures. Specifically, the filial-trained parents in both studies demonstrated a significant increase in their level of empathic interactions with their children during parent–child play sessions, a significant increase in their attitude of acceptance toward their children, and a significant reduction in their level of stress related to parenting.

Lee and Landreth (2003) researched the effectiveness of Child Parent Relationship Therapy with 36 immigrant Korean parents in the United States and their children, ages 2–10 years.

Results revealed that, when compared to a randomized control group, the 18 parents randomly assigned to the experimental group significantly increased their level of empathic interactions with their children, showed significant gains in parental acceptance, and significantly reduced their level of stress related to parenting. In a study conducted in Korea, Jang (2002) reported adapting the 10-session filial therapy methodology proposed by Landreth (1991) to study the effects of this intervention on 30 Korean families. Experimental group parents met twice per week for 4 weeks for filial therapy training and conducted play sessions with their children, ages 3 to 9 years. Compared to the 16 mothers who received no treatment, the 14 mothers assigned to filial therapy demonstrated significant gains in empathic interactions with their children. Although not statistically significant, the filial-trained mothers also reported improvements in their children's behavior, level of parental acceptance, and parenting stress. Qualitative data supported the parents' reported improvements in themselves and their children.

Kidron (2004) also examined the effectiveness of an intensive version of this model with 27 Israeli parents and their children, ages 4 to 11 years, living in Israel. The 14 parents assigned to the treatment group received 9 filial therapy training sessions within a 5-week period and had 7 filial play sessions with their children during the 5-week period. Compared to the no-treatment comparison group of 13 parents, filial-trained parents reported a significant decrease in their children's externalizing behavior problems. Results also revealed the parents in the experimental group significantly reduced parental stress and significantly increased their communication of empathy to their children.

Research Support for Child Parent Relationship Therapy: Paraprofessional Studies

Several studies have investigated the 10-session model with teachers and mentors in the school setting. Smith and Landreth (2004) examined the effectiveness of filial therapy with 24 teachers of deaf and hard-of-hearing preschool children. Compared to a control group, the 12 teachers in the experimental group significantly improved their empathic interactions with students. Children whose teachers were in the experimental group exhibited significantly fewer overall behavior problems compared to the control group children.

Using a pretest–posttest comparison group design, an innovative study by Jones, Rhine, and Bratton (2002) examined the efficacy of this model in training high school students (juniors and seniors) to be effective helpers with 4- and 5-year-olds referred for school adjustment difficulties. Thirty-one high school students enrolled in two sections of a Peer Assistance and Leadership course (PALs) participated in the study. One PALs class (n = 16) received filial training based on the 10-session model, while the other class (n = 15) received training in the traditional PALs curriculum, designed to teach high school students helping skills to mentor younger students. The Child Parent Relationship Therapy (CPRT) curriculum and training delivery format were modified to accommodate for the developmental needs of high school students and to adjust to the PALs course and school schedule. Both the filial-trained PALs and the traditionally trained PALs received training during their regularly scheduled PALs class time. The experimental treatment group practiced their skills in weekly supervised play sessions with their assigned children at the children's schools. The comparison group conducted weekly play-based mentoring sessions with their assigned children. Results from statistical analyses revealed that the PALs students trained in CPRT skills demonstrated a statistically significant increase in their empathic interactions with children compared to the traditionally trained PALs students. Compared to a randomized control group, the 16 experimental group of children who received weekly 20-minute play sessions from their filial-trained PALs demonstrated a significant reduction in problem behaviors according to parent report.

A quasi-experimental research study by Brown (2003) investigated the effectiveness of Child Parent Relationship (CPRT) Therapy adapted for use with 38 undergraduate early childhood teacher trainees enrolled in 2 sections of a required course. One class received the experimental treatment, while the other class received the comparison treatment. The experimental group of 18 teacher trainees received 10 weekly 90-minute training sessions in CPRT principles and skills and conducted 7 weekly special playtimes with their assigned children. The comparison group of 20 teacher trainees received 10 weeks of training in child guidance techniques. Results revealed that the teacher trainees in the experimental group demonstrated statistically significant increases in empathy and significant gains on a measure of play therapy attitudes, knowledge, and skills over the comparison group. In a similar study, Crane and Brown (2003) investigated the effects of filial training on undergraduate students enrolled in a human services course. Consistent with Brown (2003), the experimental group of undergraduates demonstrated significant gains in empathy, as well as in attitudes, knowledge, and skills related to play therapy.

In companion studies, Baggerly and Landreth (2001) and Robinson (2003) investigated the effectiveness of adapting the 10-session filial therapy model to train fifth-grade students in play-based mentoring with kindergarten children identified as at-risk for school success. Adapting the model to accommodate for the developmental needs of the fifth graders, training sessions were shorter and the duration of training was extended to 15 weeks. Fifteen fifth-grade students were randomly assigned to the experimental treatment and received 35 minutes of training twice a week for 5 weeks and then once a week for the duration of the 10 weeks, during which they conducted weekly play-based mentoring sessions with their assigned kindergarteners. The 14 control group fifth-graders received no training during the 15 weeks. Using pre-post measures, Robinson (2003) assessed the impact of filial training on the fifth-grade students and found that, compared to the no-treatment control group, the filial-trained students demonstrated statistically significant increases in empathic interactions with their assigned kindergarteners. Baggerly and Landreth (2001) investigated the impact of this adaptation of filial therapy methodology with fifth-graders on the behavior and self-concept of kindergarten children referred for school adjustment difficulties. Children assigned to the experimental group received 10 weekly 20-minute play-based mentoring sessions with their filial-trained mentors; control group children received no treatment during the treatment phase. Although not statistically significant, the children in the experimental group demonstrated a decrease in somatic complaints, along with improvements in self-concept, total behavior problems, externalizing behavior problems, delinquent behavior, and demandingness. Detailed observation and teacher reports supported these findings, revealing an increase in self-acceptance, self-esteem, self-confidence, self-control, creativity, and positive relationships, as well as decreases in aggression and withdrawn behavior.

The following 2 studies described adapting the 10-session filial therapy model introduced by Landreth (1991) to train preschool teachers. Post, McAllister, Sheely, Hess, and Flowers (2004) examined the impact of filial training on 17 preschool teachers and children identified as at-risk. The 9 teachers assigned to the treatment group received 10 weeks of group filial training and conducted weekly play sessions with their assigned child, followed by 30 minutes of immediate feedback. Following the initial training, teachers participated in 13 group sessions to help them generalize filial skills to their classrooms. Children who participated in play sessions with their teachers improved in three of the four composite scales of the Behavior Assessment Scale for Children (Internalizing Problems, Behavioral Symptoms Index, and Adaptive Skills) compared to a control group of children who did not have play sessions. The filial-trained teachers demonstrated significant increases in therapeutic play skills and significant increases in empathic responding during individual play sessions with their assigned children. In addition, when measured against a matched no-treatment comparison group of teachers, teachers were able to generalize the skills into their classrooms. Using data from the Post et al. study, Hess (2004) conducted a follow-up study, comparing the experimental group of teachers with a matched group of untrained teachers one year after the original training. Results indicated statistically significant differences between the trained and untrained teachers on the use of play therapy skills and empathic responses in individual one-on-one session videotapes and in teachers' attitudes about children and knowledge of play therapy skills. There were no significant differences found between the trained and untrained teachers on the use of these skills in the classroom. Additionally, the experimental group of teachers reported the usefulness of the training, including improved classroom management skills, a changed perspective on the value of including children's opinions, and increased confidence as teachers.

Modifications to the 10-Session Child Parent Relationship Therapy Model

Ferrell (2003) investigated the effectiveness of an intensive 4-weekend format of Child Parent Relationship Therapy (CPRT) compared to the traditional 10-session model and proposed a modified training curriculum to accommodate the format. While other studies have condensed the 10-session model to accommodate for the setting (Harris & Landreth, 1997; Smith & Landreth, 2003; Jang, 2000; Kidron, 2004) and have adapted the model to accommodate for developmental needs of participants (Jones, Rhine, and Bratton, 2002; Baggerly and Landreth 2001; Robinson, 2003), this study is the first of its kind to formally investigate a modification of the curriculum against the traditional 10-session format. The experimental filial treatment group (n = 13) met on 4 consecutive Saturdays, for a total of 16 hours of training, while the traditional filial therapy comparison group met for approximately 1½ hours per week for 10 weeks, for a total of 16 hours. In the intensive model, the CPRT curriculum was collapsed and reorganized slightly to provide the content and training experiences during 4-hour blocks over 4 weeks compared to the traditional model, which provides 10 two-hour training sessions. Group sizes were smaller (4–5 parents) to accommodate for the fewer number of total hours of training (16 vs. 20 hours). Children accompanied their parents to the training to provide opportunities for supervised practice of filial skills. Parent–child play sessions were structured at home and during the weekend training sessions so that children received an identical number of play sessions (n = 7) as prescribed by the traditional 10-session model. Results revealed no statistically significant differences between the intensive filial group and the traditional filial group of parents at posttesting on measures of parent stress, parental acceptance, empathic behavior, and children's behavior problems. However, the researcher noted that the parents who received the intensive filial training showed more cohesion as a group and reported a greater sense of support. Greater reductions in parenting stress by the intensive filial-trained parents supported anecdotal findings. Although not statistically significant, parents who received the traditional 10-week training showed greater gains in skill attainment, especially in the area of communicating acceptance to their children through acknowledgement of feelings. This finding suggests that while a 4-session intensive model of filial training can be considered as effective as the traditional 10-session model, parents may benefit from having more time to assimilate the new skills they are learning. The authors suggested structuring the intense training to accommodate for this limitation by asking parents to commit to continuing their home play sessions and scheduling one to two follow-up meetings with parents.

Skills of Filial-Trained Parents Compared to Graduate-Level Play Therapists

In a unique filial study, Elling, (2003) compared the skill level and amount of change due to training between 21 parents trained in the 10-session filial therapy model and 13 graduate students enrolled in a 45-credit hour, graduate-level introductory play therapy course. This study was conducted, in part, to address findings that suggest that parents can be more effective with their children than professionals (Bratton et al.). The researcher's goal was to specifically compare skill-level attainment of parents and professionals-in-training posttreatment. The author found that although the graduate students' mean posttraining scores after 15 weeks of coursework revealed a statistically significant higher Total Empathy score on the Measurement of Empathy in Adult–Child Interactions (MEACI), the two groups showed equal skill in the areas of Communication of Acceptance and Allowing the Child Self-Direction. The filial-trained parents showed greater mean change scores from pre- to posttesting. This finding would be expected given that the graduate students had received prior training in basic counseling skills, thus started with a higher skill level. Overall, while these results support that filial-trained parents can learn child-centered play therapy skills at a similar level to graduate play therapy students, their skill level does not explain the suggested efficacy of filial therapy over play therapy. These findings give credence to one of the basic premises for filial therapy first proposed by Guerney (1964): that parents have greater emotional significance to the child than does the therapist—and that it is the relationship between the parent and child that likely accounts for the powerful results that filial research has shown.

The large number of controlled studies indicating the effectiveness of the Child Parent Relationship Therapy (CPRT) model verifies that teaching and training parents in child-centered play therapy principles and skills is a viable intervention for children exhibiting a variety of emotional and behavioral difficulties.

Qualitative Studies

To date, four qualitative studies have examined dimensions of the filial therapy process in greater detail. Bavin-Hoffman,

Jennings and Landreth (1996) completed a qualitative study using a phenomenological approach to examine 20 married couples' perceptions of how their families and their couple relationships changed after a filial therapy experience. Married couples (20 females and 20 males), who completed filial therapy between 1991 and 1994, participated in semistructured, audiotaped interviews. Three recurring themes, (a) improved parent/child communication, (b) improved couple interpersonal communication, and (c) positive changes in child behavior such as children's increased self-control and a decrease in aggression, were identified from the data collected in response to the two interview questions.

Utilizing ethnographic methodology, Lahti (1993) examined and described the filial therapy process to provide an in-depth understanding of the process, the relations in progress, and effects on the parent, child, and parent/child relationship. Data were collected from 3 parents who attended 10 weekly two-hour sessions on filial therapy, and their respective three children, ages 7–9. Changes in parents entailed increases in confidence and feelings of personal power, reduction in degree of parental control and responsibility, and increased awareness of adults' and children's needs. Closer parent–child and marital relationships were described and characterized by increased, enhanced communication; adoption of more realistic, appropriate expectations; and less friction. The children's changes included increased and enhanced communication, increased responsibility for actions, decreased withdrawn and aggressive behavior, and increased feelings of happiness.

Utilizing a collective case study design, Steen (2005) examined and described the filial therapy (FT) process and adaptations discovered to be necessary in working with families who have a child with a life-threatening illness in the hospital setting. Seven parents attended 10 one- to two-hour FT sessions. Changes noted in the children included increased confidence, increased cooperation in the medical setting, increased communication with the parent and with medical staff regarding medical issues, and increased communication with the parent regarding personal feelings and issues. Changes noted in the parents included increased confidence in parenting skills; increased awareness of their children's perceptions of the environment; increased tolerance in allowing their children to struggle in and out of the medical setting, with both emotional and physical pain in order to gain coping skills; increased ability to allow their children to empower themselves; and increased abilities in limit setting.

Using the 10-session filial methodology, Solis, Meyers, and Varjas (2004) examined an African American parent's perceptions of the process and impact of filial therapy. The parent reported positive changes in the parent, child, and parent–child relationship as a result of participation in filial therapy. Additional findings included adequate treatment acceptability with regard to the structure of filial therapy training; however, the parent reported particular difficulty in maintaining a permissive and nondirective manner during the play sessions.

Additional Research Findings

Using data from 4 previous studies investigating the effects of the 10-session filial model, Poon (1998) researched the relationship between parental empathy (PE) and parental acceptance (PA) and the effect of filial therapy training on this relationship. The Measurement of Empathy in Adult–Child Interaction (MEACI) and the Porter Parental Acceptance Scale (PPAS) are two instruments widely used in filial therapy studies to measure empathy and acceptance, respectively. Results revealed a strong correlation between the two instruments, and Poon concluded that, of the two scales, the PPAS was a more cost- and time-efficient instrument than the MEACI. Based on these findings, it appears that the PPAS is a reliable self-report measure for evaluating the effects of filial therapy training on the development of parental empathy and parental acceptance.

Sweeney (1997) investigated the relationships among single parents' parental stress, empathy, level of acceptance, perception of children's problems, and child gender, and the effect of filial therapy training on these relationships. The data utilized in this investigation came from the study by Bratton and Landreth (1995). Significant correlations were found between parental stress and acceptance, parental stress and perception of children's problems, parental empathy and acceptance, parental empathy and perception of children's problems, and between parental acceptance and perception of children's problems. No significant correlations were found between child gender and any of the variables. Significant correlation changes were found in several of the measured variables (from pre- to post-) due to the filial therapy intervention. Regression analysis indicated that parental acceptance was predictive of parental empathy, parental empathy was predictive of parental acceptance, and parental stress was predictive of parental perception of problems. No significant findings of prediction were obtained with child gender.

Summary of Research Support for Child Parent Relationship Therapy

Collectively, the body of research on the effectiveness of the 10-session Child Parent Relationship Therapy model is compelling. That improvements were noted in both parents and children further demonstrates the robustness of this approach. Certainly, the research strongly supports the adoption of filial therapy, specifically the model presented in this text, as an evidence-based therapeutic modality for children and parents. It cannot be overstated that these findings do not merely suggest the value of involving parents in their children's therapy. These overwhelmingly positive outcomes from these studies appear to be the result of (a) fully involving parents as the therapeutic change agents in their children's therapy, (b) parents receiving child-centered play therapy training and close supervision from a specially trained mental health professional, (c) providing supervised experiences for parents to practice their skills with their children, and, perhaps most importantly, (d) therapist training in, and adherence to, the 10-session filial therapy curriculum.

That training occurs in a group setting adds to the efficiency of this model, allowing professionals to help more individuals in the same amount of time. Of note, these results were achieved in what would be considered by most mental health professions as a relatively brief number of sessions. We must also remind the reader that the actual number of play sessions that children received was approximately 7, due to the fact that parents do not start play sessions with their children until after the third filial training session. The efficacy of this model in so few sessions is especially noteworthy considering that play therapy meta-analytic results revealed that, across 93 studies, 35 sessions was found to be the optimum number for greatest treatment effect (Bratton et al., 2005).

These results further add credence to the meta-analytic findings of Bratton et al. (2005) that suggested that filial therapy is a more effective intervention than traditional play therapy, and in a shorter amount of time. Although at first glance these results suggest that therapists and managed care providers should advocate the use of filial training over play therapy, clinical rationale would prohibit the use of filial therapy with all parents and children. Parents who are experiencing a significant amount of emotional stress often have difficulty focusing on the needs of their children. In this case, many parents need to undertake their own therapy before they are capable of learning and facilitating the skills of therapeutic play with their children. Also, as most child therapists have experienced, many parents are unwilling or unmotivated to participate in their children's therapy. Issues of guilt, resentment, time, money, and effort are just a few of the reasons for nonparticipation by parents.

In addition to parental issues that prohibit participation in filial play therapy training, a child may not be best suited for this approach. On occasion, a child's emotional issues might extend beyond the capability of the parent. In a case where a child is significantly emotionally disturbed, a parent may not be able to provide a child with an effective therapeutic experience. Clearly, more research is needed to directly study the effects of play therapy compared to filial therapy with specific populations and issues. Yet, research supports that if a child and a parent are both firm candidates, filial therapy would be the treatment of choice (Bratton et al., 2005).

Furthermore, the strong research support for this model answers the critical need expressed in the most recent Surgeon General's report, "A National Action Agenda for Children's Mental Health" (U.S. Public Health Service, 2000), to identify proven approaches that "engage families in prevention and intervention strategies..." as a solution to the crises in children's mental health in this country (p. 8). Filial therapy fully engages parents in the therapy process, impacting current family dynamics and providing parents with skills and resources that can serve to prevent future problems.

It is our belief that mental health professionals have a responsibility to use the findings from this body of research to not only educate managed care companies, but to also to educate and work with parents, government, schools, and the medical and legal community to insure that children and their families receive the most beneficial and cost-effective treatment.

Research Studies on the 10-Session Child Parent Relationship Model

Note: An asterisk (*) in front of a citation denotes that neither the researcher nor the treatment providers for the study were directly trained and supervised by either of the authors; therefore, adherence to the 10-session CPRT treatment protocol is unknown. Studies were included because the author stated that research was conducted on filial therapy treatment that followed the 10-session model proposed by Landreth (1991).

Quantitative Outcome Studies

Baggerly, J., & Landreth, G. (2001). Training children to help children: A new dimension in play therapy. *Peer Facilitator Quarterly, 18*(1), 6–14.

Beckloff, D. R. (1998). Filial therapy with children with spectrum pervasive development disorders (Doctoral dissertation, University of North Texas, 1997). *Dissertation Abstracts International, B, 58* (11), 6224.

Bratton, S., & Landreth, G. (1995). Filial therapy with single parents: Effects on parental acceptance, empathy, and stress. *International Journal of Play Therapy, 4*(1), 61–80.

Brown, C. (2003). Filial therapy training with undergraduate teacher trainees: Child–teacher relationship training (Doctoral dissertation, University of North Texas, 2000). *Dissertation Abstracts International, A, 63* (09), 3112.

Chau, I., & Landreth, G. (1997). Filial therapy with Chinese parents: Effects on parental empathic interactions, parental acceptance of child and parental stress. *International Journal of Play Therapy, 6*(2), 75–92.

Costas, M., & Landreth, G. (1999). Filial therapy with nonoffending parents of children who have been sexually abused. *International Journal of Play Therapy, 8*(1), 43–66.

Crane, J. M., & Brown, C. J. (2003). Effectiveness of teaching play therapy attitudes and skills to undergraduate human service majors. *International Journal of Play Therapy, 12*(2), 49–65.

Elling, E. R. P. (2003). A comparison of skill level of parents trained in the Landreth Filial Therapy Model and graduate students trained in play therapy (Doctoral dissertation, University of North Texas, 2003). *Dissertation Abstracts International, 64* (06), 1983.

Ferrell, L. G. (2003). *A comparison of an intensive 4-week format of the Landreth 10-week filial therapy training model with the traditional Landreth 10-week model of filial therapy.* Unpublished doctoral dissertation, University of North Texas, Denton.

Glass, N. (1987). Parents as therapeutic agents: A study of the effects of filial therapy (Doctoral dissertation, North Texas State University, 1986). *Dissertation Abstracts International, A, 47* (07), 2457.

Glazer-Waldman, H., Zimmerman, J., Landreth, G., & Norton, D. (1992). Filial therapy: An intervention for parents of children with chronic illness. *International Journal of Play Therapy, 1*(1), 31–42.

Glover, G., & Landreth, G. (2000). Filial therapy with Native Americans on the Flathead Reservation. *International Journal of Play Therapy, 9*(2), 57–80.

Harris, Z. L., & Landreth, G. (1997). Filial therapy with incarcerated mothers: A five week model. *International Journal of Play Therapy, 6*(2), 53–73.

*Hess, B. (2004). The long-term effect of kinder therapy training on preschool teachers of children considered at-risk (Doctoral dissertation, University of North Carolina at Charlotte, 2004). *Dissertation Abstracts International, A, 65* (01), 76.

*Jang, M. (2000). Effectiveness of filial therapy for Korean parents. *International Journal of Play Therapy, 9*(2), 39–56.

Jones, L., Rhine, T., & Bratton, S. (2002). High school students as therapeutic agents with young children experiencing school adjustment difficulties: The effectiveness of filial therapy training model. *International Journal of Play Therapy, 11*(2), 43–62.

Kale, A. L., & Landreth, G. (1999). Filial therapy with parents of children experiencing learning difficulties. *International Journal of Play Therapy, 8*(2), 35–56.

Kidron, M. (2004). Filial therapy with Israeli parents (Doctoral dissertation, University of North Texas, 2003). *Dissertation Abstracts International, A, 64* (12), 4372.

Kot, S., Landreth, G., & Giordano, M. (1998). Intensive child-centered play therapy with child witnesses of domestic violence. *International Journal of Play Therapy,* 7(2), 17–36.

Landreth, G., & Lobaugh, A. (1998). Filial therapy with incarcerated fathers: Effects on parental acceptance of child, parental stress, and child adjustment. *Journal of Counseling & Development, 76*, 157–165.

Lee, M., & Landreth, G. (2003). Filial therapy with immigrant Korean parents in the United States. *International Journal of Play Therapy, 12*(2), 67–85.

*Post, P., McAllister, M., Sheely, A., Hess, B., & Flowers, C. (2004). Child centered kinder training for teachers of pre-school children deemed at risk. *International Journal of Play Therapy, 13*(2), 53–74.

*Ray, D. E. (2003). *The effect of filial therapy on parental acceptance and child adjustment.* Unpublished master's thesis, Emporia State University.

Robinson, J. Z. (2003). Fifth grade students as emotional helpers with kindergarten children, using play therapy procedures and skills (Doctoral dissertation, University of North Texas, 2001). *Dissertation Abstracts Interntional, A, 63* (12), 4234.

Smith, N., & Landreth, G. (2003). Intensive filial therapy with child witnesses of domestic violence: A comparison with individual and sibling group play therapy. *International Journal for Play Therapy, 12*(1), 67–88.

Smith, D. M., & Landreth, G. L. (2004). Filial therapy with teachers of deaf and hard of hearing preschool children. *International Journal of Play Therapy, 13*(1), 13–33.

Tew, K., Landreth, G., Joiner, K. D., & Solt, M. D. (2002). Filial therapy with parents of chronically ill children. *International Journal of Play Therapy, 11*(1), 79–100.

Tyndall-Lind, A., Landreth, G., & Giordano, M. (2001). Intensive group play therapy with children witnesses of domestic violence. *International Journal of Play Therapy*, 10(1), 53–83.

Yuen, T. C. (1997). Filial therapy with immigrant Chinese parents in Canada (Doctoral dissertation, University of North Texas, 1997). *Dissertation Abstracts International, A, 57* (04), 1498.

Yuen, T., Landreth, G., & Baggerly, J. (2002). Filial therapy with immigrant Chinese families. *International Journal for Play Therapy*, 11(2), 63–90.

Qualitative Studies

Bavin-Hoffman, R., Jennings, G., & Landreth, G. (1996). Filial therapy: Parental perceptions of the process. *International Journal of Play Therapy, 5*(1), 45–58.

Lahti, S. L. (1993). An ethnographic study of the filial therapy process (Doctoral dissertation, University of North Texas, 1992). *Dissertation Abstracts International, A, 53* (08), 2691.

*Solis, C. M., Meyers, J., & Varjas, K. M. (2004). A qualitative case study of the process and impact of filial therapy with an African American parent. *International Journal of Play Therapy, 13*(2), 99–118.

Steen, R. L. (2005). Adapting filial therapy for families who have a child with a life-threatening illness (Doctoral dissertation, University of North Texas, 2004). *Dissertation Abstract International, B, 65* (08), 4306.

Other Studies

Poon, W. S. (1998). The relationship between parental empathy and parental acceptance and the effect of filial therapy training on this relationship (Doctoral dissertation, University of North Texas, 1997). *Dissertation Abstracts International, A, 59* (04), 1080.

Sweeney, D. (1997). The relationship among single parents' parental stress, empathy, level of acceptance, perceived problems of the child, and child gender and the effect of filial therapy (Doctoral dissertation, University of North Texas, 1996). *Dissertation Abstracts International, A, 57* (07), 2883.

References

Note: All references for research publications on the 10-Session Filial Therapy Model are listed above; therefore, those references are not repeated.

Boll, L. A. (1973). Effects of filial therapy on maternal perceptions of their mentally retarded children's social behavior (Doctoral dissertation, University of Oklahoma, 1972). *Dissertation Abstracts International, A, 33* (12), 6661.

Bratton, S., Ray, D., Rhine, T., & Jones, L. (2005). The efficacy of play therapy with children: A meta-analytic review of treatment outcomes, *Professional Psychology: Research and Practice, 36*(4).

Cohen, J. (1988). *Statistical power analysis for the behavioral sciences* (2nd ed.). New York: Academic Press.

Dematatis, C. (1982). A comparison of the traditional filial therapy program to an integrated Filial-IPR program (Doctoral dissertation, Michigan State University, 1981). *Dissertation Abstracts International, B, 42* (10), 4187.

Guerney, B. (1964). Filial therapy: Description and rationale. *Journal of Consulting Psychology*, 28(4), 303–310.

Guerney, B. G., Jr., & Stover, L. (1971). *Filial therapy: Final report on MH 18264-01*. Unpublished manuscript, Pennsylvania State University, University Park.

Guerney, L. (1975). *Follow-up study on filial therapy.* Paper presented at the annual convention of the Eastern Psychological Association, New York, NY.

Guerney, L. (1997). Filial therapy. In K. O'Connor & L. Braverman (Eds.), *Play therapy: Theory and practice* (pp. 131–159). New York: Wiley.

Kezur, B. A. (1981). Mother–child communication patterns based on therapeutic principles (Doctoral dissertation, Humanistic Psychology Institute, 1980). *Dissertation Abstracts International, B, 41* (12), 4671.

Landreth, G. L. (1991/2002). Play therapy: The art of the relationship. New York: Routledge.

Oxman, L. (1972). The effectiveness of filial therapy: A controlled study (Doctoral dissertation, Rutgers The State University of New Jersey, 1972). *Dissertation Abstracts International, B, 32* (11), 6656.

Payton, I. (1981). Filial therapy as a potential primary preventive process with children between the ages of four and ten (Doctoral dissertation, University of Northern Colorado, 1980). *Dissertation Abstracts International, A, 41* (07), 2942.

Sensue, M. E. (1981). Filial therapy follow-up study: Effects on parental acceptance and child adjustment (Doctoral dissertation, Pennsylvania State University, 1981). *Dissertation Abstracts International, A, 42* (01)148.

Stover, L., & Guerney, B. (1967). The efficacy of training procedures for mothers in filial therapy. *Psychotherapy: Theory, Research, and Practice*, *4*(3), 110–115.

Stover, L., Guerney, B., & O'Connell, M. (1971). Measurements of acceptance, allowing self-direction, involvement, and empathy in adult–child interaction. *Journal of Psychology*, *77*, 261–269.

Sywulak, A. (1978). The effect of filial therapy on parental acceptance and child adjustment (Doctoral dissertation, Pennsylvania State University, 1977). *Dissertation Abstracts International, B, 38* (12), 6180.

U.S. Public Health Service (2000). Report of the Surgeon General's conference on children's mental health: A national action agenda. Washington, D.C.

Wall, L. (1979). Parents as play therapists: A comparison of three interventions into children's play (Doctoral dissertation, University of Northern Colorado, 1979). *Dissertation Abstracts International, B, 39* (11), 5597.

INDEX

C

D

E

F

J

K

L

Q

R

S

T